Human Rights...

Human Rights

The Commons and the Collective

...... Laura Westra

UBCPress · Vancouver · Toronto

20 19 18 17 16 15 14 13 12 11   5 4 3 2 1

Printed in Canada on FSC-certified ancient-forest-free paper
(100 percent post-consumer recycled) that is processed chlorine- and acid-free.

Library and Archives Canada Cataloguing in Publication

Westra, Laura Suzanne, 1933-
    Human rights : the commons and the collective / Laura Westra.

Includes bibliographical references and index.
Also issued in electronic format.
ISBN 978-0-7748-2117-9 (bound); ISBN 978-0-77482118-6 (pbk.)

    1. Human rights. 2. Environmental law. 3. Commons. I. Title.

K3240.W48 2011   341.4'8   C2011-903713-0

e-book ISBNs: 978-0-7748-2119-3 (pdf); 978-0-7748-2120-9 (epub)

Canadä

UBC Press gratefully acknowledges the financial support for our publishing program of the Government of Canada (through the Canada Book Fund), the Canada Council for the Arts, and the British Columbia Arts Council.

This book has been published with the help of a grant from the Canadian Federation for the Humanities and Social Sciences, through the Aid to Scholarly Publications Program, using funds provided by the Social Sciences and Humanities Research Council of Canada.

UBC Press
The University of British Columbia
2029 West Mall
Vancouver, BC V6T 1Z2
www.ubcpress.ca

For the members of the Global Ecological Integrity Group (GEIG),

friends and colleagues who have inspired me,
supported me, and helped me to expand my knowledge
for almost twenty years.

Thank you.

Contents

PART 3: TOWARD A NEW COSMOPOLITANISM

Acknowledgments

The argument of this book was developed and inspired by many hours spent reading the seminal work of scholars such as Roger Brownsword, Bradford Morse, Dwight Newman, Gaetano Pentassuglia, Maurizio Ragazzi, William Rees, and Tullio Scovazzi. In addition, the members of the International Court of the Environment Foundation (ICEF) (20-21 May 2010) in Rome, under the leadership of Judge Amedeo Postiglione, indicated a possible way forward, a path that may help to redress the many grave problems uncovered by my research and summed up briefly in this volume.

Special thanks are also due to the members of the Global Ecological Integrity Group (GEIG), whose research in many fields has opened new horizons for me in areas of study too numerous to mention.

I am especially grateful for the support of a Social Sciences and Humanities Research Council (SSHRC) grant ("Indigenous Rights and the Impact of Environmental Degradation on Public Health," principal investigator, Bradford Morse, University of Ottawa, Faculty of Common Law, 2008-11), under which I worked as a postdoctoral scholar. I am also extremely grateful to the SSHRC for its sustained support of the work of the GEIG from 1992 to 1999 and of my doctoral research at Osgoode Hall Law School from 2001 to 2004. Finally, I am thankful for the grant that permitted the publication of this book.

Warm thanks are also due to Diane Rooke at Osgoode Hall Law School Law Library for her ongoing research assistance and to Luc Quenneville of the University of Windsor for the excellent technical help necessary for the completion of this work.

Portions of this book have appeared previously elsewhere. I would like to thank Transnational Publishers and Earthscan for granting me permission to reprint material from my books *Environmental Justice and the Rights of Ecological Refugees* (Earthscan, 2009) and *Ecoviolence and the Law: Supranational Normative Foundation of Ecocrime* (Transnational, 2004).

Foreword

Some of the most important things in life have no physical presence. They do not exist in the "natural" world. These things are fabrications of the human mind or, sometimes, of many human minds. Psychologists and sociologists refer to such entities as mental constructs and social constructs, respectively.[1]

We can take this idea one step further. People "live" in consciousness and "know" certain things to be true or real. However, although formal knowledge may masquerade as "reality" in our conscious minds, all knowing is, to some degree, socially constructed. Some social constructs have been erected to describe corresponding real-world phenomena. For example, people from both capitalist democracies and failed communist states would agree that *the economy* refers to that set of activities central to the production, distribution, and consumption of goods and services in a specified region or country. However, capitalism and communism are themselves elaborately different social constructs; each perceives various components of the economy (finance capital, the physical means of production, markets, producers and consumers, mechanisms for distribution, and so on) and their social context (regulatory regimes, tax policies, trade treaties, private property, the public good, the role of the state and of ordinary citizens, and so on) through vastly different lenses. It is possible to give all of these elements alternative configurations and weights – the important point is that economic actors and activities exist in some form or another to serve the material needs of every society *whether or not* the people have constructed any formal concept of the economy.

Other social constructs are entirely made up: there is no corresponding structure in the natural world for capitalism or communism, for example. These ideological frames were given birth entirely through words, language, and decades of social discourse. They acquired sturdy (or not so sturdy) legs in the actual practices of economic entities, institutions, and whole nation-states, which reflected the beliefs, values, and assumptions of their adherents and acolytes. Abstractions they may be, but the ideologies implied by the terms *capitalism* and *communism* carry formidable intellectual weight. And who can dispute their life-changing effects on people and societies once let loose in the real world? Little wonder that any debate of their relative merits and weaknesses is as much charged by visceral emotion as by logical discourse.

Which brings me back to my central point. Despite their abstract or even ethereal quality, many pure social constructs contribute more to the depth and substance, to the joys and horrors of human life than do physical objects we can touch or feel (and with which we so frantically try to surround ourselves). Think for a moment about such notions as the land ethic, private property, democracy, and civil rights. And what about gay liberation? Again, none of these ideas per se has any physical manifestation; absent the human intellect, they would not exist. Yet each concept has a shared meaning for any educated person in Western society; these concepts profoundly influence how we act out our lives in both the biophysical and social worlds; they have dramatically formative influences on the lives of countless individuals and whole subgroups in society.

These are by no means trivial observations. What I am describing here is a truly unique quality of *Homo sapiens*. All other organisms respond to the biophysical world *as they find it,* their actions dictated by instinct, pre-dictable stimulus-response mechanisms, and simple trial-and-error learning. By contrast, humans create abstract concepts of such power that they actually determine how we perceive reality. Indeed, we experience both social and biophysical stimuli through socially constructed perceptual frames that help to shape both our individual reactions and group responses.

The human manipulation of reality is a universal phenomenon. All cultural narratives, worldviews, religious doctrines, political ideologies, and academic paradigms are largely social constructs. Each construct is an uneasy blend of facts and beliefs, assumptions and values. The whole is massaged and polished by social discourse and elevated to the status of received wisdom by tacit agreement among members of the social group creating the construct. The resulting perceptual frames are, of course, culture-specific – people from different cultures may therefore respond to the same political events, natural catastrophes, or other stimuli in dramatically differing ways.

Most importantly, *social constructs can carry sufficient weight to determine the fates of entire societies.*[2]

In theory, there are no limits to the diversity and form of alternative perceptions of reality, but this by no means implies that all alternatives are equally valid. In the words of Neil Postman, "You may say, if you wish, that all 'reality' is a social construction, but you cannot deny that some constructions are 'truer' than others. They are not 'truer' because they are privileged, they [become] privileged because they are 'truer.'"[3] Karl Popper makes much the same point: "What the scientist's and the lunatic's theories have in common is that both belong to conjectural knowledge. But some conjectures are much better than others."[4] What do Postman and Popper mean when they declare that there are "truer" or "better" conjectures?[5] Assuming that the purpose of a given construct is to enhance human well-being, the simplest answer in the case of constructs pertaining to physical phenomena (e.g., an aircraft design or the blueprint for a bridge) is that a "truer" construct will "map" better to the reality it purports to represent; it will be substantiated or reaffirmed by repeated observation over time. Devices, behaviours, and activities based on the construct will produce predictable beneficial results. At the very least, the construct should not jeopardize the health and safety of agents who act as if it were true. In short, the airplane will fly reliably, and the bridge will bear traffic without incident.

We can apply similar criteria even when assessing more abstract constructs (e.g., a law or regulation, a paradigm or ideology). If adopted, will the social construct "work" to further human purposes? Will it enhance individual or social well-being? Will it improve the quality of life of targeted groups or society at large? Will it enhance prospects for cultural survival in the face of rapid global change? Truer or better social constructs will generate positive responses to all these questions.

Global Change and the Social Construction of Human Rights

The contemporary world is a world of contradictions and contrasts, of extraordinary beauty and desecrated landscapes, of unprecedented wealth and chronic poverty, of material abundance and spiritual desolation. It is also an "ecologically full" world of 7 billion people, all with rising material expectations. In fact, ours is a world in *overshoot* whose human inhabitants each year consume more than the ecosphere produces and generate more wastes than the ecosphere can assimilate. Although half the human family does not yet have enough of the basics for a decent life, the global economy is already bloated. Humanity is living, in part, by depleting and dissipating so-called natural capital (both self-producing and nonrenewable resources) that took millennia to accumulate in the ecosphere.

Despite the obvious ecological conundrum, the world community has scripted a cultural narrative based almost exclusively on continuous material growth and market dynamics. The assumption is that working from this construct will "solve" the problems of landscape degradation, poverty, and social inequity while enhancing human well-being (happiness). Anyone remotely in touch with the state of the world may fairly conclude that this global economic construct isn't working.

- Growth-driven "development" is degrading the biophysical basis of human existence at an accelerating rate: the oceans are acidifying, deserts are spreading, tropical forests are disappearing, biodiversity is declining, fisheries are collapsing, soils are eroding, aquifers are falling, surface waters are polluted beyond life and use, et cetera, et cetera. The climate system and major ecosystems are approaching tipping points beyond which they may well "flip" into new equilibrium states that may not be compatible with human economic or ecological needs.
- The greatest share of national and global income growth flows to upper-income groups who need it least. The richest 20 percent of the world's population takes home 76.6 percent of the world's income; the poorest 20 percent subsist on 1.5 percent.[6] Because high-income consumers are driven by consumption, the world's most serious ecological problems (e.g., climate change) can be traced mainly to this group.
- Although recent economic growth has raised millions out of poverty (particularly in China), the absolute number of poor has never been greater. In impoverished parts of Africa, Asia, and Latin America, about 1.2 billion people still lack access to potable water, and 2.6 billion have no sanitary sewage. Almost a billion people live on less than a dollar per day, and most are calorically deprived. About 2.6 billion people or 40 percent of the human population live in poverty at less than two dollars a day, and most are otherwise malnourished. Over twenty-six thousand children die every day from poverty (meaning hunger, water-borne, and other preventable illnesses).[7]
- In this light, further income growth for the rich is an egregious misallocation of wealth and a waste of the world's resources. Beyond a certain

point – a point long past in the development of high-income countries – there is no significant positive relationship between various objective indicators of population health (longevity, infant mortality, postoperative survival, etc.) and rising incomes.[8] The same goes for subjective indicators, measures of "felt" well-being. In the United States, for example, Robert Lane describes "the strange, seemingly contradictory pattern ... of rising real income and a falling index of subjective well-being."[9]

- The income gap both between and within countries is widening. In 1960, the richest 20 percent of the world's people, living mostly in industrialized countries, took home thirty times the income of the poorest 20 percent; by 1997, they took home seventy-four times as much.[10] The problem is by no means confined to developing countries. By 2000, the richest 5 percent in the United States owned 60 percent of the nation's wealth. That is, the top 5 percent had more wealth than the remaining 95 percent of the population combined. (The United States now has the widest income gap of any high-income nation.)

- Ironically, one of the most significant contributors to declining population health and increasing civil unrest in poor and rich countries alike is income disparity. Countries with increasing inequality and deepening social divisions tend to show markedly higher rates of alcohol-related deaths, accidents, homicide, crime, violence and probably drug use.[11] Yet we actively promote national and global political economies that systematically and dramatically increase inequity. More than 80 percent of the human population lives in countries where income differentials are increasing, including Canada and the United States.[12]

Sustainability and *sustainable development* may have become watchwords among political leaders, international development agencies, and humanitarian nongovernmental organizations, but it is clear that the prevailing approach is a multidimensional failure.

And the situation shows every sign of worsening. The latest UN projections suggest the global population is headed toward 10 billion by the end of the century.[13] Climate change is accelerating; sea levels are rising; deserts are spreading; water shortages loom for hundreds of millions of people. We have passed the production peak for conventional petroleum and must now rely on more remote and dirtier sources of most fossil fuels (renewable energies are not yet significant substitutes for oil, gas, and coal). After a century of decline, commodity prices have begun to climb as demand exceeds supply and outstrips the gains from technological efficiency. Food prices in particular are at a historic high.

One cause *and* effect is that the competitive scramble for the world's remaining bounty has begun in earnest. For example, land is critical to identity, livelihoods, self-reliance, and food security. Wealthy, overpopulated land-poor countries ranging from Saudi Arabia to China and South Korea are therefore spreading their ecological footprints globally by leasing or buying up vast tracts of land in poorer countries, particularly in Africa for the production of food, fibre, and biofuels, which are shipped home.[14] Ironies abound. While Saudi investors spend $100 million raising wheat, barley, and rice on land leased to them by the Ethiopian government for export back home, the World Food Program spends even more ($116 million) to provide "230,000 tonnes of food aid between 2007 and 2011 to the 4.6m Ethiopians it thinks are threatened by hunger and malnutrition."[15] Meanwhile, subsistence farmers and existing communities are being displaced from their traditional lands and homes to satisfy the demands of foreign corporations and national states. And with vast sums of money involved, shady deals and corruption are inevitable. The government of Madagascar fell to a military-backed popular uprising in April 2009 as word spread that it had signed away rights to 1.3 million hectares of oil palm and cropland to Daewoo Logistics of South Korea for ninety-nine years.

And this is where Laura Westra's work comes in. Like many of her other writings, this book raises critical issues that have largely been ignored or deliberately repressed in mainstream debates concerning the dynamics of global ecological and geopolitical change. Can there be any more important question in international politics and law than how the global community will go about socially constructing and reaffirming the framework of individual and collective rights and responsibilities that will govern how individuals, corporations, and states interact with one another and the broader "environment" in the tumultuous decades ahead? What individual rights should remain sacrosanct, and what responsibilities should go with them? What collective rights must be constructed and honoured by all to ensure the integrity of the global commons, and how might these new rights stint the existing rights of individuals? (The private ownership of land and "natural capital" upon which many others depend for their livelihoods or well-being raises many questions in an increasingly crowded and resource-poor world.)

Clearly, the global community must develop the means to achieve balance between individual and collective interests and to recognize the critical points where individual and community rights converge.

We have already noted that the human capacity to construct alternative social realities is a unique human attribute and, fortunately, we have several other uniquely human qualities to bring to bear on the task: high intelligence and the capacity for logical thought, the capacity for moral judgment, the ability to plan ahead, and an unequalled capacity to express capacity for other people (and even other species).

If these were the only things in play, then planning a just sustainable future would be relatively easy. Logic rails against unlimited material growth on a finite planet. Indeed, our best science tells us that we are already pressing up against potentially disastrous climate tipping points. At the very least, the precautionary principle argues that we should therefore scale back on aggregate economic activity. In these circumstances, gross social inequity, already morally reprehensible, would become intolerable. Wealthy countries would naturally plan for controlled economic contraction to create the ecological space necessary for justifiable growth in low-income countries (and should be willing to do so on compassionate grounds).[16] Properly executed, policies for wealth redistribution could actually improve the quality of life in both rich and poor countries.[17]

In any case, there is certainly enough to go around (at least in the short term). Consider food: the nearly one billion poor suffering from chronic caloric deprivation are "balanced" by a billion relatively wealthy people suffering from excess weight or obesity (and don't forget that in rich countries such as the United States and Canada half our grain crops are fed to livestock). Of course, a smaller steady-state, carbon-neutral economy would lower the risks of climate change and stop the conversion of wild habitats for agriculture and other human-dominated land uses.[18] Biodiversity may actually start to recover. And, of course, intelligence and logic dictates that the world community come together to implement a human program for population control and reduction.

Intelligence, sound planning, moral logic, and compassion – it's not hard to envisage how the application of these qualities could ultimately produce an economically equitable, socially just, and ecologically secure global community. But these are not the only factors at large in today's world. Humans share with all other species a natural predisposition to expand, a tendency that is being reinforced by a well-entrenched social construct, the global growth paradigm. To complicate matters, the past half century has seen powerful interests engage in the deliberate construction of a global economic ethic that exalts short-term greed, selfish individualism, and private property rights as a means to further growth while disparaging altruism, kindness, community, and consideration of the common good. And, as if that weren't enough, the same corporate and political interests have engineered the emergence of a new age of unreason. In many countries, particularly the United States, politics is dominated not by logical consideration of the ecological, socioeconomic, and moral crises confronting citizens everywhere, but rather by faith-based ideologies (e.g., neoliberal economics and market capitalism), religious fundamentalism, climate-change denial, anti-intellectualism, and myriad other forms of magical thinking. Together, these factors have contributed to a world rife with conflict, suspicion, distrust, and (understandably) growing despair.

It is also a world seemingly paralyzed from taking action to save itself. This is particularly tragic when we recognize a singular fact: ours is a globally interconnected world of mutual interdependence bristling with nuclear weapons. An all-out economic – or military – competition for remaining stocks of vital resources will produce no winners. No person, corporation, or nation-state can go it alone, can achieve sustainability in isolation from the whole. (We would do well to remember that the first-class suites on the Titanic sank just as quickly and just as deep as the meanest steerage cabins.) In short, there has never been a greater need for clarity concerning the rights and responsibilities of individuals, corporations, and nations to ensure the continued integrity of, and popular access to, the common pool of resources and life-support functions upon which we all depend. We are dealing here with questions that affect the basis of life and the right to life itself. Perhaps for the first time in history, individual and "tribal" interests have converged with humanity's collective interests.

Laura Westra explores this ground with dogged vigour. Hers is a plea for recognition (among other things) that such basic rights "are actually and temporally prior to all other rights," that one has "no need for freedom of speech, of religion, or the right to vote or equality before the law" if one lacks basic subsistence and physical security. The idea that a civilization should be judged on the basis of how it treats its most vulnerable members is about to be tested as never before. We must succeed in protecting the ecological rights of ordinary people against the unwarranted incursions of powerful vested interests. The critical questions are as follows: Will our raucously divided world community be able to negotiate the logical, moral, and legal constructs necessary to enshrine fundamental ecological rights in the name of the common good? And if such agreements are struck, will there be time to massage, polish, and exercise these rights until they are seen as inviolable? Will governments and the corporate sector enforce and respect them?

The failure to construct an adequate framework of critical "rights to life" would be no ordinary failure. One possible outcome would be global descent into political chaos and irreversible ecological decline at the cost of millions – even billions – of human lives and the loss of untold non-human species. Even if by some miracle the world were otherwise to pull through the ecological crisis, achieving sustainability without a framework that guarantees human dignity through access to vital necessities would be a hollow achievement.

But there is something else: the collapse of this initiative would mean the failure of the global community to exploit the very qualities that allegedly elevate our species above common brutishness – high intelligence, foresight, moral character, and compassion. "*Homo sapiens* will either rise above mere animal instinct and become fully human, or wink out ignominiously, a guttering candle in a violent storm of our own making."[19] It would be tragic irony if, in the twenty-first century, this most intelligent and self-aware of species, this most technologically sophisticated of human societies, succumbs to the unconscious urgings of a myopic, narrowly self-interested, and brutishly primitive tribalism. Civilization would cease to exist. It may even mean the end of *Homo sapiens*, arguably Nature's most daring evolutionary experiment.

William E. Rees, PhD, FRSC
Professor, School of Community and Regional Planning,
University of British Columbia

NOTES

1 See Berger and Luckmann (1966).
2 See Tainter (1998); Diamond (2005).
3 Postman (1999, 76).
4 Popper (1972).
5 In this context, it is helpful to think of a social construct as a hypothesis (i.e., conjecture) that is to be tested by application in the real (social or biophysical) world. In effect, acting out any social construct represents an uncontrolled experiment.

For example, neoliberal growth-based economics and globalization theory are both elaborate social constructs that are currently playing out (destructively?) in the real finite ecosphere.

6   Shah (2010).

7   Ibid.; World Bank (2008).

8   Siegel (2006); Victor (2008).

9   Lane (2000).

10   UNDP (2005).

11   Wilkinson (1996); see also Wilkinson and Pickett (2009).

12   UNDP (2007).

13   Of course, the population may never reach such heady heights because of the various constraints detailed here.

14   These countries, with their expanding populations, will soon need the land, particularly if climate change and market competition further threaten local food supplies. Cotula et al. (2009).

15   "Outsourcing's Third Wave," *The Economist*, 21 May 2009; see also "Fears for the World's Poor Countries as the Rich Grab Land," *The Guardian*, 4 July 2009.

16   At present, global markets and money wealth enable the residents of high-income countries such as Canada and the United States to access three to five times their equitable share of global biocapacity.

17   A socially just sustainability implies that everyone would be better off. See Wilkinson and Pickett (2009).

18   *Steady-state* refers to a constant sustainable throughput of energy and material through the economy within the productive and assimilative capacities of supportive ecosystems. A steady state is not to be confused with a static state. The steady state can be dynamic, constantly changing and innovating. Sunrise sectors of the economy would be free to grow as obsolete or sunset industries are phased out.

19   Rees (2002, 267).

WORKS CITED

Berger, Peter L., and Thomas. Luckmann. 1966. *The Social Construction of Reality.* Garden City, NY: Doubleday.

Cotula, Lorenzo, Sonja Vermeulen, Rebeca Leonard, and James Keeley. 2009. *Land Grab or Development Opportunity? Agricultural Investment and International Land Deals in Africa.* London: IIED/FAO/IFAD.

Diamond, Jared. 2005. *Collapse: How Societies Choose to Fail or Succeed.* New York: Viking.

Lane, Robert. 2000. *The Loss of Happiness in Market Democracies.* New Haven, CT: Yale University Press.

Popper, Karl. 1972. "Conjectural Knowledge: My Solution of the Problem of Induction." In *Objective Knowledge: An Evolutionary Approach,* by Karl Popper. Oxford: Oxford University Press.

Postman, Neil. 1999. *Building a Bridge to the Eighteenth Century*. New York: Alfred Knopf.

Rees, W.E. 2002. "Globalization and Sustainability: Conflict or Convergence?" *Bulletin of Science, Technology and Society* 22, 4: 249-68.

Shah, Anup. 2010. "Poverty Facts and Stats." *Global Issues: Social, Political, Economic and Environmental Issues That Affect Us All*. http://www.globalissues.org/.

Siegel, Charles. 2006. *The End of Economic Growth*. Preservation Institute, Berkeley, California. http://www.preservenet.com/.

Tainter, Joseph. 1988. *The Collapse of Complex Societies*. New York: Cambridge University Press.

UNDP (United Nations Development Program). 2005. *Human Development Report 2005*. New York: United Nations Development Program.

–. 2007. *Human Development Report 2007*. New York: United Nations Development Program.

Victor, Peter A. 2008. *Managing without Growth: Slower by Design, Not Disaster*. Cheltenham: Edward Elgar.

Wilkinson, Richard. 1996. *Unhealthy Societies: The Afflictions of Inequality*. London: Routledge.

Wilkinson, Richard, and Kate Pickett. 2009. *The Spirit Level: Why Equality Is Better for Everyone*. London: Penguin Books.

World Bank. 2008. Development Indicators. http://web.worldbank.org/.

Human Rights

Introduction

After teaching environmental ethics and the politics of environmental racism for many years, it became increasingly obvious to me that environmental ethics was the locus of an ongoing battle between different positions and arguments, little of which filtered down to public policy or actual legal regimes to make a difference on the ground. My research indicated the urgency of the situation confronting millions of people affected by environmental causes ranging from climate change and the extreme weather events it engendered (for example, drought and famine in the southern continents and melting ice in the Arctic and its devastating consequences on the lives and survival prospects of peoples in the Far North), to the ongoing thrust of globalization and trade and its disastrous effects on local and indigenous communities, to the proliferation of hazardous chemicals in the developed world.

Moral exhortation, while necessary, appears to be insufficient to stem the tide of ongoing collective harms. The triumph of capitalism over the rights of the commons started a long time ago in agrarian England. But I argue that what we are facing today is the final enclosure movement, for the commons today are no longer available to the collective, for most of the natural world has been either inquinated and commodified or turned into private exploited property.[1] The early enclosure movement was the result of capitalism, but some today question whether earlier forms of capitalism can be equated with the modern notion of globalization. Richard Westra argues that "neoliberal state policy is undermining the very conditions for the existence of capitalism."[2]

At any rate, neoliberalism and globalization now dominate global governance, and they have been accompanied by increasing breaches of human rights law. The vital importance of law to attempts to redress harms persuaded me to return to school for a second PhD in law, which resulted in the publication of *Ecoviolence and the Law*.[3] As I continued to research the effects of environmental injustice on human rights, I chose areas where injustice appeared to be most obvious and to engender the gravest harm. What emerged from my research was the realization that that the rights of communities and collectives – especially those of traditional, land-based groups – were the ones most at risk. Starting with the largest collective, that of unborn and future generations, I worked on three case studies and produced a trilogy on environmental justice: *Environmental Justice and the Rights of Unborn and Future Generations* (2006), *Environmental Justice and the Rights of Indigenous Peoples* (2007), and *Environmental Justice and the Rights of Ecological Refugees* (2009).

What these case studies indicated was that, although there were numerous domestic and international legal instruments for the protection of individual rights, there were fewer for the collective. That was the reason for undertaking the present work: to research and sum up the status of the collective in regard to the commons and to discover whether there were any avenues that promised some timely progress in the defence of both, given the urgency of the multiple issues that affect basic collective human rights.

This book is not intended as a comprehensive review of all domestic and international legal instruments or related jurisprudence pertaining to the commons and the collective. It simply draws upon instruments and case law to present an argument about the need to protect collective rights and the "commons," upon which they depend for survival.

Starting with the principles, both legal and moral, that mandate the protection of the collective, Chapter 1 discusses the meaning of communities and the collective, setting the stage for a wide-ranging discussion of principles and relevant instruments. Chapter 2 highlights the discrepancy between various instruments, declarations, and UN reports on the public interest and the defence of the common good and the worst issues affecting basic rights today: climate change and world hunger. Unlike ethical arguments that, for the most part, use abstract examples with little or no ties to reality, and because law and public policy *must* be involved in ethical issues, these examples are necessary to tie my argument regarding principles to actual issues. A similar approach informs Chapter 3, in which the argument presented in Chapter 1 regarding the difference between communities and the collective is fleshed out through a discussion of the pivotal importance of traditional communities to the collective and these communities' rights, protected as they are, at least in principle.

Part 2 reverses the order of Part 1. Whereas Part 1 addresses principles first and then introduces actual issues as examples, Part 2 proceeds directly to a discussion of what is available today for the protection of human rights. Chapter 4 considers the right to development, the common heritage of mankind, and public health law, all of which are intended to reach beyond the protection of individual rights. Chapter 5 considers the relationship between state obligations and democracy and the importance and role of the latter, as the most desired form of governance today, against a background of unequal power and imperialistic nationalism.

Chapter 6 returns to the basic principles proposed in Chapter 1. It examines these principles as they pertain not only to power but also to the responsibility of states, the role and history of the United Nations, and the many obstacles to the protections of basic collective rights. The power and primacy of globalized trade and economic regimes add to these difficulties. Finally, Chapter 7 reconsiders the development of recent case law and the re-emergence in recent legal scholarship of older doctrines such as *parens patriae* (parent of the nation) and the public interest. The need to return to such moral or legal principles also underlies the proposal for a world law and for a renewed international constitutionalism based on the *Charter of the United Nations*.

The conclusion of this book in theory, then, is that we must return to robust moral and legal principles, nonderogable norms and doctrines that stand above conventions and positive law in general. In practice, however, I conclude with a plea to re-examine not only the UN's *Charter* but also its organs, its reports, and its initiatives, all of which are strong and desirable but are often not enforced because of politics rather than principles. This discrepancy seems to be the basis of the dysfunctionality of the current international law regime and its domestic counterparts. Hence, that is where transformative changes must start.

PART 1

Basic Collective Rights for Law and Morality – The Theory

1

Individual Rights and Collective Rights in Conflict: The Ecocentric Perspective and the Commons

Many centuries ago, capitalism arose in agrarian England as economic motive and competitiveness replaced traditional values during the enclosure movement. Enclosures provided the most famous redefinition of property rights: they eliminated the commons, with no regard for human rights.[1] Philosopher John Locke defended the right to property above all, although he predicated his defence on ensuring that enough land would be left to be held in common. But he also espoused the defence of improvements as needed to impose value on nature, an argument that supported the policies of his master, the Earl of Shaftsbury.

Through Locke's friendship with Thomas Jefferson, Lockean arguments filtered into the American Declaration of Independence. But these enclosure movements, brutal though they were in their effects on the people, also started what eventually became known as the tragedy of the commons.[2] What we encounter today – the primacy of the economic motive over and above human rights, including the right to a safe and healthy habitat – is the final enclosure movement. It is once again mostly the poor and dispossessed of the world who are shut out of the natural global commons.

The benefits that would have once accrued to the poor are no longer available: whatever is left of the commons has become someone's property and is used as such. Even the simplest "natural goods" – for example, clean air, pure water, safe sunlight, and safe foods – are no longer freely available, and all are unavailable to the poor. Drinking water must be bought; sunscreen is needed to protect us from the sun; removing housing from hazardous industrial operations is expensive; and food in areas of famine and that which is safe and organically grown is marginally more available but often laced with toxic substances. All are commercial goods. As E.M. Wood points out, the very notion of improvement as originally conceived is problematic: "We might like to think about the implications of a culture in which the world for 'making better' is rooted in the word for making monetary profit."[3]

What was at stake then, as it is now, was first and foremost the existence of the most basic human right: respect for human life, for human security and subsistence.[4] This was at issue long before questions of religious or sexual rights. Dispossessed farmer-tenants in seventeenth-century agrarian England had no way of supporting themselves or their families. Today, many of us, especially in developed Western democracies, can in fact support ourselves, but our life and health are nevertheless under attack.

Likening the effects of unsafe, unhealthy habitats to an attack is particularly apt because the simile emphasizes two main points connected to the law, one historical, the other moral. I describe what I term ecoviolence – that is, violence perpetrated in and through the environment and human rights.[5] Alan Boyle asks,

> Should we continue to think about human rights and the environment within the existing framework of human rights law in which the protection of human rights is the central focus – essentially a greening of the right to life, private life, and property – or has the time come to talk directly about environmental rights – in other words a right to have the environment itself protected? Should we transcend the anthropocentric in favor of the eco-centric?[6]

One can only applaud the reasoning behind the question raised by Boyle: the protection of human rights when they are isolated from their ecological basis is increasingly insufficient as the effects of climate change reduce whole cities and areas to rubble, or even eliminate them altogether (see *Native Village of Kivalina v. ExxonMobil* (2008)). Or perhaps we need to ask ourselves which human rights are protected when the unfortunate inhabitants of these areas are forced to flee and become environmentally displaced persons, a group that includes hundreds of thousands of persons, all of whom (at this time) have no protection under the law.[7]

Similarly, what of the local and indigenous communities whose inhabitants are either harmed within their own territories or forced to relocate by the pressures of unwanted and unconsented development?[8] As well, what of the rights under the present laws of all those in developing countries whose resources are no longer there because of desertification or have been eliminated and replaced with products desired by those in affluent countries? What about the many others who are the victims of economic oppression and the neoliberal policies of globalization?

Yet in these and most other cases where environmental rights may be invoked because of the impact of environmental degradation on human beings, the question is not whether to give primacy to the ecocentric viewpoint at the expense of the anthropocentric perspective. Science today clearly indicates that – at the level of basic human rights – the two are one and the same.[9] In other words, protecting human rights *starts* with protecting the ecology of our habitat, for we are, as Aldo Leopold puts it, part of the commonality of life: "All ethics so far evolved rest upon a single premise: that the individual is a member of a community of interdependent parts ... the land ethic simply enlarges the boundaries of the community to include soils, waters, plants and animals, or collectively, the land."[10]

Hence the question posed at the start of this chapter is based on a false dichotomy: environmental rights *are* human rights, as Judge Christian Weeramantry of the International Criminal Court argued in 1997.[11] Moreover, until this fact is entrenched in law and reflected in both instruments and jurisprudence, there is no hope that the respect for human rights advocated by Boyle and most legal scholars will prevail. This is a question I discuss in most of my work to date. In this book, there is another question I want to raise, for I believe that the discussion and the answers that may emerge will offer a fuller understanding of Weeramantry's argument. Are environmental rights individual or collective rights? Boyle does not address this question, and those who do discuss collective rights for the most part do not do so in the context of the environment, let alone that of ecocentrism. Collective rights in general are part of what some term third-generation or solidarity rights.[12]

According to Karel Vasak, "the last generation of Human Rights would be of more collective nature."[13] And according to Marlies Galenkamp, they will include "the right to development," "the right to environment, the right to peace, the right to co-ownership of the common heritage of mankind and the right to communicate."[14] At this time the important issues are the right to the environment and the common heritage of mankind, for the right to development is often that of corporations and neoliberal states, not that of local and indigenous communities, which, most often, have not been fully informed about, let alone asked to consent to, the so-called development imposed on them that brings harms rather than benefits. Rodolfo Stavenhagen argues that indigenous peoples "must be regarded as the victims of the so-called right to development which states attach to themselves and with which they are destroying any number of peoples within the borders of their territory."[15] Here, Stavenhagen criticizes this one aspect of collective rights from three separate angles, the globalist, the statist, and the nationalistic. The existence of the rights of states points to the presence of a collectivity that already exists in law and has rights. State rights stand alongside minority rights, peoples' rights, and indigenous rights.[16] Another collectivity – the multinational corporation – likewise possesses great and undisputed rights that should be disputed, a point I argue below.

Neither states nor multinational corporations are biological entities, although they are certainly legal entities and are, in fact, composed of biological individuals. Hence they are, *prima facie*, potentially in conflict with the rights of the biological individuals of which they are composed. The simplest examples are wars for the former and hazardous industries for the latter. A state's interest (and right) may well be to wage a war of conquest that requires the use of soldiers, whose individual survival will be at risk. In the case of a multinational corporation, an operation for the production of chemicals, for instance, will put at risk individual workers and people who live in the surrounding area.[17]

When these two collectivities are eliminated from the present discussion, what remains are minorities and indigenous communities, and the argument I propose is appropriate to both. When viewed from the perspective of basic rights and an ecocentric point of view, collectivities and individuals are two aspects of the same cosmopolitan rights. Most of the existing scholarship on either collective rights or community rights, such as those of indigenous peoples, does not start from an ecocentric perspective, nor does it demand it in support of its arguments.[18] But some scholars do acknowledge the increasing presence of community or collective rights in the law. For instance, in his seminal work on indigenous peoples' rights, James Anaya characterizes human rights as mainly "individual's demands of freedom, equality, participation and economic and physical security vis-à-vis the state" but recognizes that "concepts of group or collective rights have begun to take hold in the new articulation of human rights norms."[19]

At any rate, two basic questions emerge. What is the status of collective rights in relation to individual human rights, and can and should the policies of aggressive Western liberal governments regarding individual rights be reconciled with the existence of collective rights? The first question can be extended further for clarity. What are collective rights, and are they the same as communitarian or group rights? The clarification portion of the first question can be answered more easily than the question itself. The rights of communities and groups (and indigenous peoples, who represent the paradigm case in this category) are part of the collectivities here envisioned, yet they do not exhaust that category, even though they are often spoken of as if they represent the sum total of collectivities. As the growing case law related to such rights indicates, these groups are increasingly present in international and domestic law (see the following chapter) because they provide the best introduction to the questions under consideration. But the general term *collectivities* exceeds the concept of communities. An answer to the first question will help to clarify an even more basic question: what is the basis and nature of human rights, whether individual or collective? Dwight Newman's definitive argument embodies and supports my own conclusion, but by a different path. Newman writes: "My argument is that certain individual interests that ground duties are meaningful interests and can be fulfilled only on the precondition that certain collective interests are also rights. We can put this statement in simplified terms: if we accept certain individual rights, we presuppose certain collective rights."[20]

A somewhat compatible position is evident in Roger Brownsword's discussion of basic human rights in the concepts of human dignity as empowerment or human dignity as constraint: "In practice, though, whereas the former [human dignity as empowerment] tends to be closely associated with human rights movements aimed at giving individuals the opportunity to flourish as self-determining authors of their own destinies, the latter [human dignity as constraint] (as expressed by the dignitarian alliance) combines a (Kantian) view of what is distinctive about what defines life as civilized (and, thus, respectful of human dignity), in a particular community."[21] The main difference between the two positions on the relationship between dignity and human rights is that Newman speaks of collective rights whereas Brownsword refers to communitarian rights. I believe that the former rather than the latter better represents the universalism of both Kant and the understanding of human rights I defend. It bears repeating: communitarian rights are already more visible in both moral and legal discourse, given their connection to cultural and indigenous communities.

But I am seeking at this time to establish a connection between universal collective rights and universal individual human rights so that the limits (if any) of the latter may be defined through a fuller understanding of the former. The starting point for this discussion, including the argument leading to the answer to the first question, is the understanding of human rights that will form the basis for the connection between them and collective rights understood as universal.

Universal Principles and Human Rights

For the most part, talk about human rights, outside the realm of armed conflicts, centres on religious or sexual rights or the right to secede or to acquire national status on the part of groups. The most fundamental right – the right to life – the basis of all others has been quietly forgotten: it has become, if not obsolete, at least politically incorrect because of its possible conflict with other rights. Yet, unless we return to the defence of the most basic rights of all, as Henry Shue terms them, it will not be possible to protect humankind globally and indict those who breach those rights and punish them with a severity appropriate to the crimes.

I do not view other rights violations as unimportant. I simply emphasize that our right to make any and all choices – be they political, religious, or personal – starts with our being not only alive but also in a condition that renders us capable of thinking, acting, and pursuing various goals. As Shue argues, "part of what it means to be able to enjoy any other right is not to be prevented from exercising it by lack of security or subsistence. To claim to guarantee people a right that they are in fact unable to exercise is fraudulent, like furnishing people with meal tickets but providing no food."[22] He continues, "Basic rights are the morality of the depths"; they represent "everyone's minimum reasonable demands upon the rest of humanity."[23] Subsistence rights include the bare necessities we all need, beginning with "unpolluted air, unpolluted water, adequate food, adequate clothing, adequate shelter."[24] Although some of these subsistence rights are at least present in the language of the *Universal Declaration of Human Rights*, neither the *International Covenant on Economic, Social and Cultural Rights* (1966) nor the *International Covenant on Civil and Political Rights* (1966) specifies that the triad of safe air, water, and food – that is, elements supportive of life – is an actual right.[25]

In addition, although we may tend to think of the two international covenants as necessary to improve the lives of citizens in developing countries, Shue's triad is empathetically not present as a right of citizens of affluent, technologically advanced democracies, any more than it is a clear right in the impoverished Global South. The role of poverty in depriving people of their rights and thus of basic justice worldwide is amply documented. As Thomas Pogge writes, "severe poverty has consequences: 790 million persons are not adequately nourished, while one billion are without safe water and 2.4 billion without basic sanitation; more than 880 million lack access to basic health services; about one billion are without adequate shelter and two billion without electricity."[26] Epidemiological data also document the lack of less than healthy air, water, and food in the Global North or West, where particulates in the air, ozone layer depletion, and unsanitary water and food laced with hormones, chemicals, and other additives promote a wide range of diseases, including a cancer epidemic in citizens far removed from poverty.[27]

The first step in strengthening the principles that will sustain laws to protect basic rights is leaving behind any form of reasoning that is purely consequential in favour of a deontological approach. We need to adopt universal principles that will impose the obligation to ensure respect for life's infinite value, in the Kantian sense. Respect for life, Onora O'Neill contends, means rejecting the infliction not only of direct harm but also of indirect injury to the natural world.[28] She argues that such injury may be gratuitous (that is, undertaken simply because it is "convenient for the powerful") or systematic (taken for granted as a normal way to conduct business or govern society).[29] Either case results in deep injustice through the destruction of natural environments: "In the first place, their destruction is unjust because it is a further way by which others can be injured: systematic or gratuitous destruction of the means of life creates vulnerabilities, which facilitate direct injuries to individuals. Destroying (parts of) natural and man-made environments injures those whose lives depend on them. Secondly, the principle of destroying their reproductive and regenerative powers is not universalizabile."[30] Thus O'Neill does not advocate abstract cosmopolitanism but rather that justice should prevail globally in a practical sense, by "identifying compatible institutions and practices."[31] Although O'Neill does not clearly state it, *we all* depend on natural systems in various ways: to be deprived of them is a severe attack on life, health, and our natural function.[32] This attack now extends not only to a plurality of others everywhere but also to future generations, whose ability to survive, thrive, and have their rights protected must also be respected.[33] Our interconnectedness, to all living things and processes today and in the future, ensures that this dimension of our obligations cannot be avoided, and it represents the basis of ecological concern.[34]

Whoever the humans of the future may be, they will share our finiteness and vulnerability; therefore, in Kantian terms, "inclusive principles of indifference to and neglect of others also cannot be universalized."[35] Shue adds: "The infant and the aged do not need to be assaulted in order to be deprived of health, life or the capacity to enjoy active rights. The classical liberal main prescription for the good life, do not interfere with thy neighbor, is the only poison they need."[36] We can add all debilitated, malnourished, or weakened infants, adults, and aged, and all of us who are continually exposed to unsafe living conditions.

Grounding Human Rights

> When health is absent
> Wisdom cannot reveal itself,
> Art cannot become manifest
> Strength cannot fight,
> Wealth becomes useless
> And intelligence cannot be applied.
>
> – Herophilus (325 BC)

The connection between environmental degradation and human life, health, and normal function expressed by Herophilus rests on the inviolability of human rights. Although a detailed analysis of all existing arguments in support of these rights is beyond the scope of this book, I draw on some of them to support my own thesis that human rights extend beyond the right of the human person to the generic right to life, including our habitat. My approach is Kantian, in line with the arguments by O'Neill, Shue, and Pogge.

The foundational arguments proposed by Alan Gewirth help to shed light on the basic connection between humans and their habitats. Gewirth argues that human rights are not based primarily on human dignity and that this Kantian principle is only partially right.[37] He prefers to base "human rights on the necessary conditions of human action," for morality is intended to give rise to moral action.[38] Gewirth adds that "human rights are the equivalent to 'natural' rights, in that they pertain to all humans by virtue of their nature as actual or prospective agents."[39] He cites five reasons in support of his claim: (1) "the supreme importance of the conditions of human actions"; (2) action is "the common subject matter of all moralities"; (3) *action* is more specific and less vague than *dignity* or *flourishing*; (4) action ultimately secures fundamental moral status for persons; and (5) "action's necessary conditions provide justification for human rights – as every agent must hold that he has a right to freedom and well-being as the necessary conditions of his 'actions.'"[40]

Deryck Beyleveld and Roger Brownsword argue that the basic or generic needs that represent the preconditions of all action, including moral action, are freedom or volunatariness and well-being or purposiveness. The former are procedural, while the latter are substantive.[41] They view freedom as an instrument to well-being. I propose inverting this order. Life, health, and the mental ability to comprehend and choose precede the exercise of voluntariness and are not only necessary for it but also sufficient when all these conditions are present.

In essence, this is the argument presented here: basic rights, as defined by Shue, represent the minimum all humans are entitled to, and they are prior to all other rights, both conceptually and temporally.[42] For Gewirth as well, life and the capacities named above can be interfered with or threatened.[43] Thus, to say we have rights is to say equally that the preconditions of these rights represent something we are entitled to, not only in morality but also in law. In other words, any legal instrument that supports the existence of human rights *ipso facto* ought to proclaim the requirement that their preconditions be equally supported and respected.

Some argue that the dignity of human beings is only partially the grounds for human rights and that dignity itself is based on agency. This argument, however, allows for the introduction of at least one further point in favour of extending human rights to life and health. The introduction of preconditions means the introduction of conditions that are not only conceptually but also temporally prior to agency; therefore, the protection of these preconditions entails the acceptance of potential consequences in the protection of agency.

Arguments about potentiality are discussed rather cavalierly in the extensive literature on abortion, and they have re-emerged more recently because of the presence of the rights of the child (to be) in utero. For instance, Deborah Mathieu writes: "Thus even if the foetus is not considered a person in the moral or legal sense, there are still important interests of a person which must be weighed against those of the pregnant woman: the interests of the future child. A pregnant woman should act for the sake of the child that the foetus will become. *Her* obligations, in other words, are to her future child, not to her foetus."[44] Given that the potential for developing certain genetic conditions has been used to explain or justify abortion, it is hard to see why the future should be viewed as suspect when it is used to proscribe abortion in cases where concern for the child's future health is not an issue.[45] Beyleveld and Brownsword argue that it is not necessary to support the presumed dignity of the embryo from conception: "It is the consideration of the possibility that the zygote might be an agent (and have dignity) even though there is little evidence of this."[46] The authors continue by citing the possible rights of the pregnant woman in this respect. To destroy the fetus by removing it from its first natural habitat, however, clearly violates the preconditions of its eventual agency, even if, with the authors, we accept "the view that agency is the ground of human dignity."[47]

If we consider Peter Singer's position that rights should be grounded in sentience foundational, or even if we consider David DeGrazia's notion of nociception, we have more than dignity or even dignity-as-agency, in which the Gewirthian principle of proportionality maintains that agents have "duties to all living creatures (human or non-human) on a proportional basis."[48] A discussion of the detailed arguments for and against abortion or the use of embryos would take us too far afield. Yet even this brief analysis indicates that the presence of life ought to be the most important category to render beings worthy of respect and consideration, aside from their present or possible mental states.

Kant defends the infinite value of life, for people's generic capacities to be human, and all that they may entail, are not eliminated by adverse conditions, such as regular drunkenness. Nonhuman animals have been deemed to have purposiveness.[49] The same could be said of fetuses, for the development of their nervous systems are comparable to animals at various stages, and they certainly do not have nociception as an indication of the capacities they will possess later in their development.[50] If duties, at minimum, are owed to all beings capable of sentience and agency in various proportions, then the duty is not specific, but it can be owed to all life and to its preconditions – that is, to the habitats whose fittingness supports our own. In other words, by extending the meaning of *dignity* from its modern sense of *dignitas* to its classical Greek sense of "within the natural laws of the universe," Kant's imperatives can be placed within the more far-reaching imperatives of the principle of integrity.[51] In this case, anything that conflicts with the dignity of natural universal laws is *prima facie* suspect: it requires, at minimum, serious justification beyond preferences or economic advances.[52]

In fact, these extended rights, or the preconditions of the rights themselves, are everyone's entitlement, and those who deliberately or negligently impose harms should be considered either guilty of crimes, directly or indirectly, or complicit in their commission.

Basic Rights?

Unless we define basic rights in functional terms, as Shue does, we are almost certain to make implicit or even explicit arguments that "basic rights" are more important than other rights. By distinguishing a core group of "basic" rights that are alleged more important than other rights, one almost unavoidably devalues the remaining human rights.

– Jack Donnelly, *Universal Human Rights in*
Theory and Practice, 2003

The concept of basic rights is controversial, and Jack Donnelly lists several proposals beyond that of Shue.[53] Most of them include various civil or political rights, as well as life, survival, and subsistence.[54] But there is a difference in kind between Shue's basic rights and most of the additions found in the formulations of other scholars. The difference is that Shue's basic rights are actually and temporally prior to all other rights: you have no need for freedom of speech or religion, the right to vote, or equality before the law if you lack subsistence and security, the latter being understood as physical safety. The presence of basic rights does not, therefore, depreciate all other rights: it demonstrates the interdependence of all rights and emphasizes the need for preconditions for the actualization of all others. In addition, the temporal aspect is needed to anchor rights that will develop in the future of each human being. The child needs to be safe and to subsist to *eventually* claim the right to vote, to be a citizen of a country, or to have the right not to be tortured or taken prisoner unjustly.

All other proposed bundles of rights have, within each bundle, rights that are basic in the sense that they are prior in time and absolutely required before the rest of the bundle can be claimed or even understood. This is the reason why only Shue's interpretation of basic rights is valid, whereas all other attempts to seek a basic formulation are mixed or assume an already developed adult who is possessed of normal function, understanding and, in many cases (see for instance the language of the *International Covenant on Civil and Political Rights*), education, rather than a bare, unspecific human being. This requirement of basic rights is particularly relevant because I argue that collective rights (rather than merely communal or cultural rights), as collectives, are not limited to specific groupings, whether based on age, education, or ethnic background.

Yet Donnelly objects to Shue's list: "If one cannot *obtain* one's subsistence, one will die and thus be unable to enjoy any rights at all. But one can subsist without a *right* to subsistence. For example, mid-nineteenth century workers enjoyed no such right: if they were starving they could not advance effective or even widely acknowledged subsistence claim rights, claims against the state. Nonetheless many of them subsisted and exercised a variety of (legal) rights."[55] The same argument would apply to slaves in the southern parts of the United States before emancipation: they subsisted; they had a security of sorts, as long as they pleased their masters. Therefore, the third category of freedom Shue proposes as part of his basic rights would be equally necessary for slaves and for indentured workers during the period to which Donnelly appeals. Both human dignity as empowerment and human dignity as constraint would require all three basic rights for human beings.[56] In fact, these requirements should today exist clearly for people in developing countries, who appear to lack all three basic rights in many cases.

Yet both the argument based on human dignity and the one based on agency proposed by Gewirth, which I accept, require all three basic rights. Unless individuals can procure what they need to subsist, and unless they are free from attacks on their physical or biological existence, their freedom to will, choose, and act, their essential humanity based on agency, cannot be exercised. This freedom may be there potentially, in the sense that someone who is starving and unable to think an issue through – let alone stand and, say, vote – may still have the capacity to do so once fed and recovered. But the practices (thinking, choosing, willing, doing) that are foundational to our humanity and basic to our dignity as humans can only be actualized through the presence of the basic rights listed by Shue.

One counterargument is that even those who are incapacitated, seriously ill, or comatose (thus, incapable of any human activity) still possess the dignity of being human, and this appears to be correct. But the *exercise* of all other rights requires the initial presence of the basic categories Shue proposes, although the potential ability to exercise all the other rights is, or should be, innate. Once basic rights are understood in this sense, it is easier to view their reach as collective, especially because the harms discussed above are, for the most part, collective harms.

Poisoning a person (especially when the motive for that crime is understood) or preventing a person from developing in a normal way (perhaps by depriving a child of normal nourishment) are also crimes identifiable in domestic instruments and punishable by law. In contrast, collective harmful exposures and deprivations seldom rise to the level of international law.[57] Collective harms therefore tend to go unpunished unless, perhaps, a specific community is harmed, a case can be made for the loss of cultural integrity, or a case can be made for racial discrimination of an indigenous group. The crime still remains hard to prove, but at least there are existing legal criteria to deal with these issues to some extent, although they are still treated, at best, as torts not crimes. But no legal instrument exists to prevent such whole-sale harms before they happen, for these harms often consist of an accumulation of legal hazardous exposures, the sum of which becomes the instrument of the attack on these peoples' lives and health.[58]

It is worthy of note that while such an attack on indigenous people may at least be noted and studied and will, perhaps eventually, receive some form of redress, even such a limited recognition is not available to nonindigenous local populations who are similarly affected, such as the population of the Windsor-Sarnia area in Ontario, Canada, where heavy industrial pollution has grave health effects.[59]

In sum, Henry Shue's understanding of basic rights best supports the development of measures to protect the preconditions of human rights presently accepted and defended in international law. In addition, this interpretation of Shue's basic rights also clarifies the connection between individual and collective rights while also supporting communitarian rights as foundational to the Kantian understanding of the dignity of human beings, universally understood and applied.

Do Collective Rights Presuppose a Constitutive Community?

> The key assumptions underlying the communitarian way of thinking are twofold: first, the presence of a constitutive community and two (and related) the presence of a common good.
>
> – Marlies Galenkamp, *Individualism versus Collectivism*

John Finnis, author of *Natural Law and Natural Rights,* holds a similar position to Marlies Galenkamp, for he relates communities to the common good: "sharing of aim rather than a multiplicity of interactions is constitutive of human groups, communities and societies."[60] This "sharing of aims" leads to the consideration of the common good. Finnis discusses "our unity in human community" in four parts, and his analysis limits community and even common good to specific societies and collectives.[61] In brief, he argues that "part of our unity in human community, then, is physical and biological ... Secondly ... part of our unity in human community ... is the unity of intelligence in its capacities, its workings and its product knowledge ... Thirdly, part of our unity in human community ... is the cultural unity of shared language, common technology and so on ... Part of our unity in human community ... is the unity of common action."[62]

It is clear that points three and four can refer only to specific communities, and Finnis' reference to "communities of which one is a member" conforms to my understanding. However, the focus of this book – the universal collective of humankind in relation to human individual rights – is not what Finnis has in mind. Before turning to the types of communities discussed by Finnis (indigenous, local, and ethnic), this chapter explores the possibility of a common good and, in general, a commonality that can be viewed as universal or cosmopolitan in the political (Kantian) sense. I argue that only the first two aspects of community discussed by Finnis are appropriate from the perspective of this book. In fact, they are sufficient to support the development of this book's argument.

For the most part, the rights and goals of single communities are insufficient to support universal rights (excluding the traditional indigenous and local communities mentioned), and their often conflicting goals and practices need to be assessed from the universal standpoint of justice. In *Rights, Regulation and the Technological Revolution*, Roger Brownsword remarks that "in a world of global governance, no nation state is a regulatory island."[63] In fact, those groups that are termed societies or communities by Finnis fit better within the category Brownsword terms club cosmopolitanism.[64] As Brownsword clarifies, "By 'club cosmopolitanism' I mean a certain kind of regulatory ideal that is characteristic of a group (sometimes a trade association, sometimes a cultural club) that defines itself by reference to a set of value commitments (such as the value of access to markets and free trade, or more generally the value of freedom)." Such groups are by no means all oriented to economics or trade, for the cultural possibility that Brownsword envisages fits well within the goals and lifestyles of traditional indigenous and local communities, whose principal goal is to retain their own culture and to be allowed to transmit it to their children and future generations.[65] In contrast, the collective rights of humankind include respect for indigenous peoples' cultural integrity and their traditional lifestyles, but they are not limited by them: they strive, instead, for a universal cosmopolitanism. Brownsword defends a universal constitutive cosmopolitanism that is committed to respecting "fundamental values while, at the same time, according room and respect for legitimate local differences."[66]

I propose a somewhat different approach, for I see the rights of indigenous communities as integral to a truly universal cosmopolitanism, given that the basic values recommended here as foundational start precisely with the biological integrity of individuals, which is or should be the basic right of all humans, once its role in support of the ability to think, choose, and decide (Finnis' second point) is recognized as the precondition for that ability.[67] Instead of an either/or approach to the two forms of cosmopolitanism that Brownsword envisages, I propose that universal collective rights should start with the basic values of traditional communities and extend them to all humans, regardless of their background, religion, or location and, most of all, regardless of their preferences when these basic values conflict openly with the basic general good of all.

If, as I argue, human rights that are universally defensible must be (1) basic (in the sense defended by Shue) and in support of human biological integrity, and (2) minimally dependent on ecological integrity to ensure that (3) normal development such as the human capacity to think, understand, and choose is actualized according to the potential of each human being, then the characteristic approach of traditional indigenous communities is itself basic to collective cosmopolitan rights.

Collective Rights and Cosmopolitanism

> True law is right reason in agreement with nature; it is of universal
> application, unchanging and everlasting, it summons to duty by
> its commands, and averts from wrongdoing by its prohibition ...
> We can not be freed from its obligations by senate or people, and
> we need not look outside ourselves for an expounder or
> interpreter of it.
>
> – Cicero, *De Republica*, Book 3, xxiii

In Cicero we find one of the earliest expressions of natural law after the Stoics, whose position was far less close than was Cicero's to human law and governance. At any rate, this early statement of cosmopolitanism discloses its main tenets: (1) it is based on the eternal laws of nature; (2) these laws are the basis of absolute principles, which cannot be changed either by authority (the senate) or by popular demand; and (3) our right reason is sufficient to inform us about our obligations. This passage also implies that morality and law are not mutually exclusive.[68]

Of course, the earliest expression of cosmopolitanism can be found in Diogenes "the Dog," who originated the philosophy of the Cynics in 300 BC Diogenes was the seeker of the wise man. He lived an ascetic life while despising the niceties of society; he praised virtue and wisdom above all and was perhaps the first conscientious objector to consumerism and the primacy of trade and economics.[69] However, Cicero believed that the law of reason was applicable primarily to lands and peoples ruled by Roman law, which would appear to limit the universality of his principles. Even so, natural law in general ensures that all human beings have rights, understood in a cosmopolitan sense, and it provides the best basis for that conclusion.

Thomas Pogge, however, views (1) individualism, together with (2) universality and (3) generality, as one of the three basic aspects of cosmopolitanism. Although the second and third postulates are compatible with the position discussed so far, the first postulate, although not wrong, appears to put a somewhat different emphasis on our present understanding of cosmopolitanism: "*Individualism:* the ultimate units of concern are human beings or persons rather than say, family lines, tribes, ethic, cultural or religious communities, nations or states."[70]

Although it is correct to say that communities or cultural groups possess rights in virtue of the individuals of which they are composed, as Brownsword argues, it seems as though extreme individualism may run counter to the main goals of cosmopolitanism, as Pogge understands it, specifically institutional cosmopolitanism, which he contrasts to the interactional cosmopolitanism proposed by Shue.[71] Pogge writes, "The institutional approach thus counts a person's human right to physical integrity as fully satisfied if her physical integrity is reasonably secure."[72]

But current governance approaches already claim that persons are reasonably secure or well protected, and that claim – which has resulted in widespread harm to physical integrity, notably economic oppression, hunger, and deprivations that Pogge himself describes – is the main reason for this book.[73] Pogge, however, acknowledges that "our present global economic regime produces a stable pattern of widespread malnutrition and starvation among the poor (with some 20 million persons dying every year from hunger and trivial diseases), and there are likely to be feasible regimes that would not produce similarly severe deprivations."[74]

Perhaps Pogge's argument that current global institutional settings are not favourable to human rights can be accepted, but given the monumental difficulties involved in changing not only understandings of human rights but also global institutions, it may be best to start by clarifying obligations and trust that such a changed mindset may, in time, engender a new institutional framework for governance.

Given the "basic rights" orientation being proposed, the first step to changing mindsets is *not* to agree with Pogge's discussion of ecology:

> Now we think that this fourth reason goes beyond my institutional cosmopolitanism because there is no recognized human right to a clean environment. Why should people not be free in a degraded environment if they choose? In response, perhaps they should be, but for now they won't have had a choice. The degradation of our natural environment ineluctably affects us all. And yet most people are effectively excluded from any say about this issue.[75]

Pogge concludes that this understanding of the issue (i.e., no recognized right to a clean environment) "suggests replacing ecology with a deeper and more general fourth reason, which might be labeled 'democracy.'"[76] Unfortunately, this replacement simply cements the present faulty regimes (with their flawed democracies) of global governance and, I would argue, runs counter to the true meaning of a natural law based on cosmopolitanism. As Cicero said, neither the senate (state governments or other institutions or nonstate actors) nor the people (democracies) can free us from the absolute moral obligations that arise from right reason.

It is for this reason that I want to propose a global understanding of basic human rights – or "morality of the depths," as Shue terms it – that is collective.[77] Individual rights, freed from either Kantian or earlier traditional moral societies and elevated to ultimate choices without the constraints provided by moral absolutes, could certainly allow the choice (mostly present today) to live and die polluted, without respect for natural laws or for the biological integrity of others who will be affected by the so-called democratic choices we make.[78] Placing individual rights, coupled with democracy, above the absolutes of natural law does not, therefore, support cosmopolitanism; rather, it reinforces the present immoral institutions that Pogge criticizes at length. In other words, when the primacy of individual rights (particularly when combined with present democratic institutions) is not tied to a collective understanding of what constitutes a basic right for all, such that it evokes an equally basic obligation, then individual rights may or may not fit within cosmopolitan theory. The collectivity I have in mind is universal and general, and it should include specific traditional, ethnic, or religious communities, provided their traditions are consonant with an absolute respect for the basic rights of all. In this sense, then, the existence of basic collective rights represents the limit to all democratic choices of individuals who wish to exercise and defend their rights. Finnis discusses human rights precisely in this context, and his approach is particularly relevant to the natural law perspective of cosmopolitanism.

Nevertheless, despite the present effort to turn the relationship between individual and communitarian or collective rights on its head – in a sense, negating the progress made by individuals in the affirmation of their rights from the Enlightenment on – the possibility of using the concept of collective rights in ways that is the exact opposite of what I propose exists today. For instance, after the attacks on New York on 11 September 2000, the US administration laboured steadily to promote the "collective right" of self-defence against terrorism by allowing unprovoked attacks and wars and by eliminating many well-established individual civil and political rights. This nefarious aspect of collective rights, and their use for specific purposes by various groups, is discussed in Chapter 5. Perhaps the use of collective rights by a powerful state would fit the notion of club community proposed by Brownsword. Under the guise of protecting the common good, collective rights are used to advance the specific interests of those who would promote illegal and immoral activities under the mask of protecting common human interests instead.

Collective Rights: Chosen Goods versus the Common Good

> [The United Nations enumeration of rights is] simply a way of sketching the outlines of the common good, the various aspects of individual well-being in community. What the reference to rights contributes in this sketch is simply a pointed expression of what is implicit in the term "common good," namely, that each and everyone's well-being, in each of its basic aspects, must be considered and favoured at all times by those responsible for co-ordinating the common life.
>
> – John Finnis, *Natural Law and Natural Rights*

Finnis' point is to reconcile what he terms the modern manifesto – that is, Joel Feinberg's conception of human rights – to the common good.[79] Dwight

Newman cites Finnis in his defence of moral rights held by collectivities.[80] He defines collectivities as being based on moral rights: "A collectivity is a collection of persons such that we would still identify it as the same collectivity were some or all of the persons in the collectivity to change (provided that the collectivity identify themselves in some non-trivial way as members of this collectivity)." He adds, "a moral right is an entitlement or justified claim whose justification does not depend on whether any legal or political system is willing to recognize the right.[81] Moreover, Thomas Aquinas stated that a legal or political system that attempts to deviate from the common good according to natural law is not a legitimate government – that is, one that ought to be obeyed. It is, instead, a tyranny: "A tyrannical government is not just, because it is directed not to the common good, but to the private good of the ruler."[82]

In fact, it is each citizen's obligation to rebel against such a government, for it does not follow natural law, and it seeks to impose a form of violence rather than practise lawful governance.[83] Thus a basic understanding of natural law and cosmopolitanism supports the difference I outline between popular or even institutional choices and rules based on the common good or public interest: natural law separates citizens' choices, even when the citizens are in democratic regimes, from the moral realm.[84] Yet the common good, or the good of collectivities, is far more than a theoretical position, for it is based on basic rights: it is therefore both a high moral ideal and the lowest common denominator among the interests shared by all humankind.[85]

The common good is a high moral ideal because it is based on absolutes of morality, on principle, rather than on a specific regime or ideology. But the common good is also the lowest common ground, in the sense that basic rights do not attempt to define all the rights that correspond to the legitimate interests of all people. By remaining basic as related only to (1) the preconditions of agency and (2) the requirements of survival needed inescapably by all human beings (all of humankind, not only those who can claim developed personhood), whatever their age, location, race, religion, or ethnicity, it remains a common good for all, with no need for additional defence.

It is clear that Shue's definition of basic rights does not include all acceptable choices or disparate lifestyle preferences: it is intended to ensure that the capabilities of all agents are protected so that their eventual choices are neither pre-judged nor pre-selected. The only limit placed upon them is that any and all acceptable choices must be such that they support (or do not conflict with) the common good – that is, the good of all humankind. In a sense, they are preparatory rights, for they are intended to ensure that a specific interest in living polluted (as per Pogge's example above) is not permitted to prevail. If such an interest were supported, it would contribute to the inability of some vulnerable agents to develop their own normal capacities for agency, possibly depriving them of any human rights whatsoever.[86]

Another version of Pogge's example may be found in Joseph Raz's example of a public good: unpolluted air.[87] Raz argues that even if unpolluted air indeed represented a good for all persons, consumers and those employed by the polluting industries would have contrary interests: unanimous consent would not exist.[88] Such examples could be multiplied. It is a fact that we are globally in a dire situation because of climate change and the ecological harms that ensue, as well as the ability of corporate power to subvert the public interest. Raz's point is confirmed. For the most part, and through various methods of deceit, persuasion, and lack of interest on the part of voters, the global common interest in safe living conditions has been countered by various aggregate preferences.

Once collective interests are understood as being embodied in the common good, however, it can be argued that they not only are uncontroversial goods but are also based on absolute principles. Hence no specific regime or institution can deprive human beings of these rights and the good they represent. The common good is based on "the irreducibly collective nature of certain interests."[89] In fact, the interests of all individuals *necessarily* depend on the fulfillment of collective rights.

Neoliberalism and Globalization versus the Common Good

> Delegitimization of neoliberalism takes place not only via visible crisis – like the ecological and financial one – or by means of the enormous social polarization in many countries, but in addition through the continuing conceptual and practical criticism undertaken by intellectuals, scientists and crucial media, social movements and NGOs.[90]
>
> – Ulrich Brand and Nicola Sekler, "Postneoliberalism"

We are, or should be, in the era of postneoliberalism, given the global crisis that has emerged over the last few decades. Yet the classic treatment of human rights in international law, for instance, by Jack Donnelly, paints a contrasting picture regarding "equal and inalienable rights": "Internationally recognized human rights require a liberal regime."[91] He echoes Ronald Dworkin's dis-cussion of the government's ideal role in support of liberalism: "[govern-ments] must not constrain liberty on the ground that one citizen's conception of the good life ... is nobler or superior to another's."[92]

Donnelly notes that the start of human rights discourse can be traced to a "tactic of the bourgeoisie to protect its own interests," but the discourse has since extended globally to all people as "universal inalienable personal rights" continue to gain ground.[93] Yet if we view a specific vision of human dignity as central to the understanding of human rights and superior to modern government's choices, and if we acknowledge that Western governments were the original locus in which human rights were developed by their practices, forcing the need for human rights, then we must also accept that Western liberal governments cannot be praised for the invention of human rights. "Because," Donnelly writes, "prior to the creation of capitalist markets econ-omies and modern nation states, the problems that human rights seek to address, the particular violations of human dignity that they seek to prevent either did not exist, or were not perceived to be central social problems."[94] But if modern markets "created the new range of threats to human dignity," and – as we know – markets are at the core of the global operation of liberal-ism, then it is hard to see why we should embrace the original source of the problem, and hope that that very source might be capable of yielding a solu-tion to the problem that is created.[95]

Richard Falk puts it well: "Superpowers use space and oceans to establish their earth-girdling security systems and expose the planet as a whole to enormous risks. Also, global patterns of industrialization result in disparate disproportionate claims on energy and other earth resources by non-Third Word societies. As well, dangerous environmental hazards result and are 'exported' to Third World pollution sanctuaries or are 'externalized' to inflict various degrees of harm on the planet as a whole."[96] This passage illustrates particularly well the notion of mass violence, especially ecoviolence, as I term it.[97] The very notion of violence as described by Falk, and the detailed discus-sion in Reinhart Kössler's article especially, clearly demonstrates the collective reach of the phenomenon. It is not a specific violence directed with intent at a particular person or persons: it is a mass violence inflicted negligibly, or through wilful blindness, on persons against whom the perpetrators feel no special enmity. Still, "the infliction of violence is deemed to be humiliation for the victim ... He is palpably placed in a position of inferiority in terms of physical power, bodily integrity and also moral worth."[98] The results of the infliction of violence on a grand scale via environmental degradation "exported" to developing countries (or simply to nonwhites and other minorities in Western countries) are a manifestation of an obvious arrogance, for the racially discriminatory activities of neocolonial powers assume and, in fact, demonstrate their own superiority as the bodily integrity of aliens is attacked and their moral worth is brought into question, not in words but through actions that say "you are not like us," you are not worthy of the same respect for your human dignity.

It bears repeating: the common good, the general interest of humankind, is not and should not be limited to the wish fulfillment of the most powerful. True cosmopolitanism is all-inclusive; it is about the basic rights of everyone. Specific communities and individuals must measure their interests, hence their rights, according to this golden standard: are their wants and needs such that they can be extended to the total collectivity of humankind? It is not my intention to create two categories – the moral haves and the moral have-nots – but unless a principled position supports the interests, say, of a specific community, that community will not be part of the moral collectivity that is intended to expect at least support for life on earth.

Perhaps this position runs counter to the modern liberal attitude of complete tolerance, even respect, for all choices. But the basic question remains: will preferences x (foundational to a community as cx) or choice y on the part of another community (cy) be such that they do not negate or eliminate any basic aspect of the common good? But if cx or cy preferences are such that they impose grave harms on the human collectivity through the environment, or from their actualization, then the latter cannot be defended on cosmopolitan grounds, for it is only a limited group that benefits, while the common good is under threat.

It is only when the effects of certain communities' choices, or those of powerful aggregates, reflect and engender wide-reaching harms that we need to understand those choices as placing the community or aggregate beyond the moral community. And only groups or aggregates can produce the envisaged harms: a single individual cannot pollute on a grand scale or undertake projects that spell disaster for other communities or regions, thus committing crimes against humanity or even genocide. Hence a dumbing down of the common good, reducing it simply to the most popular choices of the majority, will not do.

If this approach seems to take too high a moral road and to depreciate democracy in the process, review the results of neoliberalism since the end of classic colonization. As Jacques Depelchin, for instance, describes it, neo-liberalism is the origin of "global warming, global pauperization, global de-humanization."[99] Nor is genocide as defined by the *Convention Against Genocide* and as codified by the jurisprudence of the International Court of Justice the result of an occasional deranged individual or regime.[100] The phenomenon is increasingly visible today, from Congo to Darfur to Palestine, although it is, technically, still limited by the intent requirement.[101]

The Public Good and State Stewardship: Beyond Consent?

> Let me focus on and contrast just two ethics – one prioritizing private rights, the other the public good: one prioritizing the autonomy of individuals, the other the good of the community; one putting a premium on informed consent, the other largely discounting or dispensing with consent, informed or otherwise.
>
> – Roger Brownsword, "Rights, Responsibility, and Stewardship"

Theoretically, it is possible to contrast a community of rights based on the individual agency of persons, in the Gewirthian sense, and the public good, if one understands the latter in purely utilitarian terms. But if the understanding of the public good defended here is re-examined, it is clear that public good is the expression of the basic rights of the collectivity or the general and ecological conditions required to ensure that all persons are able to develop normally and reach the status of thinking and willing agents without impediment. With this understanding, the difference between the public good and a community of rights based on individual agency appears blurred for two main reasons. First, the conditions that define the basic public good are applicable to a whole collectivity rather than simply to an individual's basic right as an agent. Safe ecological conditions cannot be provided only to one person's habitat, but they are necessarily general to whole areas or regions. When these conditions are present, each person will develop normally, as is their (individual) right. But the preconditions of that development and of their agency can only be present in a general way or not at all: they cannot be limited to one person and his or her rights. Second, the good of the community, from this perspective, is not a separate goal; therefore, it cannot be considered in opposition to the community of rights envisaged by Brownsword.

An example may be useful. Assume that a corporation obtains a "legal" consent for an operation that will benefit it first, as well as its shareholders and the bureaucracy or government of the country for which its activities are planned. Assume that one or more of the local people would consent for personal reasons (such as the promise of a job). Even then, if the operation is such that it would affect the normal development of people in the community and produce neurotoxic effluents to the detriment of not only present individuals but also those not yet born, then all the legal consents combined cannot possibly justify the irreversible attacks on the collectivity, regardless of whether they are deliberate or unintended.[102]

Essentially, the very respect and primacy due to the individual agency of everyone in the moral community would require the primacy of the common good. The latter would demand that hazardous activities be eliminated, despite the legality of these activities and the presence of consent on the part of both officials and of some of the persons put at risk by the activities. Yet it would be difficult to call such a decision utilitarian, given that it is based on respect for individual agency and freedom from harm rather than on the aggregate utility, without consideration of those who benefit and those who do not.

Kant himself says one cannot be moral and consent to sell or give away one's humanity – that is, individual agency and life. Neither selling oneself into slavery nor selling one's organs is permissible. No doubt, giving away one's ability to be fully human in several senses would not be consistent with the moral community's mandate of respect.[103] In such situations, the importance of the state's obligation to protect its citizens cannot be overstated. Brownsword writes: "It is arguable that rights-holders need to make some allowance for the State's responsibility as steward for the community or, more precisely as steward for those essential conditions without which the community cannot survive or function."[104] In fact, it should be mandatory for states to factor the recently researched scientific aspects of any and all operations they are prepared to license or otherwise permit into their regulatory framework, for the protection of the life and health of all citizens is their responsibility, not that of the industries in question.[105]

If one remains within the ambit of the moral community of rights, and if one accepts human agency as a fundamental justification for such rights, then one must also consider how the effects of chemical and other industrial exposures will affect the capacity of humans to be part of that moral community.[106] Deryck Beyleveld and Roger Brownsword are explicit on this point, for they recognize the existence of partial agents: "Apparent partial agents are owed duties of protection by agents in proportion to the degree to which they approach being ostensible agents – not qua partial agents – but qua possible agents."[107] Hence, not only are many of the exposures affecting the physical integrity and well-being of individuals in the community or collectivity, these individuals' very status as autonomous agents is also gravely at risk because of the neurotoxic effects of most industrial substances.[108]

Nor can those affected (partial agents) be placed in the same category as other marginal groups such as children or fetuses, because, unlike those groups, their status as agents is not potential: it is eventually actualized.[109] Their status instead may be that of intermittent or partial agents. According to Beyleveld and Brownsword, "Intermittent display of agency sometimes characterizes the behaviour of persons recovering from certain kinds of strokes or other severe brain injuries. It also sometimes characterizes the behaviour of persons with severe mental illness ... As far as the moral status of intermittent agents as such is concerned, they have dignity and generic rights when they are agents and lack these when they are not."[110] In any case, what these persons face is a demotion from their status as (normal) moral agents, in addition to the altered health status they suffer. It seems clear that to affect natural persons who are moral agents in this manner is and should be considered a seriously wrongful act. In addition, such acts are wrong from the standpoint of Kantian doctrine (or what Brownsword terms dignitarianism), given that intent, if not knowledge and lack of good will, is certainly present in these corporate activities.[111]

Much of the problem rests on the present status of environmental laws, for regulatory regimes are often fragmented and entrusted to multiple agencies and bureaucracies, the Canadian regime being a case in point.[112] These regimes lack the coherent overarching focus that would be required, minimally, to achieve results, with the notable exceptions of Sweden and the Netherlands.[113] In addition, environmental laws in Canada, for the most part, use discretionary rather than mandatory language. A simple review of Canadian domestic environmental laws, in comparison with the country's *Criminal Code*, demonstrates this point. The legal language of environmental laws is not only discretionary but also imprecise. Often, discussion of accommodation is sought with major polluters, primarily for economic reasons, for local governments are intent on retaining the benefits provided by industry (such as tax revenues and employment) and are far less committed to sustainability or public health. Speaking of the Canadian *Criminal Code*, David Boyd says: "Canada's Criminal Code is written in mandatory, legally binding language, and it is rigorously enforced."[114] Moreover, the underlying causes of criminal behaviour – "social and economic factors like poverty, lack of education, and child abuse" – are also taken into consideration and addressed in turn.[115] In contrast, discretionary language and all forms of accommodation preclude the emergence of laws and regulations that may demonstrate "clear targets and timelines" and use various well-accepted principles, such as "intergenerational equity, polluter pays, user pays, pollution prevention, full-cost accounting, life-cycle analysis, and the like."[116]

I propose considering environmental regulatory breaches as ecocrimes to bridge the gap between what is considered a real crime and what are often more destructive activities, whose effects on human rights are at least as damaging and far more hazardous. The discussion in *Ecoviolence and the Law* centres on sex or gender disputes, cases in which criminality is far more easily proven and the incarceration of perpetrators far more frequent than cases of ecological attacks on human life and health, despite the latter's irreversibility.[117] This comparison is also useful when one considers the issue of consent in sexual crimes: "no means no" is a well-established, well-used principle, invoked in a plethora of cases.[118]

Unfortunately, these categories are not employed when a corporate wrongdoer claims ignorance of the effects of his activities or, more generally, of the consequences of the manufacture or use of something their well-supported and well-informed research-and-development department should have been able to predict with a great deal of accuracy. Similarly, the lack of consent, the "no" expressed by various indigenous or local communities, is seldom heard. In fact, in these cases, serious consultation is avoided. The "consent" of central bureaucracies lured by economic advantages is accepted without question, whereas local harms are not factored into calculations of the advance of so-called development and progress.

Cass Sunstein discusses some of the "successes" of the regulatory state as he lists various reductions in exposures to safety and health hazards.[119] But he adds that although new technologies are considered carefully, the regulation of older ones is either neglected or treated with great leniency.[120] This situation confirms that there is little or no effort in domestic law, at least in Canada, to update existing instruments on the basis of new scientific information. The resulting situation is as unacceptable as, say, accepting contemporary human rights regulations based on the morality and scientific knowledge of Victorian times.

The Public Good in International Law: Jus Cogens Norms and Erga Omens Obligations

> It is hard to find examples of the operation of jus cogens in the jurisprudence of the ICJ. The Court has not yet expressly, directly and unequivocally relied on jus cogens. So far, such statements are only found in separate or dissenting opinions.
>
> – Stefan Kadelbach, "Jus Cogens, Obligations Erga Omnes and Other Rules"[121]

Do international instruments, regimes, and jurisprudence offer hope for locating a legal source that will give primacy to the common good? Since treaties, for the most part, and positive state law are concerned only with the perceived advantage to states themselves, it may be only in the states' *jus cogens* norms and *erga omnes* obligations that we may find instruments that transcend the interests of individuals and aggregates to protect the public interest. These norms and obligations are particularly relevant in that they also transcend any notion of consent, that of individuals and that of states themselves. They are the only legal expression of absolute norms beyond customary law and state practice and are, in fact, often in direct conflict with the latter. Kadelbach writes, "Violations by one party and the *tu quoque* argument may not be used to excuse wrongful acts if they conflict with peremptory law. Unilateral reprisals taken in order to force the wrongdoer to return to lawful behaviour may not transgress the limits set by *jus cogens,* since the public interests at stake are not subject to unilateral discretion."[122] The jurisprudence that appeals explicitly to peremptory law is sparse, to say the least. The two major decisions that present strong, though not direct, reference to it and that are to some extent related to our topic are first and foremost the dissenting opinion of Judge Christian Weeramantry in the International Court of Justice's *Gabčíkovo-Nagymaros* case and the court's opinion in *Legality of the Threat of Nuclear Weapons.*

NUCLEAR WEAPONS AND THE OPINION OF THE WORLD COURT

The International Court of Justice has issued an advisory opinion of great weight on the legality of nuclear weaponry. It is the first time ever that an international tribunal has directly addressed this gravest universal threat to the future of humanity.

– Richard Falk, *Law in an Emerging Global Village*

The International Court of Justice's opinion on the nuclear weapons question must be placed in the context of nuclear weapons development and the international pleadings of Australia and New Zealand. Nuclear power, in all its applications, represents one of the most hazardous products and processes on Earth.[123] As such, it demands immediate attention and legal action on several fronts: the fuel cycle, or the mining of materials necessary for nuclear power, is hazardous; it is hazardous in all its uses, not simply as a weapon; and it is especially hazardous in it disposal phase.[124] As Elaine Drape argues, nuclear power is indeed risky business from the cradle to the grave, and its effects have all the characteristics of the harms this book confronts: immediate harm to human health; delayed threats to health, life, and normal function; and long-term harm to the diversity of life and to its very survival, through direct and indirect (genetic) impacts.[125]

It is not hard to find extensive and clear philosophical support not only for the immorality of the use of nuclear weapons but also for threats intended as nuclear deterrence.[126] In law, one finds direct reference only to two aspects of nuclear power use: testing and the threat and use of nuclear armaments. This is somewhat surprising. The occurrence of terrible accidents such as Chernobyl and the routine production of low-level ionizing radiation through the peace-time operation of nuclear power stations have not been addressed officially in international law, to the best of my knowledge, although both have been discussed in the literature.[127] For instance, no legal cases have been associated with the presence of an old, often malfunctioning power station at Fermi, which lies in the United States, right over the border from Windsor, Ontario.

On the question of the legality of atmospheric nuclear testing, Australia and New Zealand instituted separate proceedings against France before the International Court of Justice in 1974.[128] Atmospheric nuclear tests clearly spread unwarranted radioactive material indiscriminately to any and all adjacent countries adjacent. Even France, which wanted to test, did not attempt to conduct tests over its own soil. France must have recognized that the atmospheric tests were neither desirable nor risk-free, for it defended its strategy. France claimed it needed to perform these last tests to end atmospheric testing altogether. This declaration ensured that "the International Court did not pronounce either jurisdiction or the merits of the cases, relying on the obligation undertaken explicitly by the French government."[129]

The importance of the case did not lie with the majority view expressed above, however. Rather, the four judges who wrote a forceful dissent (Charles Onyeama, Hardy Dillard, Jiménez de Aréchaga, and Sir Humphrey Waldock) asserted that the "object of the applicant States was to obtain a declaratory judgment" instead.[130] The pleadings in these cases show that the intentions of the states were not simply to stop France on this single occasion but to make a universal point of principle. France, according to these pleadings, had violated an important right: New Zealand's sovereign right to be free of radionuclear fallout and contamination. The court described it as a right that belonged to "all members of the international community."[131]

The obligation, especially for New Zealand, was therefore erga omnes, and all states possessed correlative rights of protection. The fact that France (with China) had not been a signatory to the *Treaty Banning Nuclear Weapons Tests in the Atmosphere, in Outer Space and under Water* was not relevant.[132] Nevertheless, the fact that 104 states did become parties to the treaty over the next ten years enabled Australia and New Zealand to argue that "customary rule had gradually emerged" in the international community and New Zealand to assert, at the same time, the erga omnes character of France's obligation.[133] Ragazzi infers that the obligation is indeed erga omnes from the following arguments found in the pleadings:

The obligation

(a) is stated in "absolute" terms (the dictum refers to "absolute" and "unqualified" obligations);

(b) reflects a "community interest" (the dictum refers to the "concern of all States");

(c) protects fundamental goods, namely, "the security, life and health of all peoples" and the "global environment" (security, life and health are also some of the basic goods protected by the four examples of obligations *erga omnes* given in the dictum);

(d) has a prohibitory content (like the four examples given in the dictum);

(e) is not owed to particular States, but to the "international community" (the dictum refers to the "international community as a whole"); and

(f) its correlative rights of protection "are held in common" (the dictum provides that "all States can be held to have a legal interest" in the protection of obligations *erga omnes*).[134]

The dictum referred to here is the one found in the *Barcelona Traction* case.[135] This argument is of foundational importance, because it introduces the principled approach sought later by the World Health Organization (WHO) in opposing the use of nuclear weapons.

In 1996, the WHO submitted a question requesting an advisory opinion on "the legality of the use by a state of Nuclear Weapons in an armed conflict" to the International Court of Justice: "In view of the health and environmental effects, would the use of nuclear weapons by a state in war or other armed conflict be a breach of its obligations under international law, including the WHO constitution?"[136] Several states argued that the question went beyond "the WHO's proper activities." The court added that "three conditions must be satisfied in order to found the jurisdiction of the Court when a request for an advisory opinion is submitted to it by a specialized agency: the agency requesting the opinion must be duly authorized, under the Charter, to request opinions from the Court; the opinion requested must be one arising within the scope of the activities of the requesting agency."[137]

Although the WHO was competent to assess and evaluate the health effects of the use of nuclear weapons, the International Court of Justice at first judged that the final condition had not been met, for the WHO was not a state able to wage a war or enter into a conflict. The UN General Assembly therefore had to bring the question to the court once again. The court held (by eleven votes to three) that neither customary nor conventional international law specifically authorizes the use of nuclear weapons, that the threat or use of nuclear weapons is not specifically permitted, and that

it follows from the above-mentioned requirements that the threat or use of nuclear weapons would generally be contrary to the rules of international law applicable in armed conflict, and in particular the principles and rules of humanitarian law; however, in view of the current state of international law, and of the elements of facts at its disposal, the Court cannot conclude definitively whether the threat or use of nuclear weapons would be lawful or unlawful in an extreme circumstance of self-defence, in which the very survival of a State would be at stake ... (the President casting his vote to break the 7 to 7 tie).[138]

This opinion, despite its ambiguous tone, was viewed as an important decision, and it shows the transition from state treaties as sole arbiters of the status of nuclear armaments to an opinion whose history and background served to bring a normative issue to the forefront of public opinion.[139]

Richard Falk traces the history of the movement that culminated in that request from several groups in civil society, for "the push to achieve elimination [of nuclear weapons] often merges with the view that weapons of mass destruction cannot be reconciled with international humanitarian law."[140] Falk shows how global opinion as well as the work of many committed nongovernmental organizations prepared the ground for the very possibility of asking for an opinion. From the time of the 1985 London Nuclear Warfare Tribunal, weapons were defined as unconditionally illegal; therefore, even the threat of their use would amount to a crime against humanity.[141]

The main point is that neither politics nor economic factors, nor even the advantage of groups of nuclear states, could be allowed to determine the use of these weapons. Therefore, the UN General Assembly and the WHO referred a difficult question to the world court, and although the question could be evaded because health, narrowly construed, not the use of weapons was the WHO's concern, the court later gave an opinion. Both the original request by the WHO and the eventual opinion implied that "Nuclear Weaponry, with its global implications, raises question of legality that affect not just the citizenry of the nuclear weapons states, but the entire world."[142] This position supports, once again, the erga omnes status of the question at least in principle, given the careful phrasing of the court's statements. Falk does not use this language to refer to either the question or the opinion, but he adds: "Although not so formulated, the radical element in this request was to transfer the question of nuclear weapons policy from the domain of geopolitics, where it had remained since the first attacks on Hiroshima and Nagasaki, to the domain of international law."[143] And if it has not transferred the question to treaty law, which is clearly both incomplete and insufficient to deal with this global threat, then Mauizio Ragazzi's argument for placing its normative aspect among the few jus cogens norms generating an erga omnes obligation appears to be correct. Another element that is present in all legal approaches to the status of nuclear power, whether weapons or testing, is the precautionary principle.

NORMATIVITY AND THE PRECAUTIONARY PRINCIPLE IN INTERNATIONAL LAW: THE GABČÍKOVO-NAGYMAROS CASE

> The protection of the environment is likewise a vital part of contemporary human rights doctrine, for it is a *sine qua non* for numerous human rights, such as the right to health, and the right to life itself. It is scarcely necessary to elaborate on this, as damage to the environment can impair and undermine all the human rights spoken of in the Universal Declaration of Human Rights and other human rights instruments.
>
> – Christian Weeramantry, separate opinion in
> *Gabčíkovo-Nagymaros Project*

Christian Weeramantry's important words were written as a separate opinion in the well-known *Gabčíkovo-Nagymaros* case. On first impression, it appears that the case – which started with a treaty, in 1977, between Hungary and Czechoslovakia to build twin dams "for the production of electricity, flood control and improvement of navigation on the River Danube" – was based on many scientific assumptions that must now be discarded.[144] In earlier times, it was common to exclusively or primarily consider the economic, and perhaps the social, dimensions of a project. It took several decades for an understanding of the real impact of some of these local economic decisions to develop, and even today it is hard to ensure the incorporation of environmental considerations in all projects.[145]

The twin dams were extremely significant, in different ways, to their countries. By the late 1980s, Miklós Németh, the Hungarian prime minister, who was facing strong opposition to the project from his country's environmentalists, had suspended all work on Nagymaros; while on the Czech side, despite some minor environmental protests, the dam was near completion.[146] Because bilateral talks broke down, the European Union convinced the parties to bring the case to the International Court of Justice. Article 2 of the judgment in the *Case Concerning the Gabčíkovo-Nagymaros Project* sets out the court's responsibility:

Article 2

(1) The Court is requested to decide on the basis of the Treaty and the rules and principles of general international law, as well as such other treaties as the Court may find applicable,

    (a) whether the Republic of Hungary was entitled to suspend and subsequently abandon, in 1989, the works on the Nagymaros Project and on the part of the Gabcikovo Project for which the Treaty attributed responsibility to the Republic of Hungary;

    (b) whether the Czech and Slovak Federal Republic was entitled to proceed, in November 1991, to the "provisional solution" and to put into operation from October 1992 this system, described in the Report of the Working Group of Independent Experts of the Commission of the European Communities, the Republic of Hungary and the Czech and Slovak Federal Republic dated 23 November 1992 (damming up of the Danube at river kilometer 1857.7 on Czechoslovak territory and resulting consequences on water and navigation course);

    (c) what are the legal effects of the notification, on 19 May 1992, of the termination of the Treaty by the Republic of Hungary.

(2) The Court is also requested to determine the legal consequences, including the rights and obligations for the Parties, arising from its Judgment on the question in paragraph 1 of this Article.[147]

The most important point arising from this case is the increasing influence of an ecological worldview in the last two or three decades, giving rise to what Jacqueline Peel terms "an almost meteoric rise in profile within the body of international law.'[148] During this period, multilateral treaties have proliferated, and one can find any number of conventions for the protection of nonhuman animals (from polar bears to whales), biodiversity, and natural systems. Yet, although soft law in the protection of the environment entered everyone's consciousness from 1972 to 1992, the global environmental situation has continued, for the most part, to deteriorate, as has the compliance of state and nonstate actors.

Another important point emerged from the case: as long as states believe that international law is mainly a question of obeying *pacta sunt servanda* (agreements must be kept) and are correspondingly cagey about entering into bilateral or even multilateral agreements that may eventually inconvenience them, any truly international dimension of the protection of the global commons will be lost. Peel argues that "the crucial test for the new rules developed by the ILC [International Law Commission] will be their ability to promote better compliance by states."[149]

The next chapter discusses both the International Law Commission's draft articles on state responsibility of 1996 and 2000 and the work of the special rapporteur, James Crawford. It presents the argument that the 1996 iteration of the ILC's Article 19(3)(d), for instance, came closest to expressing the main point of this book by defining an international crime as follows: "A serious breach of an international obligation of essential importance for the safeguarding and preservation of the human environment such as those prohibiting massive pollution of the atmosphere or the seas." The question of international crime is discussed below. For now, the main point is that we should consider the preservation of the human environment as an issue of "essential importance" and failure to uphold that preservation as a serious breach of an international obligation. When the global commons are at issue, as noted in the previous section and in Ragazzi's analysis of what constitutes an obligation erga omnes according to the dictum of the *Barcelona Traction* case, the obligation of state and nonstate actors cannot be exhausted by agreements that predate recent science by several decades and that do not recognize the global implications of all environmentally hazardous activities.

This is precisely the case in *Gabčíkovo-Nagymaros*. It may well be true that the Hungarians came to view the construction of the twin dams as an undesirable legacy of the Russian regime that had oppressed them, while the Slovaks viewed the project as an "important achievement of the Slovak nation in the modern world."[150] But regardless of whether the two states fully understood this, the main issue – as Weeramantry justly pointed out – was sustainability: "When a major scheme such as the one under consideration in the present case, is planned and implemented, there is always the need to weigh considerations of development against environmental considerations, as their underlying justice bases – the right to environmental protection and the right to development – are important principles of current international law."[151] The fact that the right to both environmental protection and to development have a strong presence in international law (for instance, Article 1 of the UN's *Declaration on the Right to Development* makes the latter an inalienable human right) does not help to solve problems arising from conflicts between the two rights, even though the *Declaration of the United Nations Conference on the Human Environment* (Stockholm Declaration) (Principle II) considers both essential.[152]

The proliferation of multilateral environmental treaties is undeniable, and the "concept of sustainable development is ... a principle accepted not merely by the developing countries, but one which rests on the basis of worldwide acceptance."[153] This is a major consideration if one keeps in mind that the science that helped to draft some of these conventions and that supports them and gives them their rationale is, for the most part, science that was not recognized twenty to thirty years ago. This fact is foundational for two major points. On the one hand, the scientific information that eventually changed the picture was not available to either Hungary or Slovakia when they signed the treaty. On the other hand, if one acknowledges this fact, any treaty signed at a time prior to the availability of full scientific information about the circumstances of the case ought to be null and void.

From the standpoint of business ethics, a similar argument is routinely made for contracts in domestic law.[154] Anyone who signs a contract to purchase a property is expected to know, and to be made aware of, the circumstances and conditions under which he or she signed the contract. If the person was not informed about all the circumstances regarding the transaction, then the signature on the contract was not given under conditions of free and informed choice. For such choice to be both free and informed, contracts must be undertaken without either coercion or ignorance.

In the *Gabčíkovo-Nagymaros* case, if knowledge of the environmental reality of the Danube ecosystem and the possible consequences of disrupting that system was not available at the time the treaty was signed, then, like any other contract in which information was not fully disclosed at the time of signing, the treaty itself ought not to be binding on either party. It seems clear that no one was attempting to commit a fraud by deliberately withholding information. Nevertheless, the fact remains: Hungary signed in good faith as did Slovakia, although neither party was fully aware of the implications of what they were signing.

That one country, Slovakia, did not deem the emerging ecological information important enough to overcome its need for cheap electric power or a national project that might enhance its status in the international community ought not render its misguided reasons for abiding by the treaty binding on Hungary. Speaking of commercial agreements, Manuel Velasquez says, "An agreement cannot bind unless both parties to the agreement know what they are doing and freely choose to do it."[155]

In addition, one of the four conditions traditionally considered significant to contractual rights and duties is that "the contract must not bind the parties to an immoral act."[156] Arguably, disrupting and, to some extent, destroying a vitally important ecosystem such as that of the Danube Delta is morally wrong because of the present and future consequences. Whatever the consequences may turn out to be, they will affect not only the present inhabitants of the area, including all the species in that natural system, but also future generations to whom obligations are due.[157]

Finally, the importance of disclosure and consent is also emphasized in biomedical ethics. The assumption is that no matter the procedure for which consent is sought, consent is specifically intended to benefit the person who is asked to consent, a presumption that is lacking for environmentally significant disruptions if the benefit is intended to be a biological benefit to the collective. The separate opinion of Judge Spotswood W. Robinson III in *Canterbury v. Spence* is a clear example of the significance of consent in this context: "The root premise is the concept fundamental in American Jurisprudence, that '[e]very human being of adult years and sound mind has a right to determine what shall be done with his own body' ... True consent to what happens to one's self is *the informed exercise of a choice that entails an opportunity to evaluate the options available* and the risk attendant upon each."[158] In international law, both the *Nuremberg Code of Ethics in Medical Research* (1948) and the *Declaration of Helsinki* (1989) address the issue of consent – although in a different context, that of medical experimentation, but still for the subjects' own good – because voluntary, fully informed consent is central to both the legality and the moral acceptability of an activity. Despite the vast difference in context, the basic lesson is clear: whether we are dealing with an economically valuable business transaction or a medically beneficial procedure, neither can or should take place without full informed consent, although in international law the stability of treaties is strongly emphasized.

In the case under discussion, neither country appeared to be fully informed of the scientific and moral implications of its actions, even as these implications and consequences became clearer and gave rise to several legal instruments in later years. As a parallel example, if a patient is informed of certain risks and consents to a procedure but then later becomes aware of new scientific knowledge that adds to the risks, surely the first consent could be revoked on moral grounds. If the precautionary principle – codified in 1992 as soft law in Agenda 21 (XV) – is also taken into consideration, the combination of these factors supports to some extent the final decision of the International Court of Justice: "B. Finds, by thirteen votes to two, that Hungary and Slovakia must negotiate in good faith in the light of the prevailing situations, and must take all necessary measures to ensure the achievement of the objectives of the treaty of 16 September 1977, in accordance with such modalities as they may agree upon."[159]

But, when the common good is at stake in the ecological sustainability of the region, the same changed circumstances that mandate and support the new negotiations would also support adding some clear limits to any "good faith" negotiation that remains purely bilateral. Recognition of this basic factor ought to move the negotiations in a different direction, one that would include impartial scientific observers, perhaps provided by the WHO and the United Nations Environment Programme, in order to safeguard the global interests of the international community. This approach would entail that the obligations of state and nonstate actors be identified as erga omnes, rather than simply bilateral commitments. In essence, because of the introduction of the precautionary principle into international law discourse, and because of its increasing presence at least after 1992, arguments about the possible (even probable) negative consequences of damming the Danube ought to prevail on those grounds alone, even without appealing to the concept of informed consent. Therefore, although Weeramantry's is only a separate dissenting opinion, its importance as a contribution to international law and as a statement of moral principle cannot be overstated.

CONCLUSION: ENVIRONMENTAL RIGHTS AS BASIC HUMAN RIGHTS

The ingrained values of any civilization are the sources from which its legal concepts derive, and the ultimate yardstick and touchstone of their validity. This is so in international and domestic legal systems alike, save that international law would require a worldwide recognition of those values. It would not be wrong to state that the love of nature, the desire for its preservation, the need for human activity to respect the requisites for its maintenance and continuance are among those pristine and universal values which command international recognition.

– Christian Weeramantry, separate opinion in the
Gabčíkovo-Nagymaros case

Although, as we noted, Richard Falk does not recognize the obvious connection, Thomas Aquinas' principles of natural law clearly places its basic locus universally in human reason and recognizes that lawmakers must *apply* (not simply repeat) these basic universal principles to their own evolving and changing societies, provided that the basic inalterable message in not lost in the application. This is simply another way of appealing to pristine and universal values or to the ingrained values of civilization, and Weeramantry does a masterful job of tracing these universal environmental values to *all* civilizations, thus neutralizing the oft-repeated critique of natural law as limited to a specific religion or even as an element of Western imperialism. Therefore the utter universality of the quest for sustainability predates colonialism, North-South conflicts, and the rise of positivism in international law. In his separate opinion in the *Gabčíkovo-Nagymaros* case, Weeramantry adds: "If the Treaty were to operate for decades into the future, it could not operate on the basis of environmental norms as though they were frozen in time when the Treaty was entered into."[160]

The related question of state responsibility is discussed in the next chapter. But the reliance on universal principles appears to be preferable to a positivistic counting of (States') heads. Fernando Tesón argues that "excessive reliance on democracy" is a flaw and adds: "Unrepresentative governments are unacceptable in International Law; the tyranny of the majority is also unacceptable, even when it appears disguised under the cloak of 'substantive deliberative process.'"[161]

The same argument, mutatis mutandis, can be made about multilateral agreements: even when they are procedurally correct and accepted by all involved international "citizens," moral correctness, justice, and fairness cannot be guaranteed until universal normativity is introduced to judge the decisions: "The positivist argument for making governmental behavior the touchstone for the validity of democracy is ultimately contingent and irrational, like most arguments from authority."[162] Tesón relies on deontology, a well-accepted antidote to utilitarian or majoritarian answers to human rights problems, to provide the needed corrective. His approach therefore supports universalism and human rights, although his basis is Kantian rather than naturalistic, like Weeramantry's. Still, speaking of *Gabčíkovo-Nagymaros*, Weeramantry says:

> Environmental rights are human rights. Treaties that affect human rights cannot be applied in such a manner to constitute a denial of

human rights, as understood at the time of their application. A Court cannot endorse activities which are violations of human rights by the standards of their time, merely because they are taken under a Treaty which dates back to a period when such action was not a violation of human rights.[163]

Jus Cogens Norms and Erga Omnes Obligations: Bridging the Gap between State Environmental Laws and Their Obligations to Humankind

A great many rules of humanitarian law applicable in armed conflict are so fundamental to the respect of the human person and "elementary considerations of humanity" that they are observed by all states, whether or not they have ratified the conventions that contain them, because they constitute intransgressible principles of international customary law. In the Court's view, these rules incorporate obligations which are essentially of an erga omnes character.

– International Court of Justice, *Legal Consequences of the Construction of a Wall*

In *Legal Consequences of the Construction of a Wall*, the International Court of Justice refers to the language of the advisory opinion on nuclear weapons.[164] The presence, however limited and muted, of jus cogens norms and erga omnes obligations supports the argument proposed here in support of the existence of cosmopolitan, collective rights that are and should be the strongest and final limitation on the proliferation of individual rights of natural and legal persons, including states.

There are a number of problems with the norms and obligations articulated, for instance, in the articles on state responsibility by the UN General Assembly in 2001, in which the term *erga omnes* is not used but the following related concepts appear instead: obligations vis-à-vis the international community, peremptory norms (jus cogens), and grave breaches of international law.[165] James Crawford, special rapporteur of the International Law Commission for the law of state responsibility, follows the classic locus in the *Barcelona Light and Traction* judgment for the categories of obligations listed in that case, although he also considers "certain obligations in environmental law, such as those involving harm to the global commons."[166] In other words, the most serious obligations of states are neither fully spelled out nor explicitly enforced by the UN. Accordingly, the two major courts (the International Court of Justice and the International Criminal Court) only deal with the most obvious and widespread instances of genocide and crimes against humanity.

Another related issue is the corresponding lack of indictments and punishments for those responsible for the breaches under consideration. Moreover, some of the states that contribute the most to the mounting number of violations of erga omnes obligations – say, to the *Geneva Conventions*, the *Convention against Torture and Other Cruel, Inhuman, or Degrading Treatment or Punishment*, and the humanitarian law convention – are not signatories to the statues of the International Criminal Court (e.g., the United States, Israel, and Iran). Although the nonratification of these basic human rights and humanitarian law treaties should not make a difference because erga omnes obligations are such precisely because no treaty or bilateral agreement may be used to escape the obligation they impose, there are few, if any, indictments of any of these states, at least in the classic cases identified by the International Law Commission: the prohibition of aggression and the illegal use of force; the prohibitions against slavery and the slave trade, genocide and racial discrimination and apartheid; the prohibition against torture; the basic rules on international humanitarian law; and the right to self-determination.[167] In addition, the German Federal Constitutional Court has added "the prohibition of cruel, inhuman or degrading treatment," crimes against humanity, the prohibition of piracy and the principle of permanent sovereignty over national resources, and even basic rules for the protection of the environment.[168]

Yet, despite the gravity of these obligations, the UN and the international community it represents appear to have little or no control over any major illegal situation that may develop. The illegal wall between Palestine and East Jerusalem and expanding settlements in illegal territories, which culminated in the 2009 attack on Gaza, indicate that nonrecognition of a state's illegal acts may have no practical effects.[169] The lack of clear condemnation and of enforcement of nonrecognition, in all its possible aspects, echoes the retreat from mandatory regulations and appropriate condemnation and punishment in Canadian environmental law instruments. This similarity is particularly grave, as the deleterious effects of policies of accommodation and tolerance of major polluters on Canada's environment and public health and on the very possibility of creating a sustainable overarching regime suggest.

I proposed considering jus cogens norms and their related obligations precisely to escape the leniency and cronyism that permitted, if not supported, ongoing crimes against humanity committed against Canadian First Nations, as well as other communities in North and South America and developing countries. A serious re-examination of these international norms and obligations is necessary to escape the ongoing disregard for human rights that results from ignoring environmental laws.

It is at the international level that we can fully appreciate the implications of concepts such as consent, harm, and precaution. Roger Brownsword analyzes these notions as he shows how one's ultimate ethical position can change our understanding of these concepts and how we need to reach a consensus position based on this plurality of understanding.[170] I address this issue further in the next chapter, but it is important here to acknowledge yet another aspect of this issue, one that emerges when the focus is not biomedical ethics but the biological integrity, hence the survival, of the collectivity of humankind. At the outset, it needs to be stated that jus cogens norms are such that, at best, they paint with a broad brush; they are not nuanced enough to apply human rights to all agents, present and potential.

It may be best to advocate the application of Kantian dignitarianism instead, so that all human beings, individually and collectively, can be judged to be under the protection of the erga omnes obligations of states, especially in their expanded categories, as proposed by the Federal German Court. Jus Cogens norms and erga omnes obligations are cosmopolitan mandates for the protection of the broadest collectivities; therefore, they are, potentially, the most likely instruments to stop or limit the hazardous individual rights fostered by globalization. I have supported policies based on a Gewirthian community of rights that give primacy to individual agency, existing or potential.[171] But at this level of discourse it seems that dignitarianism is the only position that will provide the unequivocal "no" needed for the defence of the basic right to survival of the most vulnerable people. Brownsword, however, does not seem to view this characteristic of the ethical stance he terms dignitarianism as an unadulterated blessing. He writes: "Dignitarianism, it cannot be emphasized too strongly, is a red light, not an amber light ethic; its credo is that we should not proceed at all (where activities are judged categorically to compromise human dignity), rather than we should proceed with care."[172]

In the next chapter, I discuss jus cogens norms as a potential red light, rather than an amber light, in war and peace, at the international level. Given the current status of the world – primarily in the fields of environmental protection, climate change, and respect for UN law-making and in multiple situations of ongoing humanitarian law and human rights breaches – these norms are the strongest path to collective survival, whereas an amber light would, at least for a time, maintain the status quo. Current harms would continue, without mitigation, while endless possible debates and justificatory discussions would continue. In the meantime, Rome would continue to burn.

2

The Common Good and the Public Interest: Jus Cogens Norms and Erga Omnes Obligations in a Lawless World

It is impossible to grasp international responsibility without referring to the categories of domestic law that were used to construct it through the centuries; in this sense, no concept in international law exists "of itself." But the various ways of using the analogy have often led to inconsistent assessments of the civil and criminal aspects of responsibility. For instance, denying it a criminal character because of the absence in international society of a higher centralized authority capable of imposing criminal penalties ought also to lead to denying it any civil aspect, since domestic civil legal orders similarly require the same type of authority in order to function.

– Eric Wyler, "From 'State Crime' to Responsibility"[1]

Erick Wyler refers to the birth and death of international crimes of state, from the International Law Commission's draft Article 19 on state responsibility to their demise, which was, according to James Crawford, to avoid the criminalization of responsibility.[2] Yet, to be fair, even Alain Pellet, who in 1997 wrote wonderfully "Vive le crime!" in regard to Article 19, admitted in 2006 that *erga omnes* obligations and *jus cogens* norms are seldom, if ever, used. He even questioned the possibility of their being one and the same concept: "En relevant ici encore, que la pratique est rare: comme l'a écrit Ian Brownlie, le *jus cogens* est un véhicule qui sort rarement du garage; c'est une notion dissuasive – au sens où l'en parle de dissuasion nucléaire: les norms impératives sont suffisamment ressenties come telles qu'elles dissuadent leur distinataires de passer outré."[3]

In contrast, Christian Tomuschat affirms that "the international community accepts today that there exists a class of legal precepts, which is hierarchically superior to 'ordinary' rules of international law, precepts which cannot even be brushed aside, or derogated from, by the sovereign will of two or more States, as long as the international community upholds the values encapsulated in them."[4]

A number of international law scholars have argued for and against the effectiveness of these concepts. The problem of their limited visibility and application persists, however, because of the limits of international courts (the International Court of Justice and the International Criminal Court) but most of all because of modern geopolitical realities. Blatant breaches of higher norms are not brought to the courts because of the special status of some states and their close ties with other, more powerful governments. Take, for instance, the activities of the government of Israel. Israel is presently in breach of several jus cogens norms, but other countries have had no success establishing the presence of erga omnes obligations or seeking redress for the worsening situation in Palestine, especially Gaza, the Golan Heights, and East Jerusalem.[5]

At any rate, although it is fair and correct to argue, with Pellet, that this vehicle hardly ever leaves the garage, there are some areas in which the existence of jus cogens norms and the erga omnes obligations to which they give rise are more in evidence than others: these areas include, of course, the rare but existing genocide cases at the International Court of Justice.[6] These cases place a state essentially outside membership of the United Nations; therefore, they could well represent the most serious application of *jus cogens* norms a country may face.

Jus Cogens and the Defence of the Common Good in the Nonrecognition of States

> Some still object to the very notion of jus cogens on the grounds that it creates an unwarranted normative differentiation between rules of international law based on natural law principles of a higher law and other international law rules.
>
> – John Dugard, *Recognition and the United Nations* [7]

Although some argue that jus cogens is based in positive law, if international law and international public policy are to uphold public order and the public good, it ought to have some principles to oppose those states that would, for their own particular interests, practise aggression or commit acts in conflict with the common interests of humankind.[8] In fact, some of the best-known scholars in public international law equate jus cogens with international public policy.[9] In addition, despite their distrust of Western law-making,[10] developing countries rightly connect the presence of principles that give primacy to human rights, rather than state agreements regarding trade advantage, as an appropriate and much-needed vehicle to correct abuses perpetrated by the more powerful states. These developing countries view "the concept of peremptory norms as both an immediate symbol and eventual instrumentality for restructuring the legal order."[11] Speaking of the presence of jus cogens norms and their possible defence of developing nations, John Dugard adds: "Western States may not approve of this development, but it is the price to be paid for universality of membership in the United Nations."[12]

Jus cogens norms represent the ultimate rights of the collectivity and the most wide-reaching cosmopolitan obligations of states and persons (both natural and legal). As I argue in Chapter 1, they prescribe the limits of individual choices and preferences, no matter how many states and individuals may prefer them, and each of the principal peremptory norms demonstrates the importance of this aspect of their presence. The agreements of individuals or states to promote their future utility or convenience cannot and should not be the primary governing rule of law – or of morality either.

AGGRESSION, UNLAWFUL USE OF FORCE, AND ILLEGAL TERRITORIAL ACQUISITIONS: NONRECOGNITION IN INTERNATIONAL LAW

> Non-recognition is based on the view that acts contrary to international law are invalid and cannot become a source of legal rights for the wrongdoer. That view applies to international law as one of the "general principles of law recognized by civilized nations." The principle ex injuria jus non oritur is one of the fundamental maxims of jurisprudence. An illegality cannot, as a rule, become a source of legal rights to the wrongdoer.
>
> – Hersch Lauterpacht, *Recognition in International Law*[13]

Lauterpacht's statement is a clear and important application of jus cogens, for acts in violations of such peremptory norms are illegal and, hence, "null and void."[14] In addition, all resolutions of the Security Council and the UN

General Assembly are declaratory because they "confirm an already existing duty" on the part of state.[15] As early as 1971, the International Court of Justice, in the Namibia Opinion, went beyond asserting the obligations of member states to the *Charter of the United Nations:* "The termination of the Mandate and the declaration of the illegality of South Africa's presence in Namibia are opposable to all States in the sense of barring *erga omnes* the legality of a situation which is maintained in violation of international law."[16]

When a state acquires another, in part or as a whole, by force or otherwise illegally, the acquisition is a clear violation of jus cogens norms, although an exhaustive enumeration of those norms is not available in Article 53 of the *Vienna Convention on the Law of Treaties.*[17] This lack of precision was considered a possible disruptive factor, and the International Law Commission viewed the provisions in Article 66 of the convention as necessary "for the submission of possible disputes concerning the application of Article 53 to the International Court of Justice for decision."[18] As well, erga omnes obligations are not fully enumerated in the *Barcelona Traction, Light and Power Company* case:

> An essential distinction should be drawn between the obligations of a state toward the International Community as a whole, and those arising vis-à-vis another State in the field of diplomatic protection. By their very nature, the former are the concern of all States. In view of the importance of the rights involved, all States can be held to have legal interest in their protection; they are obligations *erga omnes.* Such obligations derive, for example, in contemporary international law from the outlawing of acts of aggression, and of genocide, as also from the principles and rules of governing the basic rights of the human person, including protection from slavery and racial discrimination.[19]

The difference between crimes and delicts and the grave position of the former as breaches of absolute norms have been noted. The explicit mention of the rights of the human person also appears to include the basic collective rights that define the common good, as is proposed here, although there is no explicit inclusion of the content of such rights in the passage above. But, a review of major issues intended to give rise to erga omnes obligations reveals that peremptory norms are necessary to support the public good.

COLLECTIVE RIGHTS, STATES, AND NONSTATE ACTORS

> Witness the proliferation of international organizations, the
> gradual substitution of an international law of cooperation for
> the traditional international law of co-existence, the emergence
> of the concept of "international community" and its sometimes
> successful attempts at subjectivization. A testimony to all these
> developments is provided by the place which international law
> now accords to concepts such as obligations erga omnes, rules of
> jus cogens, or the common heritage of mankind. The resolutely
> positivist, voluntarist approach of international law which still
> held sway at the beginning of the [twentieth] century ... has been
> replaced by an objective conception of international law, a law
> more readily seen as a reflection of a collective juridical conscience
> and as a response to the social necessities of States organized as a
> community.
>
> – Declaration of President Bedjaoui, International Court
> of Justice, *Legality of the Threat of Nuclear Weapons*

As Mohammed Bedjaoui suggests, the main change is that of viewing a number of separate states as a so-called community, one that will increasingly need to come together to ensure the defence of international human rights: a law that "exists first and foremost to change abuse of power," hence "the growth of power in non-state actors, such as transnational corporations (TNCs), will require that human rights law be made applicable to them."[20]

It may surprise some to learn that fifty-one of the world's largest economies are corporations while only forty-nine are countries.[21] These figures are a clear indication of the immense power corporations yield and, even more important, of the reason why state actors should not be the sole subjects of international law while transnational corporations are permitted to join the ranks of vulnerable legal persons in need of protection, rather than being forced to feeling the effects of the restraints required to curb their power.

For the most part, states have a constitutional obligation to protect their citizens, but corporations have neither a constitution of this sort nor a wide-reaching obligation to protect: their well-known obligations are limited to the interests of their organization and those of their shareholders. Their power is not even limited in principle by explicit, legal obligations to the collectivity of humankind, and their activities produce some of the worst hazards human beings are forced to face. This is true not only because of corporations' repeated so-called accidents but also because of the ongoing dangers their normal operations represent.[22]

Therefore, as the specific content of erga omnes obligations is examined, their main function must be kept in mind: to shield the basic rights of the most vulnerable from the results of activities based on the interests of the most powerful. To connect more clearly the sparse jurisprudence on erga omnes and jus cogens to the concept of the common good required by both natural law and cosmopolitanism, we should start by considering the moral and legal obligations of the *Barcelona* dictum.

Moral Considerations beyond Legal Positivism

> In its *dictum*, the International Court wrote that certain obligations are the concern of all States (i.e., are erga omnes), "[b]y their very nature." Therefore the International Court required that the "nature" of a particular obligation, i.e., its "essential qualities or properties" be examined to ascertain whether the obligation in question is *erga omnes*.
>
> – Maurizio Ragazzi, *The Concept of International Obligations Erga Omnes*

Maurizio Ragazzi argues that when you speak of the very nature of a concept, you clearly move beyond positive law.[23] The essential meaning of a concept, therefore, cannot be found in the formal or informal agreements of states but needs to be understood as a moral absolute for the protection of the "universal validity of basic normal values": "Each of the four obligations *erga omnes* listed by the International Court reflects an exceptionless moral norm (or moral absolute), prohibiting an act which, in moral terms, is intrinsically evil *(malum in se)*."[24] Therefore, basic moral values and basic human rights represent the nonderogable obligations of states. They are the values that apply to collectives and pose clear limits to individual and aggregate nonbasic rights. The common good of humankind is based on the observance of these norms, for it limits individual natural and legal rights, which are not equally basic. In the same sense, erga omnes obligations depend on jus cogens norms;

therefore, they too provide limits to the rights of states to pursue their own interests, singly and collectively.

According to Ragazzi, the Nuclear Tests case represented an appeal to erga omnes obligations in the area of environmental law.[25] As well, Judge Christian Weeramantry's appeals to global moral values in the *Gabčíkovo-Nagymaros* case and the advisory opinion in *Legality of the Threat of Nuclear Weapons* (both discussed in Chapter 1) also refer to the basic values of the protection of life and biological integrity and the ecological integrity that supports both. These basic rights and the foundational values that support them are also in evidence in the defence of "the legal responsibility of the international community regarding world poverty."[26]

It seems, therefore, that the bias against natural law, on the one hand, and the support for state sovereignty, on the other, that appears to prevent many scholars from accepting the importance of jus cogens,[27] ought to be eliminated, unless one is prepared to deny the existence of all principles of international law and morality, beyond state sovereignty and treaties. This denial would simply represent a turn toward complete cultural and moral relativism, for it would no longer be possible to judge any state action, no matter how contrary to human rights, as wrong or to condemn such acts through the organs of the United Nations and the international courts. In fact, such a turn would imply that the international community has no values to uphold.

The main point is that all jus cogens norms impose erga omnes obligations, whereas there are so-called self-existent obligations that are binding but still based on treaties instead.[28] Their origin therefore remains contractual. Ragazzi adds:

(a) The obligations identified by the International Court in the *Barcelona Traction* case are *erga omnes*, primarily because of the intrinsic value of their content, and only secondarily because of their legal structure;

(b) the reason why special rights and remedies attach to these obligations is that these obligations are *erga omnes*, and not the other way around;

(c) obligations *erga omnes* are few in number, unlike "self-existing" obligations which are as many as the international treaties that give rise to them.[29]

Hence, according to the *Barcelona Traction* dictum, both erga omnes obligations and jus cogens norms are such because of their content, not because of procedural reasons. Thus, positivists who view jus cogens norms and the erga omnes obligations that follow from them as "the obligation to comply with treaties" are in error.[30] It is natural law theorists who understand that the basis of jus cogens lies in respect for human rights and human dignity, for they understand the nature of the term, as defined by the drafters of the *Vienna Convention*, who described such norms as peremptory (Article 53). The definition relates to the legal consequences of jus cogens: the norms are of a peremptory nature, from which no exception may be made, not even by consensus.[31]

The idea that not even consensus is sufficient to set aside these norms echoes the cosmopolitanism of Cicero (as discussed in Chapter 1): neither the authority of the senate nor the common will of the people is sufficient to overturn principles of morality and collective basic rights. At least in principle, however, this position appears to run counter to the general movement toward transforming a society of states into an international community, as per Article 53, albeit such a community remains undefined to this day.[32]

Christian Tomuschat supports the term *international community* as "a term suitable to indicate a closer union than between members of a society."[33] On the same topic, Antonio Cassese writes: "Human rights doctrine has operated as a potent leaven, contributing to shift the world community from a reciprocity-based bundle of legal relations, geared to the 'private' pursuit of self-interest, and ultimately blind to collective needs, to a community hinging on a core of fundamental values strengthened by the emergence of community obligations and community rights and the gradual shaping of public interest."[34] The connection between jus cogens and the all-encompassing moral stance of the international community, intended to support and promote *collective* human rights, is here laid bare. The connection is undeniable, and the need for such a new approach is clear, because of the "structural deficiencies of the international order" that impede the exercise of the mandates of such basic international documents as the *International Covenant on Economic, Social and Cultural Rights* or the *Convention on the Rights of the Child*.[35]

The next question is whether the scholarly recognition of this emerging approach to international law as the law of community is present only in documents and scholarly analyses while practice continues to lag behind.

Collective Human Rights and the Community of States in a Lawless World

> Although Bill Clinton signed the Statute, the Bush Administration, since it came into office January 2001, has been running an aggressive, mendacious and ill-informed campaign to undermine the ICC. Its approach to the ICC is symptomatic of a more generalized opposition to international rules and to multilateralism, and reduces the effectiveness of raising legitimate concerns.
>
> – Philippe Sands, *Lawless World*

There are two contrasting points of view on this question. The first is held by many international legal scholars who defend and discuss the emergence of what Tomuschat terms a system that "brought into existence for the first time in history the 'blueprint of a legal order not resting upon the classical doctrine of sovereign equality.'"[36] In contrast, the second position, held by Philippe Sands, is based on the stance of George W. Bush's administration, not only on the International Criminal Court – Bush "unsigned" the *Rome Statute* in May 2002 – but also, in general, on the authority of international law. The ostensible reason for this position is the so-called War on Terror.[37] It is instructive to note that the countries that did not sign (or unsigned) the *Rome Statute* are the United States, Israel, and Iran, three countries that openly flout the mandates of the UN's instruments, Charter, and resolutions on a regular basis.

But the main practical reason for seeking a community-based approach is that most problems facing the world today – environmental and public health issues such as ecological refugees, nuclear proliferation, and all trade and labour issues – are global in nature. All of these problems require regulatory regimes that transcend the capabilities of a single state.[38] And these problems are, ultimately, having grave effects on human rights. The main reason for this book – with its clear emphasis on collectivism and cosmopolitanism, hence on the rights and responsibility of humankind – is to emphasize this need, even if its mandates conflict with individual rights. Bush's unsigning is, in fact, a clear example of placing the protection of certain legal and natural persons and aggregates, and related procedures, above the public good. But most of the global issues, including drug trafficking and finance,[39] affect mostly the poor collectivity – as we saw during the recent global recession, the mounting violence in Colombia (related to cocaine traffic), and in Iraq (poppy cultivation) – while the wealthy and powerful continue to profit. Margot Salomon believes that the powerful presence of globality, the interdependence of all states and peoples, informs international law.[40]

But it is the individuality of uncaring aggregated purpose that (1) creates or aggravates most of these global problems, and (2) it is the powerful "purpose" that actively discourages the application of even the most high-sounding millennium goals in international law. Essentially, many instruments are potentially capable of saving or at least helping humanity, but for the most part, the significant environmental, public health, and human rights components of these documents can only be found in their preambles. However, most of these legal instruments are non-enforceable because powerful interests prevent even the observance of those instruments that already link genocide, or crimes against humanity as obvious nonderogable norms, to clear human rights violations. Even worse, the inescapable and well-proven connection between environmental degradation (including climate change) and public health is still not explicitly acknowledged in any instrument or court, except for the rare dictum or separate opinion, such as the famous separate opinion of Christian Weeramantry discussed above.

The problem is that even these judicial pronouncements, be they separate opinions or dicta, appear in court judgments. They are produced *after* some event or case in which the connection between the environment and human rights is clearly present, but the harm has already occurred. In contrast, that connection ought to be made explicit in all instruments, domestic and international, to ensure that it can be used to prevent the grave harms that arise when the connection is ignored. So far, to my knowledge, there has only been one proposal, by Judge Amedeo Postiglione, to establish an environmental court.[41] To date, such a court has not been officially considered, let alone established. Environmental law, however, continues to exclude the most recent scientific research on the interface between human health and the environment.

The most evident and best-known environmental issue today is global warming, even though it was denied or ignored by the Bush administration. Bush said: "I oppose the Kyoto Protocol because it exempts 80 percent of the world, including major population centres such as China and India from compliance, and would cause serious harm to the US economy."[42] Of course, there is no rule of international law that requires a state to become a party to a treaty.[43] The question of jurisdiction is another problem that is largely ignored by legal scholars. Coupled with a general malaise about committing to international legal principles, this problem renders the achievement of justice almost impossible.

A QUESTION OF JURISDICTION: ENVIRONMENTAL HARMS, HUMAN RIGHTS, AND THE JURIDICAL DEFICIT

> On February 28, 2002 ... Judge Wood's opinion found that the plaintiffs' allegations met the requirements for claims under the *Alien Torts Claim Act,* in that the actions of Royal Dutch Shell and Anderson constituted participation in crimes against humanity, torture, summary execution, arbitrary detention, cruel, inhuman and degrading treatment and other violations of international law.
>
> – *Wiwa v. Royal Dutch Petroleum Co.* (2002)

Environmental harms and human rights violations are hard to prosecute from the standpoint of jurisdiction. Should the nationality of all those affected be considered? Should *all* those who contribute to the harms be held accountable, including complicit states, corporate bodies, and incorporated companies within a multinational corporate empire? And how should a diffuse harm, originating from multiple actors, be analyzed in terms of the three aspects of jurisdiction: jurisdiction to prescribe, jurisdiction to adjudicate, and jurisdiction to enforce?[44]

The first aspect raises the question of which court and, therefore, which state has the authority "to prescribe rules that impact the conduct and behavior of individuals" outside its own national borders. The second addresses the most obvious question: which state has the right to rule on a matter that might have taken place outside its borders and might not have caused harm to its own citizens? The third raises a more difficult question (in practice): how to enforce a court's decree?[45] The problem is exacerbated because changes to human rights and international humanitarian and economic law have given international organizations and even individuals (both biological and juridical) "some measure of international legal personality."[46] David Bederman analyzes these aspects of jurisdictional problems from the Lotus presumption, which allows states "to assert jurisdiction to the maximum limits allowed."[47] And he does so in light of US law, especially section 403 of the 1978 Restatement (Third) of the Foreign Relations Law of the United States. The paramount role of several standards emerges from the criteria listed in this document – that is, the need to use what is "most reasonable," (only with respect to (b)), "comity," and the balancing of interests, before applying the doctrine of forum non conveniens.[48] One of the most recent and important examples of unclear and conflicted jurisdiction is apparently being addressed and is on the way to being resolved in the United States in *Wiwa v. Royal Dutch Petroleum Co.* (2002). (This case was concluded with a favourable judgment in 2009.)

In the case's opinion and order, Judge Kimba Wood addresses the question of jurisdiction and gives the disposition of the case:

> Plaintiffs filed the first action against the corporate defendants on November 6, 1996 and filed an amended complaint on April 29, 1997. By Order dated September 25, 1998 ["1998 Order"], the Court found that the corporate defendants were subject to personal jurisdiction in New York, but dismissed plaintiffs' amended complaint on forum non conveniens grounds. On appeal, the second Circuit Court affirmed that the corporate defendants were subject to personal jurisdiction, but reversed the Court's forum non conveniens dismissal and remanded the action for further proceedings. See Wiwa v. Royal Dutch Petroleum Company, et al., 226 F.3d 88 (2d Cir. 2000). Plaintiffs filed a new action against Brian Anderson on March 5, 2001.
>
> Presently before the Court are: (1) defendants' motion to dismiss the actions for lack of subject matter jurisdiction; (2) defendants' motion to dismiss claims for failure to state a claim for which relief may be granted; (3) defendants' motion to abstain on the basis of act of state doctrine; and (4) defendant Anderson's motion to dismiss on the grounds of forum non conveniens. For the reasons stated below, the Court grants defendants' motion to dismiss pursuant to Fed. R. Civ. P. 12(b)(6) with respect to two claims only: Owens Wiwa's Alien Torts Claim Act claims, 18 U.S.C. § 1350 ["ACTA"], founded on an alleged violation of his right to life, liberty and security of person, and his ACTA claim for arbitrary arrest and detention. Plaintiffs are given 30 days from the date of this Order to replead those claims. Defendants' motion to dismiss is denied in all other respects.

There are both positive and negative aspects to dealing with this case under the *Alien Torts Claim Act*. It is indeed highly desirable to make oil corporations accountable for the havoc they wreak.[49] But it is insufficient to highlight the most obvious and serious aspect of the tragedy in Ogoniland while ignoring the causal nexus between environmental crimes, citizens' resistance, and the state-corporate terrorist activities that ensued. That no international environmental tribunal exists today to bring justice to the ecocriminals supports Judge Postiglione's pleas for the necessity of such a tribunal.[50] Justice Weeramantry, however, disagrees with the need for more courts, preferring instead to ensure the appropriate education of judges.[51]

In essence, Nigerian citizens in the area had no resource when their lands and waters were degraded and, with them, their only food supply. Had the ecocrimes been brought to an appropriate forum, perhaps the gross human rights violations now in the court might not have occurred. Properly trained judges would have been the best option, at that stage.

After the murder of Ken Saro-Wiwa, a Nigerian author and activist, in November 1995, I prepared a case study with the help of documents provided by Amnesty International, the Goldman Prize Organization, and Dr. Owens Wiwa, brother of the deceased.[52] The case includes both genocide and ecocide, as Saro-Wiwa himself described it. After the continuing and unrelenting practice of gross human rights abuses – ranging from the suppression of peaceful protests for irreversible damages to the land and waters of the Ogoni people to rapes, organized military raids, and slayings, culminating with the murder of the Ogoni 9, including Ken Saro-Wiwa – no international body brought the perpetrators to justice.[53]

The main point is that "any company that profits from crimes against humanity should be brought to justice wherever they are," and the most appropriate forum for such a legal exercise should be the one best able to mount a successful prosecution.[54] What is at stake in this case is not only the defence of the most basic human rights but also the defence of our common environment or habitat, and this issue is not even mentioned.

In his discussion, Judge Wood clarifies the reach of the *Alien Torts Claim Act* and of the *Trafficking Victims Protection Act* with respect to the case:

A. ATCA and TVPA

Plaintiffs premise jurisdiction over their international law claims on the ATCA, 28 U.S.C. § 1350, and general federal question jurisdiction, 28 U.S.C. § 1331 (1993). The ATCA provides that "the district courts shall have original jurisdiction of any civil action by any alien for a tort only, committed in violation of the law of nations or a treaty of the United States." 28 U.S.C. § 1350. Section 1350 was enacted in 1789, but was rarely invoked until the Second Circuit's 1980 decision in Filartiga v. Pena-Irala, 630 F.2d 876 (2d Cir. 1980). In Filartiga, the Second Circuit "recognized the important principle" that ATCA "validly creates federal court jurisdiction for suits alleging torts committed anywhere in the world against aliens in violation of the law of nations." Kadic v. Karadzic, 70 F.3d 232,236 (2d Cir.1995).[55]

This paragraph brings out the requirement for an international crime in violation of the law of nations, in other words, for violations encompassing breaches of erga omnes obligations. In some sense, it is insufficient to view these crimes as torts, but the presence of universal, nonderogable obligations, breached in the cases the Alien Torts Claim Act considers, paves the way for further criminal prosecutions, especially since the International Criminal Court came into force on July 2002.

In a much simpler and lower-profile case, Ward v. Canada (Attorney General) (2002), the Supreme Court of Canada upheld a similar principle. It was a sealing case in which Ford Ward was charged with using his fishing licence to kill certain seals and sell their pelts in violation of federal laws enacted in the common interest for the protection of seals and their habitat. Although Ward justly claimed he had a valid licence to pursue his chosen occupation, the Supreme Court of Canada argued that section 27 of the Marine Mammals Regulations prohibits the sale, trade, or barter of young harp seals and that it falls under the federal power over fisheries, "which is not confined to conserving fish stocks, but extends more broadly to maintenance and preservation of the fishery as a whole, including its economic value."[56] Notably, economic value is clearly not the primary consideration in the case; rather, the main concern is the "management of fisheries as a public resource."[57]

It may seem strange to turn to a case such as R. v. Ford Ward, a case in which no human rights violations were at issue, for comparison with the murder, destruction, and torture present in the Ken Saro-Wiwa case. What they have in common is, first, the choice of jurisdiction and law instrument based on whatever best supports the common interest and, second, an environmental issue that is evident in Wiwa v. Royal Dutch Petroleum but not mentioned in analysis of the case. Yet the facts show that ecological concerns were indeed the starting point and foundation of the Ogoni's protest, which was on behalf of their basic rights.[58]

Ward is a case in which a court upholds federal prescriptive jurisdiction, whereas *Wiwa v. Royal Dutch Petroleum Co.* is about interpretive adjudicative jurisdiction. In addition, the common-interest institutional function for one state (Canada) is quite different from the actual scope of the *Alien Torts Claim Act*. Nevertheless, it can be argued that the appeal to the common interest is the key that links the two apparently disparate cases. Even the Canadian case, ostensibly about the Canadian common interest, has several features that may bring *Ward* closer, in principle, to the erga omnes requirements of the *Alien Torts Claim Act*. These features are consideration of Europe's negative assessment of seal-hunting practices and the consideration, through that issue, of animal rights (a universal issue), even if it is primarily its Canadian economic aspect that emerges.

Both cases uphold universal common interests in some measure. Both cases also point to the fact that, when the environment is at issue, there is, as Postiglione argues, a juridical necessity and a social necessity for the institution of an international environmental court that would use the power of erga omnes obligations to promote the universal common good.[59] That such a court does not exist and that there has never been even an ad hoc international environmental court today points to what I, inspired by Postiglione's words, will term a juridical deficit: "The deficits of legality and justice are real and present, because, as well as having scientific, technical, economic and administrative instruments, the necessary role of the judicial system in jurisprudence must be considered."[60]

Only an international environmental court would be the appropriate institution capable of hearing environmental cases and of issuing decrees with erga omnes efficacy. Postiglione offers a number of reasons why an ad hoc international environmental court should be established:

1 It is important to have jurisdiction beyond the means to resolve state conflicts, as indicated by Article 34.1 of the International Court of Justice.
2 On environmental matters, it is imperative that NGOs be granted access to justice.
3 The legal principle of transboundary responsibility for damages beyond state jurisdiction has a primary and categorical character (erga omnes) that is hard to defend through legal actions between states but can best be sought by society as a whole, citizens and NGOs.
4 Many of the conflicts arising from multilateral treaties cannot be solved through the voluntary cooperation of arbitral decisions but require erga omnes obligations.

5　The political basis of consensus is limited to about 45 states (out of 180), but the accelerating global ecological crisis requires immediate preventive measures.

6　The International Court of Justice at The Hague has created no real body of jurisprudence in the last fifty years (only two arbitral cases) and no obligatory decisions.

7　The proposed new ad hoc court would add a specialized, positive, and interdisciplinary institution, without disrupting the unity of the present international juridical system.

8　The obstacle of state sovereignty can be mitigated through a statute that proposes an acceptable model for international order and peace, without interfering with the primary responsibility of states to protect the environment within their jurisdictions.

9　Through the evolution and growth of a culture of human rights, it is anachronistic to view environmental matters only as a state responsibility; by their very nature, human rights and the environment are substantially universal and in the common interest.

10　There has been a rapid growth of international environmental law, and this body of law is ready for a global institutional organ.

11　New models of multilateral conventions (climate, biodiversity, desertification, the sea, and the like), as well as the requirements of general information, participation, and access would benefit from more than proposals for measures such as ombudsmen, which fall far short of the mark.

12　States have a legal obligation to protect the common resources of the planet for future generations. There cannot be room for the violence of globalization and of the world economy, for they foster a deficit of law and justice.

13　Today, there is neither a convention nor statute to reform the International Court of Justice or to reconstruct an ad hoc court to establish a true and real environmental jurisdiction, despite the political interests of governments.[61]

Postiglione adds that only an innovative instrument could address international global damage. Society and all its citizens bear the brunt of ecological harms; therefore, it is fair that society should be allowed to protect itself when states fail in their duty to do so.[62]

The Aarhus Convention of 23-25 June 1998 recognized the right of all persons to full information and to access to justice. How are these rights to be achieved in the present context? Since 1976, the European Court of Justice in Luxembourg has also recognized the right of those suffering environmental extraterritorial harms to have access to justice beyond their borders.[63] These rights become even clearer when one considers the relationship between health and environmental damage as supported by the World Health Organization as well as its 1999 London Declaration.[64]

TRANSNATIONAL ECOLOGICAL DISASTERS: TORTS AND CRIMES?

> The right to access to ecological justice is present in several international legal instruments, but there does not exist an ad hoc Convention to acknowledge that each person, as subject of international law ... has a right to access to a supranational organ for all environmental matters.
>
> – Amedeo Postiglione, *Giustizia e ambiente globale*
> (author's translation)

Ken Saro-Wiwa spoke of genocide, ecocide, and omnicide, long before he and his fellow activists were killed. He called the corporations companies unholy for what they were doing *ecologically* to Ogoniland and, therefore, to his people. In essence, his words likened Royal Dutch Shell Oil practices to murder, whether the killing was direct – that is, through the use of conventional weapons – or occurred through poisoning and bulldozing a habitat upon which the Ogoni had depended for centuries. The difference between ecological disasters on the one hand and violence against humans on the other was one of degree not of kind, and the recent *Alien Torts Claim Act* case does not accurately reflect the origins of the human rights violations: the environmental degradation of the region. One can understand both the activists and the lawyers and their desire to use whatever "facts" are most likely to make their case, and we can also celebrate the pubic recognition of the crimes and recognize their gravity. There is no question that this is a positive step forward, although John Terry writes: "Although the idea of pursuing torturers for damages rather than jailing them may strike some as a second best solution, the tort remedy is an important complement to, and in many ways a more useful mechanism than, the criminal remedy."[65]

No matter how important the possibility of turning to the *Alien Torts Claim Act* to bring (some) justice to cases involving egregious human rights violations within the global community may be, the approach assumes that all resulting harms are compensable. My argument is, in part, that ecocrimes are forms of assaults and even crimes against humanity. Monetary compensation is, therefore, insufficient to compensate victims, as it is in regard to both assaults and homicides in common law. In the Canadian case *R. v. Ewanchuk*, Madam Justice L'Heureux-Dubé describes the assault of a young woman (even without the addition of rape) as "an attack on human dignity." Ewanchuck was tried and found guilty, even though he handed $100 to the victim "for the massage" as she left the trailer where she had been confined. The "payment" did not cancel the wrong he had inflicted on the woman, and I do not believe that even a substantial fine should ever be considered to replace the criminal charge of sexual assault.

Another aspect of this difficulty is discussed in another well-known international case, the *Bhopal* case. The question of *forum non conveniens* was raised by the United States courts, with far less moral credibility than in *Wiwa v. Shell* (2009) case, given that it was a US-based multinational corporation, Union Carbide, that was negligent and even delinquent in its practices and, therefore, responsible for the slaughter that ensued in India. Philippe Sands acknowledges the importance of these procedural obstacles, and he proposes considering the domestic alternative for transnational disputes.[66] He shows that, at times, European domestic courts, influenced by international law, may be able to deal with these cases, at least when the country where the case is tried is one of the parties to the dispute (as was the case for Union Carbide in *Bhopal*). He cites a number of cases in support of his position, ranging from river pollution (Italy and France), to airborne pollutants for an electric power plant (Germany and France), to a fishery dispute (Italy and France), to a mine versus a garden nursery (Germany and the Netherlands).[67]

Sands also appears to think highly of the International Joint Commission (US-Canada) and the potential role it could play, especially when facilitated by the 1909 US-Canada *Boundary Waters Treaty*.[68] In contrast, my earlier discussion about the lack of success of international instruments indicates that this potential has not come to fruition to date, if we judge its success from the standpoint of the conditions of the Great Lakes rather than from the lack of serious litigation on environmental issues arising in the area. Another example Sands adduces is that of section 7(1)(b) of the *Canadian Clean Air Act*, "which enables the Canadian Government to prescribe national standards to control emissions 'likely to result in the violation of a term or terms of any international obligation entered into the government of Canada relating to the control or abatement of air pollution in regions adjacent to any international boundary or throughout the world.'"[69]

Once again, the border areas between Canada and the United States – from Windsor, Ontario, and Detroit, Michigan, to Toronto, Ontario, and Buffalo, New York – are among the most polluted areas in both countries. They exhibit a number of hot spots, areas with extremely high concentrations of disease, high rates of morbidity and fatality, and a large number of reproductive anomalies, for both humans and animals.[70] Although Sands and others such as Richard Falk see an important role for domestic courts, in the context of Canadian federal and provincial instruments, the function of environmental regulations is frustrated by corporate economic interests and their supporting governmental bureaucracies intent on consolidating their power rather than protecting the health of their citizens and the common habitat.[71]

A Lawless World and Global Warming

> Now, however, almost every decent person recognizes that it would be most equitable and efficient for those countries which have benefited the most from lax environmental controls over the past 200 years to bear the burden of immediate actions to address global warming.
>
> – Philippe Sands, *Lawless World*

Aside from the thorny procedural issues discussed above, climate change is perhaps the most well-known global problem today. The desire of major powers such as the United States to avoid even the possibility of domestic economic harms has led to misinformation campaigns and inaction and eventually to the collective harms with which we are now familiar. Although the origins of global warming lie in the presence of various hazardous gasses, the results we see today – from glacial melts to desertification, from tsunamis to tidal waves – render water as the main actor in most climate change disasters.

In *Lawless World*, Sands traces the torturous process that led to the signing and ratification of the Kyoto Protocol and the Framework Convention.[72] He acknowledges that the process leading to the protocol was not driven by sound science but by the quest for consensus and that the United State's resistance to principled cooperation was perhaps the major obstacle to a better and faster agreement. He also notes that those who denigrated the words of the International Panel on Climate Change (IPCC) and the Kyoto

Protocol only saw its problems rather than the fact that it was, and is, only the international community's first step toward the protection of the collective rights of humankind.[73]

Breaches of collective rights are occurring almost everywhere at this time, but they are particularly visible in Arctic regions. Yet even in these regions, at best, the lawyers employed by Aboriginal communities treat these human rights breaches as torts. One particular case – *Native Village of Kivalina v. ExxonMobil* – merits a mention here because although the Kivalina were not successful, the case dealt with water issues in relation to an indigenous community.[74] The Village of Kivalina is an Inupiat Village of approximately for hundred people: "Kivalina is located on the tip of a six-mile barrier reef located between the Chuckchi Sea and the Kivalina and Wulik Rivers on the Northwest Coast of Alaska, some seventy miles north of the Arctic circle."[75] The case reveals the dangers, in contrast to the health-giving and even sacred aspects, of water when it is at its most harmful – that is, when it becomes a destroyer of peoples' territorial integrity. Arctic sea ice is melting because of global warming, which has been actively fostered by ExxonMobil and many other US and multinational corporations through CO_2 emissions. As a consequence, the village is no longer protected from winter storms. The village is being destroyed by increasingly severe storms, and as the "ground crumbles from underneath it ... critical infrastructure is imminently threatened with permanent destruction. If the entire village is not relocated soon, the village will be destroyed."[76] The Kivalina's claim is not simply being advanced by a few members of an indigenous community: the US Army Corps of Engineers and the US Accountability Office agree that the village must be relocated, and they estimate the costs to be from US$85 million to US$400 million.[77]

The substance of the case hinges on the culpable actions (and omissions) on the part of multiple corporate defendants. However, an even more significant issue was not even considered in the case – the cultural and territorial rights of the Kivalina. Even if the US government spends $US400 million to relocate the inhabitants of the village, their land and their religious and cultural rights will be lost, for most Aboriginal peoples' lives are tied inextricably to the area they have always occupied. Removed from their traditional lands, their survival as a people will no longer be possible, even if the lives of individual citizens are saved. One could argue, then, that water's natural function is affected by polluters, that polluters change water's true nature from a giver of life to a deadly threat.

Of course, the arguments offered by the lawyers in the case are conservative. They refer to the federal common law of public nuisance, even though the villagers' health, home, and family life are clearly affected.[78] As well, more protection might well have been available to them, had they been mainstream Americans, say from Boston or New York – in other words, racial discrimination appears to have been involved to some degree.

WATER AS DANGER AND THE NEGATIVE CONSEQUENCES OF CLIMATE CHANGE

> Globalization, with the inequalities it promotes, challenges if
> not threatens the integrity of human rights law, precisely because
> it uses human rights as a means of furthering itself.
>
> – Antony Anghie, *Imperialism*

No doubt, storms and floods existed from time immemorial, and the story of Noah's Ark bears witness to one of the earliest examples in history. But in modern times, the dangers of water originate with climate change: severe glacial melts; the warming of the oceans, which results in hurricanes, tidal waves, and tsunamis; and excessive warming and desertification, which has led to starvation and resource wars, especially in sub-Saharan Africa.

Those who live closest to the land, not only indigenous and northern communities but also those who live in island states and coastal towns, bear the brunt of these negative impacts. Tracing the causal connections between globalized human industrial and economic activities and climate change reveals its impact on the world's waters. The lawyers for the plaintiffs in *Kivalina* lay out the historical background of the village's impending destruction. The case merits careful analysis, because, whatever our location, we are all affected in various measures by climate change. We need to understand not only what climate change is but also what it does and how it operates in purely scientific terms. We need to understand its institutional and policy implications. The *Kivalina* case was tried before the US District Court of California, San Francisco Division, and it cites as defendants not only ExxonMobil but also another twenty-three corporations. The case opened with a detailed analysis of the causes of global warming under three main headings: "Oil Companies," "Power Companies," and "Coal Companies." The companies all contributed deliberately to the global warming that caused "Kivalina's special injuries."[79] In addition, "Kivalina further asserts claims for civil conspiracy and concert of action for certain defendants' participation in conspiratorial and other actions intended to further the defendants' abilities to contribute to global warming."[80]

Global warming is also defined briefly in another recent case, *People of State of California v. General Motors Corp.*, as follows: "Global warming [is a] change of climate which is attributed directly or indirectly to human activity that alters the composition of the global atmosphere and which is in addition to natural climate variability observed over comparable time periods."[81] In *Kivalina*, the plaintiffs claimed that defendants "knew of or should have known" the results of their continued "substantial contributions to global warming," specifically in relation to Arctic coastal communities such as Kivalina. Additionally, some of the defendants conspired "to create a false scientific debate about global warming in order to deceive the public."[82] The attorneys for the plaintiffs stated that Kivalina had asserted a claim for public nuisance under federal common law[83] and under state law[84] and were right to do so because defendants either reside in California or have "substantial or continuous and systematic contacts with the state of California."[85] These connections also ensured that the venue chosen was legally appropriate.

After relating the amount of CO_2 emissions on the part of each defendant, the defendants each acknowledged that they were indeed emitting hazardous gases.[86] However, ExxonMobil stands out for two main reasons. The first is the large quantities of its emissions: "ExxonMobil has interest in more than 80 Cogeneration facilities in more than 30 locations worldwide, with a capacity to provide about 3,300 megawatts of power. These facilities now supply more than 90 percent of ExxonMobil's power-generating capacity in its refineries and chemical plants worldwide. These emit hundreds of millions of tons of CO_2."[87] In addition, ExxonMobil also owns and operates coal mines. The second is that the company took the lead "in industry efforts to disseminate false information about global warming."[88]

THE *KIVALINA* COMPLAINT AND CIVIL CONSPIRACY ALLEGATIONS

In January 2001, a report from the Union of Concerned Scientists produced a comprehensive report regarding the disinformation tactics used by ExxonMobil "to delay action on the issue."[89] The company,

* *Manufactured uncertainty* by raising doubts about even the most indisputable scientific evidence. Adopted a strategy of *information laundering* by using seemingly independent front organizations to publicly further its desired message and thereby confuse the public.
* *Promoted scientific spokespeople* who misrepresent peer-reviewed scientific findings or cherry-pick facts in their attempts to persuade the media and the public that there is still serious debate among scientists that burning

fossil fuels has contributed to global warming and that human-caused warming will have serious consequences.

* *Attempted to shift the focus* away from meaningful action on global warming with misleading charges about the need for "sound science."[90]

Substantiating the civil conspiracy allegations, defendants ExxonMobil, AEP, BP America, Chevron, Conoco Phillips, Duke Energy, Peabody, and Southern, who were all participants in the campaign to deceive the public, opened by denying the existence of global warming. Later, they attempted to demonstrate "that global warming is good for the planet and its inhabitants or that even if there may be ill effects, there is not enough scientific certainty to warrant action."[91] The misinformation disseminated made use of industry-formed front groups, "fake citizen organizations," and "bogus scientific bodies, such as the Global Climate Change Coalition ('GCC'), the Greening Earth Society, the George C. Marshall Institute, and the CoolerHeads Coalition."[92]

Under the leadership of the most active defendant, ExxonMobil, these companies funded global warming skeptics and professional scientific experts, many of whom were not qualified to publish their work in scientific journals, and all of whom were also funded and supported by trade associations such as the Edison Electric Institute and the National Mining Association. The most important front group was the Advancement of Sound Science Coalition, formed in 1993. Originally a public-relations company for Philip Morris Tobacco, the coalition was the inspiration for the term *junk science* to refer to industry-sponsored science. The manufactured science was created for Philip Morris and other tobacco companies to deny the links between smoking and cancer and, in general, the effects of second-hand smoke. Their targets were "older, less educated males from large households who are not typically active information seekers" and "younger, lower income women."[93]

The International Panel on Climate Change working groups have been documenting the unfolding of global warming and the increasing presence of emissions, both CO_2 and methane (for the latter, see Chapter 3), through regular meetings at international forums.[94] According to the plaintiffs in *Kivalina*, "Carbon dioxide levels in the atmosphere have increased by 35 percent since the dawn of the industrial revolution in the 18th century, and more than one-third of the increase has occurred since 1980. The current level of carbon dioxide in the atmosphere is higher than any time in the last 20 million years. The current level of methane in the atmosphere is approximately 250 percent higher than pre-industrial levels."[95] In other words, despite the efforts of industry's representatives, and of the defendants' various "citizens' groups," the effects of global warming put all the inhabitants of Kivalina at grave risk, for their property and their very location is on the brink of being destroyed. The parallel with Big Tobacco, prior to the convention that set up strict parameters for tobacco's use and forbade any practice that may inflict second-hand smoke on others, is undeniable.[96]

A clear difference between the two issues, however, is that, at least initially, the use of tobacco is an individual choice, even though the habit that ensues eventually represents a form of addiction that can no longer be described as a free choice. The addiction itself is the result of the deliberately planned chemical composition of cigarettes, which makes the resulting use a forced activity. In contrast, the extreme effects of global warming on northern peoples and other indigenous communities are not the consequence of choices made by these people, even at the start, for their traditional lifestyles do not include the overconsumption and overuse of energy endemic to most affluent Western societies. It is the choices of Western societies, rather than their own, that have resulted in the gross breaches of human rights they are forced to endure.

There is a dissonance between the choices that foster global warming and the recipients of the effects of those choices, effects they, for the most part, had no part in creating. Thus the painstakingly drafted case presented to the San Francisco court in *Kivalina* seems to be understated, at least insofar as it presented its first claim for relief: "federal common law: public nuisance."[97] Although the term used, *public nuisance*, cannot begin to truly characterize the "substantial and unreasonable interference" with the Kivalina's public and human rights, the attorneys acknowledge the role of the defendants in the ongoing crisis when they add: "Intentionally or negligently defendants have created, contributed to and/or maintained the public nuisance."[98] In addition, the complaint itself recognizes the *sui generis* aspects of the plight of Kivalina's residents:

258. Plaintiffs do not have the economic ability to avoid or prevent the harm.
259. Plaintiffs due in part to their way of life, contribute very little to global warming.

Given the effects of the defendants' actions, and the results that ensued, it may seem appropriate (though not formally acceptable in a US court of law) to view this case as involving criminal activities. The Canadian criminal law category of wilful blindness can also be used to bridge the gap between knowingly committing actions that would eventually deprive populations of their human rights and the refusal to accept the inescapable effects of actions embraced and fully understood on the part of the defendants.[99] The same critique applies to the second claim for relief, "state law: private and public nuisance," which claims relief under "state statutory and/or common law of private and public nuisance."[100]

More interesting is the third claim for relief: civil conspiracy.[101] The deliberate actions on the part of the defendants sought to (1) mislead the public regarding the existence and effects of global warming, (2) mislead the public regarding efforts to discredit sound science on global warming, (3) mislead the public regarding further efforts to delay their own inevitable costs (while ignoring or discounting the "externalities" that resulted in human right breaches and, eventually, in the destruction of towns and communities, for the Kvalina case), and (4) eliminate an indigenous community as such. All these activities were pursued in concert by the "conspiracy defendants," as described in the fourth claim for relief: "279. Defendants have engaged in and/or are engaging in tortious acts in concert with each other or pursuant to a common design."[102]

At the time of writing, neither the requested trial by jury nor the relief for the damages suffered by Kivalina has been awarded. The trial is extremely important: just like the Inuit petition submitted to the European Court of Human Rights, and aside from its value in providing relief for the affected persons, the case ties climate change to water, not only storming oceans, warmed by the effects of climate change, but also melting ice. Finally and most significantly, the plaintiffs are using the few vague and incomplete legal categories presently available in domestic law to pinpoint the role of multinational corporations and the complicit governments that allow their activities to inflict incompensable harms that can only be described as crimes against humanity.[103]

This is only one example of cases that should be won with ease. By the same token, other Arctic and small island states ought to sue those who found the conditions of climate change on the one hand but belittled their existence and impact on the other. Although the perpetrators are hard to identify in a case of such diffuse harm, the home states of these corporations can also be viewed as complicit in the industrial activities that perpetrated the harm and should be held responsible. The case is not only an example of the lawless present, the influence of powerful states, and the economic interests of individuals but also an example that reveals the results of shunning principles and ignoring the rights of the collectivity.

The Swine Flu Pandemic: Individual Corporate Rights versus Collective Human Rights

> Sewage-filled lagoons at a pig farm in eastern Mexico – a product of the North American Free Trade deal – are suspected of creating ground zero conditions for swine flu in this country.
>
> – Linda Diebel, "Mexican Outbreak Is Really 'NAFTA Flu'"

Smithfield Farms, the farm identified by Diebel in 2009, has operated Carroll Farms since 1994 in La Gloria, Mexico.[104] One can blame lax or nonexistent environmental laws in the area for the disaster, for they ought to prevent the dumping of raw sewage into a pond, but the same corporation was fined US$12.6 million in 1997, when the United States Environmental Protection Agency (USEPA) discovered raw sewage in a river flowing into the Chesapeake Bay. So, the corporation was well aware that what it was doing was wrong and apparently decided to move into an even more permissive environment than the one it had left behind.

Local groups in the area of Smithfield's present operation have been asking to have the farm closed "pending extensive environmental and health reviews of an operation that raises 950,000 pigs a year and does not have a sewage treatment plan."[105] But the problem is not confined to Mexico or to states in the NAFTA pact, for farms are not required by law to have sewage treatments either in the United States or, as we shall see, Canada. The World Health Organization has raised its pandemic alarm to the highest level, not because of the gravity of the threat or the number of deaths thus far (about 160 as of 3 May 2009), but because most countries are now involved in the pandemic, not only in North America but also in Europe and Asia. Mexico officials have closed schools, churches, and holiday functions as people circulate and work wearing protective masks.

The situation in Mexico is not, however, the result of an accident, it is part of an ongoing lawlessness that ignores collective rights to life and health in favour of the individual gain of legal persons and aggregates. Diebel describes Smithfield's general operations:

> In a 2006 article on Smithfield's Virginia operations, *Rolling Stone* reported "[the] pigs live by the hundreds or thousands in warehouse-like barns in rows of wall-to-wall pens (and) trample each other to death. The floors are slatted to allow excrement to fall into a catchment

pit under the pens, but many things besides excrement can wind up in the pits: afterbirths, piglets accidentally crushed by their mothers, old batteries, broken bottles of insecticide, antibiotic syringes, still-born pigs.[106]

Eventually, as pressure builds in the pits, pipes are opened and "everything bursts into a large holding pond."[107] Because this is a normal routine, the operation considers the contamination that ensues simply collateral damage, and such public health hazards continue as a normal part of doing business.[108] That the mother plant was located in Virginia is also part of what Robert Bullard terms dumping in Dixie, a practice that refers to dumping hazardous industrial pollutant in areas inhabited by African Americans.[109] The transfer of the operation to Mexico appears to simply extend the tradition of such hazardous sittings into other nonwhite and impoverished areas.[110]

The Mexican outbreak therefore continues the ongoing racist practices of violent polluting industries that refuse to respond to laws, regulatory regimes, or even, simply, consideration of human rights. Those who dare to protest are often jailed, as were Guadalupe Serrano Gaspar and four other activists. According to an article published by *La Jomada* on 26 April 2009, the activists were jailed after describing the holding ponds, which do not have a special membrane to prevent the spread of "excrements and chemical residues" as well as "foetid odours that infest the whole valley." The Mexican author gives 20 January 2006 as the date when Smithfield Carroll Industry was expelled from Virginia because of the hazards associated with its operation.

As far as the recent pandemic was concerned, the Canadian government's response was to change the name from swine flu to H1N1 Influenza A so as not to harm the pork "industry." Aside from the ridiculous equivocation on the name, Prime Minister Stephen Harper was perfectly correct to referring to the operation as an industry. Unfortunately, such operations are still considered farms under Canadian environmental law; therefore, they benefit from exceptions to all prohibitions regarding pollutants and hazardous substances.[111] On 4 May 2010, the front page of The *Globe and Mail*, the Canadian national newspaper, stated "The Pork Industry in Panic as Pigs Catch the Flu."

MORE PIG FARM DEATH AND MORBIDITY: WALKERTON, ONTARIO

One of the shortcomings of protecting human rights through, for example, the general exceptions raised at the dispute settlement

stage, is that it does not serve the wider purpose of reconciling
human rights with trade and economic development which places
the realization of human rights among the very objectives of
trade rules.

– Margot Salomon, *Global Responsibility for Human Rights*

In May 2000, an outbreak of the deadly E. coli bacteria struck Walkerton,
Ontario, a small rural town, killing as many as eighteen people, although according to later official sources, the total deaths acknowledged by provincial
authorities was only seven. The initial public outrage started with a question:
how could this happen in an affluent democracy such as the Province of
Ontario? In early June, banner headlines such as "Ontario Ignored Water
Alert" multiplied as the circumstances, background, and implications of the
case became clear: "Ontario's Environmental Ministry warned as early as 1997
that shutting down its water-testing labs could lead to the kind of water
disaster that has hit Walkerton, Ont. and killed at least seven people, internal
documents show."[112] As a general approach, Ontario's premier, Mike Harris,
had pursued a policy of (1) privatizing water-testing services without ensuring
that medical officers were informed if harmful bacteria were detected; (2)
revising Ontario's drinking-water objectives by shifting the treatment costs
to municipalities, without guaranteeing that smaller municipalities would
continue to keep tabs on water quality; (3) disbanding "teams charged with
inspecting municipal water-treatment plants"; (4) and giving priority to
"infrastructure projects to aid economic development."[113] Harris had stated
clearly and repeatedly, as part of his election platform, that provincial debt
reduction would be his main objective, not the protection of the environment
and public health.

Despite the opposition of the Liberal Party and many environmental and
human rights groups, Harris had been re-elected for a second term in 1999
precisely because of his "pro business/lower taxes" platform. But the general
public assumed that basic safety would be ensured for all citizens, that public
health would not be or become an issue. Yet it would be difficult for Harris
to claim ignorance of the trends in Canadian water issues.

The Walkerton incident is unexpected in a country such as Canada, especially in one of its richest and most populous provinces. It is important to
keep in mind, however, that the Walkerton case was never completely decided
by the courts. Therefore, Walkerton is only discussed here as an example of
an ecodisaster that can happen anywhere, even in a democratic country and

close to home, not only in a developing country under a military regime. Walkerton is also different in that the ecocrimes committed are systemic, institutional, and the result of practices that are either legal or taken for granted, not the result of some specific activity by a specific actor or actors, as is often the case in other cases, such as those in *Bhopal*, or the Saro-Wiwa case in Ogoniland.[114]

Normally, case studies include a clear chronology and perhaps details not only about the facts at issue but also about the individuals or companies involved. Although I describe, broadly speaking, some of the political and regulative background against which the Walkerton events unfolded, I make no effort to provide a specific chronology of events or to indict a specific individual, company, or group, as is normally done in case studies. What I hope to do is show the nature of ecocrimes that are systemic, diffuse, and institutional. Walkerton is a clear example of this sort of disaster. I therefore argue that breaches of environmental regulations are ecocrimes and ought to be treated as such, not only as quasi-crimes, and that the "emergent risks" posed by ecocrimes are not easily dealt with either by tradition or by regional or national means, let alone by a weakening system that supports deregulation.[115] Ecocrimes are not sporadic, occasional offences; they are institutional forms of violence often practised through nonpoint pollution – that is, pollution that does not come from one identifiable source in the careless and often negligent pursuit of other goals, mostly economic. I then turn to the question of moral and legal responsibility and the way regulatory breaches are viewed in common law. It is important to understand these breaches as real crimes. Unlike other ecodisasters, primarily in developing countries or in North American minority neighbourhoods, Walkerton was the result of legal, institutionalized practices. No illegal acts were committed, and there is no taint or racism.[116]

After considering the governance aspect and the regulatory framework, I then turn to the question of corporate responsibility for ecoviolence. This responsibility does not rest equally on corporations and on businesses in general, and it does not have the good of the people as its primary concern. Whether megafarms or a single farm operation was the major trigger for the disaster, the relationship between democratic governments, their regulatory systems, and public safety must be re-examined to assess their failure to meet their protective obligations.[117]

The economic interests of institutions, corporations, and individuals, appear to pose the gravest threats to the possibility of achieving environmental security. Some argue that the root of the problem is the form of governance of the country affected by environmental disasters. But, as we shall see, even in a country with no dictator or other repressive form of governance, citizens may be at serious risk. In the Walkerton case, practices that have documented harmful effects were permitted to protect the ability of industry to provide abundant meat at low prices, thus enabling everyone to buy and eat as much as they desire. Although catering to public preferences is often viewed as one of the goals of liberal democratic governance, in this case preferences were in direct conflict with the public good. In brief, a diet based on animal meat and fat, laced with various chemicals, as required by factory-farming conditions and the economic interests of industrial producers, is as harmful to humankind as illegal drugs. Not only is such a diet harmful to public health, it has serious implications for public health services, which are strained to the limit by the recurrence and growth of "Western man diseases," such as cancers and heart disease.[118] The true beneficiaries of factory farming are the corporate owners of these operations and, perhaps, the bureaucracies that may get rewarded for their support.

After much prevarication and name calling among politicians, the problem at Walkerton came to a head on the front page of one of Canada's most conservative and pro-business newspaper (a victory in itself). On 7 June 2000, Andrew Nikiforuk's special report in the *Globe and Mail*, titled "National Water Crisis Forecast," pointed to the problem. The report was based on an interview with Canada's foremost water ecologist, David Schindler, from the University of Alberta, who predicted that "the combined effects of climate change, acid rain, human and livestock wastes, increased ultraviolet radiation, airborne toxins and biological invaders will result in the degradation of Canadian freshwater on a scale hitherto unimaginable."[119] Once again, as had happened for many years, the underlying ecoviolence was not isolated as a major issue, and the list of problems Schindler outlined were, at best, viewed as separate problems, each requiring an individualized response. Schindler, correctly, views all separate effects as arising from a combined, unified cause. I call the cause disintegrity, or that condition of climate, air, and land that engenders and sustains multiple water disasters. The lax attitudes cited by Schindler are also the basis of much of the stress that fosters climate change. A lack of moral imperatives that demand responsibility, not simply rights, and support appropriate laws and regulations is fundamentally at fault.

We need at least a certain percentage of the earth to be left as wild or undeveloped in order to provide all life with nature's services.[120] We also need to keep the remainder, both land and water, in a state of health.[121] Most of all, we need to accept, as Schindler does, the ecosystem approach as a holistic means to understanding the problems and to designing and implementing a solution.

Walkerton is an example of the general acceptance of practices and policies chosen under the same problematic conditions as those outlined in the discussion of contingent valuations.[122] We can address the choices that resulted in the litany of disasters described by Schindler. In most cases, including that of Walkerton, reductionist rather than holistic end-of-pipe solutions were (and are) sought, and the institutional response is limited to an effort to isolate the failure of government, bureaucrats, or others to monitor the grave conditions of the natural systems involved, including air, water, and land. But no effort or even mention is made of isolating the underlying causes, the practices and choices that North Americans (in this case, Canadians) have made over the years that have brought these environmental matters to a head. Schindler states that "People don't appreciate the impact of multiple stressors on our water supply, and we have a history of underestimating problems. And when you put all these things together, nasty things tend to happen."[123] Only the holistic approach truly captures the reality of what is happening. Therefore, so long as we continue to view each problem as arising from a separate stressor, we will accept individualized, fragmented responses as adequate. I argue that only when we understand the role of multiple stressors on a system, can we start to move toward appropriate public policies.

The Walkerton disaster shows precisely the role of multiple stressors on ecosystems, as well as the multiple instances of violence arising from these stresses. The violent attacks combine to affect human health at the most obvious levels. An outbreak of disease (engendered by E. coli) in the water supply and the resulting infection, morbidity, and fatality for men, women, and children is undeniably a violent attack, fostered by disintegrity, including the lack of appropriately sized wild areas and environmental degradation.

Diet Choices, Preferences, and Megafarms

This section does not address the indefensible violence against animals in factory farms: it has been documented all too well in many books and evaluated and discussed by many ethicists. Descriptive works such as *Slaughterhouse; Prisoned Chickens, Poisoned Eggs;* and *Milk: The Deadly Poison* tell a shocking story of violence and inhumanity.[124] Philosophical works such as *The Case for Animal Rights* and *Animal Liberation* discuss and analyze the practices that support our preferred affluent Western diets.[125] Jeremy Rifkin's *Beyond Beef: The Rise and Fall of Cattle Culture* ties unethical diet choices to the global injustices engendered by overuse and overconsumption that are as hazardous to our environment as they are to our health and to the survival of those in impoverished countries in the Southeast. Aside from questions relating to the responsibility and accountability of the bureaucrats, businesses, and institutions of Walkerton, there is a question that was not raised in the newspapers: why was this sort of hazardous business encouraged to locate in the area, without imposing limits or other regulatory restraints on where and how it should operate? The underlying motive is primarily economic, if we consider the business operations involved. When we consider the motivation of the Ontario government, the economic motive, even if present through business support, is normatively insufficient and legally suspect. Governments should not license or permit to operate operations that do not function for the public good.

Examples of environmentally hazardous operations include the opening up of highways with multiple lanes and large hospitals with copious toxic wastes. Both examples indicate that the side effects – intrusion into the wild for the former, hazardous waste for the latter – should be mitigated. Yet the public good is served by both operations. Clearly, both should function in a more environmentally safe manner in order not to give rise to double-effect harms to the public. But the basic usefulness of highways and hospitals cannot be denied.

We also need to consider the question of diet preferences that lead not only to farms producing meat in traditional ways – that is, keeping animals in natural conditions of life – but also to factory farms, which are intended to produce large quantities of meat at prices low enough to enable most citizens of affluent Western democracies to eat abundant meat at all meals. But factory-raised animals must be fed large amounts of antibiotics and other chemicals to keep them alive in unnatural conditions of confinement, and they are also fed growth hormones and other medicines to bring them as soon as possible to full size and the market. The question, then, is whether this progress is indeed in the public interest, or whether the harms imposed are significant enough to justify legal countermeasures to control these practices.

In relation to both the human right to be free from harm and the justice dimensions of the environmental effects of cattle culture, Rifkin outlines the effects, such as famine, in developing countries. When cattle are fed grains that could feed hundreds of thousands of people in the South and instead produce meat to suit the taste preferences of those who can afford it, this is not only an environmental wrong, it is also a breach of justice. Of course, even turning everyone in developed countries to vegetarianism, in the interest of global justice, would not be enough, unless the monumental distribution and political problems were settled first.[126] The science supporting this position is readily available, and so are the normative analyses of these practices.[127]

For most philosophers, it is the unspeakable violence against individual animals that is the target of their arguments. I accept these arguments as given and will not attempt to compare or evaluate them, as there is an abundant literature that has already done much of that work. I will, however, use their joint (though nuanced) agreement that the violence perpetrated upon animals in the quest to meet consumer preferences is immoral. Accepting this argument means accepting that what takes place in factory farming is institutionalized, legal violence. What must be added is that the violence eventually returns to us, magnified and unexpected, when we exercise our right to enjoy what we prefer to consume. The ecoviolence that boomerangs back to us follows through these stages: ecoviolence in agricultural practices leads to ecoviolence through ecosystem disruption, representing both violence to the system and to us through its health effects, the consequence of which is ecoviolence against both individual and public health. The latter, in turn, includes several interrelated but separate attacks. It is both sad and puzzling that we accept these attacks fostered by a global economic enterprise that supports a hazardous diet for all who want it and can afford it, without regard for the resulting "Western man's diseases" or for the violence upon which the diet itself is based.

Thus, beyond the violence against so-called farm animals, the question about the common good raised in the previous section demands answers. It is not enough to say, look at what happened at Walkerton and what the Government of Ontario or of Canada did or did not do. Why did we empower politicians, freely and democratically chosen, to support such hazardous choices? These choices are, at the same time, a threat to our health, to other living creatures, and to our joint habitat. Of course, another question comes first: Can we truly claim that our preferences are truly our own and freely chosen? Does our knowledge of the consequence of our preferences, spotty and incomplete though it is, render us complicit in the violent results of those preferences? And, most puzzling of all, what leads even the citizens of democratic countries, where at least some information is available to them in principle, to participate in practices that are ultimately going to harm them?

Diet choices are manipulated by those who gain from selling food that is harmful when it is grown, processed, and even consumed.[128] This issue touches each one of us as closely as we can be touched: our immediate survival depends both on our nourishment and on our habitat. Both are under attack, as we are, from current diet choices. We are bombarded with advertisements for fatty, unhealthful food choices we know are harmful to our health and to that of our children. In addition, at least in Northwest democracies, we also know that our government's bureaucracies have other priorities than the protection of human health. Mike Harris candidly admitted that his priority was reducing the debt and supporting business. This frank confession was uttered while a television interviewer raised questions about the unprecedented spread of disease and the mounting number of deaths and while yet another agricultural community, St. Thomas, discovered E. coli in the water of a local nursing home.

The connection between diet choices and the E. coli outbreak starts with the existence of megafarms that produce what we believe we need and we are entitled to have, together with the morally culpable negligence of those whose responsibility it is to protect our life and physical integrity. The Walkerton example shows the sequence of events leading to the disaster. The stage is set by a political system that only pays lip service to the common interest in ecological and health protection, as legally established by national environmental acts, such as the *Canadian Environmental Protection Act* (1999) and by the bi-national (Canada-US) regulatory mandates of the *Great Lakes Water Quality Agreement* (1987) but does not really incorporate the binding requirement "to protect and restore the integrity" of the Great Lakes waters and their basin, with all that it would imply for the conduct of business in the area.

The second step is the election of a government that implements disastrous ecological and health deregulation under the heading of bringing about a "common sense revolution" that openly places economic interests above environmental protection and the basic rights of Canadians. Note that each step can be deemed normal routine, a legal aspect of institutionalized practices. But the megafarms raise public and individual health problems that do not arise from small family farm operations such as the ones that were present in Ontario for years. Consider, for instance, hog farming. In a *Globe and Mail* feature titled "Fear of Farming," Alana Mitchell, John Gray, and Real Seguin cite some "porcine statistics":

12 million: Canada's current (record) hog population
36,000: number of hog farms in 1986
13,000: number of hog farms today
280: pigs per farm in 1986
917: pigs per farm today[129]

Similar percentages are present in Ontario and in Quebec, where bovine statistics report equally large numbers and rapid growth. The phenomenal growth of megafarms indicates public and individual health problems that do not arise from the operation and the products of the small family farm operations of the past. The epidemic proportions of Western diseases, all fostered by cheap fat and meat products, is related to our diet. The World Health Organization has publicized the benefits of the Mediterranean diet and contrasts it starkly with the practices of affluent Western countries. (Italy, both a Mediterranean and a Western country, boasts the most longevity in the world today.) We are taught, enticed, and convinced to prefer unsafe diets, whereas what is healthy and safe is presented as harmful. We should eat meat never, or no more than once a month at best; chicken (normally raised or free range), once a week, at most; fruits, vegetables, olive oil, grains and natural starches, and fish, daily.

We reap the result of ignoring the reality of our needs and our best interests at our own cost, and at the cost of those who are disproportionately affected by our practices. These injustices range from the use of grain protein for feed (thus limiting protein intake to those who can afford it in meat form). This practice, as many have shown, deprives those who are starving to satisfy our taste preferences.[130] We also reap the results at many other levels, for agribusiness and factory farms have grown enormously. Farmers themselves suffer, at minimum, noxious odours and other discomforts. The Hern family has watched the factory farm evolve up close. For the better part of 140 years, members of the family happily farmed twenty acres near Kirkton, which is fifty kilometres north of London, Ontario. Then newcomers moved into the neighbourhood. "I now have 10,000 hogs one mile from my bedroom," David Hern says: the result is waste equal to that produced by forty thousand people. But there is more involved than a bad smell. The threat to neighbours and to the rest of us is real: hog waste, like cattle manure, is not treated. Cattle and hogs can transmit E. coli through their feces or, in the case of cattle, from their hides after butchering. Some US research shows that cattle raised in overcrowded feedlots in Nebraska and those fattened in Midwest feedlots are breeding grounds for E. coli, which was found in 72 percent of the lots investigated.[131]

The factory farm is, therefore, the source of severe individual and public health threats, but it is also, at the same time, the source of serious environmental damage and the epitome of gross disregard for the life, health, and integrity of individual animals. There is more than a casual connection between these forms of violence and the harm that eventually rebounds to us. It is worth noting that J. Baird Callicott in his classic treatment of the topic, "Animal Liberation: A Triangular Affair," although he does not argue on the side of animal ethics, strongly indicts agribusiness practices.[132] He says of the consumption of meat: "Meat, however, purchased at the supermarket, externally packaged and internally laced with petrochemicals, fattened in feed lots, slaughtered impersonally and, in general, mechanically processed from artificial insemination to microwave roaster, is an affront not only to physical metabolism and bodily health, but to conscience as well."[133]

We distance ourselves from the violent treatment meted out to animals that we only encounter, eventually, as slabs in a supermarket cooler. Similarly, we tend to think of agribusiness as just business – that is, as something un-related to suffering or violence, just a normal, legal part of everyday life. In fact, we admire and even treat as celebrities those with thriving businesses. Even environmental damage is often thought to be something else, something other than and unrelated to violence or health. When we see violence against animals, environmental violence, and violent attacks on our health for what they really are, the connection becomes clear, as does the cause-and-effect sequence and the eventual deadening of our ability to be morally awake and emotionally sensitive to violence in all its forms.

Eventually, the violence has a boomerang effect. Difficult questions re-main unanswered. For instance, why do we continue to accept a meat-based diet and these practices with their tripartite violence – to nonhuman animals, to natural systems, and to human organisms – as inevitable? Underlying all three types of violence is a global injustice: the pursuit of institutional prac-tices that decimate biodiversity, despoil nature, and reduce those in de-veloping countries to famine-stricken masses.[134]

It may be possible to at least understand, if not condone, such a cluster of immoral choices and preferences, if the results produced unadulterated good for the choosers. However, the opposite is true. Given what goes into the meat and the milk we consume – the hormones, antibiotics, and other chemicals, together with the dirt and contamination to which all these prod-ucts are exposed through the slaughtering and butchering processes – it is clear that they present grave threats to health, even beyond diet considera-tions.[135] Jeremy Rifkin reports an accidental experiment as it happened to Danish nationals. Because of the naval blockade of 1917, "the Danes were cut off from incoming shipments of food. The government was subsequently forced to begin to ration out food, and encourage the country to give up its meat, and eat mainly a potato-based diet. In time, some three million people became vegetarians and the death rate from disease fell some 35 percent.[136]

The reverse is shown by the increase of cancer and heart disease in Japan, a country that is moving away from its traditional low-meat diet. Of 2.1 million deaths in the United States, 1.5 million are due to dietary factors, primarily high consumption of cholesterol and fat in meat. The hormones, synthetics, and other substances – including bioengineered and transgenic substances that are present in the feed and, therefore, in the animals we eat – add to the now well-documented health risks. Perhaps the most publicized of recent times has been the presence of bovine growth hormone (BGH) followed by the infamous outbreak of mad cow disease.[137] In conclusion, the violence practised on animals to support our choices and preferences for certain foods is tied to the violence we receive from these choices and preferences in our diet.

Each offence must be punished in accordance with its specific facts, but pollution offences must be approached as crimes, not as morally blameless technical breaches of a regulatory standard.[138]

One of the key elements in the Walkerton tragedy may well be the legislative and regulatory framework in Ontario. Even before the tragedy happened, the Canadian Environmental Law Association's *Intervenor* described the situation in Ontario's farming communities under the heading "Rural Ontario: Industrial Hog Barns, Industrial Waste."[139] One form of waste, antibiotics, are fed to pigs because "thousands of animals are kept packed together in huge barns, sows producing more piglets and piglets fattened for the shortest possible time before slaughter."[140] Animals under these violent, inhumane, and unnatural conditions require antibiotics to survive to market. The spring 2001 issue of *Nucleus*, the magazine of the Union of Concerned Scientists, makes the same point in "Pearls before Pigs."[141] Too many antibiotics, which can be considered key to human medicine, are "routinely fed to livestock"; some of the antibiotics are tetracycline, penicillin, and erythromicin, all of which are used for healthy livestock. Although the European Union has banned growth hormones, promoting the use of antibiotics, in the United States, for instance, their use has increased by 50 percent.[142] It is almost obscene to think of using medication in this way, for the profit of some, when children in developing countries are dying from lack of some of the same medications.

Nevertheless, these statistics further support the point made in the *Intervenor*: the threats arising from intensive livestock facilities are even more immediate. Intensive livestock facilities produce enormous quantities of highly toxic manure. A single hog produces two tons of manure per year. Ontario's 4 million hogs produce as much raw sewage as the entire human population of the province, without the benefit of a single sewage treatment plant.[143] This waste is the most hazardous aspect of these industrial farming operations, a fact later confirmed by a study of the general conditions and background to the events in Walkerton. In addition, "the odour associated with a hog barn is dramatically worse than the odour which comes with a normal farming environment," and the odour of manure itself, can have "severe health impacts."[144] The article's author, E. Bruckmann, adds: "Manure contains over 150 gaseous compounds, including hydrogen sulfide, ammonia, carbon dioxide and methane. Residents living near intensive livestock facilities report headaches, nausea, and the exacerbation of asthma and respiratory problems."[145]

Even before the Walkerton tragedy, it was clear that the existing regulations were completely inadequate. As long as what amounts to a hazardous industrial operation continues to be improperly defined as farming, the nature of the actual operation is not properly understood and cannot be controlled realistically.

LESSONS FROM THE WALKERTON CASE

What can be learned from this Canadian case, beyond the obvious importance of a safe, healthy environment as the foundation of human rights in general? Several issues emerge to demonstrate that Seveso, Bhopal, and Sandoz, well-known disasters, are not the only way to produce disastrous conditions that impose grave harms on children and future generations. A regular industrial operation is hazardous to environmental and human health on its own, even before human error occurs to compound the problem. At first sight, Walkerton, too, is a disaster. But the presence of normal, accepted practices, licensed and promoted by a government that views "cutting red tape" and facilitating business operations as its first priority, rather than the protection of citizens from harm, tells a different story.

Unfortunate government priorities are the underlying cause of disasters and regular business operations in which neither the health nor the safety of the public is viewed as the main responsibility of democratic institutions that owe their very existence and raison d'être to the public it is elected to protect. The argument that can be used against Walkerton's many factory farm operations is the same as those that can be brought to bear against industrial chemical, pesticides, and other harmful activities. Although these industries may offer increased consumer choices and low price products, they are not in the best interests of most citizens, at least not with the conditions under which they operate.

Earlier I indicated the deleterious effects of the increased availability of an unhealthful diet, one based on too much fatty protein, laced with antibiotics and other chemicals made necessary by the conditions of mass production. This availability is not a benefit but a hazard to most citizens. The same can be said of chemicals designed to make smells or dirt disappear with ease, or to make weeds disappear from our lawns and golf courses, or to kill pests indiscriminately, along with insects best adapted to safe crop rotation. Even the greater availability of out-of-season fruits and vegetables, part of our ecological footprint that is damaging developing countries and eliminating local traditional agricultural practices, is not quite the boon to our health it appears to be, for they are most likely laced with chemical residues and far lower in nutritional value than normally grown food.[146] Fungicides and other chemicals are increasingly added to prolong the shelf life of products that are neither grown nor manufactured (e.g., bread) in the same area where they are grown.

The obligation of legislators and monitoring officials is clear in these and all similar cases: to ensure that public health is protected at the source, by not permitting chemical companies to perform in-house assessment of their products and by demanding testing by independent agencies. Academics who publish their work or defend a doctoral thesis are forced to name and accept only the reviews of referees and examiners they have kept at arm's length so that no bias or cronyism can interfere with the quality of their work. How much more important to ensure that the general public is not harmed by inappropriate relationships between the testers of products and processes and the industrial giants that produce and direct them. It is wrong to mislead the public, but it is even more wrong to poison or otherwise physically harm an unsuspecting citizen or, even worse, a child.

The responsibilities of these outside guardians should include a thorough examination of all products and processes from cradle to grave. Because the interests of the general public and those of corporations are not at the same level, these guardians should also ensure that corporate citizens are kept away from these procedures and not allowed to sit at a negotiating table. Because of corporations' immense economic power and advertising and marketing campaigns (which are intended to promote, not simply to inform), and because of the presence of protective trade secrets laws, the public never makes free and informed contributions to these discussions of policies. The tragedy at Walkerton was not simply a tragedy of human error. It was the result of systemic practices, for the most part, and their negligent and violent results. These practices are founded on a total disregard for basic human rights to safety and health as primary obligations of law and governance.

Supporters of the status quo will respond by saying that many of the products that are hazardous both in their manufacture and use – plastics, medicines and medical equipment used in hospitals and elsewhere, additives to make food safer in the long term, cheap and mass-produced cars, information equipment, and so on – are vitally important not only to the economy of nations but also to the good of humankind. The question, however, remains: *who* decides *where* and *how* even ostensibly beneficial products are made, and *who* controls and enforces their continued safety?

During the Walkerton disaster, roughly as many people were killed or severely and irreversibly harmed as during the infamous 9/11 attack in New York. Yet no war on unsafe industry has been instituted; in fact, the military establishment in the West is on expanding, adding to the industrial violence to which we are already exposed. It is noteworthy that global change is an exacerbating factor everywhere, as it was in Walkerton, where unusually heavy rains led contaminants to spread to the affected wells. All industrial enterprises depend on oil as a basic source of energy, and the recent decision of the Bush administration to open up Alaska for exploration will further destabilize the climate and increase all the risks, especially in developing countries, while postponing sounder decisions that may promote alternative energy sources and even alternative consumer lifestyles.

The conflict, as suggested earlier, is between the freedom of certain groups to pursue their interests as they see fit and the public interest. This conflict is complicated further by the fact that many grey areas are present within it. For instance, many so-called consumers would probably choose their freedom over the security and safety not only of distant peoples but also of people in their own community: they may not be prepared to question the ultimate wisdom of the choices they embrace or the moral implications of such choices.

ANOTHER FOOD-RELATED DISASTER: BHOPAL

During the night between 2 and 3 December 1984, a lethal gas known as isocyanate was released from a chemical plant operated

> by Union Carbide India Limited (UCIL) in the city of Bhopal,
> State of Madhya Pradesh, India. In the most devastating industrial
> disaster that has ever occurred, about 2,660 persons died (the
> exact number will probably never be ascertained) and between
> 30,000 and 40,000 sustained serious injuries.
>
> – Tullio Scovazzi, "Industrial Accidents and the Veil
> of Transnational Corporations"[147]

In the *Bhopal* case, the rights of a legal entity prevailed. Union Carbide Corporation (owning all but 22 percent of the shares of Union Carbide India Limited [UCIL]) conducted an operation intended ostensibly for the production of abundant food, based on the use of hazardous chemicals.[148] Thus, once again, an industry committed to the production of hazardous materials was neither fully restrained at its inception nor was an additional corrective measure applied to compensate for the fact that even the scant public protection that may have existed in the home country (the United States) would not have been present at its location in India.

Aside from the dangers of using powerful chemicals in food production, such as the presence of residues, the harms resulting from spraying crops with these chemicals (for a parallel example, see *Ecuador v. Columbia* in Chapter 3) and from the production of the chemicals themselves means the possibility of a disaster is always present. Thus, in addition to chemical companies being allowed to produce regardless of the possible harms that may ensue, even mass disasters such as the Bhopal case have historically been relegated to the realm of torts.[149] Suffice it to say that it was alleged that trying the case in India would provide a *forum non conveniens*, as the absence of those responsible for Union Carbide would be a problem for the court. Even more problematic was Union Carbide's motion to dismiss. The case was only one of many dismissed when "brought by foreign citizens and residents, involving foreign accidents, because they are far more appropriately and conveniently tried in the foreign forum."[150]

Aside from attempts to ignore the carnage caused by Union Carbide and the insurmountable difficulties involved in flying witnesses to the United States instead or interviewing persons who are not familiar with either the languages or the laws of Western countries, Union Carbide's motion to dismiss also stated: "The complaints allege claims of negligence, strict liability, nuisance, and ultra-hazardous activity on behalf of Indian citizens living in India which must be decided in accordance with Indian principles of law, policy and socio-economic standards."[151] Aside from the obvious critique that can be brought against this disingenuous pronouncement, it is aimed at escaping the grave responsibility for the disaster, the main point is that "negligence, strict liability, nuisance and ultra-hazardous activity" still sounds like something that can be redressed as compensable, at least in elevated monetary terms.

The approach I propose instead is to accuse Union Carbide of crimes against humanity, for the gross breaches of human rights that its operation implied under normal circumstances and for the disaster its operation created. In this hypothetical case, the International Court of Justice at The Hague or, eventually, the International Criminal Court at Rome would provide appropriate forums to judge what amounted, minimally, to mass manslaughter. One would hope that this change of venue would help to eliminate carelessness and recklessness, especially when it is directed to those in developing countries or, in North America, to people of colour.

Corporate crime or institutional crime of this sort must be treated as such because, for the most part, the victims suffer incompensable harms. The question of intent becomes moot: neither in Walkerton, Ontario, nor in Bhopal, India, can those who lost a child or a parent be compensated. It is therefore false to consider and try these crimes under a heading that, even in the best of circumstances, will not elicit a just disposition in a court of law. Disasters of this magnitude make it obvious that both the quantitative and the qualitative parameters of environmental harms have changed dramatically in recent times because of the exponential growth of technological power and the corresponding scientific knowledge that demonstrates the multiple implications of each case. What is particularly interesting about the resolution of the *Bhopal* case is the novel position taken by the Indian government. With the object that claims arising out of the accident should "be dealt with speedily, effectively, equitably and to the best advantage of the claimants," India enacted the *Bhopal Gas Leak Disaster (Processing of Claims) Act, 1985*. It attributes to the central government of India "the exclusive right to represent and act in place of (whether within or outside India) every person who has made, or is entitled to make, a claim for all persons connected with such claim for all purposes connected with such claim in the same manner and to the same effect as such persons."[152]

In the case of the *Bhopal Gas Leak Disaster Act*, India enacted a form of *parens patriae* (parent of the nation) doctrine, noting that, as states in the 1985 legislation, the victims were impoverished and, therefore, unable to sustain a protracted court battle. Thus the court held that "the conventional adversary system would be totally inadequate"; therefore, "the State in the discharge of its sovereign obligation must come forward. The Indian State because of its constitutional commitment is obliged to take upon itself the claims of the victims and to protect them in their hour of need."[153] This adoption of the parens patriae doctrine is particularly relevant, for twenty years later the same doctrine would be used explicitly in a New York appellate court in *State of Connecticut, et al. v. American Electric Power Company,* a case brought against corporate persons in the defence of the basic rights of the collective, this time regarding climate change (see Chapter 7).

Conclusion

> Article 38(1) of the ICJ Statute lists the sources of international law upon which the Court can draw when determining disputes. The Court may apply "the general principles of law recognized by civilized nations," separate and independent conventions, and international custom.
>
> – Margot Salomon, *Global Responsibility for Human Rights*

As the above discussion of climate change reveals, neither domestic nor treaty law can actually support collective human rights, even when these rights run counter to the specific interests of one or more states. In addition, neither has the character of nonderogability essential to the protection of universal human rights that, according to Judge Tanaka, are "included in the general principles mentioned in article 38(1) of the ICJ Statue."[154]

Whether such obligations are derived from their natural law origins, the general obligation to respect human rights in the *International Covenant on Economic, Social and Cultural Rights* derives from the "inherent dignity of the human person."[155] The same position was also present in the Nuclear Weapons Opinion, and it is reinforced in the International Court of Justice's opinion on the *Legal Consequences of the Construction of a Wall in the Occupied Palestinian Territory* and in the judgment reaffirming the principles of the *Convention on Genocide* in the case *Armed Activities on the Territory of the Congo.*[156]

Essentially, then, from 1980 to 2006 there was no shift in the position of the United Nations and the International Court of Justice on the foundational character of the norms requiring respect for the dignity of the human person, from the right to self-determination of peoples (see the next chapter) to the right of survival of individuals and communities – in other words, to the right to food, water, resources, and a safe environment. These norms, as noted, are not fully specified, but they will "be further refined by the interpretation and application of various judicial bodies.[157] Their presence cannot be ignored, and their status cannot be denied. As for natural law itself, Judge Tanaka writes: "A State or States are not capable of creating human rights by law or by convention; they can only confirm their existence and give them protection: the role of the state is no more than declaratory."[158]

This chapter considers some of the forces that militate against the use and application of nonderogable principles, including solidarity, universality, and enforcement and legal standing.[159] The bias against principles is constantly in evidence as business-as-usual attitudes (the individual and aggregate interests of natural and legal persons), and the quest for power by states on the international stage combine to raise constant obstacles to the moral and legal rights of the collective and what is suggested by basic individual morality. The main characteristic of morality is that it supersedes individual gain, choices, or pleasure, and this characteristic is something that has been established since the inception of moral reasoning and is evident, for instance, in ancient Greek philosophical thought.

3
Communities and Collectives: The Interface

．．．．

> One of the first characteristics of liberal philosophical theories
> is that the moral agent is conceptualized in individualistic terms.
> That is, individuals are thought to be the only actors which
> may have moral standing. Collectivities are seen as either the
> summation of individual human beings or eventually, as
> fictitious, possessing no existence beyond that of the individuals
> who collectively compose them. As Kymlicka has noted, within
> liberal ontology, there does not seem to be any room left for
> constitutive communities having moral standing as a collectivity.
>
> – Marlies Galenkamp, *Individualism versus Collectivism*[1]

To clarify the difference between communities and collectivities, not only in theory but also in terms of the reality of such rights, I return to the argument presented in Chapter 1. In that chapter, I argue that the starting point, the reason to seek collective rights that are cosmopolitan (that is, universal and binding), is the lack of an ecocentric position in law, such that individual, aggregate, and community rights are affected. This starting point must be kept in mind as the most basic consideration because it is foundational to the right to life, including the right to water, to food, to health and normal development, for all may be gravely affected by the ecological conditions in which we live.

This starting point remains the gold standard to which regulatory regimes, conventions, and community standards must comply. These regimes need to accept this basis for whatever lifestyles, goals, and beliefs people require beyond that. In addition, Cicero's point about the insufficiency of both authority and popular choices as final arbiters of policy decisions is important for this goal.

In the first chapter, I also asked whether the community and the collective should be viewed as the same. The answer was clear: they are not. To repeat, the collectivity is at least the totality of humankind, although one would add the community of all life as well.[2] Communities may be foundational to the recognition of basic rights or they may not: many groups and communities, especially aggregates of individual natural and legal persons, hold beliefs and accept practices that are entirely contrary to the common good of humankind. Hence, although Article 27 of the *International Covenant on Economic, Social and Cultural Rights* states that "in those States in which ethnic, religious or linguistic minorities exist, persons belonging to such minorities shall not be denied the right in community with other members of their group, to their own culture, to profess and practice their own religion, or to use their own language," this article supports the rights of minorities, and it does so, Marlies Galenkamp argues, on the basis of an individualistic bias.[3] This article speaks against discrimination, on any grounds, against any group, but it is inconclusive and insufficient. Chapter 2 discloses the dire results of unrestrained individual or aggregate rights when they are affirmed without consideration for the collectivity. Should people in over twenty-five countries become ill and risk death because of the interests of the pork industry and because a great majority of people in the world like to eat that meat?

This is just one of examples cited but, in general, our freedom to act extends only so far as the possibility of harming another human being, thus conflicting with his or her right to be free from harm. Therefore, basic justice ought to mandate that such foundational moral principles be extended to the legal obligations of both states and individuals. As well, the right of communities, aggregates, and minorities alike should extend only so long as their actions cause no harm within and outside their chosen group. Even in a group or aggregate that has a preference, say, for eating pork, the members of the group have the same rights as vegetarians not to be harmed and to receive full information about the risks involved. Hence we are still operating within the individual perspective we are attempting to transcend.[4] Therefore the concept of minorities does not, on its own, support collective rights. However, after decolonization, another notion emerged – that of peoples' rights, a term left undefined in UN instruments but intended primarily to fit certain groups, formerly occupied or oppressed. Galenkamp writes: "Although theoretically the term 'peoples' might be used to denote a broad collection of subjects, varying from oppressed groups, populations, communities, nations and ex-colonies, in actual state practice its legitimate used tends to be restricted to those peoples who have been under Western colonial rule. A vivid illustration of this tendency is provided by the practice concerning the right of peoples to self-determination."[5] Because decolonization left peoples to form their own nations, emphasizing "state sovereignty and territorial integrity," such communities acquired rights.[6] But the emergence of "new states" and this approach in general are not the same as supporting the universal, collective rights I seek to defend. Thus, there is no need to discuss this political/legal point of view further. Because Galenkamp seems to confuse collective with community rights, her work does not advance my argument.[7]

The rights I seek to defend are fully moral and acceptable only insofar as they do not permit individual rights to trump (as Dworkin has it) the basic rights of the collectivity.[8] I trace these basic rights back to natural law, although that is not the only path to reach them, as is indicated by Henry Shue's work, for they appear to be both moral and legal at the same time.[9] Hence, in response to Galenkamp's claim that "we may say that rights serve as an important kind of constraint on the pursuit of social goods,"[10] I argue that the converse is true. The common good, as a distinctive (though basic) human goal, places a final constraint on the pursuit of individual rights.

This is the argument of Chapter 1, while Chapter 2 explores the possible legal aspects of this nonderogable constraint.[11] At this time, however, the legal aspects are only tenable at the highest level, and there is strong legal support for absolutes at the level of respect for life, preserving the human dignity of prisoners, and protecting against racial and gender discrimination. This support, however, is primarily limited to the area of physical aggression or other attacks on the respect due humanity. These are the accepted forms of obligation based on *jus cogens* norms, as indicated by the dictum in the *Barcelona Traction* case (see Chapter 2). Based on these principles and legal instruments, the limits here proposed to the rights of individuals and aggregates are both moral and legal.

Communities of Rights and the Collectivity: The Role of Traditional Communities

An aggregate interest has from the outset an odd feature in that it is non-neutral in respect to potentially trivial changes in the collectivity's membership. An aggregate interest will vary based on both changes in the interests of continuing members and changes in membership. Even a very minor change in a collectivity's membership could change the aggregate interest, if for instance a new member's interests diverged in the appropriate way. This feature is arguably problematic in a *collectivity*, for the defining features of a collectivity as opposed to a set include that it remain the same collectivity even with changed membership.

> – Dwight Newman, "Collective Interests and
> Collective Rights"

Once again: my starting point is to support not only a community of rights – that is, a community of agents free to make informed and reasoned decisions for themselves as individuals – but also components of the moral community that defines them.[12] My starting point also requires that the basic rights supported would be those of the universal collectivity and that these rights would be basic in the sense that such rights would be ensured only when a moral community is physically or biologically capable of reaching decisions and of exercising and defending its own rights, beyond the most basic ones, which simply support the community's survival and normal capabilities. To clarify my point further, there is no conflict between "social good" (or, better, "common good") decisions and those that support the freedom of agents to act morally (with the full exercise of their normal faculties). Collective rights must simply meet two basic conditions: they must be primary, both conceptually and temporally, and they should not extend beyond their basic nature to usurp the decision-making agency of individuals within the community of rights, such as Brownsword defines it.[13]

These conditions must be kept in mind when considering the role that communities can play in relation to the notion of a collectivity. In fact, we should do something that liberal thinkers and others abhor – that is, we should rank the interests of individuals and aggregates, which may well be incomparable from the standpoint of law.[14] Many will resist any attempt to rank goals and preferences, the equality of which (other than those that are clearly illegal) represents both a modern trend and the development of rights within the UN as it appears to follow an ongoing project to support the freedom of choice.[15]

Yet, if the development of rights within international law is considered, the extension of rights deals primarily with individual rights and individual activities, especially within the area of sexual mores. Roman emperors advocated *panem et circenses* to keep the populace quiet and satisfied, no matter what else was happening in the empire. *Panem et circenses* can loosely be translated as "food (consumerism?) and entertainment" (the latter includes sexual preferences), both of which are viewed as almost sacred within affluent Western countries.

In contrast, it is harder to add community and collective rights to the roster of conventions and other legal instruments. Witness, for instance, the agonizingly slow pace of the ratification of the "Draft United Nations Declaration on the Rights of Indigenous Peoples."[16] Collective decision making, however, is not necessarily decision making for the common good; it is, at best, a way of aggregating social preferences, unconstrained by the non-derogable obligation to choose one option over another.[17] Dwight Newman states, "Given that an interest is something that makes someone's life go better, then a collective interest is something that makes a collectivity's life go better."[18] Although true, this is too mild a statement to describe collective interests, if they are understood as a common good. Without restraints on other choices and interests, neither survival nor moral capacities or developments are ensured when the common good of the collectivity, understood in our sense, is not given primacy. Thus, the collective interest must be understood as far more basic than whatever makes "life go better," although the latter is true.

This collective interest is why communities should be approached and considered in a similar vein and ranked, as Newman proposes, for individual interests. Communities are such when they are more than aggregates or sets of individuals who may share one goal while also holding many different lifestyle preferences and beliefs. However, this ranking would be a futile exercise, given the great number of present, past, and future communities, assembling an endless variety of peoples and purposes.

The best way to proceed is to single out a specific sort of community, one that is rare but still in existence today. It will hold within it the seeds of the values and beliefs that make it unique, and its characteristics will be representative of the common good we require. Traditional indigenous or local land-based communities manifest the characteristics of unity of belief and practice and respect for their habitat and the creatures they share it with. These communities exemplify the collective quest for the common good. In addition, these communities share another major characteristic. At least in principle, they are protected by legal instruments and regimes, both domestic and international, although in practice such protection is either limited or, in many cases, non-existent. Analyzing the conditions that make such communities unique or – as it is described in law, *sui generis* – reveals communities that are both inspirational and a clear constitutive part of the collectivity of humankind because of their basic tenets.

WHO AND WHAT DEFINES AN INDIGENOUS COMMUNITY?

> We thus accept that there are no fixed cultural traits that
> objectively constitute the identity of a given ethnic group. To
> the contrary, ethnic identity is constructed by individuals in their
> social interactions. When we encounter another person, we rely
> on certain traits ("markers") to classify that person as belonging
> to our group or to another group (e.g., language, behaviour, skin
> colour, etc.). There are no markers that are objectively or naturally
> more important than others. However, when a large number of
> people generally agree on such markers, we can conclude that an
> ethnic group exists.
>
> – Sebastien Grammond, with Lynne Groulx, "Finding
>   Métis Communities"

This passage raises a number of questions, two of which have not been explored here: How are indigenous communities "found" in law?[19] Who defines them? Sebastien Grammond examines these questions in relation to a group that is indigenous to Canada but separate in many ways from Canadian First Nations: the Métis. This is a particularly significant community, because it has, in law, been defined to some extent by trial judges.[20] In addition, the Supreme Court of Canada "may give advice as to the legal "tests or principles that must be applied" to decide whether a specific community is indeed Métis.[21] This stipulation indicates the important role played by judges, lawyers, and witnesses in establishing the ethnic boundary that defines a Métis community.[22] In the major case *R. v. Powley*, the accused were not allowed to participate because the factual aspects of the case were not in question, but the witnesses and the defence lawyer were indeed Métis. At any rate, if we exclude race as a marker (for it appears objectionable in this context), as a way of defining a community, some other identity markers that emerge are "ancestry, recognition by others, way of life, efforts towards self-government, economic activities, language and art."[23]

For the purpose of this discussion, who is or is not a Métis is less important than the general considerations that lead to the definition of an indigenous community. In particular, it is significant that, most often, such groups are defined by nonindigenous persons – in other words, from outside: "In the Canadian context, the government has, since 1850, assumed the power to define who the indigenous peoples were, and did so in an unjust divisive and exclusive way."[24] This is a persistent problem, present in various countries, including those where colonizers had the effective power to define the colonized. The "potential for oppression" in these situations is undeniable.[25]

Definitions of indigeneity, even if imposed by legally appointed individuals and bodies, may well be internalized by community members or recognized by them. But, in principle, indigenous claims of identity that are based on cultural practices may conflict with the "constructed" identity that originated from outside the community. This is an important aspect of the issue, for we are attempting to define a model community in such a way that its principles and lifestyle demonstrate the need for curbing, in general, individual rights in favour of the rights of the collectivity. How and who defines such communities is therefore basic to my argument .

The importance of the legally accepted definition of any indigenous group cannot be overstated, for the group's hunting, fishing, and trapping rights, all of which are basic to its survival, depend upon such definitions to support their acknowledged sui generis lifestyle.

INDIGENOUS PEOPLES' RIGHTS IN INTERNATIONAL LAW

> International law is not only rules. It is a normative system harnessed to the achievement of common values, values that speak to all of us.
>
> – Rosalyn Higgins, *Problems and Process: International Law and How We Use It*

The first thing to note is that there is not one absolute definition of indigenous peoples in international law, although the various definitions are increasingly emerging, both as players and participants in UN instruments and other documents.[26] The main international law instrument that attempts to define indigenous peoples and their rights is the International Labour Organization (ILO),[27] which treats as indigenous the following groups:

- peoples whose social, cultural and economic conditions distinguish them from other sections of the national community;

- peoples whose status is regulated wholly or partially by their own customs and traditions;
- peoples who descend from populations that inhabited a country at the time of conquest or colonization;
- self-identification of a group as indigenous or tribal is regarded as a fundamental criterion.[28]

There are legal instruments that are relevant to both indigenous peoples and their environment, but only two of them are legally binding: the afore-mentioned ILO convention and the *Convention on Biological Diversity*.[29] James Anaya traces the rights of indigenous peoples to the earliest times of international law, when they emerged as a topic of discussion after Christopher Columbus's so-called discovery of America.[30]

The maltreatment of the "other Indians" is clearly documented in the writings of Roman Catholic missionaries such as Francisco de Vitorias, as is the natural law basis for critiques of this ongoing practice.[31] Despite later criticisms of natural law-based arguments for human rights,[32] the natural law approach provides the best basis for an all-embracing system of human rights protection, a system that Grotius later attempted to separate somewhat from its doctrinal origin: "Grotius moved toward a secular characterization of the law of nature, defining it as a 'dictate of right reason' in conformity with the social nature of human beings."[33] Nevertheless, it is only because natural law claims a supranational source for its moral perspective (it is not, therefore, simply humanist)[34] that natural law could and can be claimed a judge of positivist laws. In natural law, a law that violates the moral code is not truly a law at all.[35]

A century after Grotius, Emmerich de Vattel wrote the *Law of Nations*, in which he argued that natural law should be applied to nation-states as it was to individuals.[36] This approach was perhaps foundational to the correct positivist law preference; it can also be viewed as the origin of the application of individual rights and norms to corporate legal entities. Both developments proved to be highly damaging to the individual rights of the natural person. In modern times, the size of humanity's ecological footprint renders these rights particularly vulnerable if the individuals at risk are part of an indigenous population.[37]

In sum, the shift from natural law's protection of all individual basic rights to positivism's subsumption of individuals under the category of nation-states papers over vast differences that exist, for instance, between minority groups and dominant groups, the rich and the poor, colonizers and colonized.

The lack of recognition of these fundamental differences is highly damaging to indigenous peoples, for indigenous people are slowly attempting to regain, singly and collectively, rights they might have retained historically under a different conceptual understanding of the law.

To apply international law regarding indigenous peoples to First Nations and other Aboriginal groups, the first steps are to see whether they fit within existing definitions of indigenous peoples, to discover what binding or suggestive legal instruments exist that are relevant to the protection of the groups' interests, and to determine what soft law instruments may be used to the groups' advantage. In addition to the covenants listed above, the *Earth Charter* should also be included because it strongly supports the ecological integrity of all habitats and natural entities and respects indigenous peoples.[38]

PROTECTION OF INDIGENOUS PEOPLES THROUGH INTERNATIONAL MECHANISMS

The next question is whether any group or body exists to monitor the regulatory instruments for the protection of indigenous peoples. Most legal scholars acknowledge that these protections are not adequate, that there is a protection gap between human rights legislation and the problems faced by indigenous peoples.[39] Some of these problems are the "impacts of development projects on indigenous communities, the implementation of enacted domestic laws to protect indigenous rights, the relation between formal state law and customary indigenous law, indigenous cultural rights, indigenous children, indigenous participation in policy- and decision-making processes, and various forms of discrimination against indigenous individuals."[40]

The UN's Committee on the Elimination of Racial Discrimination has the authority to monitor human rights implementation and has adopted procedures to address all circumstances that could be viewed as early warnings of situations that might escalate.[41] This approach was urged by Aboriginal groups in Australia. The committee often invokes the principle of self-determination (even in dealing with Canada, considering Canada's report in 1992 and the dispute between the Mohawks and the Government of Quebec in which the question of self-determination was raised).[42]

The Inter-American Commission on Human Rights investigated the situation of several Amazonian communities and noted that "the right to life and to physical security and integrity is necessarily related to and in some ways dependent upon one's physical environment."[43] This particular point cannot be overemphasized. In fact, when Cherie Metcalf and James Anaya list two major models of indigenous rights – the cultural integrity model and the self-determination model – I believe they overlook an even more basic model: the biological or ecological integrity model.[44] I believe this model is foundational to all considerations involving Aboriginal peoples, with special emphasis on the seventh generations rule and the legally binding international covenants, including the *Convention on the Rights of the Child*.

THE THIRD MODEL AND INDIGENOUS ENVIRONMENTAL RIGHTS

> The "indigenous" perspective or world view is one of embed-
> dedness and holistic integration and sharing, in which the
> environment is embedded within the identity and the existence
> of humans.
>
> – Kate Kempton, "Bridge over Troubled Waters"

The "right to life and to physical security," protected in *Convention No. 169*, is clearly a description of rights that Henry Shue calls basic: the right to security and to subsistence.[45] These rights precede, both conceptually and chronologically, both civil and political rights and economic, social, and cultural rights. The use of normal functions and the capacity for independent agency both depend on an individual developing in environmental circumstances that permit and foster, rather than hinder, a human being's normal development.[46] The biological integrity of individuals is entirely dependent on the ecological integrity of their habitat.

In the case of indigenous peoples, including First Nations, the requirement for a healthy environment is vital. Large cities and industrial centres *may* be able to mitigate some of the disastrous environmental conditions that affect us, including the effects of climate change, but these conditions may not be available to peoples who live closer to the land and are entirely dependent upon it for their survival. In addition, as was clear in the case of the city of New Orleans and Hurricane Katrina, even in a wealthy country, in a fully developed area, a city cannot count on escaping disaster. Of course, other seaside populations in developing countries and island states face even more disastrous conditions.

The problem, even for landlocked groups, is that, despite the work of several decades of conservation biologists, including Michael Soulé and Reed Noss, the need to ensure that conservation and respect for an area's integrity implies the presence of buffer (or corridor) areas, as well as the designated "core" areas, in order to ensure the security and survival of the targeted flora and fauna intended for protection.[47] Unfortunately, this requirement, although absolutely necessary to the achievement of protection goals, has largely been ignored. Any natural reserve and, of course, any First Nation needs a surrounding buffer of sufficient size to ensure that the populations and species within the protected areas are not affected by any pollutants, toxins, and effluents that may affect the mandated conservation.[48]

Recent work by the European Environmental Agency (EEA) and the World Health Organization details the risk of exposing *all* populations to pollution and climate change, and it indicates that the problem is particularly acute for indigenous peoples in several areas: "Arctic human populations are at risk due to the long-distance transport of bio-accumulative substances, with the Arctic as an important sink and the dependence of indigenous populations on traditional diets exposes them unduly to chemicals accumulated in the food chain. Europe and other developed countries have a clear responsibility for the global body burden of chemicals. This raises issues of equity and global responsibility."[49] Both wildlife and children serve as canaries or sentinels, giving early warnings of the effects of chemicals, especially those that are bioaccumulative, persistent, and toxic. Links between climate change and health are emerging in scientific research as well, and these changes "particularly affect vulnerable groups ... raising issues of equity."[50]

The lacuna in environmental and human rights law was evident in a recent discovery regarding the Aamjiwaang First Nation in Canada's "Chemical Valley" near Sarnia, Ontario.[51] Scott Munro, general manager of the Sarnia-Lambton Environmental Association (financed by Shell Canada, Imperial Oil, and thirteen other large Chemical Valley firms), has asked for further research to be sure of that data, a familiar ploy when facts emerge that may threaten the status quo. But the fact is that there are twice as many girls than boys being born in the community, a finding greeted with alarm by environmental groups. Pollutants such as hormones and endocrine disruptors in general are altering parents' hormonal makeup: "The sexual characteristics of the child are determined during early development and are under the control of estrogen in girls and testosterone in boys. Under normal circumstances, the sex ratio is higher than one, i.e., more boys than girls are born. Several studies have reported a small but significant decrease in the sex ratio of several European countries."[52] It is worth noting that following Italy's Seveso dioxin spill in 1976, the ratio of girls to boys was forty-eight to twenty-six. Because thyroid hormones are essential for normal brain development, especially in the first weeks of pregnancy, much more could also be said about a number of neurodevelopmental disorders related to PCBs, insecticides, herbicides, and phthalates.[53]

The question is, what type of environmental heritage are parents being forced to pass on to their children? Theses effects of pollution cannot be ignored, even if our normal approaches to epidemiology and toxicology do not quite capture them: "We probably have to abandon the classical toxicological dogma of cause/effect relationship at the individual level and extend it to the generational level."[54] Consideration of future generations is one of the pillars of First Nations knowledge and belief. In contrast, to ignore the evidence of the harm perpetrated on First Nations by practices that the Ontario and Canadian governments ought to regulate, alter, or eliminate altogether may not be intentional genocide but could be termed wilful blindness in criminal law or an attack on the human person in international law.

Nor are these harmful effects a recent discovery. Theo Colborn discovered similar effects in the bird, mammal, and marine life in the Great Lakes.[55] It was yet another "canary in the mine" situation that was not heeded at the time. Nor was the study unrelated to human health. According to the European Environment Agency, "One way of understanding how environmental exposures affect health is to study animals in the wild. Despite many differences, many fundamental physiological processes in animals and humans are identical or very similar. An effect in wild animals carries a strong implication that a similar effect may occur in humans in a similar exposure situation."[56] Thus, we can say with some confidence that these effects on First Nations deny them their biological integrity, their natural functions. And much like the elimination of species documented by Colborn and others, especially in the Great Lakes area, these effects indicate the presence of conditions amounting almost to genocide. Ken Saro-Wiwa described the chemical alterations produced by the operations of Royal Dutch Petroleum in Ogoniland, Nigeria, as forms of genocide and omnicide, because the security and subsistence of his people was being systematically eliminated.[57]

In sum, the biological integrity of indigenous peoples, including First Nations, is dependent on the ecological integrity of their living environment, and it is their access to environmental regimes that singles out their specific habitat conditions. Both the cultural integrity and self-determination models to which Anaya and Metcalf appeal are important, but they do not meet the basic conditions needed for individuals and groups to thrive. For all three models, the presence of existing international legal instruments emphasizes the importance of environmental and human rights law.

The Cultural Integrity Model

> The current treaty-based framework of international environmental law is poorly equipped to accommodate non-state players with equivalent-to-state rights within the area of environmental management.
>
> – Cherie Metcalf, "Indigenous Rights and the Environment: Evolving International Law"

Like the third model I propose, the cultural integrity model is supported by the Organization of American States' proposed declaration on indigenous peoples, which explicitly addresses the right to cultural integrity.[58] The same can be said of the self-determination model – that is, both models are firmly based in human rights instruments. For that reason, both models pose problems for state sovereignty.[59] In both cases, the holistic approach to environmental rights, typical of the indigenous worldview, is fundamental.

However, the difference between these two models and the ecological integrity is that the latter addresses the most basic human rights of all – the right to life, health, and normal function – whereas the former assumes the presence of those conditions and proceed to add further rights to protect other possible choices. The self-determination model replicates the *International Covenant on Economic, Social and Cultural Rights,* whereas the cultural integrity model appears to be in line with the *International Covenant on Civil and Political Rights.* In order to benefit from the protection of the activities under either covenant, normal intellectual abilities and physical capabilities are required. The main point is that all three models require the presence of a safe and healthy environment, both for the general habitat and for the land itself. The indigenous peoples traditional lifestyle, which is lived close to the land, renders them particularly vulnerable.

The cultural integrity model emphasizes the value of traditional cultures in and of themselves and for the rest of society. According to Principle 22 of the *Rio Declaration,* traditional cultures and the knowledge they possess must be protected: "Cultural protection for indigenous peoples involves providing environmental guarantees that allow them to maintain the harmonious relationship to the earth that is central to their cultural survival."[60] In other words, indigenous peoples' biological *and* cultural integrity are entirely dependent on protecting the ecological integrity of the areas they occupy. Any consideration of the economic value of these areas and forests is equally dependent on that protection.

Both Article 8(j) of the *Convention on Biological Diversity* and the *Convention to Combat Desertification* incorporate cultural integrity as an indigenous environmental right to be protected.[61] The *Declaration on the Establishment of the Arctic Council* of 1996 ensures that "indigenous groups gained status as permanent participants in an international inter-governmental forum for addressing environmental concerns affecting them and their ancestral lands."[62]

The cultural integrity model has two aspects. The first emphasizes the closeness between the environment and the traditional lifestyle of indigenous peoples, a closeness that in fact defines and delimits their cultural presence as a people. The second focuses on traditional knowledge, especially the value of that knowledge to the global community. The first aspect is akin to the ecological model I proposed earlier and complementary to it, but the second aspect may be problematic because indigenous groups are not valued for themselves as much as for their instrumental value, as holders of specific, commercially valuable knowledge.[63] If traditional knowledge is viewed as intellectual property, it can be concluded, as does Dinah Shelton, that the best way to protect the environmental rights of indigenous peoples is through intellectual property law.[64] I believe that this emphasis is misplaced because the traditional approach of indigenous peoples to the land, for instance, is one of deep kinship and respect, for it and all the creatures it supports and all its processes are not viewed as a commodity.

Several articles of the *Convention on the Rights of the Child* are far more appropriate for the protection of indigenous peoples' cultural integrity. The convention is also an instrument that has been ratified by almost the entire global community (with the exception of the United States and Somalia).[65] Article 30 states: "In those States in which ethnic, religious or linguistic minorities or persons of indigenous origin exist, a child belonging to such a minority, or who is indigenous, shall not be denied the right, in community with other members of his or her group, to enjoy his or her own culture, to profess and practice his or her own religion, or to use his or her own language." Here, the respect for cultural integrity of children is easy to adapt to indigenous teachings, especially the seventh generation rule; that is, the importance of basing all political group decisions on a consideration of the seven years before and after the time of such decision.

If indigenous people are to survive as peoples rather than being assimi-lated into the larger society, *both* their biological integrity and their cultural integrity must be treasured, the latter not as a commodity but as a living tradition of great value necessary to survival.

The Self-Determination Model

Self-determination is a powerful expression of the underlying tensions and contradictions of international legal theory: it perfectly reflects the cyclical oscillation between positivism and natural law, between an emphasis on consent, that is, voluntarism, and an emphasis on binding objective legal principles, between a "statist" and a communitarian vision of world order.

– Antonio Cassese, *Self-Determination of Peoples*

The self-determination model appears to be the most firmly entrenched in international law.[66] Self-determination is a pre-eminent topic in scholarship on United Nation's law; therefore, it is the easiest model to defend. But even this model is not free of difficulties. The very concept of peoples in this context is hard to define. Limiting peoples to postcolonial groups is insufficient, and an understanding of peoples that includes whole populations is unnecessarily inclusive and too state-centred. Any definition based exclusively on ethno-nationalist theory also ignores the existence of overlapping groups and com-munities, all of which benefit from a definition based on human rights.[67] Perhaps the best approach is found in the Great Law of Peace as defined by the Iroquois Confederacy (the Haudenosaunee): "The Great Law of Peace ... describes a great tree with roots extending in the four cardinal directions to all peoples of the earth; all are invited to follow the roots of the tree and join the peaceful co-existence and cooperation under its great long leaves. The Great Law of Peace promotes unity among individuals, families, clans, and nations while upholding the integrity of diverse identities and spheres of autonomy."[68] The right to self-determination therefore does not necessarily mean that any and all groups have rights to independent statehood, although decolonization itself is indeed based on self-determination. Essentially, self-determination requires governing institutions where peoples "may live and develop freely on a continuous basis."[69]

The Early History of Self-Determination

Despite the importance of the concept of self-determination and its consistent presence in international law, there is no "comprehensive legal account of the concept."[70] Nor is the concept's prominence of recent origin, which might explain this lacuna. Lenin declared the importance of self-determination to the freedom of peoples.[71] The concept of internal self-determination, given its origin, was necessarily based on socialism. The concept of self-determination had three aspects: (1) it maintained that the ethnic or national group could freely decide its own destiny; (2) self-determination would be applied after military action, to decide on the appropriate allocation of territories; and (3) self-determination would be the basis of anticolonialism and the liberation of colonized territories.[72] For Lenin, liberation would be accomplished by secession: "In the same way as mankind can arrive at the abolition of classes only through a transition period of the dictatorship of the oppressed classes, it can arrive at the inevitable integration of nations only through a transition period of the complete emancipation of all oppressed nations, i.e., their freedom to secede."[73]

In contrast to Lenin, as Antonio Cassese points out, Woodrow Wilson, the US president, viewed self-determination as free choice and, ultimately, self-government, which would be accomplished through orderly, progressive reform.[74] Lenin, in contrast, called for an immediate halt to colonial rule, thus undermining present power structures by admitting the right of minorities to separate from the state. Nevertheless, aside from political principles, "state sovereignty and territorial integrity remained of paramount importance."[75]

During and after the Second World War, these political principles (e.g., self-determination and self-government) emerged as international legal standards, although, at first, they were applied only to Europe, not to indigenous populations. Even in Europe, however, "self-determination was deemed irrelevant where the people's will was certain to run counter to the victors' geopolitical, economic and strategic interests."[76] This point is worth keeping in mind, as *victors* may be understood today to include "powerful states and corporations." In 1941, Franklin D. Roosevelt and Winston Churchill drafted the *Atlantic Charter* and "proclaimed self-determination as a general standard governing territorial changes, as well as a principle concerning the free choice of rulers in every sovereign State (internal self-determination).[77]

Although internal self-determination is important because it strengthens the ability of indigenous groups to stand up to those who would exploit them and perhaps provides them with a stronger voice in the governance of the host country, it is not sufficient to support indigenous rights. Even the UN's *Charter* fails to define either external or internal self-determination, and despite the wording of Article 1(2) and Article 55(c), the document does not impose hard and fast obligations on member states. Its merit lies primarily in it being the first multilateral treaty to include self-determination. Article 1(2) states that the purpose of the United Nations is to "develop friendly relations among nations, based on respect for the principle of equal rights and self-determination of peoples, and to take the appropriate measures to strengthen universal peace." Article 55(c) states that the UN's goal is to promote, inter alia, "universal respect for and observance of, human rights and fundamental freedoms for all without distinction as to race, sex, language or religion."

After the Second World War, both eastern Europeans and developing countries wanted to interpret Lenin's definition of self-determination in terms of anticolonialism, whereas Western countries were not immediately willing to accept his conception.[78]

DEVELOPING COUNTRIES, SELF-DETERMINATION, AND THE IMPACT OF NEOCOLONIALISM

> For developing countries, self-determination meant three things: (1) the fight against colonialism and racism; (2) the struggle against the domination of any alien oppressor illegally occupying a territory (an idea that was fostered largely due to the insistence of the Arab states after 1967 with the case of Palestine in mind); (3) the struggle against all manifestations of neocolonialism and in particular the exploitation by alien powers of the natural resources of developing countries.
>
> – Antonio Cassese, *Self-Determination of Peoples*

The international covenants on civil and political rights and economic, social, and cultural rights are clear on the topic of the political and economic aspects of self-determination. Article 1, which is common to both covenants, states: "All peoples have the right to self-determination. By virtue of that right they freely determine their political status and freely pursue their economic, social and cultural development ... In no case may a people be derived of its own means of subsistence."[79] These rights appear to be unequivocal, and they stand unless a "public emergency which threatens the life of the nation" and which is proclaimed officially (Article 41) permits a state to disregard them. Yet many cases brought before the courts by indigenous groups are deemed "not to rise to the level of the law of nations." Cassese points out: "The problem lies not in understanding the nature of the right, but in ensuring State compliance."[80]

In contrast, it is clear that the collaboration between states and multinational corporations violates Article 1(2) of the covenants. The presence of "complicity" between these actors when the deprivation of necessary resources results in genocide demonstrates yet another criminal aspect of these cases in international law. At the present time, dispossessed people can, at best, seek compensation, even though many of the harms perpetrated against them are simply incompensable. (See Article 47 of the *International Covenant on Civil and Political Rights* and Article 25 of the *International Covenant on Economic, Social and Cultural Rights*, both of which reiterate "the inherent right of all peoples to enjoy and utilize fully and freely their natural wealth and resources.")

Since 1945 and the proclamation of the *Charter of the United Nations*, self-determination, primarily in its internal form as self-government, has been accepted in law. But self-determination is primarily a goal, with no specific obligation imposed on states to accept it, even in this weakened form.[81] Nevertheless, in 1971 the International Court of Justice gave an advisory opinion on Namibia. The UN had set up Namibia in 1946 as a separate state, "under the direct responsibility of the United Nations," because South Africa had refused to acknowledge it as a separate territory with a separate, freely elected government.[82]

But our main concern is the disenfranchised victims of globalized development, cases in which resources, lands, water, and ways of life are taken or destroyed. The states in which these groups live, in general, respect neither the law of self-determination nor the mandates of international law regarding indigenous rights to resources. Nor is the principle of territorial integrity fully appreciated in its quantitative and qualitative aspects. Paragraph 6 of the UN General Assembly's Resolution 1514 (XV) states: "Any attempt aimed at partial or total disruption of the national unity and territorial integrity of a country is incompatible with the purposes and principles of the Charter of the United Nations."[83]

The problem becomes more complex when the argument for interference with self-determination is extended to encompass the standpoint of economic neocolonialism. Article 1 of the 1977 *Geneva Protocol* to the four 1949 *Geneva Conventions on the Protection of Victims of War* "supports the thesis that the right to self-determination is considered to arise when a State dominates the people in a foreign territory using military means."[84] In the protocol, the phrase *alien occupation*, the meaning of which lends itself less easily to an interpretation linked to economic development, militates against the interpretation I propose. But "it should be added that the United Nations and a minority of States – Mexico, Afghanistan, Iraq and Pakistan – considered economic exploitation of a foreign State (chiefly in the form of neocolonialism) a breach of self-determination."[85]

At best, what is addressed in the protocol is the issue of economic interference in the affairs of a separate state. The concern of this book, however, is the exploitation and domination of specific peoples. How should *indigenous peoples* and *land-based minorities* be defined in this regard? Should local people, especially those based in the African continent, be included in these categories?

DECOLONIZATION, SELF-DETERMINATION, AND NATURAL RESOURCES

> The term "indigenous" refers to those who, while retaining totally or partially their traditional languages, institutions and lifestyles which distinguish them from the dominant society, occupied a particular area before other population groups arrived.
>
> – Manuela Tomei and Lee Swepston, *Indigenous and Tribal Peoples: A Guide to ILO Convention No. 169*

Who are indigenous peoples? And how do we resolve the grave problem of evaluating the well-documented gross violations of human rights under the categories of neocolonization or second conquest in a way that lays bare their insidious and racist aspects, particularly when these violations masquerade as development or trade, which are both well protected under international law?

S.K. Date-Bah considers some of these questions from an African perspective.[86] It is clear that local peoples in the African and Asian continents may lack the protections (weak as they are) that are available to indigenous peoples elsewhere, despite their long history in certain areas. Therefore, present clear-cut definitions might exclude too many people affected by corporate development. The major difficulty, however, remains the need to consider that vulnerable people suffer economic domination, exploitation, and depriva-tion of resources. These deprivations are promoted and protected either as free trade or simply as economic development, and they are imposed with or without outright force, and sometimes even through the force of the law itself.

The argument I want to propose and develop is that the ecofootprint of developed Western countries is the foundation of the second conquest and a direct attack on both the right to survival and the right to self-determination of indigenous and local populations. However, if decolonization is now a major principle of international law, and a *jus cogens* norm, then the elimina-tion of the practices that impose the precarious conditions forced on local and indigenous peoples by corporate actors, with the cooperation of state governments and the support of international trade laws, should represent an obligation *erga omnes* on legal individuals as well as states.

FURTHER CRITIQUES OF THE SELF-DETERMINATION MODEL

Self-determination, however, may well include "free" developments that run contrary to moral development or just institutions, or even ecologically sound ones. Even the collective will of the people may be based on misinformation and falsehoods and may lead to conditions that do not represent the best interests of all, although the decisions leading to these conditions may be the result of free self-determination.

Paul Gilbert discusses self-determination in the context of ethnicity and national identity and suggests "that the proper grounds for a group's claim to statehood are that it is living or could live a decent communal life which would be protected or enhanced by statehood."[87] For Gilbert, then, a volun-tarist model of self-determination is not sufficient to establish a group as entirely separate: it is "not [only] what people desire, but [also] what is desir-able for them, that generates that right." Gilbert does, however, acknowledge that such a group will be in the best position to judge what is its most desir-able choice.[88]

This is, indeed, what James Anaya concludes, and he cites Ian Brownlie on the topic. For people the best option may simply be to live in a political order that enables them to live as a distinct group, with a different character, and "to have their character reflected in the institutions of government under which it lives."[89] A noncontroversial definition proposed by Cherie Metcalf is closer to the environmental requirements of indigenous peoples in general, and First Nations in particular: "This model recognizes a limited form of self-determination in which indigenous peoples have internal sovereignty rights over their own cultural, social, and economic development, including the exclusive ability to control and manage indigenous lands and resources."[90] This definition does not attempt to redefine *peoples*, but its meaning is clear. In addition, this definition is consonant with the UN's "Draft Declaration on the Rights of Indigenous Peoples," which includes one of the strongest statements of the rights of indigenous peoples in the context of international law.[91]

At first sight it may seem as if the emphasis on environmental land issues makes the self-determination model quite similar to the cultural integrity model. But in this model, individual peoples' rights to their lands are based on their rights to control their own social life and development. A troubling corollary of this approach is that there is, at least in principle, no necessary connection between a group's free choices and an ecologically sound policy. However, Article 39 of the draft declaration states: "Indigenous peoples have the right to have access to and prompt decisions through mutually acceptable and fair procedures for the resolution of conflicts and disputes with States, as well as to effective remedies for all infringements of their individual and collective rights. Such a decision shall take into consideration the customs, traditions, rules, and legal system of the indigenous peoples concerned." Thus, at least this article recognizes the essential presence of tradition and customs, although it stops short of making the presence of such traditional choices mandatory for legitimizing an indigenous people's or First Nation's choices.

Perhaps this is the most disturbing aspect of this model. If self-determination is the ultimate value, aside from any other consideration, then in theory (although most likely not in practice) an Aboriginal group could decide to rent its land to a Monsanto affiliate, a chemical company, or any other hazardous industry, as long as it was the general will of the people to do so.

Although all three models include positive aspects for First Nations, the third model, the biological or ecological integrity model, might be the best choice (on its own or in conjunction with either of the two other models) to provide and ensure a solid and sustainable ecological foundation.

The Model Community and the Public Good

An Aboriginal First Nation may have a collective interest in hunting and fishing in its ancestry homeland. Leroy, an individual member, may have a significant individual interest in his individual legally recognized hunting and fishing rights, insofar as they provide him a source of subsistence, which is obviously important to him as an individual. But, following the reasoning here, we can say that his individual interests, while not wholly derivative from, are nonetheless secondary to the primary collective interest.

> – Dwight Newman, "Collective Interests and
> Collective Rights"

Collectivities have a primary interest in the type of communal right discussed by Newman because it is nonexclusionary in character. When the ecosystem has been protected, the whole indigenous community enjoys the results without exception. The individual interests of members in that community are secondary, but they exist and are not denied by this emphasis on the collective rights or interests of the community.

The collectivity of humankind likewise has a primary interest in the ecological integrity of any area on Earth. Hence, our basic rights as individuals are present and existent but secondary to those of the collectivity. The collectivity also remains the primary source of the obligation to ensure the protection of these interests and rights. This is a nonderogable obligation, one the collectivity must meet as a whole, although there may well be different degrees of responsibility to ensure that the obligation is met.

An indigenous community such as the one discussed by Newman differs radically from, say, Roger Brownsword's moral community (see Chapter 1) because of its commitment to interpersonal morality – that is, all of the community's lifestyle choices and activities are neither limited nor prescribed by its obligations and commitment to its dealings with the earth, its habitat.[92] It may well be a moral community whose members are committed to dealing morally with one another and to respecting humanity. However, a community of the highest moral character that does not share the indigenous community's commitment to the earth and its obligation to ensure its protection through the generations would not fit the definition of a model community in our sense.

Does such a community actually exist today? Is there more than one? Without any claim to having performed exhaustive social research worldwide, I propose, as a test, that every time an indigenous or local community says a clear no to development, they demonstrate their status as a model community. Even if they believe a small part of the developer's promises of advancement, these communities prove their existence as model communities, not only by what they are but also, especially, by their unfailing opposition to what they do not want to be. Most of the cases that appear before US courts under the *Alien Torts Claims Act*, for instance, fall under this rubric.[93] We can therefore concur with Newman's conclusion "that certain individual interests that ground duties are meaningful interests and can be fulfilled only on the precondition that certain collective interests are also rights. We can put this statement in simplified terms: if we accept certain individual rights we presuppose certain collective rights."[94]

These collective rights and obligations do not interfere with various possible moral communities – that is, communities committed to a high level of interpersonal morality as individual members interact with one another or even make collective plans. But the collectivity, as it is envisaged here, is indeed presupposed by any such community; in fact the collective obligations based on interests and rights that precede any and all communities, both temporally and conceptually, are presupposed. Finally, as Newman states: "An individual interest *necessarily depends* on a collective interest if and only if the individual interest either does not meaningfully exist, or cannot meaningfully be fulfilled in the absence of a collective interest being fulfilled."[95]

The individual right to life and normal development, which is basic to the right of freedom of choice and all civil and political rights, depends absolutely on the collective right to a safe environment. Members of indigenous communities who live a traditional, even "undeveloped," lifestyle, represent the only existing model for these collective interests, rights, and corresponding obligations, regardless of any other interests or life plans they may have. For the most part, the model these traditional indigenous groups provide is neither admired nor followed by the majority of people, whose lifestyle not only contrasts with theirs but also is such that its ecofootprint gravely affects their (and our) collective rights.

This argument is not dictated by a romantic view of "noble savages." Considerations of ecological integrity, which supports the biological integrity of human beings, demand that safe environmental conditions be viewed as basic for the collective rights of all. They represent the common good, and as such, they ought not to be treated as individual rights or limited to the rights of those who can afford to be insulated against an unsafe habitat. Denise Réaume asks, "Can there be rights to public goods?" but she also acknowledges that the answer "cannot ignore the nature of the good at issue."[96]

My argument is that the physical conditions of a community's habitat are necessary for the inhabitants' survival and health. Protected areas of ecological integrity and buffer zones are necessary to ensure the health and survival of local flora and fauna upon which these communities depend. In contrast, the overconsumption prevalent in affluent countries is unsustainable and is engendering hazardous global conditions such as climate change and its resulting droughts, glacial melts, sea rises, and other extreme weather patterns. Therefore, local communities and indigenous peoples who choose to live a traditional lifestyle, respectful of their environment and mindful of the seventh generation rule, represent model communities, worthy of respect and emulation, within limits. At least, they point to the direction the world's people must follow in order to reduce or mitigate the ongoing harms. No doubt, First Nations and others are free to deal with tar sand developers, but given the developmental and neurotoxic harms that have been documented, such projects do not fit the model proposed here.

A recent article by David Tabachnick titled "Writing on Water" explains why common property institutions support an "environmentally, democratically just society," whereas societies that depend entirely on individual rights do not.[97] He discusses the example of rural Guinea, where people "preserve the role of common property as a social welfare system and democratic check on elites."[98] He adds that Guinea is by no means the only African country where such an approach is chosen, as both Sierra Leone and Nigeria follow similar systems. Families and future descendants are viewed as the appropriate recipients of land in order that it can be held and protected in perpetuity.[99] In contrast, in England after 1688, "landed gentry controlled the state and did not permit most people to vote. The gentry were able to force the enclosure of common property land the state awarded exclusively as individual land titles to selected members of what had been common property communities, taking away common property rights without compensation and without the possibility of legal appeal for the rest of the community."[100]

In other words, the appeal to the traditional lifestyles of First Nations can be supported by other nations' common property systems. As in England, the loss of a community's traditional approach to property represented a significant loss of rights for those who were deprived not only of property but also of the means to implement their cultural beliefs and the time-honoured ways of participating in their nation's governance.

The pivotal importance of having protected areas of ecological integrity adds a third dimension – on top of respect for land and a communitarian approach to governance – to the special position proposed for Native Americans, First Nations in Canada, and other traditional communities in all continents. It was this dimension that first directed me to researching indigenous peoples.[101] My work on ecological integrity began in 1992 after I read the *Clean Water Act* (US, 1972) and the *Great Lakes Water Quality Agreement* (1978, rat. 1988). Both cited integrity but left it undefined. Funding by the Social Sciences and Humanities Research Council of Canada (SSHRC) from 1992 to 1999 and by NATO in 1999-2000 enabled a small group of scholars to convene yearly and invite major scientists and scholars from other disciplines to collaborate on our attempts to understand the meaning and the role of integrity. That initial small group started growing steadily, as most participants wanted to remain with the group after their first experience as presenters.

The Global Ecological Integrity Group's research started with an analysis of integrity from the standpoint of biologists, ecologists, and earth scientists. Later, William Rees joined and stayed, and the group incorporated the importance of ecofootprint analysis into its work. After 1998, when epidemiologists and medical doctors joined the group, the biological integrity of single individuals was also studied. This aspect of our work culminated in a meeting at the offices of the World Health Organization in Rome, Italy, in December of that year, and the publications of our findings, together with those of others from the WHO, who published in 1999.[102]

In 2000, legal and political scholars joined the group, especially those who had worked in the specialist groups of the International Union for the Conservation of Nature and the Earth Charter. By this time, the group numbered about 250 people (our full membership list now has about 400 names), and several people in the group published various volumes individually and as a group.[103]

Thus, the significance of the traditional lifestyle of various land-based communities is supported through three separate but converging aspects of their chosen existence and form of governance: conservation, health, and human rights. For instance, Joseph Raz argues that one "has a right only if one's well-being or interest is a sufficient reason for holding some other person(s) to be under a duty."[104] An example of a public good could be that of a cultured society.[105] Réaume recognizes that it may be hard to impose onerous duties on others, in order for the collectivity to have a cultured society. However, her intuition about the *nature* of the good being the key seems right, as does the position of Raz regarding the acceptance of collective duties only on the basis of serious interests.

I suggest that the duties entailed by my position support the most basic of all public goods. A cultured society is a worthwhile goal, but it is an optional one, whereas the conditions required for life, health, and normal development are neither optional nor desirable for some, while others may have other priorities. Whatever other interests people may have, the desire to survive and to be able to function as normal human beings, with all the expected character and mental abilities, comes first and is universally desirable.

Not only are traditional communities part of the collectivity, they also serve as a model of a group whose values are universally valid. In addition to their role as models, at least in principle, their rights are protected in law, for they have rights many others do not possess, because of their sui generis characteristics. The reality, however, is that the law offers less protection than we may expect, because traditional communities, because of their special vulnerability, are often the first harmed by globalization and the activities of industries and other commercial operations. Hence, the first question is, what is the reality encountered by traditional indigenous societies? Second, if indigenous groups indeed have a particular protection in law, why is humanity in general's dependence on the environment not similarly recognized?

An Example of Ongoing Harms: Development and Indigenous Peoples in South America

> Indigenising development also implies having ethno-sustainability as a principle, means and goal of development. A holistic view of the complex Indigenous reality is thus required. This is needed in order to go beyond the hegemonic logic that puts the economic dimension of life as an overwhelming determinant of all others.
>
> – Gersen Boniwa, "To Dominate the System and Not Be Dominated by It"

Is it possible to indigenize development? Can development and traditional indigenous values be reconciled? The discussion that follows, about indigenous peoples in Brazil, Colombia, and Ecuador, is, as Gersen Boniwa suggests, based on two premises: (1) despite the problems connected with it, it is futile to fight against modern development, and (2) there may be ways of successfully indigenizing development so that its apparent inherent contrast with indigenous traditions, beliefs, and lifestyles can be reconciled. Both premises can, however, be questioned. Solid scientific research increasingly demonstrates that we need to humanize industrial development so that its activities, processes, and products are not in direct conflict with human rights to life, health, and normal development.[106] Lawrence Gostin writes, "A legislative choice to prefer collective health and well-being over individual interests deserves respect and insulation from aggressive judicial scrutiny. This is broadly the judicial approach to public health regulation that affects personal autonomy."[107]

The personal autonomy that must be restrained is far less that of natural persons than that of legal persons, except in cases involving personal sexual choices or the nondisclosure of HIV status, for instance.[108] It is regrettable, however, that while the criminal law remains alert and responsive to new scientific discoveries on the one hand and to negligent criminal behaviour on the other, neither environmental nor trade law is prepared to consider criminal negligence and wilful blindness as it evolves apace with modern science, especially on the part of corporate actors.[109]

If law is essential for creating the conditions for people to lead healthier and safer lives," as Gostin argues, then its main efforts ought to be directed precisely to the restraints necessary to protect humanity in general and the most vulnerable in particular from the results of industrial activities in a post-cautionary world.[110] Only when this goal has been achieved will we be able to assess whether some indigenous communities may be capable of maintaining their culture and traditions while retaining their health and safety and accepting some humanized, or perhaps even indigenized, form of development.

At this time, I find it problematic to simply accept the futility of fighting development. Perhaps Gersen Boniwa needs to consider two aspects of on-going development as the most problematic aspects of globalization itself. The first is that both energy and resources – that is, the material foundations of industrial development – are disappearing at a steadily increasing pace, as is demonstrated in ecological footprint analysis.[111] The second is that the harms engendered by this situation are becoming well known even to the general public. Their awareness includes climate change and the economic collapse that has joined the ongoing ecological collapse, so that almost all nations and people feel the effects of both.

As far as the second premise is concerned, the model community proposed by me is one that says no to development. Although some communities may want to attempt to participate in some modified or indigenized forms of development, not all would. In fact, their attitude to changes of lifestyle might contribute toward the isolation of different indigenous groups, in the effort to recognize those who might fit our understanding of a "model community" (without, however, demeaning those who do not). The current realities of the interface between development and indigenous lifestyle, however, are such that it is hard, at this time, to hold much hope for any possible reconciliation, no matter how well-intentioned the project may appear to be. The ongoing, legally sanctioned health disaster affecting indigenous people in Colombia and Ecuador demonstrates the difficulties involved in any such project.

PLAN COLOMBIA AND THE INDIGENOUS PEOPLES OF THE COLOMBIA-ECUADOR BORDER REGION

> Relying partly on Vitoria's naturalist theory of international law, Brazil recognized the right to primordial occupation of land. While, under the pre-1988 Constitution, lands occupied by "forest dwelling aborigines" were part of the "patrimony of the Union," i.e., property of the federal government, those lands were inalienable, and it was prescribed that the Indians "shall have permanent possession of them, and their right to exclusive usufruct of the natural resources and of the useful things therein existing [was] recognized."
>
> > – Siegfrid Wiessner, "Rights and Status of Indigenous Peoples"[112]

Although the passage above refers to Brazil rather than Colombia or Ecuador, the status of indigenous peoples in the latter, in relation to the governments of their respective countries, is similar, although Colombia has the additional problem of what Siegfried Wiessner terms the "fog war of narcoterrorism."[113] Colombia's Constitution has a new "unit of protection for human rights (*accion de tutela*)." In addition, Colombia recognizes the collective property rights of indigenous peoples, offers official protection for Native languages and dialects, guarantees indigenous peoples a share in oil and mining royalties, and shows respect for indigenous peoples' cultural identity through the national education system.[114] Although indigenous peoples enjoy a protected position within the country, the US and the Colombian governments established a contract to combat the illegal drug trade in the area. "The agreement, labeled Plan Colombia, involved the eradication of illegal crops in Colombia, using the aerial herbicide Roundup, which was produced by the American chemical company Monsanto."[115]

Is this plan an effect of development? Perhaps not in principle, but neo-colonialism – the economic or political power of a stronger and richer state over a poorer and weaker one – is indeed a major aspect of globalized development. The problem is that glyphosate, the major component of Roundup, cannot be directed only to the coca plants, for it is sprayed aerially. On 24 January 2002, the UN Commission on Human Rights stated that "reports indicate that the mixture likely contains herbicide concentrations that are more than five times greater then levels [permitted] for aerial application."[116] Because the airplanes fly over the border region between Colombia and Ecuador, the indigenous population of Ecuador is constantly at risk, far more so than the coca growers of Colombia. In addition, the indigenous peoples of this impoverished region have little or no access to health care or other social services.[117]

The position of the US agencies is that any possible negative results caused by their activities "would be more than compensated by their extensive financial contributions, in the name of social and economic development."[118] Can these activities be considered in any way as forms of advancement or as positive development for the affected countries? The health and the very physical survival of the indigenous communities in the border area and Ecuador are gravely at risk, as are the basic necessities of their survival: crops and water.[119] The violations of human rights are obvious, and the UN's high commissioner for refugees recognizes the reality of the situation: "Ecuador is arguably Colombia's most vulnerable neighbour and has suffered profound effects from both Colombia's internal conflict and Plan Colombia. Problems on the border include drug-related violence, increased rates of crime, kidnappings, the forced migration of Ecuadorians from their homes, effects on human health and the environment from the aerial spraying of coca that drifts across the border, and food insecurity."[120] It is therefore, indigenous peoples who have been gravely affected, not drug lords, and even the Plan Colombia has not achieved its goals, other than to promote, and therefore enrich, Monsanto (a US-based multinational corporation), at the expense of the health, safety, and cultural integrity of affected and displaced persons in local indigenous communities. These activities and their results are in direct conflict with the mandates of Article 7 of the UN's *Declaration on the Rights of Indigenous Peoples*, which assures indigenous peoples "life, physical and mental integrity, liberty and security of person."[121] In addition, the survival of traditional culture should be equally protected, for all activities that may affect indigenous lands or resources are in violation of indigenous rights.[122]

This case is neither unusual nor the first attack on indigenous rights and survival in the area: oil companies have also carried out "development" in the region for some time, with grave effects on the health of local populations, especially in Ecuador and the Amazon region.[123]

Despite the efforts of the US government to maintain secrecy, the substance sprayed was identified as glyphosate herbicide, manufactured by Monsanto under the brand name Roundup, although it was later established that the herbicide was, in fact, Roundup SL, "considerably more toxic than Roundup Ultra."[124] The health effects have been known for some time: "Aerial spraying has a significant negative effect on the lives of large numbers of people, particularly the rural poor in Colombia. There is strong evidence linking spraying with serious human health effects; large-scale destruction of food crops; and severe environmental impacts in sensitive tropical ecosystems. There is also evidence of links between fumigation and loss of agricultural resources, including fish kills, and sickness and the death of livestock."[125] The Cofán people of the Putumayo Province complained to their health department of "dizziness, diarrhea, vomiting, itchy skin, red eyes and headaches, and similar reactions were reported in Ecuador near the Colombia border, in the Sucumbio Province, as well as in Mataje, Esmeraldas.[126]

In September 2001, the Ecuadorian Indians who lived near the Colombian border filed a class action suit against DynCorp, the company in charge of the spraying in Colombia.[127] The physical and monetary damages were evident, as was, and is, the loss of cultural integrity and identity of these peoples, many of whom had to abandon their homes. Aside from the question of whether this sort of globalized industrial activity can be stopped, or at least humanized (that is, modified to respect human rights), these events raise a number of other questions related to human collective rights.

HUMANIZED OR INDIGENIZED DEVELOPMENT? LACUNAE IN LAW

> One can paradoxically have a democratic state grudgingly concede on substance rather than principles and an undemocratic state pro-actively concede on principles rather than actual protection.
>
> – Gaetano Pentassuglia, "Evolving Protection of
>   Minority Groups"

Having considered the public health disasters, the next question is, what does international law have to say about transnational activities? According to Gaetano Pentassuglia, there have been three movements in the legal history of minority protection. The first occurred after the disintegration of three multinational empires: Austria-Hungary, Prussia, and the Ottoman Empire. The second occurred after the Second World War, when international human rights were used as a substitute for minority rights.[128] From the point of view of my argument, this approach was a wrong turn, one from which we have not yet recovered, despite the increasing number of instruments intended for the protection of minorities, many of which remain within the ambit of individual rights but some of which are indeed concerned with people. Pentassuglia puts it well: "The human rights approach of the time was meant to remove 'ethnic particularism' from the code of rights available to everyone."[129]

The most important aspect of the conflict between individual and collective rights can be found here: human rights without provision for specific communities is what informs, for instance, operations such as the Plan Colombia spraying of Monsanto's Roundup. No doubt, just as the US State Department's response to the indigenous claimants indicated, the small print describing the conditions of use for the product were quite detailed and worthy of study:

1. The scientific review article cited by the State Department as justification for the spray campaigns assesses the hazards from "present and expected conditions of use" of Glyphosate herbicides. However, the term "present and expected conditions of use" of glyphosate implies adherence to the manufacturer's recommendations. For example, the Manufacturer's label for Roundup Ultra warns against applying the herbicide "in a way that will contact workers or other persons, either directly or through drift." The label also calls for the removal of livestock before spraying and waiting periods of 2 to 8 weeks before harvesting crops or using sprayed areas for grazing. The label warns against contact of the "herbicide with foliage, green stems, exposed non-woody roots or fruit of crops ... desirable plants and trees, because severe injury or destruction may result." These conditions are not met in Colombia, where airplanes apply herbicides over acres at a time with no prior warning to land owners.

In the U.S., such a failure to follow the label instructions would be
a violation of Federal law.[130]

Even if we consider the use of Roundup permissible in the general sense, the
conditions of its use make it unacceptable. It is worth noting that, after a
recent case in the Canadian Province of Quebec, where a small town eliminated the use of pesticides for health and environmental reasons, even the
Province of Ontario has eliminated the use of pesticides or herbicides for
cosmetic use.[131]

But the mode of application in Colombia offers no protection to vulnerable people. The specific conditions and lifestyle of the affected populations
eliminate any hope that the required safeguards may be in place. In fact, it
appears that the domestic legal structure, as well as the social and health
services infrastructures, is, in practice, unable to deal with the actual problems
created by the spraying operations, despite constitutional guarantees.
Therefore, this is just one obvious practical aspect of the need for specific
minority-community rights, in which the actual "face" of the affected group
would be understood and respected.

According to Pentassuglia, the third movement was "defined precisely
by minority-related standard setting as a way of integrating minority provisions into the international framework of human rights beyond cases of
gross abuse."[132] A number of international instruments have tried to do
justice to indigenous communities and other local minorities, culminating
with the Declaration on the Rights of Indigenous Peoples, passed by the UN
General Assembly in 2007, despite the opposition of countries such as the
United States, Canada, Australia, and New Zealand and the abstention of
eleven others.[133] We are clearly living in an era after the third movement. The
UN's declaration and the 2005 Plan of Action define all possible future
instruments.[134]

The third movement is the basic ground of a fourth movement envisioned
by Pentassuglia, one that has the potential to ensure that not only international law but also domestic instruments help concentrate attention on
and define the full extent of protection needed for minorities and indigenous
communities. If any movement is to succeed in ensuring protection for traditional and indigenous communities, the connection between the ecological
conditions of the territories they occupy and their health and survival must
be explicitly acknowledged and codified in law.

In fact, many national constitutions today recognize the importance of
ecology and environmental protection, at least in principle. However, there

is no corresponding movement to connect the ecological integrity of the habitat to the biological integrity of the individual (human) organisms who live in it, let alone an effort to devote special attention to the specific vulnerability of particular communities.

Constitutional Protection of the Environment in Colombia and Ecuador: A Brief Overview

> It is the duty of the State to protect the diversity and integrity of the environment to conserve areas of special ecological importance, and to foster the education for the achievement.
>
> – *Constitution of Colombia*, 1991

The clear commitment to nature and to indigenous rights expressed in Colombia's Constitution is proceeded by several related statements, all of which appear to be in direct conflict with what is happening on the ground in that country:

- Every individual has the right to a healthy environment.
- The laws must guarantee the Community's participation in the decisions that may affect the environment.
- The state must also cooperate with other nations in the protection of the ecosystems in border areas.

If these are constitutional mandates, it is hard to see how the government of Colombia could even enter into the Plan Colombia with the United States, let alone permit the human rights violations that ensued.

It is even harder to see how Ecuador's new Constitution, a unique and inspirational document, could allow the country to tolerate the toxic operations taking place at its borders. The articles approved by Ecuador's Constitutional Assembly on 7 July 2008 state the following:

Rights for Nature

Art. 1. Nature or Pachamama, where life is reproduced and exists, has the right to exist, persist, maintain and regenerate its vital cycles, structure, functions and its processes in evolution. Every person, people, community or nationality will be able to demand the recognition of rights for nature before the public organisms. The application and interpretation of these rights will follow the related principles established in the Constitution.

Art. 2. Nature has the right to an integral restoration. This integral restoration is independent of the obligation on natural and juridical persons to the State to identify the people and the collectives that depend on the natural systems. In the cases of severe or permanent environmental impact, including the ones caused by the exploitation of non-renewable natural resources, the State will establish the most efficient mechanisms for the restoration, and will adopt the adequate measures to eliminate or mitigate the harmful environmental consequences.

Art. 3. The State will motivate natural and juridical persons as well as collectives to protect nature; it will promote respect towards all elements that form an ecosystem.

Art. 4. The State will apply precaution and restriction on measures in all the activities that can lead to the extinction of species, the destruction of ecosystems or the permanent alteration of the natural cycles. The introduction of organisms and organic and inorganic material that can alter in a definitive way the genetic patrimony is prohibited.

Art. 5. The persons, people, communities and nationalities will have the right to benefit from the environment and from natural wealth that will allow well-being. The environmental services cannot be appropriated: their production, provision, use and exploitation will be regulated by the State.

Articles 4 and 5 appear to specifically address the problems encountered by local or traditional inhabitants.

It appears that even constitutionally entrenched protections for the environment and the peoples who depend upon in are insufficient within a context of corporate and neoliberal state power. An international instrument, if it is to be effective in a national setting, has to be explicitly included in the domestic constitution or charter of the nation, but the converse does not hold. The articles cited from the new Constitution of Ecuador should be inserted and explicitly adopted in the international instruments mentioned thus far. Only then can these provisions be appealed to in international courts, to help curb and redress the sort of abuses we have cited and other similar, but common, situations.

Yet it must be acknowledged that even the Constitution of Ecuador does not explicitly link environmental degradation and disintegrity to human rights. For instance, people and communities have the right to benefit from and to achieve natural wealth rather than the right to the protection of their life and health. Similarly, even the European Court of Human Rights, the only forum to link the environment to human rights, makes use of Article 8 of the European Charter, which protects the "right to one's home and family life," instead of addressing directly the right to life, dignity, and health.[135] The few cases that the court decided in favour of the plaintiffs were individual human rights cases and, for the most part, did not involve minorities or indigenous peoples. In fact, in the well-known case of Sandra Lovelace, the decision came down in favour of individual rights versus group rights, although it is debatable whether the decision reached was indeed the correct one.

The Sandra Lovelace Case and the UN's Human Rights Committee: Individual Rights versus Community Rights

> Article 27 [of the *International Covenant on Civil and Political Rights*] articulates "rights of persons belonging to" cultural groups, as opposed to specifying rights held by the groups themselves. It is apparent, however, that in its practical application, article 27 protects group as well as individual interests in cultural integrity.
>
> – James Anaya, *Indigenous Peoples in International Law*

The best-known case in which Article 27 has been applied in a way that extends cultural integrity to a group is *Ominayak and the Lubicon Lake Band v. Canada*, in which "economic and Social activities of a group (that is, of the Lubicon Cree FN), were found to be in conflict with the Province of Alberta, as it granted oil and gas exploration leases within the aboriginal territory of the Cree, to several corporations. The U.N. Human Rights Committee, General Comment No. 23 (50) acknowledges the importance of the integrity of their lands to the cultural integrity of Indigenous Peoples":[136]

Culture manifests itself in many forms, including a particular way of life associated with the use of land resources, especially in the case of Indigenous peoples. That right might include such traditional activities as fishing or hunting and the right to live in reserves protected by law. The enjoyment of those rights may require positive legal measures of protection and measures to ensure the effective participation of members of minority communities in decisions which affect them.[137]

If, according to Article 27, indigenous persons have the right to express their culture "in community with other members of their group" – especially because culture is not the result of the activities, beliefs, and practices of a single individual but is communitarian in its own nature – then it seems clear that both the primacy of community rights and the inescapable connection between ecological and cultural integrity are firmly established.

In *Lovelace v. Canada*, however, individual rights were taken to be primary.[138] Sandra Lovelace was a Status Indian of the Tobique First Nation who married a non-Indian. After her divorce, she wanted to return to her community. Section 12(1)(b) of the *Indian Act*, however, did not permit the "return" of women in her situation, only of men. The right of return was originally denied to Lovelace by the First Nations community, for the return entails the provision of housing and other community benefits. At any rate, the UN's Human Rights Committee decided in favour of the individual in this case because it recognized that her right to practise her language and culture existed only in the First Nation of her origin, as no "such community exists" anywhere else.[139]

The conflict is clear. Did Lovelace have an individual right to practise and live her culture, or did the Tobique community have a communal right to maintain the common property of the First Nation and available housing exclusively for members of that community? It is unclear whether Lovelace had any mixed-blood children who might have inherited and, in fact, whether considerations of that sort might have influenced the rule in the *Indian Act*. In the latter case, the group's position would be better designed to protect and support the cultural integrity of the group and, ultimately, even the right of individual members to continue to enjoy their own culture, in the only place where it could be found.

The main point, however, is that the cultural integrity of indigenous communities rests on specific territory because traditional practices can continue only so long as the ecological integrity of the area is protected. Therefore, it is by supporting the primacy of the rights of these communities that we learn and appreciate which aspects of the common good are equally applicable to the collectivity of humankind. In other words, the protection of the ecological integrity of all regions is basic but, for nonindigenous communities, a specific location in which such protected and safe natural conditions can be enjoyed is not necessary for either their identity or their cultural practices.

Other cases that pit individual rights against community rights include cases within indigenous communities, including cases in which individual legal persons want to initiate or continue activities to which these communities object.

COLLECTIVES AND COMMUNITIES: *AWAS TINGNI V. NICARAGUA*

In *Awas Tingni v. Nicaragua*, the Inter-American Court of Human Rights held that the state of Nicaragua, by allowing a foreign company the right to log on the Awas Tingni's land, had violated the rights of the community. The Dominican-owned company, Maderas y Derivados de Nicaragua, SA (MADENSA) had been granted about forty-three thousand hectares of land for their logging operation in 1993. Pressure from the World Wildlife Fund, however, convinced the Nicaraguan government to ask MADENSA to suspend operations until environmental regulations could be put in place.[140]

Although lawyers from the Iowa Project (Indian Law Resource Center), at the request of the Awas Tingni, asked that all concessions be revoked as unconstitutional according to Nicaraguan law, the government attempted "to have the constitutional defence 'cured' by securing a *post hoc* ratification of the concession by the Regional Council."[141] Eventually, and through another legal action, the concession was cancelled. Despite this important success, the question of the Awas Tingni's land tenure was not addressed, let alone resolved. The community and its legal representatives presented the case to the Inter-American Court of Human Rights, and the case was decided on 31 August 2001.[142]

There were two main problems with granting title, according to the government of Nicaragua. The first was that the listed members of the community numbered no more than three hundred or four hundred, and the more recent census only listed one thousand members, too few to require a deed to sixteen thousand hectares, which was requested by the legal representatives, James Anaya and Andres Mejia Acosta, in 1993: "The State, in turn, has argued that the extent of the territory claimed by the Mayagna [Suma] is excessive, bearing in mind the number of members of the Community determined by the official census, and that the area claimed by the Community is not in proportion to the area it effectively occupies."[143]

The second problem was the government's claim that the Awas Tingni's main village had only been established in 1940. This claim contradicted the community's claim to traditional historical occupation, and other indigenous groups had similar land claims in the general area.[144] Witnesses before the Inter-American Court stressed that land, in all its variety, was vital for "their cultural, religious and family development" and that territory was not only necessary for their hunting and fishing activities included several sacred hills and places where fruit trees grow. People were accustomed to walking through the areas in silence, "as a sign of respect for their dead ancestors, and the great Asangpas Muijeni, the spirit of the mountain, who lives under the hills."[145] According to the testimony of Rodolfo Stavenhagen, indigenous peoples are those social and human groups who can be identified culturally and who have maintained a historical continuity with their ancestors, from the time before the arrival of the first Europeans.[146] Stavenhagen added that historical continuity could be established not only through self-identification but also through the use of a pre-Hispanic language.[147]

Under Article 25 of Nicaragua's Constitution (1995), indigenous peoples have the right to juridical protection; in other words, to prevent the group's access to the judiciary is an act of discrimination.[148] In fact, Article 25 declares that states are obliged to offer all legal remedies against "acts that violate their fundamental rights," and Article 5 reaffirms the existence and rights of indigenous peoples. Article 5 guarantees political pluralism and respect for the sovereignty of all nations and states: "[Nicaragua] is opposed to any form of discrimination, and it is anticolonial, anti-imperialist, anti-racist and rejects all subordination of one state to another State." Article 89 adds that "the communities of the Atlantic Coast have the right to maintain and develop their cultural identity within national unity, to their own forms of social organization, and to manage their local affairs according to their traditions."[149]

Nicaragua was responsible for violating the Awas Tingni's relationship with its lands and natural resources under a combination of breached articles of the *American Convention on Human Rights:* Article 4 (the right to life), Article 11 (the right to privacy), Article 12 (freedom of conscience and religion), Article 16 (freedom of association), Article 17 (rights of the family), Article 22 (freedom of movement and residence), and Article 23 (the right to participate in the government).[150]

In this case, then, the doctrine of *uti possidetis* (as you possess) is appropriate because the Awas Tingni's traditional presence in the area strengthened their interdependence with *those* lands and no others. In 1998, the government of Nicaragua drafted a bill titled "Organic Law Regulating the Communal Property System of the Indigenous Communities of the Atlantic Coast and the Bosawas" to formally provide legal instruments "to regulate and provide borders for indigenous lands." It was approved as Law No. 445 in December 2002.[151]

Aside from granting monetary compensation to the community, the court unanimously decided that Nicaragua should create "effective mechanisms for the delineation, demarcation and titling of property of indigenous communities," pursuant to Article 2 of the *American Convention on Human Rights*.[152] The court also decided unanimously that the state "must abstain from any acts that might lead the agents of the state itself, or third parties acting with its acquiescence or its tolerance, to affect the existence, value, use or enjoyment of the property, located in the geographical area where the members of the Mayagna (Sumo) Awas Tingni Community live and carry out their activities."[153] Therefore, in addition to being a groundbreaking judgment that upholds the collective land rights of an indigenous group, this judgment breaks new ground by ensuring that a state cannot acquiesce to or tolerate activities that may affect "the existence, value, use or enjoyment" of the newly allocated lands. Although this particular point in the court's decision refers explicitly to the period *before* the "delimitation, demarcation and titling of the corresponding lands" could be carried out, the *principle* supporting the argument remains the same, once the scientific evidence is understood. If it is wrong to affect the existence, value, and use of the lands through activities that may affect their natural functions and services, then industrial or extractive activities just outside the lands' established borders should also be forbidden, for the same reason.

The court's decision was based neither on the tenets of conservation biology nor on those of public health. But the principle upon which it based its decision may well be adapted to reflect both. Understandings of the protection of indigenous territories can and should incorporate the science developed since the 1970s, demonstrating beyond a doubt the effects of industrial/extractive activities beyond the borders of a specific territory, unless the territory is protected by a properly sized corridor or buffer zone. In this case, Nicaragua had not fulfilled its international obligations, "because of the particular acts and omissions of legislative, executive, and judicial agencies that, in the aggregate, resulted in failure to protect indigenous land rights."[154]

The Inter-American Court of Human Rights found that Nicaragua had "an inadequate legislative and administrative framework to address land titling procedures" and had inappropriately allowed logging on traditional lands, without indigenous consent.[155]

INDIVIDUAL CHOICE VERSUS CULTURAL INTEGRITY

The 1988 case *Ivan Kitok v. Sweden*, heard by the UN's Human Rights Committee, stressed indigenous peoples' right to cultural integrity. However, the case did not involve a corporate enterprise or foreign individuals as many other cases involving indigenous rights do.[156] The case demonstrates the interdependence between cultural and ecological integrity, although the former is its main focus.

Ivan Kitok, a Swedish citizen of Sámi ethnic origin (he was half-Sámi), claimed it was his right to participate in the traditional cultural activities of his people. He claimed that he belonged to a Sámi family that had practised reindeer breeding for a hundred years. "On this basis the author claims that he has inherited the 'civil right' to reindeer breeding from his forefathers as well as the rights to land and water in Skatium Sami Village."[157] Kitok referred to the fact that, in order to protect the reindeer-breeding programs, both the Lapp Swedish Crown and the Lapp bailiffs had decided that any Sámi who engaged in any other profession for a period of three years would lose his status. His name would be removed from the rolls and would not be re-entered unless by special permission.[158]

This is not, therefore, a case of an indigenous group against a state (except for the fact that the rules are promulgated by the Swedish state) or a trans-national corporation. The conflict is between a Sámi individual and the Sámi group – that is, it is a conflict between individual and group rights. *Lovelace v. Canada* dealt with a similar dynamic, but in the *Kitok* case the very real possibility of exceeding the carrying capacity of Sámi lands put an entirely different spin on it. Pasture areas for reindeer husbandry are limited; therefore, it is simply not possible to let all Sámi exercise reindeer husbandry without jeopardizing this objective and running the risk of endangering the existence of reindeer husbandry.[159]

Of the estimated five thousand Sámi who live on the Sámi land at issue, only two thousand are actually Sámi members. The others are assimilated, which conflicts with Article 27 of the *International Covenant on Civil and Political Rights*. Of the total Sámi population of about fifteen to twenty thousand, most have no special rights under Swedish law (although they do have some language rights) because they are either half-Sámi or they have been assimilated. Only a small number enjoy specific hunting and fishing rights. In addition, the members of the half-Sámi population are forced to pay four to five thousand Swedish krona in order to belong to the Sámi association. In the four main states where Sámi people still exist – that is, Sweden, Finland, Norway, and the Kola Peninsula region of Russia – they represent only a small percentage of the population. In Sweden, where the Sámi number twenty thousand, they still represent only 2 percent of the population. Only 10 percent of the Sámi in all nations are presently involved in their traditional occupation of reindeer herding.[160]

In *Kitok,* the court commented that "the important thing for the Sami people is solidarity among the people (folksolidaritet), and not industrial solidarity (narigssolidaritet)."[161] The 1964 royal committee had wanted to make the reindeer village *(renby)* "an entirely economic association." It favoured those with many reindeer; herders received a new vote for every hundred reindeer. Reindeer herding, however, is essentially a cultural activity, and Article 27 of the *International Covenant on Civil and Political Rights* states: "In those States in which ethnic, religious or linguistic minorities exist, persons belonging to such minorities shall not be denied the right, in community with other members of their group, to enjoy their own culture, to profess and practice their own religion or to use their own language." The Human Rights Committee in *Kitok* decided that "a restriction upon the right of an individual member of a minority must be shown to have a reasonable and objective justification to be necessary for the continued viability and welfare of the minority as a whole."[162] Kitok was permitted to graze and farm his reindeer and hunt and fish, but "not as of right."

What makes this case particularly interesting is that it makes the cultural integrity and ecological integrity of the group primary and the right to self-determination secondary. Cultural integrity is based on indigenous territorial rights, and the latter are inseparable from their ecological integrity. Indigenous peoples are defined by their special relationship to the land, as this aspect of their culture is inseparable from what gives them their uniqueness and their special rights. Thus the possibility of an indigenous group denying this tradition and choosing options deleterious to its cultural background and, therefore, identity must be considered.

At Fort McMurray, Alberta, a First Nation has entered into a lucrative business arrangement with Shell Oil to participate in the oil sands boom. This decision negates most of the major aspects of the group's identity, which is the basis for the special status the group enjoys in international and domestic law. Yet Ron Sandler has argued that to take into consideration such decisions takes away First Nations' basic human rights to freedom of choice, thus to self-determination: "This seems paternalistic and inconsistent with other bundles of property rights afforded to other entities (e.g., States) in international law, and therefore a double standard."[163] Sandler suggests that individuals "cannot violate their own rights."[164] However, at least from a Kantian point of view, this is certainly not true: morality prohibits people from selling themselves into slavery, selling their body parts, or allowing themselves to be dehumanized.

It is also important to note that individual rights and group rights may be different. In addition, indigenous peoples have special community rights that extend beyond those each member holds as an individual. Hence, the claim advanced here is that the community cannot make choices that contradict its essential identity (upon which its special status and rights are based) and retain those rights. In fact, a single group member cannot choose ways that may jeopardize the community's survival and, thus, their rights.

In principle (though not necessarily in law), the First Nation at Fort McMurray should retain the same individual rights as all human beings and the same corporate rights as any other business entity, but perhaps it should not claim any special rights that accrue to it as an indigenous community while it continues its industrial operations. In law, First Nations are defined by their unique interdependence with the land and their respect for it, which is both traditional and mandatory in their culture. If First Nations choose to ignore that aspect of their identity, the latter could and should be brought into question, and their rights can be differentiated according to the different spheres within which they operate.

Conclusion

It is only in relation to indigenous communities that individual human rights and community rights are joined with the right to a specific territory, and the conditions of the territory are an integral part of those rights. In some sense, this difference is appropriate because, for the most part, nonindigenous identity is not tied to a specific habitat. Various nonindigenous cultures, ethnicities, and religions, and the practices related to them, are not dependent on a particular area. It is therefore just to emphasize the sui generis right of indigenous communities as separate and distinct from those of the global community in general.

It is not just to ignore the role played by ecological integrity and a safe, non-toxic habitat in relation to all humanity. The scientific evidence is both abundant and robust in this regard, yet no human rights instrument renders this connection explicit, beyond (at best) alluding to a healthy or safe environment, with no specific description of what that may entail. In addition, to protect our basic collective rights, there are no regulatory regimes in international law that follow through with restraints for legal corporate persons, either separately or in conjunction with the governments in which the corporate activities are pursued.

Indigenous communities, therefore, are vital to understanding both the importance of our ecological base and the necessity of inserting basic needs into enforceable legal regimes. It would be hasty, however, to conclude that the problem would be resolved if such regimes were to exist. Although the constitutions of countries such as Colombia and Ecuador employ clear and decisive language for the protection of human health and even for the protection of the environment itself, local communities have found no redress for human rights breaches arising from ecological disintegrity and various forms of pollution and environmental exposure in their own countries. They have been forced to present their case to the International Court of Justice.[165]

It is instructive to read the explanation provided by Ecuador, as it institutes proceedings against Colombia:

(a) Colombia has violated its obligations under international law by causing or allowing the deposit on the territory of Ecuador of toxic herbicides that have caused damage to human health, property and the environment;

(b) Colombia shall indemnify Ecuador for any loss or damage caused by internationally unlawful acts, namely the use of herbicides, including by aerial dispersion, and, in particular:

   (i)   death or injury to the health of any person or persons arising from the use of such herbicides; and

   (ii) any loss or damage to the property or livelihood or human rights of such persons; and

   (iii) environmental damage or the depletion of natural resources; and

   (iv) the costs of monitoring to identify and assess future risks to public health, human right and the environment resulting from Colombia's use of herbicides; and

(v) any other loss or damage; and

(c) Colombia shall:

(i) respect the sovereignty and territorial integrity of Ecuador.[166]

It is even more instructive to see the instruments invoked by Ecuador: "Article XXXI of the American Treaty on Pacific Settlement (officially known as the 'Pact of Bogota') of 30 April 1948, to which both States are Parties. Ecuador also refers to Article 32 of the 1988 United Nations Convention against Illicit Traffic in Narcotic Drugs and Psychotropic Substances."[167]

Many scholars, from international lawyers to environmental ethicists and social scientists, rejoiced when Ecuadaor adopted its new Constitution in 2008. Yet it appears that indisputable harms remain nonjusticiable in the country and that recourse to an international court is necessary. The case should be followed closely to better understand what role international law can play to better protect basic collective human rights.

The examples adduced in Part 1 bring us closer to understanding human rights as public rather than private reasons for action. This understanding leads to what George Pavlakos terms "a much deeper transformation to our understanding of agents and their status, one that goes beyond the individual-community divide."[168] Pavlakos does not address the difference between communities and the collective in the sense employed in this book. But his Kantian analysis of the issue supports my argument, as does some of the work of Joseph Raz on the interface between freedom and autonomy, on the one hand, and persons reducing some of that autonomy by following the legitimate rules of international law and human rights, on the other hand.

If, as Pavlakos argues, "agents acquire the status of persons by virtue of their capacity to handle reasons," and if communities – or, as I would say instead, the collective – exercise their reflexive capacities as persons by following public practices that support that capacity, then the moral and legal reasons to support collective basic rights coincide.[169] In addition, such choices do more than validate the rational humanity of each person. By refusing to condone the ongoing primacy of private and aggregate interests in most sectors over the absolute value of the interests of those being exploited by those interests, the choice of basic collective rights also supports Kant's formula: "So act that you use humanity, as much in your own person as in the person of every other, always at the same time as end and never merely as means."[170]

In "The Problem of Authority: Revisiting the Service Conception," Joseph Raz states, "In postulating that authorities are legitimate only if their directives enable their subjects to better conform to reason, we see authority for what it is: not a denial of people's capacity for rational action, but simply one device, one method through which people can achieve the goal *(telos)* of their capacity for rational action, albeit not through its direct use."[171] Thus, if we accept the congruence of individual rational capacity and the willingness to follow the authority of rational rules (which, themselves, are legitimated by their reasons, rather than simply by consent), then collective rights are basic in theory as well as in practice. By protecting the right to normal development proposed as a basic collective right, together with the right to survival with all that it entails, the presence of basic collective rights reaffirms and supports humanity itself, in the Kantian sense. By supporting these rights, we respect our own, by not allowing any form of slavery to diminish us or others affected in a like manner.

Determining whether the presence of indirect autonomy is sufficient to influence public policy, with or without the addition of democratic consent, or whether it renders these rules and the institutions that enforce them legitimate is beyond the scope of this work. But each of the examples explored in the previous chapters affirms the presence of robust legal instruments capable of eliminating most of the practices that harm the collective; therefore, the related jurisprudence would have led to the support of the biological integrity of individuals and communities. At the same time, those legal instruments would have helped to strongly reaffirm the humanity and the dignity of all those affected and their right to protection.

PART 2

Collective Rights, Globalization, and Democracy – The Practice

4
Collective Basic Rights Today

Unlike the principles on sovereignty and non-intervention –
a typical expression of the Grotian model, to which dissensions
in the world today have given a new lease of life – the principle
imposing respect for human rights, like the ban on the threat or
use of force, is typical of a new stage of development in the
international community following the Second World War. It is
in fact competing – if not at loggerheads – with the traditional
principles of sovereign equality of states and non-intervention.

– Antonio Cassese, *International Law*, 3rd ed.

The evolving importance of human rights in international law, which extends
well beyond the simple observance of accepted state relations, is foundational
to the United Nations' system and is reflected in *erga omnes* obligations. It
would, however, be premature to say that human rights have become increasingly collective or, even less, environmental since 1997, when Judge Christian
Weeramantry offered his dissenting opinion before the International Court
of Justice in *Gabčíkovo-Nagymaros* (see Chapter 1). This chapter examines the
various aspects of international relations that reflect presently accepted principles. Only after determining what today constitutes a justiciable human
right can we address whether existing rights can be extended to protect basic
collective rights.

Even in the absence of a specific instrument or legal regime that explicitly
links environmental rights to the human rights to life and health, the most
commonly acknowledged "new" rights are collective – for instance, the right
to food (or freedom from hunger) and the right to development.[1] That many
of the other evolving human rights are also collective rights is also indicated
by the Millennium Development Goals. Antonio Cassese lists many new

aspects of human rights that are present in state obligations today (see below). These obligations are, for the most part, directed toward collectives, not individuals. And some of the more novel aspects of human rights stem from states deviating from the standards of sovereignty to protect human rights – for instance, by extending the power to legislate and enforce laws to exercise "universal legislation on terrorism."[2] In principle, such power is intended to protect people within or without the specific enacting state from acts of terrorism, not for the protection of a specific individual.

In principle, *legal equality* means both that people should be treated equally and that there should be equality among states.[3] The citizen's right to protection of both life and property abroad has a long history, but new kinds of interventions in the affairs of states – for instance, economic pressure or coercion; bringing about political destabilization; or instigating, fomenting, and financing unrest in a foreign country – are attacks on the rights of collectivities. In addition, one may wonder whether international law bans powerful states from resorting to more subtle forms interference, such as radio propaganda, economic boycotts, withholding economic assistance, or influencing international monetary and financial institutions with a view to stifling weak states economically.[4] All these forms of interference represent serious attacks on the life of the targeted people and on their ability to survive and pursue their chosen paths without hindrance. A simple example is the so-called development imposed by multinational corporations, which is directed by wealthy Western states toward local and indigenous communities in the Global South (see Chapter 2).

It is unclear whether some of these forms of coercion may indeed be viewed as "threat or use of force." According to the UN *Charter*, the threat or use of armed force must not be resorted to against states or peoples who have a representative organization (that is, national liberation movements) and fall into one of the categories entitled to self-determination (colonial peoples or peoples under foreign occupation or racist regimes).[5] One example that illustrates this issue is Israel's "acquisition" of the occupied Palestinian territories and the expanding settlements.[6] Another example involves the concept of anticipatory self-defence and the United States' declared "war on terrorism."[7] The main question is whether Article 51 of the *Charter of the United Nations* permits pre-emptive strikes, the legality of which has been claimed primarily by Israel and the United States in recent times.[8]

In general, the international community does not approve of extending the concept of self-defence in this manner, and the Israeli attack on Palestinian camps in 1975 and on the Gaza strip in January 2009 have evoked general condemnation. When Israel attacked an Iraqi nuclear reactor in 1981, only the United States "shared the Israeli concept of self-defence."[9] Given that the maintenance of peace is the "supreme value" of the UN, any interpretation of Article 51 that endangers peace is generally regarded as too subjective and arbitrary (as well as open to abuse) to be considered legally acceptable.[10]

New forms of state power must, therefore, be considered carefully. Although they are introduced ostensibly to support human rights (the right to safety, for instance), their true effects may be directly in conflict with human rights protection, as long as the notion is understood in a comprehensive, universal sense. If economic coercion is impermissible, then most of the legal cases involving indigenous communities can fall under the rubric of economic coercion. These cases range from the denial of customary work and provisions to facilitate the forceful removal of Chagossians from their island, to the limitation of the conditions required to support the traditional lifestyle of the Ogoni in Nigeria, to the Mayan population of Sipakapa's resistance to Glamis Gold Corporation.[11]

If all instances of impermissibility were monitored and enforced, the collective rights of these people might be protected. It is worth mentioning that many forms of development that employ force assume consent on the part of the residents. In fact, the World Bank employs investigative panels to hear all complaints against its operations and the consultation period that should have preceded them. As far as giving redress in such cases, the World Bank has a good record, but not all damages are compensable. In addition, a peoples' right to consent cannot be compensated financially once they have lost their chance to exercise such a right. In all cases of imposed development, one needs to consider that although the principle of *volenti non fit injuria* (to a willing person, no harm is done) exists, the fact that harmful forms of "development" have been imposed by an outside power on an unconsenting community ought to make the harms that result subject to criminal prosecution.[12] This is what the indigenous peoples of Ecuador alleged in their recent case before the International Court of Justice against Columbia and US-sponsored spraying by DynCorp (see Chapter 3). In addition, from the moral point of view, consent to activities that are contrary to the dignity of humankind is not morally right, at least according to Kant; someone who is forced to agree to sell an organ or submit to inhumane conditions of labour in order to survive is not exercising free consent. Nevertheless, the very consideration of some of these novel issues widens the reach and diversity of the human rights of collectivities and, at least in principle, the obligations of single states and the international community as a whole.

The Need for Extended Collective Rights

Major global problems in the areas of economy and ecology have their origin in consumerism, for the size of the ecofootprint of affluent Western countries prevents the establishment of the institutions and forms of governance needed to redress starvation, exploitation, hazardous development, and economic oppression in the so-called developing world.[13] Many have addressed this issue, and many more have advocated radical changes in the culture of the Western world, for they acknowledge the immense difficulties of bringing about changes in a culture that has been established and nurtured for decades. Amitai Etzioni writes:

> So what kind of transformation in our normative culture is called for? What needs to be eradicated, or at least greatly tempered, is consumerism: the obsession with acquisition that has become the organizing principle of American life. This is not the same thing as capitalism, nor is it the same thing as consumption ... As long as consumption is focused on satisfying basic human needs – safety, shelter, food, clothing, health care, education – it is not consumerism. But when the acquisition of goods and services is used to satisfy higher needs, consumption turns into consumerism – and consumerism becomes a social disease.[14]

When one accepts as a given consumerism as Etzioni describes it, it is difficult to remember that North American consumerism is not the only way. For those of us who originated in Europe, for instance, the things that traditionally made a human being worthy of respect or admiration were family name, an aristocratic or professional background, or education. All of these qualities were deemed far superior to the ability to excel at trade and business. It took a long time to spread the American or Western-based disease of consumerism to the rest of the world, even though the United States and its allies cleverly promoted such a "choice" worldwide. Today, however, the global community, including the United Nations through its Millennium Development Goals, increasingly recognizes that there is no time for a slow turnaround of culture and practices to ensure humanity's survival.[15]

THE UNITED NATIONS MILLENNIUM GOALS AND COLLECTIVE RIGHTS

> Our world is marked by enormous inequalities in economic
> starting places. Some are born into abject poverty with a
> 30 percent chance of dying before their fifth birthday. Others
> are born into the civilized luxury of the western middle class.
> These huge inequalities have evolved in the course of one
> historical process that was pervaded by monumental crimes of
> slavery, colonialism and genocide – crimes that devastated the
> populations, cultures and social institutions of four continents.
>
> – Thomas Pogge, "The First United Nations
> Millennium Development Goal"

Thomas Pogge's main focus is the relationship between hunger and poverty
and their eradication, the first United Nations Millennium Development
Goal. Although the first goal is laudable, there is no novel thinking here: the
Millennium Development Goals (see Figure 1) are, for the most part, an effort to reshuffle and expand the present institutional system, while remaining
firmly "within the box."

FIGURE 1

The Millennium Development Goals and targets

Goal 1: Eradicate extreme poverty and hunger
> TARGET 1: Halve, between 1990 and 2015, the proportion of people whose
> income is less than one dollar a day
> TARGET 2: Halve, between 1990 and 2015, the proportion of people who suffer
> from hunger

Goal 2: Achieve universal primary education
> TARGET 3: Ensure that, by 2015, children everywhere, boys and girls alike, will
> be able to complete a full course of primary schooling

Goal 3: Promote gender equality and empower women
> TARGET 4: Eliminate gender disparity in primary and secondary education,
> preferably by 2005, and to all levels of education no later than 2015

▶

◀ Figure 1

The Millennium Development Goals and targets

Goal 4: Reduce child mortality
> Target 5: Reduce by two-thirds, between 1990 and 2015, the under-five mortality rate

Goal 5: Improve maternal health
> Target 6: Reduce by three-quarters, between 1990 and 2015, the maternal mortality ratio

Goal 6: Combat HIV/AIDS, malaria and other diseases
> Target 7: Have halted by 2015 and begun to reverse the spread of HIV/AIDS
> Target 8: Have halted by 2015 and begun to reverse the incidence of malaria and other major diseases

Goal 7: Ensure environmental sustainability
> Target 9: Integrate the principles of sustainable development into country policies and programmes and reverse the loss of environmental resources
> Target 10: Halve, by 2015, the proportion of people without sustainable access to safe drinking water
> Target 11: By 2020, to have achieved a significant improvement in the lives of at least 100 million slum dwellers

Goal 8: Develop a global partnership for development
> Some of the indicators listed below will be monitored separately for the Least Developed Countries (LDCs), Africa, landlocked countries and small island developing States.
> Target 12: Develop further an open, rule-based, predictable, non-discriminatory trading and financial system
> Target 13: Address the Special Needs of the Least "Developed Countries
> Target 14: Address the Special Needs of landlocked countries and small island developing States
> Target 15: Deal comprehensively with the debt problems of developing countries through national and international measures in order to make debt sustainable in the long term
> Target 16: In co-operation with developing countries, develop and implement strategies for decent and productive work for youth
> Target 17: In co-operation with pharmaceutical companies, provide access to affordable, essential drugs in developing countries
> Target 18: In co-operation with the private sector, make available the benefits of new technologies, especially information and communications.

There is quite a bit that can be said about the possible relationship between the Millennium Development Goals and the current state of human rights. Indeed, as Philip Alston has it, the phrase "ships passing in the night" best describes the disconnect between the two.[16] However, my reasons for reaching this conclusion are entirely different from those adduced by Alston. The main problem with the Millennium Development Goals and their related targets is that they do not take into consideration the role that ecological conditions play in regard to human rights and the unsustainability of "business as usual," or even of development, in its present form. For instance, Goal 1 has as a prerequisite a much more robust formulation of Goal 7, to ensure environmental sustainability. And Target 9, in fact, proposes an oxymoron – sustainable development – which is in direct conflict with Goal 1 and Target 10, for it is the ongoing practices of development, most often touted as sustainable, that are causing the current food crisis. The reasons for unsustainability are well known: desertification, climate change, pollution, and the inappropriate use of grains and cereals in Western diets and vehicles (see Chapter 2). None of these factors are even mentioned in the goals. These omissions and the fact that overcoming climate change is neither a goal nor even a target in the Millennium Development Goals confirm their moderate and highly selective nature.

Another glaring problem, given that water is far more necessary for survival than food itself, is the mention of safe water as only a target: it should be Goal 2. Human beings – especially local, land-based, and indigenous communities – can survive briefly without the implementation of Goal 2, important though it is, but no one can survive without water.[17] Given that both hunger and the lack of safe water affect children most severely, ensuring safe water would also serve to reduce the maternal mortality ratio (Goal 5). Most significantly, however, Goal 4 should precede Goals 2 and 3, as should tighter controls over chemical and industrial exposures, which are not mentioned.[18] The whole list suffers from a blind spot regarding the main global issues affecting the world today. This oversight is also evident in Goal 6. Targets 7 and 8 refer to diseases, but there is no mention of the World Health Organization's commitment to public health.[19] Finally, neither the goals nor the targets in any way address the special and urgent needs of indigenous peoples, a glaring omission.[20] For instance, Target 11 addresses the issue of "slum dwellers" but makes no reference to the global situations that produce forced migrations, which in turn produce slum dwellers.

The main issue is the need to establish international law regimes that stop the production of harmful chemical substances; to change laws that permit practices that foster climate change; and to qualify "development" so that it is always safe, undertaken with consent, and respectful of the traditional lifestyles of those communities who prefer to follow their own path. In conclusion, the Millennium Development Goals tend to support *some* civil and political rights (the rights of women, the right to education) but gloss over most of the major collective issues: ecological collapse; climate change; corporate attacks on the right to life, health, and normal human development; the impact of consumerism and the large ecofootprint of Western countries in the Global South; and the collective cultural and ecological rights of indigenous peoples and other land-based communities. The very presence of development goals, rather than the goal of achieving and strengthening human rights, demonstrates a grave lack of concern for the results of historical process such as colonization, genocide, and slavery. These harms demand redress, at the very least, or even justice, not development, which is either a modified version of past crimes or simply more of the same.

The Right to Development?

> "State responsibility," simply put, is the name public international law gives to the normative state of affairs which occurs following a breach by a state of one of its legal obligations (whether that obligation derives from treaty law, customary law, or other recognized sources such as "general principles of law").
>
> – Craig Scott, "Translating Torture into International Tort"

State responsibility includes both positive and negative obligations, and given the grave differences in the economic situation of citizens around the world, the issue of development is of central importance. In September 2000, the open-ended Working Group on the Right to Development, established by the Commission on Human Rights, produced a document on the right to development.[21] The document covers all aspects of poverty and hunger alleviation, but it also indicates the grave problems associated with the right to development and the concept of development. The first problem is related to the question, whose right is it? Presumably, development should be a right of those who are not yet developed – that is, poor people in "developing countries." In fact, the right to development is intended as a remedy for the problems those persons encounter, to redress "the effects of poverty, structural adjustment, globalization and trade liberalization on the prospects of the enjoyment of the right to development in developing countries."[22]

Development, then, is related to the removal of poverty; it is, from the start, an economic goal, one to be implemented as a process of "economic, social, cultural and political development" so that all "human rights and fundamental freedoms can be fully realized."[23] Much of the language of *The Right to Development* is patterned on the work of Amartya Sen.[24] But reliance on the work of even a famous economist carries its own pitfalls. Paragraph 6 of the document affirms that "to have a right means to have claim to something of value on other people, institutions, the state, or the international community, who in turn have the obligation of providing or helping to provide that something of value."[25] No doubt, Sen would acknowledge that "something of value" includes more than the obligation to provide the economic means to relieve hunger or thirst.

But it is unclear, with their globalizing drive to develop the undeveloped, whether the creators of this document took into serious consideration the right of people *not* to develop, if they so choose. Economic development goes hand in hand with certain grave costs, first and foremost, the risk of losing rights to traditions and cultural lifestyles. One need only to consider the abundant jurisprudence initiated by indigenous and local communities who have tried to say no to development but whose voices are neither heeded nor respected.[26] The "something of value" these people treasure is the right to be free not to develop, to not lose the "freedom to choose their lifestyle and their children's future." In these cases, the "perfect obligation" of states and other nonstate agents should be to respect agents' choices, especially when they represent the will of these communities.[27] The preferred means of viewing state obligations – that is, "the Kantian view of imperfect obligations," which is applicable to anyone who is in a position to help – is no better if it excludes the choice not to develop.[28]

It is the starting point of *The Right to Development* that is problematic: the assumption that development unqualified (that is, not educational, moral, artistic, cultural, and so on) is the answer to poverty and hunger, despite numerous examples to the contrary. Consider, first, who truly benefits from the commercial activities associated with development. The first group to benefit are the multinational corporations that come to mine, extract, log, build and, in general, develop an area rich in resources. The impassioned pleas of those suffering the effects of these activities, mostly unrestrained by either environmental or public health mandates, ought to demonstrate that freedom is and must be understood as both negative and positive. Freedom is the right to develop *and* the right to embrace and maintain the status quo.

The second group that benefits is the bureaucracies and governments of the affected countries. At best, officials may receive a part of the profits enjoyed by the corporate actors involved; at worst, they gain roads and other infrastructure and military or paramilitary support for their warlike actions.[29] If these elites are part of undemocratic governments or outright military dictatorships, then any hope of trickle-down benefits is eliminated. This happened, for instance, in Ogoniland at the time of the rule of dictator Sani Abbacha in the 1990s.[30] The *Vienna Declaration* states categorically that "human rights and fundamental freedoms are the birthright of all human beings; their protection and promotion is the first responsibility of governments."[31] When Royal Dutch Shell arrived to bring its development to Ogoniland, however, the Ogoni people had a comfortable traditional lifestyle, cultivating their land and fishing. Ken Saro-Wiwa, author and activist, termed the destruction that accompanied oil extraction ecocide and omnicide. It was only in 2009 that Royal Dutch Shell Petroleum paid 15.5 million in damages for Saro-Wiwa's murder. The company did not, however, take responsibility for multiple murders, rapes, and other incompensable harms it had perpetrated.[32] Although the Ogoni eventually received some compensation, not all local communities today are so lucky.

For the most part, development is aimed at economic profit, not at maintaining the health and freedom from want of peoples. Development often destroys, alters, or removes the resources upon which local communities depend. Climate change does the rest, even when a community is not located on an island, a coastal zone, or the high Arctic. Essentially, then, the "imperfect duties" of state and nonstate actors listed in paragraph 8 of *The Right to Development* – to ensure freedom to maintain and retain the cherished values of communities and to eliminate or at least reduce poverty and hunger – should have started long ago, long before the present impasse was reached. These obligations should include saying no to activities that harm the natural ecological basis upon which most of the world's people depend; saying no to international instruments such as GATT's Article XX that place the environment and public health behind trade; and saying no to the political and economic support of corporate bodies whose activities and human rights records demand careful scrutiny and regulation rather than friendly cooperation.

All that *The Right to Development* demands is that the right to development be understood as the right to a process that requires the cooperation of all interdependent states. The form development should take should include "a sharp increase in GDP, or rapid industrialization, or an export-led growth."[33] Paragraph 15 acknowledges that development may not reduce poverty and that there may be no commensurate "improvement in social indicators of education, health, gender development or environmental protection."[34] The placement of environmental protection last, rather than first, as a basic right is a further symptom of misunderstanding what constitutes a real basic right, which would indeed be "the entitlement of every human person as a human right."[35] Hence, this document's definition of development, even with the unremarkable additional of *sustainable* (which is unspecified and mostly misunderstood), is flawed and incomplete.

The loss of cultural and ecological integrity is not compensated for by the introduction of Western improvements, especially when they arise from a project that lacks consent. In fact, the overwhelming use of resources and energy already in existence, fostered by overconsumption in affluent Western countries (as indicated by ecological footprint analysis) casts all further industrial development in doubt.[36] Not only are most of development's effects extremely deleterious to life on Earth, in general, and to the most vulnerable people in impoverished developing countries, specifically, but also there is neither energy nor materials enough on Earth to expand the industrial enterprise and bring it to all countries, to "raise" them to the level of growth present in the West today.

Sustainable development remains an oxymoron, for any form of development (beyond the intellectual, cultural, or moral kind) is intrinsically unsustainable and physically unachievable. Perhaps the only positive aspect of *The Right to Development* is that the right is viewed as a collective rather than an individual right. But even that plus cannot begin to offset the its numerous deficiencies. However, international instruments aimed primarily at collectives are few and far between; therefore, it is necessary to devote careful study to each one to see whether any support can be found for the position of collectives today.

BHUPINDER CHIMNI ON AMARTYA SEN, DEVELOPMENT, AND INTERNATIONAL LAW

> The Sen theory of development is less successful in its analysis of ... features of social processes and structures that are critical to the practical realization of the goal of development. Like critical theorists in general, Sen "tends to be better at emancipation from then emancipation to, and still weaker on how to get from here to there."
>
> – Bhupinder Chimni, "The Sen Conception of Development and Contemporary International Law Discourse"

In addition to the problem mentioned by Bhupinder Chimni, the second main problem with the concept of the right to development rests on the practical, scientific facts that underlie sustainability or, better yet, the integrity of the areas slated for development. As the quote by Chimni suggests, most of the international literature relating to the right to development follows in the footsteps of Amartya Sen's *Development as Freedom* (1999). But Chimni is, if anything, too kind to Sen, despite his fame and his general acceptance. Freedom, as understood by Sen – that is, within a capitalist, globalized world – may well be the precise opposite of any desirable state to be gained by an impoverished person in the Third World.

As Chimni demonstrates, Sen's approach is flawed. One can be kind and say, with Chimni, that Sen's conception of the right to development is a great improvement on the notion of development that prevailed in earlier times, a notion that is entirely related to a country's GDP. In addition, one could also acknowledge that his notion fits well within the present state of international law: "There is a striking parallel between Sen's vision of development and contemporary international law (CIL) discourse on development. It explains why the Sen thinking on development is readily accommodated in CIL."[37] Or, in contrast, one could start with the facts of this accommodation and note that the right to development is both indiscriminate and ineffective. It is indiscriminate because it treats any activity that would add industrialization and tradable commodities to a developing country as an unalloyed boon. It is also ineffective because it is viewed, as Sen does, as an individual right to freedom (primarily understood as the possession of civil and political rights), rather than as a collective right to improve a group's living conditions.

Because Sen's work is part of mainstream international law scholarship, he "does not identify and interrogate those processes and structures in the international system that prevent the realization of accepted goals of development ... [and] that there are deep structures that constrain the pursuit of the common good through international law."[38] In fact, for the most part, the proliferation of human rights instruments tend to increase personal freedoms at the expense of the common good. Individual rights are often ineffectual for remedying the grave problems of the most vulnerable people in the world. One cannot forget, as Sen appears to do, that the individual freedom of natural persons is more than offset, and most often limited, not by communitarian concerns but by the rights of wealthy and powerful *legal* persons. Thus, upholding the freedom of individuals as the "basic building blocks" of development represents a patent untruth.[39] In some cases, this freedom may represent one of the factors necessary to reduce hunger and poverty, which should be the true goal of any development process. But the fact that Sen does not critique the primacy of capitalism or growth shows that he does not understand that solutions will come only with a radical reordering of the political and economic conditions of globalization.

Until the material conditions necessary for the normal and healthy development of human beings are recognized as basic and common rights, the individual freedom to participate in civil and political processes will be meaningful only if each human being is healthy and not facing starvation. Chimni is therefore correct when he says that Sen's analysis "does not seriously explore specifics in the context of the real-world situations. In simultaneously supporting liberalization of the market and the goals of investing in education and health facilities, he tides over the tensions between the two sets of goals."[40]

Democracy and free political discussion are not, in themselves, sufficient to improve the abject social conditions found in much of the developing world.[41] At every Group of Eight meeting, noisy and often violent political arguments express the dissatisfaction of social groups around the world with the results and the processes of neoliberal market activities, which are advocated by the most powerful states and entrenched in much of today's international law. Yet, despite the continued and consistent presence of these political critiques and the freedom to express them (the latter is often limited by repression and containment on site), there has been neither significant change nor any obvious improvement on the ground, even for the most basic of rights, the right to food and water.[42] Hence, Chimni is correct once again when he states, "In sum, Sen is the classic liberal who has faith in the institution of the market and the State to deliver, even under a capitalist dispensation. His notion of democracy is also an idealistic one, where political power, political economy and struggle are absent. His liberal humanism therefore remains problematic."[43]

THE IMPORTANCE OF SOIL SECURITY

In February 2009, the Secretariat of the United Nations Convention to Combat Desertification published *Securitizing the Ground, Grounding Security*. The document highlights the importance of forging a coalition to combat desertification, land degradation, and drought (DLDD) in the present context of climate change. Doing so will deliver benefits to all by ensuring reliable access to food and water and sustainable livelihoods and by protecting biodiversity.[44] The goals named by this document are far closer to what is needed by impoverished people. These are necessities for a "new concept of security policy, through its relations with climate, water, soil, health and survival, in order to stabilize the regions at risk."[45] Thus, the interrelation between nature and human activities is central here, rather than human activities without the clear and explicit protection required on behalf of nature, to ensure "health and survival." Because this document is not a treaty or a declaration of the UN, deviating or continuing to deviate from its recommendations is not a wrongful act of state or nonstate actors. Nevertheless, *Securitizing the Ground, Grounding Security* is an authoritative statement relating to the present status quo, based on science, but closely linking the research on factual conditions to human and even humanitarian rights. It recognizes the interface between a degraded environment and regional conflict.[46]

Land degradation is a global environmental and development issue. Up-to-date, quantitative information is needed to support policy and action for food and water security, economic development, environmental integrity, and resource conservation. According to *Securitizing the Ground*, lands affected by DLDD cover from 33 percent to 41 percent of the earth, 6 percent in Africa.[47] In this document we find what is missing in the *Right to Development* document – that is, consideration of the real, on the ground, challenges to human survival, including climate change, water security, and the food crisis.[48] Furthermore, it also acknowledges that the doubling of food demand by 2050, the increased use of biofuels, and "modernization processes and

livelihood changes" will produce effects that "in the context of globalization ... can be harmful to local communities whose customary rights are not
sufficiently recognized."[49] In other words, the document acknowledges that
collective and community rights are primarily affected at the most basic level
of survival. In contrast, the *Right to Development* emphasizes individual freedom an important but overrated concept.[50]

Despite the awkward neologism, the three phases of the evolution of
DLDD should be included in formal international instruments, and they
should provide the basis for judgments in cases involving local and indigenous communities and in the preparation of binding international instruments. The three phases are scientific agenda setting and research (scientizing),
political action (politicizing), and upgrading to a security issue (securitizing).[51]
Although no conference of the parties has explicitly included these issues,
the United Nations Convention to Combat Desertification has effectively put
DLDD on the international political agenda. In addition, DLDD was explicitly
viewed as a security issue during the UN Security Council's 2007 debate on
climate change.[52]

Both conditions for survival and the "security of citizens"[53] are concerns
that apply to collectives, and the right to social security emerged in Article
22 of the *Universal Declaration of Human Rights*. These conditions concern
the international community (in fact, humankind itself), with particular
reference not to states but to "the vulnerable groups that are most exposed
to these emergent DLDD security issues, exacerbated by anthropogenic climate change."[54]

Securitizing the Ground is perhaps the first international document to
consider "the ground" under two separate though connected aspects: the land
as territory, basic to national sovereignty, and the land "as soil that produces
essential ecosystem services, including food for living organisms."[55] The issue
is also fundamental to understanding the rising number of forced migrations
and raises the question: "How can the societal consequences of hunger, dis-
tress migration and in some cases of conflicts be curbed, and the impact be
reduced by rapid response, preventive action, early warning and peacebuild-
ing?"[56] When one considers the magnitude of the problems engendered by
DLDD and, in general, by anthropogenically fostered ecological degradation,
it is obvious that proactive strategies will be absolutely necessary. The amount
of time required to reproduce viable soil or to re-establish trees and forests,
in combination with the costs involved, will gravely impede the elimination,
or even the mitigation, of the human rights and humanitarian crises described

in *Securitizing the Ground*.[57] What is needed is legal and political strategies to stop ongoing and increasing ecological disintegrity.

It is not fair to say, as *Securitizing the Ground* does, that "besides the top-down scenarios of the ... UNEP [United Nations Environment Programme], the sources of these strategies, policies and measures require an active involvement of the people affected by DLDD at the local level."[58] Neither industrial development nor climate change is a result of the actions of people in sub-Saharan Africa and other severely affected areas; therefore, there is a strong component of injustice in these issues, as well as in the expectation that the victims will work alongside the responsible parties to redress the harms they have suffered. Moreover, given that these victims were unable to stop either industrial development or the overconsumption of materials and energy that precipitated climate change, it is, at best, naive to expect them to be active participants in any successful policy to alter the situation that oppresses them. Counselling adaptation ignores the injustice suffered by affected peoples and appears to be practically inappropriate.[59]

The recommendations of the II International Symposium on Desertification and Migration, held in Almería, Spain, on 25-27 October 2006, should be analyzed in this context. The recommendations can be summarized as follows:

1   Multidisciplinary studies should include an analysis of migration, including its causes and consequences. The United Nations Convention to Combat Desertification (UNCCD) should promote scientific and technological developments that will enhance economic activities in arid areas.

2   A research, training, and coordination centre on desertification and migration in Spain should be considered and become a partner of the UNCCD Secretariat. The UNESCO initiative on the Decade of Education for Sustainable Development (2005-14) may offer a political framework to reduce desertification and migration.

3   The Plataforma Solar de Almeria, as a leading centre for the development of solar energy in Europe, may become a focal point for training experts from DLDD-affected regions that could be co-financed by the EU and international financial institutions.

4   A trilateral initiative of Spain, Mexico, and Germany to cooperate in research on climate change, desertification, migration, and renewable energies potential in drylands could be pursued in the OECD framework. Involving financial institutions such as the World Bank is also recommended.[60]

Securitizing the Ground remains an informed and useful analysis of the causes of DLDD and other forms of disintegrity, rather than part of the solution. It is excellent because it connects human rights issues to scientific facts on the ground, but it does not explicitly point a finger at the practices that engendered the dire situation described so well in the "scientizing" portion of the document. Until the "politicizing" and "securitizing" phases of DLDD deal with the source of the problems, publications such as *Securitizing the Ground* can only recommend band-aid solutions, incapable even of mitigating, let alone changing, the current situation.

The Common Heritage of Mankind and the Relevance of Cultural Goods

> In our search for an Ariadne's thread to lead us through the intricacies of international relations, we stumble upon a new concept creeping in and out of the intricacies of international reality: the "common heritage of mankind."
>
> – Antonio Cassese, *International Law in a Divided World*

In the historical development of international law, powerful Western countries have tended, as much as possible, to support the status quo through respect for the freewill of states and by upholding custom and positive law. In contrast, both developing countries and those in eastern Europe, albeit for separate motives, have supported the formation of principles and rules beyond those based on the agreement and cooperation of states. Antonio Cassese's insightful analysis shows that although a "Hobbesian or realist tradition" prevailed in earlier times, one in which each country took a self-defensive position in regard to other states, a later Grotian or internationalist conception of state interaction emerged and emphasized "co-operation and regulated intercourse among sovereign States."[61] Finally, the universalist "Kantian outlook" emerged, "which sees at work in international politics a potential community of mankind, and lays stress on the element of 'transnational solidarity.'"[62] The latter approach, together with a strong thrust toward the emergence of *jus cogens* norms and *erga omnes* obligations, is the preferred agent of change of developing countries as they press "for quick, far-reaching and radical modifications."[63] In contrast, eastern European countries "prefer to proceed gingerly, believing as they do that legal change should be brought about gradually, as much as possible through mutual agreement."[64]

Nevertheless, both eastern European and developing countries joined in support of Article 53 of the *Vienna Convention on the Law of Treaties*, which was signed in 1969 and came into force in 1980. Cassese remarks:

> To developing countries, the proclamation of *jus cogens* represented a further means of fighting against colonial or former colonial countries – as was made clear in 1968 at the Vienna Conference by the representative of Sierra Leone, who pointed out that the upholding of *jus cogens* provided a golden opportunity to condemn imperialism, slavery, forced labour and all the practices that violated the principle of equality of all human beings and of the sovereign equality of all states.[65]

For eastern European states (such as Romania and Ukraine), jus cogens was viewed as a "means of crystallizing once and for all the 'rules of the game' concerning peaceful coexistence between East and West."[66]

Despite the support of both of these blocks, Western countries were initially on the defensive before bowing to the inevitable will of the majority and the need to espouse norms consistent with their own legal traditions.[67] It was the weakest countries, those most disempowered by Western alliances and treaties, that enthusiastically supported an approach that characterized the "new" law. E. Jiménez de Aréchaga of Uruguay termed these developments "a flagrant challenge to international conscience."[68]

I argue that we are all disempowered in the face of mounting environmental threats to our health and survival and the monolithic powers that support global trade and current economic policies instead of life. Perhaps that is why we see protest groups joining forces with protesters not only from developing countries but also from Western environmental and animal defense groups.

At any rate, Cassese summarizes the three principles that emerged and were codified at the Vienna Convention: restrictions on the previously unfettered freedom of states, the democratization of international legal relations, and the enhancement of international values as opposed to national claims.[69]

A controversial principle is arising within the "new law" paradigm, one that has not quite lived up to its true potential: the principle of the common heritage of mankind. The concept appears *prima facie* to be a step forward. However, Patricia Birnie and Alan Boyle, state:

An important factor contributing to the classification of living resources as common property is that they have generally been so plentiful that the cost of asserting and defending exclusive rights exceeds the advantages to be gained. A regime of open access in these circumstances has generally been to everyone's advantage. However, as [Garrett] Hardin has observed, the inherent logic of the commons remorselessly generates tragedy, as the availability of a free resource leads to overexploitation and minimizes the interest of any individual state in conservation and restraint.[70]

THE COMMON HERITAGE OF MANKIND

Law does not spring anew; old concepts evolve and new ones emerge to fit new fields of human enterprise. In this manner, the unique historical developments manifesting themselves in the emergence of a North-South cleavage have been responsible for the introduction of a new international legal concept, the Common Heritage of Mankind Principle (hereinafter referred to as CHM). As noted by Goedhuis, there are four essential elements defining this new principle: (1) the area under consideration cannot be subject to appropriation; (2) all countries must share in the management of the region; (3) there must be an active sharing of the benefits reaped from the exploitation of the area's resources; and (4) the area must be dedicated to exclusively peaceful purposes.

> – Bradley Larschan and Bonnie Brennan,
> "The Common Heritage of Mankind Principle
> in International Law"

The common heritage of mankind (CHM) appears, at least *prima facie*, to be a wonderful addition to the small arsenal of ecologically constructive concepts. Nevertheless, the language employed in its definition clearly shows its deficiencies. If an area is ecologically sensitive and, in that sense, important enough to fit the CHM concept, then both managing it and exploiting it may be contrary to the continued preservation of the area, a goal implicit in the designation "CHM." All future generations of mankind would be deprived of any benefit whatsoever if the area were both managed and exploited.

The area's preservation would be far better served if both present and future generations of humankind were managed instead – to control their exploitive activities and even exclude them from the area designated as a common heritage. The area's existence and the natural services it may provide for all life, both within and without its immediate confines, is what is primarily at stake.[71] In essence, future generations of mankind can only benefit from nonexploitation, which, in turn, is based on regulated restraint or the management of present human enterprise.

Although the CHM principle is not yet established as either a treaty obligation or an obligation erga omnes, and although it remains a political principle at this time,[72] it has emerged in international discourse because developing countries are seeking a new international economic order. Developing nations, disempowered by free trade and the economically and politically powerful G8, are attempting to influence public policy opinion, at least in regard to areas "outside the traditional jurisdiction of states: the deep seabed, outer space and, to a lesser degree, the Antarctic."[73]

This book is concerned with the national systems of Earth, so only the deep seabed and Antarctica are relevant to my argument. The first point worthy of note is that the CHM principle is too accepting of the status quo; therefore, it is not capable of protecting our common heritage, because the natural patrimony of mankind also lies in areas not of interest to affluent Western states. Oceans, old forests, lakes, rivers, and all other areas in which biodiversity still abounds are surely part of the global commons and should be protected before their tragic loss deprives all life of the support they provide.[74] In other words, the reference to the "benefits" of exploitation is clearly an oxymoron, unless one interprets *benefit* in a purely economic and short-term sense, which appears to be contrary to the letter and spirit of a principle aimed at benefiting mankind as a whole, not simply a rich minority.

Should we consider the global commons *res nullius* (nobody's property), despite the tragic consequences that may follow the free and unrestricted appropriation of these areas by technologically advanced countries and other legal persons bent on immediate economic exploitation? Or should we consider it a *res communis* (public domain), together with air and sunlight?[75] The separate opinion of Judge De Castro in regard to the International Court of Justice's *Fisheries Jurisdiction* case (1974) clearly shows the fallacy of this approach: De Castro stated that "fish stocks in the sea are inexhaustible."[76] But neither clean air nor safe sunlight (see Chapter 1) are currently available to most people on Earth, and fish stocks are often depleted and have crashed into extinction.[77] The CHM principle should be applied as *territorium extra commercium* (territory outside commerce), as Bin Cheng proposes, except that instead of "management, exploitation and distribution," our concern should be its preservation, non-manipulation, and respectful treatment. These concepts, not the former, would ensure that mankind, as such, can enjoy the benefits of unspoiled nature. Cheng's discussion of these concepts is worth quoting at length:

> While territorium extra commercium and territorium commune humanitatis (or CHM) shared the same characteristics that they cannot be territorially appropriated by any State, they differ in that the former is essentially a negative concept, whereas the latter is a positive one. In the former, in time of peace, as long as a State respects the exclusive quasi-territorial jurisdiction of other states over their own ships, aircraft and spacecraft, general international law allows it to use the area or even abuse it more or less as it wishes, including the appropriation of its natural resources, closing large parts of such space for weapon testing and military exercises, and even using such areas as a cesspool for its municipal and industrial sewage. The emergent concept of the common heritage of mankind, on the other hand, while it still lacks precise definition, wishes basically to convey the idea that the management, and exploitation and distribution of the natural resources of the area in question are matters to be decided by the international community (or simply the contracting parties, as in the Moon Treaty?) and are not to be left to the initiative and discretion of individual States and their nationals.[78]

Bradley Larschan and Bonnie Brennan, in contrast, are concerned primarily with distributive issues. They argue convincingly that defining certain areas as protected under the CHM principle appears, in practice, to protect only the Group of 77, because the "one nation–one vote procedure of the Assembly is cosmetic."[79] The Security Council empowered to make executive decisions is dominated by states "on the basis of investments, social system, consumption, production, special interests and equitable geographical distribution."[80]

My concern is long-term preservation, not the contemporary distribution of the economic benefits of the global commons. The distributive approach, as Cheng points out, permits the patrimony of mankind to be used as a cesspool, which is hardly appropriate to the common heritage of mankind.[81] Even with the concept's weaknesses, it would have been highly desirable to retain the use of the principle, beyond open spaces, the moon, and the deep seabed.[82] The Antarctic Treaty System, established in 1991, protects the Antarctic and related ecosystems "in the interest of mankind as a whole," but our most obvious common heritage, the air we breathe, has not been so protected. Rather, the global climate has been referred to as a common concern. In other environmentally related preambles, such as that of the 1972 *Convention for the Protection of World Cultural and Natural Heritage*, the expression used is "world heritage of mankind."[83]

In contrast, referring to any aspect of the commons as a property resource eliminates the requirement of respect and preservation and substitutes an approach that only requires "fairness of allocation procedures." The latter approach will not support ecojustice as a combination of intragenerational and intergenerational justice. Rather, this approach retains an economic or procedural flavour, described by James C. Wood as "maintaining quality, allocating capacity, and controlling access."[84] I argue that we are facing the final enclosure movement as the tragedy of the commons reaches its final stage.[85]

To propose, as Wood does, "stable institutions [that] include equitable arrangements, efficiency, assumed expectations through compliance monitoring and graduated sanctions" is to misunderstand both the nature and the gravity of the situation.[86] It is not simply a matter of slowing down the inevitable elimination of the resource base through procedural fairness and "assurance games."[87] Rather, it is a matter of not viewing the earth as property to be divided and exploited, even when fairness is employed. We should, instead, consider the earth as composed of natural systems whose integrity and support is essential to our survival.[88] The protection of ecosystemic function supports our own functions, as the WHO has indicated, both in the present and in the future, starting with this generation.[89]

The most well-known collective rights of humankind, listed under the heading of common heritage of mankind, include not only natural but also cultural goods. Francesco Francioni lists five categories of cultural goods: the first is covered by conventions that deal with their protection in war time; the second addresses the problem of illicit traffic; the third covers goods of "exceptional importance of universal value for the whole of mankind"; the fourth is complementary to the laws governing the seabed and underwater resources; and the fifth concerns intangible cultural goods – that is, those present in the oral and artistic patrimony of ancient cultures.[90]

As I argue in Chapter 3, the protection of cultural goods serves to cement the right to cultural integrity possessed by various traditional communities. Together with the right to religious practice, the right to cultural integrity is one of the most solid collective rights presently in existence. Because the connection between cultural and biological integrity is easy to trace and defend for traditional communities, I propose these communities as models to emulate in the defence of collective survival rights. Given the importance of intangible and cultural goods, the fifth category of cultural goods outlined by Francioni should be considered an integral part of collective rights.

CULTURAL AND INTANGIBLE GOODS AS PART OF OUR COMMON HERITAGE

> Il est évident que la sauvegarde du patrimoine culturel immaterial s'insère dans l'objectif général de la protection des droit humains, entendus dans la plupart des cas au sens de *droits de collectivitées.*
>
> > – Tullio Scovazzi, "La Convention pour la
> > sauvegarde du patrimoine culturel immatériel"
> > (emphasis added)

Cultural and intangible goods are important collective rights because of the interface between UNESCO's instruments regarding cultural intangible rights, Article 27 of the *International Covenant on Economic, Social and Cultural Rights*, and the UN's *Universal Declaration of Human Rights*. Tracing the connection to human rights is not only necessary to better understanding cultural rights, it also serves as a limit to cultural community rights, as I argue in Chapter 1. For instance, the cultural right to female genital mutilation is not a collective right and defensible as such. In fact, female genital mutilation is an example of a non-universal, non-collective community right not related to the environment.

As of 2005, the protection of cultural goods is supported by 180 countries.[91] Cultural goods unite the international community, as do certain aspects of the material heritage of mankind, and both contribute to the unity and integrity of the international community of nations. In principle, it should not be difficult to protect intangible goods, for intellectual property is well protected in law. However intangible intellectual property is not protected as such: it is the author of the property that enjoys the protection of law.

In 1989, UNESCO passed a resolution (a soft law instrument) to protect traditional culture and folklore. Today, folklore enjoys a lower status than other forms of culture and is limited, for the most part, to activities of commercial (touristic) interest.[92] However, all levels of intangible cultural goods, regardless of their level of "culture," are protected only if they contribute to sustainability. Any traditional practices that involve the destruction of animal species or the massive degradation of natural landscapes no longer fall under UNESCO's mandate.[93]

Most traditional cultural practices, however, are put at risk by ongoing disintegrity and environmental degradation. Protecting the ecological basis of these traditional practices is integral to fulfilling UNESCO's directives.[94] Tullio Scovazzi relates a number of current examples. For instance, the Carnival of Oruro in Bolivia, which combines ancient pre-Colombian rites with Christian liturgy, is threatened by the increasing desertification of the Andean Altiplano. Similarly, in Bolivia the Kallawaya's healing arts, which demonstrate an outstanding medicinal knowledge of animals, plants, and minerals, are under threat. Kallawaya itinerant healers understand various local ecosystems and the medical properties of over 980 species. However, the lack of protection available to indigenous communities, as well as the politics of Big Pharma, threatens the very existence of this traditional knowledge. The polyphonic chants of the Aka pygmies of the Central African Republic, a complex form of voice counterpoint accompanied by percussion and string instruments, are likewise endangered, as are the traditional lifestyle and very existence of Pygmies, because of the disappearance of wildlife caused by deforestation and the exploitation associated with tourism.[95]

These examples could be multiplied but, essentially, it is not only the biological existence of these indigenous communities that is at stake but also their cultural existence and, hence, their survival as peoples. Traditional knowledge and arts are an irreplaceable part of the heritage of humanity. Other social factors may also interfere with the protection and preservation of intangible goods, such as social pressures, globalization, and religious and secularist forces. Nevertheless, indigenous peoples' connection to local environments, the basis of their cultures, renders cultural and intangible goods a valuable example of a protected collective right.

Public Health as a Collective Right

> The right to health is a legal instrument – a crucial and
> constructive tool for the health sector to provide the best care for
> patients and to hold national governments and the international
> community to account.
>
> – *The Lancet,* "The Right to Health: From Rhetoric to Reality"

In 2000, the UN Committee on Economic, Social and Cultural Rights adopted General Comment No. 14 on the right to the highest attainable standard of health. The main value of this document is its mandate to state governments, which must be understood against the background of the limited prescriptions of the *International Covenant on Economic, Social and Cultural Rights (ICESCR)*. My main focus here is on these existing legal instruments and the possibility of adapting or modifying them to support recent science regarding the life and health of human and nonhuman beings in the context of severely altered natural systems.

Nonhuman animals have been sentinels of health for a long time (recall the "canary in the mine" example); therefore, mounting rates of extinction confirm that the environment, the habitat we share with other creatures, is no longer safe. The only binding legal document in which reference is made to the protection of human health is the *ICESCR*, especially Articles 11 and 12:

Article 11

1. The States Parties to the present Covenant recognize the right of everyone to an adequate standard of living for himself and his family, including adequate food, clothing and housing, and to the continuous improvement of living conditions. The States Parties will take appropriate steps to ensure the realization of this right, recognizing to this effect the essential importance of international co-operation based on free consent.

2. The States Parties to the present Covenant, recognizing the fundamental right of everyone to be free from hunger, shall take,

individually and through international co-operation, the measures, including specific programmes, which are needed:

(a) To improve methods of production, conservation and distribution of food by making full use of technical and scientific knowledge, by disseminating knowledge of the principles of nutrition and by developing or reforming agrarian systems in such a way as to achieve the most efficient development and utilization of natural resources;

(b) Taking into account the problems of both food-importing and food-exporting countries, to ensure an equitable distribution of world food supplies in relation to need.

Article 12

1. The States Parties to the present Covenant recognize the right of everyone to the enjoyment of the highest attainable standard of physical and mental health.

2. The steps to be taken by the States Parties to the present Covenant to achieve the full realization of this right shall include those necessary for:

(a) The provision for the reduction of the stillbirth-rate and of infant mortality and for the healthy development of the child;

(b) The improvement of all aspects of environmental and industrial hygiene;

(c) The prevention, treatment and control of epidemic, endemic, occupational and other diseases;

(d) The creation of conditions which would assure to all medical service and medical attention in the event of sickness.[96]

In 1985, the United Nations Economic and Social Committee (ECOSOC) "created the CESCR [Committee on Economic, Social and Cultural Rights] as a subsidiary organ to undertake its review of reports on the measures which [state parties] have adopted and the progress made in achieving the observance of the rights recognized [in the *ICESCR*]."[97] The need for monitoring has arisen because although the *ICESCR* contains specific substantive rights (unlike the *International Covenant on Civil and Political Rights [ICCPR]*, which uses language such as "everyone has the right to" or "no one shall be"), it employs much weaker utterances.[98]

Much has been written about the stronger presence of the *ICCPR* in comparison to the *ICESCR* and the consequent need for monitoring on the part a special commission or other UN organ. The World Health Organization, for example, monitors the responses of all signatories to the *Convention on the Rights of the Child* and sends observers to various locations to judge each country's progress firsthand.[99]

The *ICESCR* limits the obligation of state parties "to the maximum of its available resources" and states that the obligation "is one of progressive realization."[100] However, because progressive realization is an open-ended concept, the binding obligations supported by this covenant appear to be substantially weaker than those supported by the *ICCPR*. Nevertheless, the CESCR has produced a series of general comments on the progressive implementation of its goals.[101] General Comment No. 14 lists all positive and negative aspects of the right to health within a "tripartite framework through which states must respect, protect, respect and fulfil the right to health."[102] Benjamin Meier writes:

> Under a state obligation to "respect" the right to health, a state must now interfere with the negative rights necessary to realize health. Looking beyond the state and its agents, the obligation to "protect" the right to health requires a state to ensure that others, including non-state actors, do not violate this right; lastly, the obligation to "fulfill" the right to health mandates that a state must take positive measures to ensure the full enjoyment of the right to health.[103]

General Comment No. 14, in its analysis of the normative content of Article 12, explains that the "right to be healthy" is not the meaning of the right to health: the latter is intended to encompass "determinants of health" beyond vaccines and basic medications to fight infectious diseases.[104] Meier contrasts public health with medicine, which is also discussed in General Comment No. 14: "The term 'public health' refers generally to the obligations of the government to fulfill the collective rights of its peoples to 'conditions in which people can be healthy.' Whereas medicine focuses primarily on individual curative treatment in clinical settings, public health – a form of social medicine – protects and promotes the health of entire societies."[105]

Dealing as it does with society and communities, public health requires regulations and legal instruments to implement the collective rights it supports. States are therefore charged with the implementation and regulation of public health. But not all public health models lend themselves equally well to the facilitation of the protection of citizens. Benjamin Meier traces the history of public health through three periods. The microbial model of public health, which prevailed until after the Second World War, eventually gave way to the behavioural mode of disease, which lasted until the early 1990s. Finally, the rise of the ecological model has led researchers to examine the underlying structural determinants of health.[106] The microbial model, for instance, with its emphasis on objective conditions, lends itself far better to government controls than, say, the behavioural model, in which suggestions or regulations originating from a government office may well conflict with individual freedoms, as has happened for a long time with tobacco regulations.

Recently, a number of scholars, including Anthony McMichael, Jonathan Patz, and Mervyn and Ezra Susser, have placed emphasis on the phrase *environmental conditions* because air, climate, water, and food are all under attack by globalization and climate change.[107] In the final analysis, environmental conditions and even a healthy environment should be taken into consideration and even coupled with human rights. Yet the vagueness of both expressions remains: what is a healthy environment? Is it a sustainable one? An environment that simply produces well for the present is not enough, unless strict conditions are put in place for the protection of areas of integrity of a sufficient size to support long-term health.

In General Comment No. 14, Article 12.2(b), "The right to healthy natural and workplace environments" is discussed under para. 15, and the article mentions "the prevention and reduction of the population's exposure to harmful substances such as radiation and harmful chemicals or other detrimental conditions that directly or indirectly impact upon human health." In addition, even under "industrial hygiene," the comment only calls for "the minimization, so far as is reasonably possible, of the causes of health hazards inherent in the working environment." There is no attempt to define the meaning of "reasonably practicable," or to explore why any hazard in the work place should be considered to be "reasonable" at all. Para. 16 in the same document addresses the details of Article 12.2(c), "the right to prevention, treatment and control of diseases," but environmental safety, as a "social determinant of good health," is the only environmental reference. Thus, even in a document devoted entirely to substantive issues regarding the implementation of the *ICESCR*, the question of the ecological conditions of the environment is not discussed as a separate issue. Gender issues and HIV/AIDS receive far more attention than what may constitute an impermissible alteration of local ecologies.

Para. 27 on indigenous peoples comes closest to this goal, for it states: "the vital medicinal plants, animals and minerals necessary to the full enjoyment of health of indigenous peoples should also be protected." Furthermore, it adds that "the Committee considers that development-related activities that lead to the displacement of indigenous peoples against their will from their traditional territories and environment, denying them their sources of nutrition and breaking their symbiotic relationship with their lands, has a deleterious effect on their health." This statement is a significant understatement, for it belittles what amounts to an ongoing crime against humanity.[108] Indigenous communities severed from their territories and traditions cannot, for the most part, survive as peoples. In addition, although attacks on indigenous and local communities are the most obvious and visible examples of the globalized development leading to what I term ecocrimes, para. 27 does not go beyond the obvious.[109] Although affluence and dwelling in more developed towns and cities may serve to insulate people in general from the effects of ecological disintegrity, environmental disasters may destroy even that precarious balance, as we saw, for instance, in the aftermath of Hurricane Katrina, which has had a legacy of internally displaced persons and all the health hazards that the condition entails.[110]

Yet the gravest health problems and their corresponding human rights breaches arise from conflicts over resources or, if we seek out the original cause, from disintegrity, biotic impoverishment, and other consequences of negligent use.[111] Essentially, we continue to deplete the biotic diversity and the ecosystemic processes of areas and regions at our own peril. As well, the fact that those who destroy or gravely affect natural systems and those who bear the brunt of the destruction belong to different groups of peoples makes this an increasingly foundational issue of justice and human rights.[112]

The Real Meaning of the Right to Health

It has been shown that external agents have as great an influence on the frequency of illness as on its fatality; the obvious corollary is that man has as much power to prevent as to cure disease ... Yet medical men, the guardians of public health, never have their attention called to the prevention of sickness; it forms no part of their education ... The public does not seek the shield of medical art ... till the arrows of death already rankle in the veins.

– William Farr, *Vital Statistics*

Perhaps, as Lawrence Gostin notes, a "vibrant conception of the common" is the most important aspect of public health.[113] But the meaning of *common good* is not obvious, although health is indeed an overarching collective right. When William Farr wrote, it was already known that prevention was not at the forefront of the concerns of society or state governments. If, as Gostin argues, the physical protection of citizens is the first concern of any government, then health care should be extended beyond all other services expected from democratic governments, and it should start with preventing exposure to elements that are widely known in the twenty-first century to harm health and cause morbidity and early fatality.

If we consider the progression of the focus of public health – from infectious to communicable to noncommunicable diseases – it is clear that even the poorest countries are now facing the "epidemiological transition from infectious to non-communicable diseases."[114] In earlier times, infectious diseases were the main concern of public health. But, just as many infectious diseases appeared to have been conquered, others returned again.[115] Gostin writes: "Disease amplifiers are principally man-made and therefore controllable. Human beings congregate and travel, live in close proximity to animals, pollute the environment and rely on an overtaxed health system. This constant cycle of congregation, consumption, and movement allows infectious diseases to mutate and spread across populations and boundaries."[116] Although Gostin explains that "ecosystem degradation has multiple health effects" and notes the consequences of human-animal interchange, particularly the "overuse and inappropriate use of pharmaceuticals" by animal agriculture, he does not go far enough.[117] As Chapter 2 shows, industrial beef and pig farms are extremely hazardous. From the drug overuse cited by Gostin, to overcrowded conditions, to unsafe butchering and distribution, to the effects of untreated animal manure, the operations need to be radically overhauled or eliminated.[118]

When the collective rights of all citizens are considered first (as they clearly are, or should be, in public health law), and when the responsibilities and obligations of governments are taken seriously, then it seems clear that the protection of the health of all should start *before* persons become ill and health care is required. Gostin writes:

> Yet, just as infectious diseases move and change, so do the NCDs [noncommunicable diseases]. The global rise in NCDs reflects significant transformations in diet habits, physical activity levels, and

tobacco use worldwide. The process of industrialization, urbaniza-
tion, economic development, and increasing food market globalization has led to harmonization of behavior. What was once culturally
attractive primarily in industrialized countries has gained popularity
all over the world.[119]

Although many of these factors leading to ill health represent deliberate
(though often manipulated) individual choices, the major determinants lie
beyond such choices, for they depend on the interface between state governance and multinationals corporations' choices for development.

An article titled "Health Systems and the Right to Health," published in
The Lancet in 2008, presents the argument that the *Universal Declaration of
Human Rights* of 1948 "laid the foundations for the right to the highest attainable standards of Health" and concludes that "right-to-health features
are not just good management, justice, or humanitarianism, they are obligations under human rights law."[120] Gostin also cites the International Sanitary
Regulations, adopted by the member states of the World Health Organization
(pursuant to the WHO's powers under Article 21). These regulations were
renamed the International Health Regulations in 1969, and they were fundamentally revised to include many global pandemics, such as HIV/AIDS,
SARS, avian flu, the Marburg virus, and even bioterrorism, in 2005.[121] Article
1 of the regulations defines a public health risk as "an event that may adversely
affect the health of human populations, with emphasis on one which may
spread internationally or may present a serious and direct danger."[122] However,
it is not simply infectious diseases that fit well within this definition: risks
can also include events and practices that may affect the health of human
populations or present "a serious and direct danger." Hazardous pollution,
climate change, and industrial activities – including those aimed at development, particularly extractive and mining operations – all fit within this
definition. The public health effects that follow these developments and
activities have been documented with solid and abundant evidence by the
World Health Organization, the European Environmental Agency, and scientists too numerous to name. These activities or practices and their effects
should therefore fall under the heading of "evident and clear threats to public
health," and it should be part of the responsibility of states to oversee, correct,
mitigate, or even eliminate them.

If we accept the claims advanced by *The Lancet* article and Gostin's
work in general, then the right to health appears to be a collective right par

excellence, or the clearest example of a collective right that no one can refuse to consider as primary and basic. The right is not only to health care *after* exposure to various chemicals, a degraded and unproductive environment, anthropogenically produced climate change, desertification, and famine but also to normal human development *prior to* being exposed to harmful situations.

For a number of reasons, it is unfortunate that neither legal scholars nor experts in public health have clearly declared the obligation of states and other nonstate actors to work toward public health through prevention. First, preventive measures will significantly reduce and even eliminate the suffering of millions who either have not chosen the source of their health problems (such as cigarette smoking, which is chosen, at the start) or have not consented to the situations that engender those problems. Second, it is far more equitable to reduce or prohibit altogether the activities that cause the harm than it is to attempt to redress the harms once they have occurred. Third, many of the harms, after they have been imposed on a population, are incompensable: abnormal births or children who acquire grave diseases, both mental and physical, are clear examples.[123] Fourth, the cost of prevention to states and other responsible bodies is a fraction of the costs associated with attempting to redress harms to public health after they have occurred. In many cases, states themselves have either supported or helped to promote the harms (e.g., by licensing unsafe operations, by not signing conventions intended to curb industrial harm, or by accepting support from corporations producing unsafe conditions). For example, one can compare the cost to states of prohibiting unsanitary conditions in so-called animal agriculture and legislating that, like human waste, waste originating from these industrial operations no longer represents an "agricultural exception" but *must* be treated like human waste before being released into the environment to the cost of the ongoing H1N1 or swine flu epidemic.[124] There is no doubt that states would lose substantial support from the food industry, as they did once they stopped supporting tobacco smoking, but the increased cost of meat everywhere that would result, would also ensure less consumption and, therefore, help to redress environmental harms and discourage the overconsumption of unhealthy products that cause obesity and plethora of other diseases, from diabetes to heart disease to cancer.

The right to health represents a prime example of a collective human right that should not to be weighed and balanced against the preferences, economic or other, of natural and legal individuals and aggregates. The human right to life and survival is a basic collective right, perhaps the first of all such rights. The next chapter considers how some of these basic collective rights fare in the courts, especially, but not exclusively, in international law. But even if it is the case that these collective rights remain in the realm of *lex ferenda* (future law), it is necessary to discuss, defend, and promote them today.

5
Globalization, Democracy,
and Collective Rights

> The whole congregation of the children of Israel complained
> against Moses and Aaron in the wilderness. The children of Israel
> said to them, "If we only had died by the hand of the Lord in the
> Land of Egypt, when we sat by the fleshpots and ate our fill of
> bread. For you have brought us into the wilderness to kill the
> whole assembly with hunger.
>
> – Exod. 16:2-4

Aside from what Moses and God himself thought of the requests of the
Children of Israel, this passage seems to express, in a nutshell, the argument
of this book in simple words. The statement can be divided into three separate but connected arguments. First, hunger is the first human consideration,
the most basic need of all people. Second, ensuring the survival of the people
they command and lead is the first responsibility of leaders. Third, these basic
rights and responsibilities precede, for all people, the civil and political rights
to which they may be entitled.

In other words, contrary to the argument of Amartya Sen, and following
Bhupinder Chimni, freedom is *not* the first requirement of impoverished,
starving people in the Third World in their quest for so-called development
(see Chapter 4). The Hebrews professed to prefer slavery itself to the hunger
that accompanied the liberation they enjoyed with Moses. And their request
for food was judged to be acceptable. God himself, through Moses, informed
the people that their (just) request would be met that food would be given
to them, just enough to satisfy their hunger. It is also worthy of note that
those responsible for the welfare of the Hebrews, a responsibility arising from
their status as leaders, accepted that the very boon they had bestowed upon
these peoples, that of freedom from slavery, was not sufficient to remove
their *primary* obligation to provide for their people's survival.

In biblical times, the situation was much simpler than it is today. Whoever was the leader – the chief of a city, region, or group – was responsible for the welfare of the citizens of his community. Today, responsibility for the citizens of a given area or nation has given way to a diffuse responsibility for the human rights of all those affected by the decisions of all countries' leaders. In fact, *erga omnes* obligations entail that every leader can be held responsible for any and all human rights breaches anywhere, for those involving their own citizens and for those involving the citizens of other nations (at least in principle), provided that the harmful practices originated in their state.

In other words, leaders' responsibilities haves increased exponentially, as has the potential for harm associated with numerous human activities.[1] In contrast, at the time of Moses, communities could object democratically to a ruler's decision and except almost immediate results and redress for their plight. Today, however, those who are deprived of necessities or otherwise oppressed in democratic countries, and those who readily and noisily defend and proclaim their rights through marches and protests, only succeed in bringing some of the worst issues to the attention of the media. So far, no ruler or government has responded immediately to redress human rights violations reported so clearly and quickly shown on television or other media outlets. We know about the outrageous situation in the occupied Palestinian territories through the UN's reports.[2] We are regularly informed about the effects of climate change on island communities, indigenous and local communities, and the people of the Arctic. We see images of hundreds of thousands of refugees in the Democratic Republic of Congo, Sudan, and elsewhere. We see their abysmal living conditions, their hunger, and their lack of water, medicine, and human dignity.[3]

Yet our international legal institutions appear to be unable or unwilling to respond to the many human rights crises that develop almost daily, and these crises show no sign of decreasing, let alone of disappearing. This factual reality raises another issue, also present in Sen's discussion of development: the problem of democracy in two senses, that is, as it is now, according to Sen and others, and as it should or could be.

State Obligations and Democracy: The Interface

Last, but not least, Sen stresses the importance of democracy to the realization of the goal of development as freedom. "Developing and strengthening a democratic system is an essential component of the process of development." The significance of democracy, he stresses, is what he calls "three distinct virtues:" (1) its intrinsic importance, (2) its instrumental contributions, and (3) its constructive role in the creation of values and norms.

> – Bhupinder Chimni, "The Sen Conception of
> Development and Contemporary International
> Law Discourse"

The first of Chimni's three virtues of democracy, its intrinsic importance, can be accepted without argument. The second and third virtues, however, need qualification and elaboration, if not outright rejection, if we consider democracy *as it is today*, rather than as it was (in antiquity, for instance) or as it could be and should be in the future.[4] I argue that the meaning and role of democracy was severely criticized by both Plato and Aristotle and that the institution has not developed in ways that address and respond to those critiques today.[5]

Democracy, in today's institutions, is based on procedural, not substantive moral principles. In most Western countries, democracy is allied with power and nationalism, and it does not support universalism. Democracy is intended to give an equal voice to all citizens; however, the citizens of two conflicting countries cannot resolve their dispute by democratic means, for the democratic rule stops at the borders. An equal voice for all exists neither in international law, where wealthy states buy or coerce compliance from weaker, poorer states, nor in domestic law, where wealthy and powerful cliques prevail even when large numbers of protesting people voice their objections. Finally, as even Moses noted, democratic governance cannot take the place of or supersede governance that respects *all* human rights, starting with the right to life (survival).

To be fair, I could also list democracy's best historical traditions and the many reasons why it gained its high profile to show that it could, again, be a shining beacon. As Ron Engel notes, "democracy denotes a complex tradition of human thought, action and experience."[6] Debates and conflicts are, therefore, to be expected. In fact, the expression of disagreement, even of strongly voiced opinion, is an important aspect of democracy; however, it is not enough if the redress of grievances does not follow. Engel proposes separating "thin" from "thick" interpretations of democracy or, better yet, the democratic ideal. He embraces the latter because thick interpretations cherish the traditions from antiquity on and the ideal they embody. In contrast, thin democracy (a product of post-Westphalian politics) is also known as procedural democracy, liberal democracy, or the democratic process: it embodies and emphasizes civil and political rights, culminating in so-called free elections. The thick interpretation of democracy has a long tradition of mutual respect and aid, starting with the tradition of natural law, which originated with the Greeks, and continuing through the Stoics, Grotius, and even Kant to finally flourish (in American thought) in the ideas of Jefferson, Lincoln, and Martin Luther King Jr.[7]

Engel's argument is convincing as long as he speaks of democracy as an idea, as a metanarrative that is, essentially, a work in progress.[8] My debate is not with the ideas that thick democracy incorporates, and even less with the traditions from which Engel argues it has developed. Nor is the present work an appropriate locus for such a debate or for a thorough examination democracy's potential as a force for human good. But I will reiterate that democracy's present "thin" instantiations do not merit the honour they receive and will not until the problems to which they are prey are brought to light and corrected.

The relevance of current instantiations of democracy to my argument are evident in a few examples, beginning with the recent practice of using renditions to apprehend and transport so-called terrorists for the purpose of torture and interrogations. This practice is particularly challenging because democratic states use the concept of collective rights to explain, defend, and sanction immoral actions and practices. A second example is the plight of the peoples of Chagos, removed illegally from their island by two great democracies.[9] Finally, the aggressive, illegal practices of the democratic state of Israel against Palestine show no consideration for international law, the decisions and pronouncements of the UN, or overwhelming global condemnation.

KHALED EL-MASRI AND THE CASE OF EXTRAORDINARY RENDITION

The right to truth about gross human rights violations and serious violations of human rights law is an inalienable and autonomous right, linked to the duty and obligation of the State to protect and guarantee human rights, to conduct effective investigations and to guarantee effective remedy and reparation. This right is closely linked with other rights and has both an individual and social

dimension and should be considered as a non-derogable right
and not to be subject to limitations.

– UN, Commission on Human Rights, *Study on the
Right to the Truth*

In Chapter 1, while trying to define collective rights in contrast to individual
rights, I note that the approach was bound to be viewed as suspect, given that
the concept of collective rights has been used recently to deny not only the
civil and political rights of individuals but also their right to life. Of course,
all domestic legal systems include the protection of state secrets but, most of
all, they include the invocation to collective interests, such as national security
and the public order.[10]

In 2006, the UN's Human Rights Committee expressed concern because
the United States, contrary to Article 7 of the *International Covenant on Civil
and Political Rights,* had invoked the "state secrets" principle to forbid access
to information regarding a case about torture, or cruel, inhumane, and degrading treatment:

> The Committee is moreover concerned by numerous well-publicized
> and documented allegations that persons sent to third world coun-
> tries in this way were indeed detained and interrogated while re-
> ceiving treatment grossly violating the prohibition contained in
> Article 7, allegations that the State party did not contest. Its concern
> is deepened by the so far successful invocation of state secrecy in
> cases where the victims of these practices have sought a remedy
> before the state party's courts.[11]

A case in point is that of Khaled El-Masri, a German citizen who became
involved in a web of extraordinary renditions, a clear example of the extreme
injustice that may follow the invocation of state secrecy.[12] The states involved
"managed to combine torture, forced disappearances, denial of justice and
other violations" in their treatment of El-Masri.[13]

The whole sequence of events in the case stemmed from the assumption
that even though it is forbidden to inflict torture within the territory of one
state, it is allowable to do so if the foreigner is tortured in another country. The
first state could then eventually make use of the information or confessions

obtained.[14] All states are involved in this torture circuit, that is, the state who captures but also the state that permits its territory or its airplanes to be so used, as well as the state that received and tortures the man.[15] The program was set up after September 11 by the CIA, and it reflects the greatly enhanced powers of the CIA.

El-Masri was captured in Macedonia on 31 December 2003 and was transported by US agents to Afghanistan, where he was tortured and kept prisoner until 28 May 2004. He had no access to a lawyer, an official of his country, or family members. He was then taken to Albania and then to Germany, where he was freed.[16] His "testimony" was not important to any country's security. According to the European rapporteur,

> The story of El-Masri is the dramatic story of a person who is evidently innocent – or at least against whom not the slightest accusation could ever be made – who has been through a real nightmare in the CIA's "spider web," merely because a supposed friendship with a person suspect at some point in time to maintain contact with terrorist groups. El-Masri is still waiting for the truth to be established, and for an excuse. His application to a court in the United States has been rejected, at least in the first instance; not because it seemed unfounded, but because the government brought to bear so-called "national security" and "state secrecy" interests. This speaks for itself.[17]

The terms *national security* and *state secrecy* are intended to convey collective rights of such grave import that (apparently, more than all individual human rights established in law – for instance, the *Convention against Torture*) they do not allow any derogation from its mandates for any reason.[18] The *Convention against Torture* and the *International Covenant on Civil and Political Rights* include the right to life and the right to humane treatment and other related rights. The right to "judicial guarantees essential for the protection of moral rights," guaranteed in the *American Convention on Human Rights*, is particularly relevant.[19]

The question I propose is a grave one. If states that are the main subjects of international law, as well as the ostensible bastion of human rights protection, use the concept of collective rights in contrast with individual human rights and in conflict with any notion of human dignity, how can their interpretation of the concept be avoided?

Extraordinary Renditions and the Implications of the CIA's Long-Term Detainees

> When territories wanted for violations of U.S. law are at large
> overseas, their return for persecution shall be a matter of the
> highest priority ... If we do not receive adequate cooperation from
> a state that harbors a terrorist whose extradition we are seeking,
> we shall take appropriate measures to induce cooperation. Return
> of suspects by force may be effected without the cooperation of
> the host government.
>
> – Bill Clinton, Presidential Decision Directive
> NSC-39, U.S. Policy on Counterterrorism,
> 21 June 1995

When President Clinton presented this directive in June 1995, he spoke of suspects, the term employed to describe not only persons against whom there is evidence of criminal activity but also persons who have not been formally charged and convicted after a trial. A suspect is quite distinct from someone who has vague, unproven connections to terrorist activities. The decision directive was originally intended for the FBI, an agency that would not have had the capacity to deal successfully with local intelligence agencies, whose cooperation would have depended on relevant treaties regarding extradition.[20]

When the CIA took over this mandate, its actions were governed entirely by immediate political convenience to achieve "prevention."[21] It eschewed the directive's instructions to collaborate with foreign counterparts and to employ the related instruments of international law, many of which had been ratified by the United States.[22] Renditions therefore remain outside the ambit of legal procedures, both those based on international law and those based on domestic criminal process.[23]

In 2001, Condoleezza Rice spoke of the need for adaptation to ongoing terrorist threats and added that "renditions save lives," a clear appeal to US citizens' collective right to protection and the government's responsibility in that regard.[24] This further extension of the presidential directive was based on another classified directive signed by George W. Bush on 17 September 2001.[25] This memorandum of notification "allows the CIA to render terrorists without governmental approval and establishes measures restraining individual freedoms, without due process of law (i.e., a formal indictment)."[26]

The extraordinary rendition program allows, and in fact encourages, illegal and often violent seizure and ensures the transfer of individuals to countries where torture is practised and legal. The "results" of interrogations and torture are then returned to the CIA as the "product" of the circuit. Matteo Winkler outlines three problems with this sequence. First, the possible application of the *male captus bene detentus* rule (the rule that states that an inappropriate capture of a suspect still allows for a legitimate trial to follow) is unclear, and some courts have rejected it outright. Second, the male captus rule applies to criminal trials, not to the interrogation of a possible suspect. Third, forced abduction is illegal, especially when a country's intelligences services are not competent to allow for such a disregard of their country's sovereignty.[27] Finally, even the issue of the legality of capturing suspects is a minor concern given the "very absolute" ban of torture in law: "Torture is unquestionably illegal under international law. Indeed, its prohibition is provided by a norm of *jus cogens*, making it non-derogable and unjustifiable under all circumstances."[28]

The El-Masri case is but one (and not the worst) rendition case. Abu Omar was abducted from Italy in 2003 and brutally tortured by Egyptians. He suffered electric shocks to his genitals and excruciatingly loud music, which rendered him incontinent and partially deaf.[29] Other cases include that of Jamil Qasim Saeed Mohammed, a Yemeni citizen abducted in 2001, and that of Mamdouh Habib, who was taken from Pakistan to Egypt in the same year.[30]

THE CANADIAN POSITION: MAHER ARAR AND STATE INTERESTS

On Sept. 26, U.S. authorities arrested Mahar Arar on a routine stopover in New York while he was waiting for a connecting flight home to Canada. Arar was born in Syria, but he lived in Canada for more than twenty years and was a Canadian citizen.

– Mario Silva, "Extraordinary Rendition"

Maher Arar was detained because he had listed Abdullah Almaki, another Canadian citizen suspected of terrorist activities, as an emergency contact on a rental application. He was denied legal advice and a telephone call. After the Canadian counsel assured him he would be returned to Canada, he agreed and signed a document to that effect. Despite that assurance, Arar was sent to Jordan instead, where he was beaten and interrogated before being sent to Syria and then to Afghanistan. At that point, he "confessed to having links to terrorism" in the hope of avoiding further torture.[31]

In 2003, Arar was released to the Canadian embassy. He had yet to be charged with any crime, either in the United States or in Canada. Canada's government "established a Commission of Inquiry to investigate and report on the actions of Canadian officials in relation to Maher Arar," in February 2008.[32] The work of the commission suggested that those who had provided the information on Arar to their US counterparts had been wilfully blind to what would follow and, correspondingly, equally linked to Canadian obligation under the *Convention against Torture*.[33] Arar brought action against the United States under the *Torture Victims Protection Act* (1991, ratified in 1992), but the case was dismissed because of "national security" considerations.[34]

This is the main point at issue: if and when *universally* agreed upon human rights (in our sense of rights of the collectivity of humankind) are set aside and viewed as secondary because of considerations related to collective national interests, the national interests given as primary are those of a specific community instead.[35] National security is indeed a right of citizens, but the universal rights that are contravened through the practice of extraordinary renditions – that is, renditions to torture, rather than to justice, as was originally intended by President Clinton – is not acceptable either in law or morality.

Forced Relocations, War Crimes, and Genocide: *Bancoult v. McNamara*, the Diego Garcia Case

> The plaintiffs in this case are persons indigenous to Chagos their survivors or direct descendants ... they bring this action against the United States and various current and former officials of State and the Department of Defence ("the individual defendants") for forced relocation, torture, racial discrimination, cruel, inhuman and degrading treatment, genocide, intentional infliction of emotional distress, negligence and trespass.
>
> – *Bancoult v. McNamara* (2003)

Although the Chagos Archipelago comprises fifty-two islands administered by the British government, it is leased to the United States, and the United States is responsible for the islands under the *British Indian Ocean Territory Agreement*. In the late 1960s and early 1970s, the entire Chagos population was moved to Mauritius and Seychelles to allow a US military facility to settle in their space. The original inhabitants were not allowed to return and were offered no compensation to help ease their transition into a new environment and the loss of their homes.[36]

Those who had not left voluntarily were forced onto "overcrowded ships for Peros Banhos and Salonen, from whence they eventually were taken to Mauritius and Seychelles."[37] The US Congress went ahead with the construction of a military basis on Diego Garcia Island, despite hearings in which multiple human rights violations were detailed, ranging from a failure to provide relocation assistance, to harsh removal conditions that cause injuries to the survivors, including miscarriages, to eventual living conditions that still include poverty, unemployment, and other deprivations.[38]

Before the judgment proper in *Bancoult v. McNamara* was decided, the individual defendants all claimed that they had been obeying their superiors' orders, based on "the statutory immunity granted to the Federal Officers under the Federal Employee Liability Reform and Tort Compensation Act."[39] The gravity of the effects of the forced removal, however, bring to mind the Nuremberg Principles, international law's denial of such claims of immunity. If the individual defendants were eliminated from the action (justly or unjustly), the United States would be the sole defendant. However, all those who knowingly perpetrated the actions against the Chagossians violated the tenets of international law: Pursuant to the *Alien Tort Claims Act*, 28 U.S.C., section 1350, "the district courts shall have original jurisdiction of any civil action by an alien for a tort only committed in violation of the law of nations or Treaty of the United States."

The plaintiff's claims were also disputed on the grounds that "they had failed to exhaust their administrative remedies." The Chagossians, however, were not allowed to return to their home base, now a US military basis, nor to the other islands, where the United Kingdom was not likely to offer an impartial forum after having entered into an agreement with the United States that had led to the very actions in question.

Another issue was the judicial expertise of the court, as it was required to pass judgment on US policy:

> Neither our federal law nor customary international law provide standards by which the court can measure and balance the foreign policy considerations at play in this case such as the containment of the Soviet Union in the Indian Ocean thirty years ago, and today the support of military operation in the Middle East. The court

concludes that it is ill-equipped to review the conduct of the military operation challenged in this case, because they implicate foreign policy and national security concerns.[40]

Essentially, if the US government's political branches had made a decision thirty years earlier, the court was not prepared to second-guess that decision.[41] Of course, even if the court was not prepared to question either the decision of the US government at the time or its rationale, the *way* those decisions were carried remains untouched by this argument. Even if a country's political or other decisions cannot be judged under the *Alien Tort Claims Act*, "Article 2(3) of the Torture Convention explicitly states that 'An order from a superior official or public authority may not be invoked as a justification for torture.'"[42] Torture is forbidden by *jus cogens* norms, and so is genocide; therefore appealing to this article is inappropriate.

This point was also made clearly in the *Filártiga v. Peña Irala* case.[43] The US Supreme Court recognized that the law of nations "may be ascertained by consulting the work of jurists writing professedly on public law; or by the general usage and practice of nations, or by the judicial decisions recognizing and enforcing the law."[44]

Nevertheless, it must be acknowledged that "unlike the criminal remedy, there is no treaty that clearly obliges or even authorizes courts to take jurisdiction over civil actions respecting torture committed abroad with the exception of the US; there is no domestic legislation in any other country that expressly grants courts jurisdiction with respect to these matters."[45] Because the *Alien Tort Claims Act* permits individual citizens to sue for torture and other such injuries, without the far more complicated requirements of initiating a criminal action in the International Court of Justice or International Criminal Court, this avenue is preferred by claimants in various venues: "While it is premised on the principle that victims of torture much be compensated, its true role in many cases is admittedly symbolic: the third country tort remedy provides recognition for, and emotional vindication of, the victims of torture and places moral and political pressure on rights abusing governments."[46]

FURTHER REFLECTIONS ON A BRITISH-AMERICAN LEGAL BLACK HOLE

While geophysical extension to a state's dependent territories is indeed discretionary under article 56 of the European Convention, that position has sarcastically been described as "the human rights black hole doctrine," given that, by the same token, the UK now treats the Geneva Conventions III and IV of 1949, the Human Rights Covenants of 1966, the UN Convention Against Torture of 1984, and the Statute of the International Criminal Court of 1998 as inapplicable to BIOT [British Indian Ocean Treaty].

> – Peter Sand, "Diego Garcia: British American Legal
> Black Hole in the Indian Ocean?"[47]

Peter Sand's work connects, at least conceptually, the Diego Garcia case (*Bancoult v. McNamara*) to other current black hole situations, which include the ongoing Guantánamo Bay legal "no man's land" and renditions. In all cases, the total disregard for collective human rights and for previously agreed upon legal infrastructures originates explicitly with the doctrine of the primacy of national security. The latter is clearly placed above any other principles and legal instruments, even above generally accepted jus cogens norms.

A further connection can be found in CIA rendition flights, by which prisoners were detained and interrogated on ships anchored in the Diego Garcia lagoon, "hence in British internal waters rather than on land."[48] Apparently, rather than attempting to justify the legal breaches, the United Kingdom, like the United States, decided to simply distance itself from the situation by relying on technicalities and by insisting on national security and on state secrecy doctrines, weak as they are, both logically and legally.

The denial of human rights in *Bancoult v. McNamara* is a denial of both individual rights and the rights of a community. Sand cites several legal instruments that were ignored or bypassed to further state aims. Yet he does not cite the *International Convention on the Elimination of All Forms of Racial Discrimination*, although such disregard for all rights of a community could only be based on (or at least fostered by) the belief that the occupying countries had a right to exercise their power without respect for the dignity of human beings not the citizens of those countries.

When this aspect of the harm suffered by the Chagossians is added to the others, it is clear that universal human rights were ignored from the start. A further problem emerges when the basic collective rights of all are considered, this time from the standpoint of yet another legal black hole, that of the international environmental laws that were transgressed.[49] Although the British Indian Ocean Territory Conservation Policy Statement of October 1997 was committed to treating the whole archipelago "in accordance with the 1972 World Heritage Convention," as it was named part of a natural

heritage site, this commitment was still "subject only to defense requirements."[50] Hence, once again, the particular meaning of a country's self-
defence was central, although no one from Chagos had attacked either the
United States or the United Kingdom, justifying the forced removal of the
island's whole population.

But military necessity precluded treating Diego Garcia as a protected area;
in fact, it permitted the introduction of a number of grave threats to the island's environment, including illegal fishing by Sri Lankan shark-fin poach-
ers"; mining coral as an "aggregate material for airfield construction"; and
the introduction of alien plant species and other activities, such as fuel spills,
that pose serious threats to marine life.[51] Basic collective rights are at stake,
as ecological degradation is a threat to us all. Of course, the harm arising
from biotic impoverishment and environmental disintegrity is neither immediate nor visible, but it is grave.

THE END OF THE STORY: *R (ON THE APPLICATION OF BANCOULT) V. SECRETARY OF STATE FOR FOREIGN AND COMMONWEALTH AFFAIRS*

> On 3 November, 2000 the Divisional Court (Laws LJ and Gibbs J)
> gave judgment in favour of Mr. Bancoult. They decided that a
> power to legislate for the "peace, order and good government" of
> the territory did not include a power to expel all the inhabitants.
>
> – *R (On the Application of Bancoult) v. Secretary of State
> for Foreign and Commonwealth Affairs*[52]

Beyond the *Alien Tort Claims Act* trials, Bancoult and other Chagossians also
attempted to find justice from the other super power involved in the case:
the United Kingdom. In his judgment of the case, *R (On the Application of
Bancoult) v. Secretary of State for Foreign and Commonwealth Affairs*, Lord
Hoffman described the original lifestyle of the inhabitants of Chagos as one
of working for the "Company" (Chagos Agalegal Company Ltd.), tending
coconut trees and producing copra and keeping gardens, chickens, and pigs
to provision the company and provide for its workers. Despite their lack of
education and their simple lifestyles, they had "a rich community life, the
Roman Catholic religion and their own dialect, derived from the French."[53]

In this case, the main points of contention for the Chagossians were
based on their history of interaction with the United Kingdom:

1   The British Indian Ocean Territories Order had made the Chagos Archipelago a separate colony.[54] The order had also appointed a commissioner for territories who had the power to "make laws for the peace, order and good government of the territory." Therefore, the inhabitants retained British citizenship.[55]

2   In 1966, the British government had corresponded with the government of the United States. The result was to grant a lease of at least fifty years to the latter, to establish a base on Diego Garcia, and to occupy other islands as required. In 1967, the UK government bought out the company, which was only allowed to run the coconut plantations until July 1971, when the United States required vacant possession. This request prompted the commissioner to make the Immigration Ordinance of 1971, section 4(1) of which provided that only a special permit would allow the former inhabitants to re-enter the territory.

3   From 1968 to 1971, the UK government removed the whole population to Mauritius and Seychelles. No force was used, but officials stated that the company was ceasing its operations and that no more supplies would be available to Chagossians.[56]

4   The whole operation had showed a "callous disregard for their interests," and the members of the community had been left to fend for themselves in the "slums of Port Louis." The ordinance denying them the right to return had been prompted by US concerns about nonaligned countries objecting to the construction of a military base in the Indian Ocean.[57] (In more recent times, objections could be raised about renditions flying into the base or taking place, with torture episodes, in ships anchored just beyond Chagos. The miserable conditions of the Chagossians in Mauritius, their poverty and unemployment, prompted negotiations between Mauritius and the United Kingdom that culminated in a grant, now depleted by inflation, to 595 Chagossian families. The Chagossians sought legal advice and, with the support of Michael Vencatessen, issued a writ in the High Court in London. At trust fund of 4 million pounds sterling was eventually set up in Mauritius in exchange for abandoning all claims. The agreement was signed by most Chagossians.)

5   After the Divisional Court's judgment in favour of Bancoult on 3 November 2000 had effectively quashed section 4(1) of the Immigration Ordinance as *ultra vires*, Robin Cook, the foreign secretary, had announced a feasibility study on resettling the Chagossians in their former territory. He concluded his press release by saying, "This government has

not defended what was done or said thirty years ago. As Lord Justice Laws recognized, we made no attempt to conceal the gravity of what happened. I am pleased that he has commended the wholly admirable conduct in disclosing material to the court, and praised the openness of today's foreign office."[58] The points that remained in contention were the Chagossians' right to return and the very legality of the Constitution Order and the Immigration Order, not to mention their irrationality, for "the Orders were not made in the interest of the Chagossians, but in the interest of the United Kingdom and the United States."[59] The government's authority to remove persons of British citizenship from their chosen residence, without (at any time) providing compensation was also questioned. Lord Hoffman and the other lords recognized the impact of the law made for a colony, citing Blackstone: "But no power on earth except the authority of Parliament can send any subject of England out of the land against his will; no, not even a criminal." The Crown and its appointed commissioner, therefore, had no authority to transport anyone against their will by what, essentially, were threats of starvation to them and their families.[60] (But even the acknowledged wrong that had been done at the time did not result in a favourable judgment. The main problem was the costs and logistics of total resettlement, although the Chagossians were permitted to return for a time, to visit family graves and the like.)

Were the Chagossians ecological refugees? Perhaps not. But they were in the sense that their migration, like many others, was forced by lack of resources and economic pressures from outside, although the main causative factors were clearly political. Their case is worth studying in detail because of the different treatment they received from the US then the UK courts. The former appealed to procedural flaws in the case, while the latter tackled the factual elements of the case head-on and admitted its own fault in regard to the series of events outlined above.

Because the entire British-American agreement was based on national security concerns, the human rights of the people indigenous to the area were simply not viewed as relevant. In contrast to the nonderogability of the international instruments discussed above, the US administration did not consider the issue of human rights important enough to counsel restraint or, better yet, a change of location. And the relocation occurred long before 9/11.

In fact, although the UK courts showed a much more sensitive approach than the more recent decision of the House of Lords, the UK was a full partner from the start in the project, which could not have been planned or concluded without its full cooperation. The collective rights of self-defence and national security were pitted against the rights of the community and, given the gravity of the violations that occurred, also against both the United States' and the United Kingdom's obligations toward the international community as a whole.

State Obligations and Concrete Collective Rights

> The danger, as Donnelly points out, is that "everyone" does not mean each (every) person, but rather defers to the "average individual, an abstract collective entity." And even "he" is assured gains only in the future.
>
> – Margot Salomon, *Global Responsibility for Human Rights*[61]

This paragraph from *Global Responsibility for Human Rights* appears in a chapter devoted to development, in which Salomon emphasizes the need for human-centred globalization and growth coupled with respect for human rights. Chapter 4 of this book reveals the impossibility of achieving the latter, and I raise grave doubts about both globalization and development and their effects on human rights. Yet Margot Salomon's statement may provide the key needed to unlock a correct understanding of *collective human right*. It shows that when the term *collective human rights* is understood in a manner that supports renditions or forced removals in defence of the collective interest, it no longer corresponds to the understanding presented in this book.

The key lies in the definition of *abstract collective entity*, which is indeed the meaning attached to *collective interests* when they are invoked to protect state secrecy and national security. That is also the meaning behind the dubious benefits of *development* as a "greater supply of goods and services ... made available through growth to everyone."[62] In both cases, it is only an *abstract* collective entity that some are ostensibly seeking to protect or benefit.

But neither the specific protection nor the benefit are defined to show how development may fit the needs and requirements of the collective – that is, the real, concrete human entities, singly and jointly, that may be affected:

"Human rights law established a binary relationship between right holders and duty-bearers. It exists not only to protect people from abuse of power (initially foreseen at the hands of the state), but to secure a normative framework within which the individual is understood to have claim on the conduct of the state."[63]

Nevertheless, legal regimes are neither coherent nor coordinated with one another in regard to human rights.[64] The most glaring discrepancy is the token primacy given to human rights over trade, economic policies, and development. For instance, the Preamble to the *Marrakesh Agreement Establishing the World Trade Organization* describes "free trade as an objective of a system aimed at the fulfillment of basic human values."[65] This laudable sentiment, however, remains a nonenforceable sentence in a document that was developed as separate and distinct from all human rights instruments. It is therefore hard to expect any similarity of purpose between international laws and human rights regimes: "Human rights norms should always be taken into account when interpreting international trade and investment obligations ... trade law is basically treaty law. Its interpretation must be taken into account and be consistent with the hierarchy of norms in international law, reflecting, for instance, the status of some human rights as peremptory norms, *erga omnes*."[66] Yet, despite the rhetoric of human rights supremacy and the existence of erga omnes obligations in international law, "the WTO's powerful enforcement mechanism (and the comparatively weaker human rights mechanism) would seem to be giving international trade *de facto* supremacy."[67]

Market strategies are promoted in terms of "aggregate benefit," which is based on unsustainable growth because trade laws aimed at development most often ignore or sacrifice human rights and environmental and health protection.[68] But, for the most part, Western democracies and even developing states are quite comfortable with this approach, although no one controls or monitors the trickle-down effects intended to benefit the concrete "everyone," instead of supporting and entrenching powerful elites in developing countries and wealthy and powerful multinational corporations in the developed world.

To clarify the meaning not only of *collective rights* but also of *collective* or *national interests* – as they are appealed to in the cases discussed above and, in general, in the literature – the definition presented here must be revisited. Because many scholars use *collective rights* interchangeably with *community rights* or *community interests*, I borrow a subtitle from Will Kymlicka to once again explore the ambiguities of collective rights.[69]

The Ambiguity of Collective Rights

> We can now see why the term "collective rights" is so unhelpful as a label for various forms of group differentiated citizenship. The problem is partly that the term is too broad, and partly that it fails to distinguish internal restrictions from external protection. But a deeper problem is that it suggests a false dichotomy with individual rights.
>
> – Will Kymlicka, *Multicultural Citizenship*

Although I agree wholeheartedly with the final sentence of this paragraph, Will Kymlicka does not differentiate between group-differentiated rights, which I term *community rights,* and collective rights, properly understood. Kymlicka does, however, recognize that *collective rights* is too broad a term to be limited to the use he proposes for it. The distinction he makes between internal restrictions (understood as internal regulations within the community, based on the cultural specifics of a group) and external protection from all forms of encroachment from outside, which is the group's right, is also well taken. Provided that the basic survival rights of all are not under attack, collective rights, as I define them, do not dictate all forms of regulation among individuals or communities.

Following his understanding of the issue and of the communitarianism-individualism dichotomy, Marlies Galenkamp writes: "both the strong communitarian and the extremely individualistic approach can be argued to be too one-sided, since both tend to reify one aspect of reality at the cost of other aspects."[70] When applied to concrete realities, both are indeed limited and incomplete, for both exclude what I consider the primary but what Galenkamp defines as the "less paradigmatic forms of collective rights, such as the right to a healthy environment and the right to development."[71] But her understanding does not clearly separate communities from the collectivity. She adds, "collectivities may also be viewed as moral agents and consequently may be qualified as right bearers."[72]

Kymlicka couples indigenous and francophone communities in the Canadian context because he defends the limits of internally regulated practices (subject to the corrective influence of human rights doctrine and legal regimes), with their nearly absolute right to external protection, which for First Nations would include not only the right to their traditional territories but also to their traditional practices, such as hunting and fishing. Most of all, it would include the right to hold their territories in common against the possible encroachment of the industrial society that surrounds them.[73] Francophones would also have a similar absolute right to their culture and their language, which must be protected from external "attacks" of any sort. But neither community has the right to flout basic laws of Canada (or international laws) against aggression, murder, and the like. However, because both of these "realities" represent national or quasi-national entities, communities (or even aggregates such as their "national interests") could be used against basic collective rights, as I show in earlier discussions of situations in which such interests were elevated to the status of ultimate rights.

Galenkamp sees the right to a healthy environment, as well as the right to development, as a "kind of alleviation of the theoretical tension" between individual and community rights.[74] However, neither Kymlicka nor Galenkamp acknowledge the existence (or even the possibility) of collective basic rights that include both the individual and communitarian or group rights they discuss and are foundational to both. Kymlicka, for instance, pits individualists against collectivists, for the latter also have rights *qua community*, flowing from "the community's interests in self-preservation."[75] This understanding certainly allows us to "rethink the liberal traditions while advancing multiculturalism," as Kymlicka suggests.[76] However, it does not prevent us from using the concept of such communities or aggregates, or even nations, in the same way that previous US administrations have used the concepts of national interest or national security (and the underlying motivation of self-preservation), in direct conflict with both individual and collective basic human rights (in the sense of the right to physical integrity and survival), as well as the individual right to due process and freedom from detention and torture.

One needs, therefore, to accept rights that include but are more fundamental than community rights, the right to national survival, or the survival of one's way of life or political regime. In this sense, Republican elites of the previous US administration had no right to plan and practise extraordinary renditions in the name of national interests, and the First Nations of Alberta have no right to support and promote their prosperity, if it entails entering into trade alliances with oil corporations that are developing the highly toxic tar sands.

Not all communities are alike, and their interests, projects, and goals are equally diverse. Like individual rights, communitarian rights should be considered morally and legally neutral (hence acceptable in principle), unless they conflict with the basic rights of humankind – that is, our collective rights (see Chapters 2 and 3).

State Responsibility: Direct and Indirect

> State responsibility, simply put, is the name public international law gives to the normative state of affairs which occur following a breach by a state of one of its international legal obligations (whether that obligation derives from treaty law, customary law or other recognized sources such as "general principles of law").
>
> – Craig Scott, "Translating Torture into International Tort"

In addition to this definition of state responsibility, Craig Scott also distinguishes between direct and indirect state responsibility and describes the obligations arising under public international law as either positive or negative. This question is whether, in addition to the responsibilities and obligations Scott correctly applies to a state "following a breach of one of its international obligations," there is a more far-reaching obligation to ensure the existence of regulatory regimes and instruments that would prevent the various breaches from occurring or, at the very least, significantly reduce their impact and occurrence, at both the national and the international levels?

Scott's main focus is the role of multinational corporations in the indirect obligation of states, because, most often, activities that result in human rights breaches originate from these corporations. Perhaps most important, from this point of view, is the obligation of states to "create harmonization between international legal obligations and domestic law if the courts actively and rigorously rely on this principle of interpretation."[77] This approach supports the proactive view of the legal responsibility of states, for it ties the latter with the obligation entrenched in international law. Although public international law deals primarily with the interaction of states, after the adoption of the *Charter of the United Nations*, "public international law has increasingly begun to assign rights to individuals *qua* human beings, thereby reaching inside the governance structure of States."[78] Therefore, the regulation of legal persons within national borders remains the responsibility of states, as is the protection of the human rights of citizens, not only within the state but also outside its confines, in certain cases. When the legal entity's activities threaten the human rights of noncitizens, because of their far-reaching effects, they should remain under state control.

Perhaps the best way of understanding the complex interaction between states, natural individuals (within and without a state), and the legal individuals that transcend all borders is to view the applicable legal instruments as part of transnational law, which includes elements of both national and international law and private and public law.[79] The main concern is to recognize the primacy of human rights in law and to defend not only the rights of natural individuals but also the basic rights of the collective, given that no clearly binding instrument exists to ensure this protection today.

Because the operation of multinational corporations and, in general, trade is the major source of threats to human rights, the World Trade Organization and, more generally, the laws governing economic transactions are critical considerations. The power of the World Trade Organization is in direct conflict with the corresponding weakness of human rights enforcement. Thus, it is necessary to keep this reality in mind, although there may be an "economic dimensions of human rights."[80]

The most important point is that no right to trade deserves to be recognized.[81] Economic liberties may well be an important component of certain human rights, but they cannot simply be coupled with basic rights, be they individual or collective, aside from the related right named in Article 15 of the *International Covenant on Economic, Social and Cultural Rights*, in which the emphasis is on the individual right to one's own creative activity, not on the right to trade, let alone to profit.[82] Philip Alston also cites Article 15, then adds: "Much more importantly, any such rights arising out of WTO agreements are not and should not be considered to be analogous to human rights. Their purpose is fundamentally different. Human rights are recognized for all the basis of the inherent human dignity of all persons. Trade-related rights are granted to individuals for instrumental reasons."[83] In that case, the responsibility of states is primarily the recognition and defence of the human rights, both individual and collective, that originate from respect for the inherent human dignity of all persons. All other rights merit acknowledgment and protection only if they do not conflict with the foundational aspect of rights, as defined above. To better circumscribe and explain collective rights, the question of nationalism and national defence must be considered.

STATE RESPONSIBILITY AND NATIONAL PROTECTION: COLLECTIVE OR COMMUNITY RIGHTS?

The rhetoric of the secretariat of the United Nations creates a weak independent sense of global identity that arises from some identification with longer-range planetary concerns. The secretary general, perhaps even more than the Pope, speaks with a voice of conscience oriented toward the morality of the whole human species rather than on behalf of a particular segment.

– Richard Falk, *Human Rights and State Sovereignty*

In 1984, Richard Falk was acknowledging the difficulties involved in the United Nations' position, but his words apply equally well to the situation today. The United Nations speaks with an authoritative voice, but it can, at best, "provide a global frame for statist logic" because its own activities are limited by the will of individual states, especially that of superpowers. The global thrust to cosmopolitanism, or universality, is therefore constrained by states that belong to the United Nations and the lack of a capable monitoring and corrective infrastructure.[84] It therefore falls to a number of international nongovernmental organizations (INGOs) – such as Amnesty International, the International League for Human Rights, and others – to actively promote human rights and denounce abuses. These and other transnational actors – such as the World Council of Churches, the Third World Forum and, more recently, Greenpeace and the Earth Charter Organization – cannot impose sanctions or enforce legal instruments, but their impartial, well-informed, and passionate defence of human rights commands respect and remains influential, at least in so far as a public opinion is concerned.[85]

The inhibiting presence of statism and sovereignty presents a further obstacle when intervention is called for and, in general, impedes any possible progress these transnational organizations may produce. Therefore, the next question is, what is the impact of nationalism on human rights? I have noted its impact when powerful states equate collective human rights with national protection or security and deem all other human rights secondary. But all human rights that are protected by jus cogens norms impose an erga omnes obligation on states, and these obligations cannot be dismissed by any other appeal. But to describe the way collective interests are used by the United States and other states that collaborate with it is not to explain why the right to survival or self-defence of *any* state should be equated with the ultimate collective rights of humanity.

If the political history of the state is considered, the *polis* of Aristotle's time was the guarantor and the basis of the moral and intellectual development of all its citizens. As a social and political animal, a human being could only be properly habituated to virtue within a well-governed polis, led by a moral man.[86] However, this foundational claim is no longer valid. In comparison with Aristotle's polis, the modern liberal democratic state embodies a significant improvement as far as its procedural aspects and several individual human rights are concerned. In contrast, the very idea of morality or intellectual and contemplative development is anathema today; instead, the freedom to choose one's morality and the shape of one's intellectual development are viewed as foundational. In addition, cultural and religious communities are accepted, and even viewed as worthy of respect in most cases, unless they contravene the main tenets of liberal democracy. Kymlicka, for instance, argues that "access to societal culture is essential for individual freedom."[87] He also speaks of minority cultures as being analogous with states.[88] It is often generally assumed that states are uninational and, whatever their background or ethnic allegiance, they can be considered as such, even if this claim is not made explicit.[89]

Even in Canada, a country well known for its multiculturalism and recognized for its welcoming and respectful approach to multiple ethnicities and religions, especially First Nations and its founding cultures (anglophones and francophones), the state is intended as a unifying entity, and this is reinforced by common public holidays and the equal status of the two major official languages. Perhaps more than any other state, then, Canada demonstrates why states cannot claim the privilege of embodying the collective: in Canada, as elsewhere, states represent an *aggregate* of communities that differs from but is related to how communities represent an aggregate of individuals. Neither states nor communities can be taken as the embodiment of basic collective rights. Kymlicka writes, "But, as I have emphasized, all political theories must accord recognition to certain forms of group differences and support certain cultural communities. This is inevitable in any theory that confronts issues of language policy, public holidays, political boundaries and immigration rules. This is as true of liberal individualists and socialist internationalists as of conservatives, communitarians and postmodernists."[90]

Indeed, *certain* communities and *certain* groups must be recognized and supported. The correlative implication is that many will not merit either recognition or support. And, to permit a distinction between two categories (of communities), the concept of basic collective rights should be broad enough to allow us to discriminate in a good way between those of the communities that do and those that do not represent a moral community, in the sense advanced by Roger Brownsword (see Chapter 1).

Clearly, then, an indiscriminate aggregate of such communities – the United States is one such example – cannot claim its absolute right to survival without also defending its moral status. Nor can it claim that right to be so strong that all other collective and individual human rights must be suspended (let alone denied) to effect its defence. Hence, Richard Falk's global perspective and conclusions can be supported, at least in part. Falk writes:

1 The general inability to deal with severe violations of human rights is one of the principal weaknesses of the prevailing system of the world order.
2 This weakness is structurally linked to the distribution of power and autonomy among sovereign states and cannot be overcome without the emergence of a new system of world order.
3 The prevailing world order has a high tolerance for severe violations of human rights, especially if the harmful effects are confirmed within territorial limits ...
8 The organs of the United Nations, in the event of a substantial consensus, can contribute to the mobilizing process. But they are limited by geopolitical rivalry and partisanship, and as a consequence, the United Nations response to severe violations has been mainly symbolic and highly selective.[91]

Falk's conclusions, especially the final one, were prophetic. In 2009, when he was appointed the UN's special rapporteur to Palestine, after John Dugard, Falk was denied access to complete his mandate by Israeli authorities. In fact, the limited role that some states permit the United Nations to play in relation to collective human rights becomes even more precarious when nationalism and religious intolerance join hands, as was the case in the relationship between Palestine and Israel, which culminated in the construction of the illegal wall, the expansion of illegal settlements and, finally, in war.

National Protection and Religious Beliefs: Israeli Policies and the Palestinian Situation

Every human being has a legitimate claim to respect from his fellow human beings and is in turn bound to respect every other. Humanity itself is a dignity; for a human being cannot be used merely as a means by any human being ... but must always be used at the same time as an end.

– Kant, *The Metaphysics of Morals*

Israel's rampant nationalism is based on a revisionist view of the history of the region, one based on the Bible. The region was colonized and held by many rulers, including Roman emperors, but only the Bible provides an explanation for the Israelites' roots: the land belongs to them because it was given to them by God; therefore, no one else, no matter their history or ethnicity, has the right to occupy the territory. Because their nationalism is based in religion, it is not open to considerations of humanitarian or human rights law. Nor is it open to moral considerations, neither Kantian respect for human dignity nor utilitarian concerns for the consequences of policies that do not achieve the ostensible aims of self-protection and peace. Nor are the policies pursued by Israel conducive to the elimination of anti-Semitism. Although Israeli policies are associated with "being Jewish," not only most of the international community but also many persons of Jewish origin, within and without the state of Israel, are increasingly disenchanted with the government's party line. Israel's standard response to critiques of its policies is that these policies must be, one and all, based on anti-Semitic sentiments.

It is amazing how many people are cowed and embarrassed by such an illogical argument. Having grown up in Mussolini's Italy, I am well aware of the strong current of antifascism that prevailed in and out of Italy during and after the regime. But no one ever suggested that antifascism corresponded to a general feeling of hate or disrespect for Italy and its people, let alone for their culture or their arts. Similarly, the growing distaste for Israeli policies and actions, especially for Israel's disregard for all international law and for the specific mandates of the United Nations, does not reflect anti-Semitism any more than the international movement against apartheid in South Africa reflected hate and disrespect for African people.

The reality is that recent Israeli policies manifest a decidedly un-Kantian belief that a strong, unshakeable trust in their own excellence (or the worth of their nation and its future) justifies, in principle, any use, legal or illegal, of others as a means to achieve the aims of their nation. Thus, before discussing the status of collective rights in the Israeli war against Gaza, it is necessary to understand Palestine's position before the war, hence what prompted the ongoing token attacks against the occupying force that so engage Israel.

It is common knowledge today that Israel led the war in 1967 that turned Palestinians into a nation of refugees. It is also known that Israel did not respect the green line (the boundary set and acknowledged by the United Nations) but continued to expand into Palestinian territory not only from natural population growth but also from ongoing immigration. The United

Nations has clearly spoken against this encroachment in occupied territories as well as on the question of the illegal wall erected by Israel:

> In the West Bank, the continuation of the Wall ... has continued despite a ruling by the International Court of Justice (ICJ) that the Wall is illegal and Israel is obliged to cease the construction of the Wall and to dismantle it. Neither the Advisory Opinion of the Court on the *Legal Consequences of the Construction of a Wall in Occupied Palestinian Territory*, rendered on 9 July 2004, nor the subsequent resolution of the General Assembly approving the advisory opinion (ED/10-15) have succeeded in curbing Israel's illegal actions.[92]

What were the specific conclusions of the International Court of Justice in its advisory opinion 9 July 2004? It is remarkable that the summary of the opinion notes that "there have been serious repercussions for agricultural production and increasing difficulties for the population concerned regarding access to health services, education establishments, and *primary sources of water*."[93] The erection of the wall, in addition to other provisions regarding the occupied Palestinian territories, led the court to express the opinion that Israel had breached a number of international legal instruments, including "articles of the 1907 Hague Regulations, the Fourth Geneva Convention, the International Covenant on Civil and Political Rights, the International Covenant on Economic, Social and Cultural Rights, and the United Nations Convention on the Rights of the Child." The opinion also refers to Israel's obligation to guarantee access to Christian, Jewish, and Islamic Holy Places.[94]

Palestinian refugees escaped an intolerable occupation and war situation only to find themselves in an ongoing situation of violence that includes physical aggression, economic oppression, and deprivation of basic rights, including the right to subsistence and the right to survival for themselves and their families. In these situations, the first response of the international community is usually humanitarian relief, if the situation warrants it. But an overly speedy "movement from humanitarian aid to development assistance" is not desirable for Palestinian refugees because, despite their flight, they are still enmeshed in a situation where illegal aggression dominates.[95] This aggression includes the imposition of indiscriminate punitive measures on civilians and the erection of an illegal wall that not only divides Palestinian communities (such as those in Eastern Jerusalem) but also separates Palestinians from fertile soils closer to the green line and, hence, from the subsistence to which they have a clear right in international law. These actions and situations imply that the war has not fully abated.

The conflict is not likely to abate in the near future if one considers the remaining roadblocks to peace and a legal, two-state solution. John Dugard explains why the present reforms "fail to address the principal institutions and instruments that violate human rights and humanitarian law in the Occupied Palestinian Territory – settlements, the Wall, checkpoints and roadblocks, the imprisonment of Gaza, and the continued incarceration of over 7000 Palestinians." The presence of closed zones, with only one gate, "seriously curtail[s] access to health services, education, basic consumer good, food and water in the West Bank."[96] The setting up of additional annexed territories, through the location of the illegal Wall, is clear evidence of Israel's plans regarding Palestine, plans that do not appear to include mutual respect between two sovereign states.[97]

Some would argue that Palestine is not a state. In contrast, I am guided by the work of James Crawford.[98] Crawford argues that, on 14 May 1948, the UN General Assembly appointed "a United Nations mediation in Palestine, *inter alia* to promote a peaceful adjustment of the future situation in Palestine."[99] Immediately after, a provisional state council proclaimed the independence of Israel.[100] Thus, Israel became a state through its secession from Palestine. Crawford also refers explicitly to "the Creation of the State of Palestine" between 1988 and 1999.[101] In November 1988, the Palestinian National Council "proclaimed the establishment of the state of Palestine on our Palestinian territory with its capital, Holy Jerusalem"[102] F.A. Boyle, in "The Creation of the State of Palestine," likewise states that the Palestinian Declaration of Independence has been "definitive, determinative and irreversible."[103] As Crawford adds, Palestinian statehood is also based on four detailed propositions on what makes a state.[104]

The law that requires Palestinian residents of East Jerusalem to obtain permits from the Israeli military authorities to move toward Ramallah, where most of the residents have "strong work, family and cultural links," is also representative of a brutally repressive regime.[105] This is especially the case if one considers that Palestinians in East Jerusalem were asked to choose between maintaining their cultural ties outside of the city or losing their homes in the city. An absentee property law enabled Israel to confiscate property in East Jerusalem without compensation, on the grounds that "the owner was not resident in Jerusalem."[106] That law has been halted temporarily, but there is no guarantee that it will not be reinstated at a later time.

Palestinian refugees, therefore, have more in common with war zone civilians than they do with convention refugees or internally displaced persons. The international human rights laws that are breached daily are too numerous to list. As Dugard suggests, this is the time to ensure that UN decisions are respected and implemented without delay. For the rest of the international community, the time for appeasement has passed.[107]

The current disregard for the refugees' racial, economic, cultural, and religious rights is evident in a sentence describing some of the many such situations encountered by the UN rapporteur:

> [I] met with a man in Anata who was compelled to watch a Caterpillar bulldozer destroy his land for the construction of the wall, despite a Court injunction to stop construction; spoke with a family in Abu Dir whose hotel on the Jerusalem side of the wall had been seized by the IDF as a security outpost and witnessed the monstrous Wall around Rachel's Tomb, that has killed a once vibrant commercial neighbourhood of Bethlehem. Although Rachel's Tomb is a site holy to Jews, Muslims and Christians, it has effectively been closed to Muslims and Christians.[108]

Dugard's reports are somewhat dated and, like the other UN reports consulted, cautiously hopeful about the possibility of change for the better. On 6 March 2008, however, Amnesty International UK, CARE International UK, CAFOD, Christian Aid, Médecins du Monde UK, OXFAM, Save the Children, and Trocaire issued a new report titled "Gaza: Humanitarian Situation Worst since 1967." The report provides statistics on the following key issues: poverty, economic collapse, basic services, and health. All in all, the situation of Palestinian refugees in the illegally occupied lands is worsening, not improving, and both the occupation and the collective punishment of communities such as those inside the Gaza blockage (1.5 million people) are illegal and immoral. The need for intervention by the international community is urgent. The unique position of Palestinians, refugee or internally displaced, requires a strong and novel approach that extends beyond present attempts at peace building. Dugard puts it well:

> In the opinion of the Special Rapporteur, negotiations should take place within a normative framework, with the guiding norms to be found in international law, particularly international humanitarian

law and human rights law, the Advisory Opinion of the International Court of Justice, and Security Council Resolutions. Negotiations on issues such as boundaries, settlements, East Jerusalem, the return of refugees and the isolation of Gaza should be informed by such norms and not by political horse-trading.[109]

National Protection and the Case of Operation "Cast Lead"

The struggle for hegemony in the world is decided for Europe by the possession of Russian territory; it makes Europe the place in the world most secure from blockade ... The Slavic people, on the other hand, are not destined for their own life ... the Russian Territory is our India and, just as the English rule India with a handful of people, so will we govern this our colonial territory. We will supply the Ukrainians with headscarves, glass chains as jewellery, and whatever else colonial people like. My goals are not immoderate; basically these are all areas where Germans *(Germanen)* were previously settled. The German Volk will grow into this territory.

– Adolf Hitler, "18 September 1941"

Hitler's racist disregard for the rights of peoples is evident in his speech of 18 September 1941, in which he clearly articulates his disregard: expansionist and imperialist goals are only sought where weak, impoverished, or otherwise vulnerable people stand in the way. Although Hitler treated the Jewish people with unspeakable inhumanity (far beyond the "headscarves and glass chains" awaiting the Ukrainians), perhaps the final sentence of this quote offers the best and clearest response to the Israeli reliance on the Biblical statement to the effect that "he was taking no man's land, only taking back what had been before in the hands of the enemy."

The latter statement could also have been uttered by Greek rulers in reference to the *Magna Grecia* regions of Italy, by Phoenicians in reference to Tuscany, or by Germans in reference to Lombardy. Essentially, nationalism can and does eventually end in imperialism, for a nation's growth dictates it (or, more accurately, it did dictate it, when the practice was tolerated and even encouraged by European rulers). In recent times, the economic imperialism of globalization has bypassed the structures of the United Nations while still permitting, and in fact fostering, unfair and often violent control of regions, peoples, and resources.

At any rate, Israel does not choose to trade with Palestine because it would, first of all, have to recognize it as another state, as an equal in the international community, something it is clearly not prepared to do.[110] What Israel has chosen to do instead, in the war on Gaza, is eliminate Palestinians through constant expansion and through restrictive and harmful practices devised to eliminate any chance Palestine may have of becoming a dignified nation with a healthy economy. The facts of the Israeli war against Gaza are well known. The recent case study by Amnesty International is as thorough on the issues involved as it is on the legal breaches it demonstrates:

> At 11:30 a.m. on 27 December 2008, without warning, Israeli forces began a devastating campaign on the Gaza strip codenamed Operation "Cast Lead." Its stated aim was to end rocket attacks into Israel by armed groups affiliated with Hamas and other Palestinian factions. By 18 January 2009, when unilateral ceasefires were announced by both Israel and Hamas, some 1,400 Palestinians had been killed, including some 300 children and hundreds of other unarmed civilians, and large areas of Gaza had been razed to the ground, leaving many thousands of homeless and the already dire economy in ruins.[111]

According to the report, there were many disturbing aspects to the offensive, including the following:

- the wanton destruction of civilians and civilian objects, which violates the principle of distinction, for international humanitarian law prohibits both indiscriminate or disproportionate attacks and collective punishment
- the shooting of women and children who posed no threat to Israeli soldiers, either at short range or with high-precision weaponry, by operators who "can see even small details of their target and even strike moving vehicles" (these weapons included US-made Hellfire Missiles
- the use of highly incendiary substances – such as white phosphorus, which burns on contact and continues to burn – that should never be used in highly populated areas
- the obstruction of access to – and, at times – direct attacks on medical care and humanitarian aid

- the introduction of border closings and bans on the entry of construction materials to Gaza, leaving 1.5 million inhabitants without bomb shelters to protect themselves[112]
- the ban – before the war, during hostilities, and after the ceasefire – on independent observers, international human rights monitors, journalists, and humanitarian workers entering Gaza.

Israel's breach of international human rights instruments was pervasive throughout the hostilities. Homes and public buildings were destroyed without justification. Warning leaflets were dropped by Israeli planes prior to some attacks, but because civilians could not leave Gaza and were often shot at when leaving their homes, the "warning" simply intensified their panic and terror. The already fragile infrastructure and economy of Gaza was destroyed.[113]

Israeli's rationale for the offensive – that so-called militants could be hiding in homes or other buildings – was too general. International human rights law – including the law of occupation, well-entrenched rules of *jus ad bellum* (the right to wage war), and *jus in bello* (justice in war) – show that Operation "Cast Lead" ran the gamut of war crimes, crimes against humanity, and rules on the conduct of hostilities. War was not officially declared, and Israel made no reasonable attempts to seek peace. Israel also made no attempt to safeguard civilians, observe the rules against inflicting collective punishment, forced relocations, or evictions, and it disregarded the rights of medical personnel and UN officials. The operation is an irrefutable example of the violent, lawless, and criminal results of nationalist policies when they are driven to extreme lengths and placed above all aspects of human rights.

Conclusion: The Limits of Nationalism for Collective Rights

This chapter ranges over a broad landscape that includes globalization, democracy, sovereignty, nationalism, and the place of collective human rights in all of these areas. It reveals that democracy, even in the cradle of democracy, is no guarantee of either individual or community and collective rights. States or nations would be better understood as aggregates of various communities, more or less worthy of support and respect, according, first, to the treatment each accorded to universal basic rights, as well as other considerations.

Although colonialism, like slavery, is dead, the economic oppression and the primacy of trade over human rights are alive and well. Although freedom and the right to self-determination are entrenched in law, they, like development, are dubious purveyors of human rights, especially the basic collective ones defended here. And what of "nationalism"? This chapter explores several examples of the multiple evils that may arise from unmitigated nationalism. Yet surely peoples have the right to be treated as such, to form and support a nation that fosters and defends their culture, their ethnicity, and their beliefs? These questions, which are related to the limits not only of formal state sovereignty (already at issue because of a variety of problems that exceed the borders of any state) but also of nations and their leaders, need to be examined in some detail. What are the obligations of states and the United Nations in regard to basic collective human rights, whose support is absolutely necessary for the survival of life on Earth?

6

Cosmopolitanism, the Moral Community, and Collective Human Rights

The previous chapters explored several aspects of collective human rights in relation to governance, both domestic and international, and a number of problems became apparent:

- The elimination of colonizing powers has left a moral vacuum (at least in principle), a vacuum that is not often filled by democratically elected rulers in developing countries, whose commitment to the rights of its own citizenry, let alone those of humankind, is for the most part limited or nonexistent.
- The rampant nationalism of many states borders on imperialism or the exercise of hegemonic power in relations with weaker, poorer nations.
- The real limits to the effectiveness of self-determination affect both individual and collective human rights against the background of a global, trade-related development agenda.
- Transnational organizations play an influential but limited role in the promotion of human rights.
- There is no explicit moral discourse in either domestic or international law, even in well-established, democratic nations.
- It is difficulty to fit a universalist or cosmopolitan position within the present legal system, which is based on the sovereignty of national communities.
- This difficulty extends to international legal systems, for the United Nations is strongly influenced by the most powerful nations.
- Economic considerations take precedence over basic collective human rights (to life, health, and normal development) and even over individual and communitarian rights when they conflict with the overall power of trade.

- There are no binding instruments expressly intended to address these problems and, in general, the obligations of both national and international law to ensure that basic collective human rights are protected and enforced globally.

This chapter explores these problems in turn, beginning with the problem of nationalism introduced in the previous chapter. I then examine some of the legal instruments that could prove to be a starting point to build a governance infrastructure to meet these challenges.

Nationalism and States: The Moral Vacuum and the Pursuit of Growth

> Virtue then is a settled disposition of the mind determining the choice of actions and emotions, consisting essentially in the observance of the mean relation to us, this being determined by principle, that is, as the prudent man would determine it. And it is a mean state between two vices, one of excess and one of defect.
>
> – Aristotle, *Nicomachean Ethics*, XIX, 95

Because Aristotle views virtue as the mean between excess and deficiency, he would expect the concept of limits to intervene when rampant nationalism suggests to a leader continued, unrestrained growth and expansion. Of course, to even consider whether any aspect of Aristotelian or other moral doctrine is worth pursuing today, we need to start by questioning two basic assumptions upon which most public policy and law are based today: (1) the need for unlimited economic growth and (2) the irrelevance of moral arguments regarding both democracy and liberalism once procedural practices are in place.

It is even more necessary to clarify the radical assertion regarding colonialism that opens this chapter. It is important to applaud the demise of colonialism, but it is also necessary to understand that the self-determination of peoples is necessary but not sufficient to ensure the protection of human rights. Neocolonialism is all around us, and it fosters hegemonic practices that tend to eliminate even the nominal accountability of earlier kings and rulers. The latter, at least in principle, were accountable to their citizenry, to the church, and to public opinion in a way that market forces, free trade, and globalization are not, not even in principle. This is not a defence of *noblesse oblige* on the part of rulers, many of whom had neither heart nor conscience, it simply means that institutions such as the World Trade Organization and, in general, all organizations that give primacy to trade also tend to demonstrate neither heart nor conscience and can neither be replaced by a better ruler nor sued.

It should also be kept in mind that the new rulers of previously colonized countries tend to support their own interests without any restraint. Even at best, some of these self-governing nations, such as Canada's First Nations, cannot even attempt to redress the major harms to which their people have been subjected because they cannot control international legal regimes. Canada, for instance, "speaks" for First Nations in international forums, such as meetings about climate change, most often without seriously taking into consideration their rights. Canada has being dragging its feet, or worse, in regard to its Kyoto obligations while Inuit are suffering from a series of disasters caused by global warming: ice melts, the disappearance of animals from their hunting and fishing grounds, and overwhelming pollution in the Arctic.[1] Examples of the first sort of harms to collective rights can be seen in most of the self-governing countries in sub-Saharan Africa. Noncolonial rulers are mostly happy to squander their peoples' resources – the collective human rights of present and future generations – for immediate gain.

To be fair, even the most sensitive and progressive African ruler can do little to remedy the effects of the global economic situation in which he finds himself. Similarly, even the most progressive Inuit governance cannot redress what is happening to Arctic peoples today. Yet the fact that self-governance is important in the face of ongoing human rights abuses but often promotes ongoing disregard for human rights with no accountability, aside from the weak and overburdened UN and its ad hoc tribunals, is a problem that is not fully recognized. Palestinians were better off with British passports, and Nigerians were worse off under the dictatorship of Sani Abbacha than under the rule of almost any European power. The UN tribunals can, at best, address the crimes of one or more individuals, but they do not and cannot address a global situation and systematically harmful forms of governance to effect meaningful change.

However, before discussing the limits of nationalism, if any, its meaning should be clarified. Paul Gilbert has studied the question at length, particularly in the context of England and Ireland and the problems of nationalism in that context. Much can be learned from his analysis of the concept of nationalism. Some have proposed that nationalism is "a certain type of sentiment, a feeling of loyalty."[2] In that sense, nationalism may be considered to be akin to patriotism, or the love of one's country. However, although nationalism may give rise to the sentiment of patriotism, the two are not the same. Many of the practices that are sometimes identified with nationalism are simply the means through which loyalty is cultivated.[3] The history and culture of a nation may well be the basis of patriotic feelings; so too may be the "constitutional commitments" that are the focus, for instance, of the American "melting pot" – a type of nationalism that may give rise to both practices and sentiments.[4] Yet, in the United States, for instance, we could say that it is precisely because of the strong sentiments of patriotism related to that constitutional commitment that many patriotic Americans now criticize the nationalistic policies of the administration of George W. Bush. At any rate, Gilbert argues that the rise of the modern state, founded upon a clearly defined nation within its borders, is "what lies at the heart of the legal conception of nationality."[5]

Nevertheless, the legal sense of a nation is not the sense that all nations rely upon, especially strongly nationalist states such as Israel (see Chapter 5). The other sense of nation, used by anthropologists, for instance, includes some sense of ethnicity and race, as well as language. In general, "nationalism is a doctrine that implies particular political goals, which themselves presuppose the development of the modern state. Moreover, nationalism is a modern phenomenon, and the concept of the nation it employs is a modern concept unintelligible outside its modern political context."[6] Gilbert adds that while both the legal and the scientific or anthropological concepts of a nation are descriptive, the political concept of a nation "occurs in a context of debate."[7] Patriotism, therefore, like the love of parents or family, is a somewhat uncritical sentiment, one that may persist and thrive even as nationalistic practices and policies are criticized as unsuitable for representing the real notion of the historical homeland. In contrast, nationalism defines a political stance or program, and it is often cited as justification for practices that may not be consonant with the original tenets that define the homeland and its main principles. One example is the effort to legitimize policies or practices contrary to the US Constitution and the intentions of its founding fathers by naming one of the agencies entrusted with perpetrating those illegal and immoral acts "homeland security" rather than "national" or "state security."

One wonders whether attachment to the beliefs of the moral community, even when these beliefs include patriotic components specific to a certain nation, should be viewed as Sir Patrick Devlin viewed the moral community in his famous 1959 lecture: "I return to the statement that I have already made that society means a community of ideas; without shared ideas on politics, morals, and ethics, no society can exist ... For society is not something that is held together physically; it is held by the invisible bonds of common thoughts."[8] These invisible bonds may explain the sentiments of which Gilbert speaks and the practices that ensure that the sentiments are fostered and not forgotten. But things are different since H.L.A. Hart responded to Lord Devlin's lecture in 1959 with the publication of "Immorality and Treason." Hart argued, with J.S. Mill, that harms to others alone provide the litmus test for what can logically and legitimately be considered punishable by law.[9] The whole debate seems to be highly relevant to the questions at hand: What is a nation? What is its relation to a moral community (see Chapter 1)? Should a moral community define a nation?

It should also be kept in mind that I consider the possibility of judging communities more or less moral *only* in regard to collective basic rights. My argument is not based upon ranking communities as more or less worthy by judging their relative lifestyles, let alone their sexual mores. The sole criterion is whether respect for the life and basic rights of all is viewed as foundational to the obligations, both legal and moral, of the national community. Yet Hart's position is harder to accept today than it was in the late 1950s. A sentence from the conclusion of his essay demonstrates this point: "As Mill saw and de Tocqueville showed in detail long ago in his critical by sympathetic study of democracy, it is fatally easy to confuse the democratic principle that power should be in the hands of the majority, with the utterly different claim that the majority, with power in their hands, need respect no limits."[10]

It is also equally necessary to critically assess the "seamless web of morality" that Devlin advocated, for it does not take as given the tenets of liberal democracy, as Hart himself recognized.[11] The most powerful present-day instantiations of liberal democracies appear to subscribe precisely to the "no limit" policies that Hart decried. Clear examples of the latter are offered in Chapter 5, especially extraordinary renditions and the unprecedented extension of national powers.

A similar position is evident in the policies of Israel (with the support of the United States). A state intended originally to be patriotic in the good sense of the term is now prey to unlimited nationalism and, ultimately, imperialism. Gilbert is correct to list the conditions that could render a nation a state, including "language culture" and a unitary "value culture."[12] However, he considers whether either condition entails the right to statehood:

I consider four types of argument for a right to statehood on the basis of a group's possession of its own value culture. The first seeks to preserve the values enshrined in that culture; the second to preserve the values of it. Both are susceptible to the criticism that the relevant values may not be worth preserving. They are incidental to a particular group, not definitive of a kind of group with a right to statehood. The third type of argument responds to such criticism by asserting a right to statehood in order to preserve cultural rights. But none of its various versions seems to secure the desired conclusion. The fourth type sidesteps the criticism by declaring that only those groups with shared values can enjoy shared statehood successfully.[13]

Gilbert's careful analysis demands further discussion. From the point of view of my argument, what is most significant is that neither shared cultural values nor other values (though necessary to define a national community that could aspire to statehood) are sufficient to ensure that statehood would be *right*. In addition, even "a common history and tradition" may not suffice.[14] At any rate, all communities require critical assessment before entrusting them with the power of a state.

Nationalism, the State, and Imperialism

The community that constitutes a nation is not necessarily, so far as one can see, a community with a common good. It therefore cannot benefit from the ethical advantages of such a community in arguments for statehood.

– Paul Gilbert, *The Philosophy of Nationalism*

Paul Gilbert's criterion for the right to statehood can be used to rank national and other communities in general. If a national community is not committed to the common good, even a combination of common language, common values, and common tradition and history may not be sufficient to give such a community the power of a state. According to Gilbert, even a lengthy tradition is insufficient: "If such faith in the past were justified, tradition nationalism would have a strong argument for statehood, since it would be able to claim that a continuing society existed by virtue of customs which a state could enforce, and, what is more, that this society provides the only secure setting for its members to act morally."[15] The argument proposed in this passage echoes Aristotle's statement on the need for a certain society to en-sure the moral development and the habituation to virtue citizens need. But, of course, what Gilbert is questioning is that even a lengthy common history does not ensure that both the tradition and the values it supports and defends will be worthy of support. The possibility of self-determination and even of statehood for a national community depends on the conditions the com-munity would need to meet to deserve that distinction.

I pose a different question. How can we judge a national community on its position regarding collective human rights, or on its moral worth? And even if cultural tradition, history, and specific values are present, the question remains, what are the plans and goals of the nation, in other words, what does it perceive to be its mission?[16] Because I am considering the moral worth of states, not only that of nations hoping to attain self-determination and statehood, the importance and moral status of their mission is of primary importance.

European imperialism – including that of Hitler, the German colonizers of the Herero people in South West Africa, and the Spanish, English, and French occupiers of North and Central America – was undertaken to enlarge national borders through the acquisition of other territories and to strengthen nations' trade positions.[17] In all cases, a belief in a cohesive nation with com-mon cultural values and a common history and tradition was present, and the goals and mission of each country were viewed as superior to whatever similar claims indigenous and local communities might have had in that regard. Their difference, their distinct forms of governance from that of the colonizers, was sufficient to ensure total disregard for individual and com-munity rights. In fact, the stronger the belief in national tradition, history, and mission, the greater the disregard of communities that might have pre-sented an obstacle to that mission.

Thus, the first and gravest harm of imperialistic expansion is to the com-munitarian and individual rights of other peoples. Because imperialistic expansion entails the acquisition of space, the use of territories for economic purposes unrelated to the traditional local practices of the colonized peoples, collective basic rights are also at stake. In addition to the acquisition of space, local resources are also used to meet the needs of the colonizers. In the process, the agricultural basis of self-support for local people is destroyed, and collective basic rights are put under attack.[18] Resources are used for general commercial purposes rather than for the satisfaction of local needs. Often, local, time-honoured practices are disregarded as products more valuable to the occupiers-colonizers, or those with whom they intend to trade, are chosen instead. At any rate, these colonizing missions are seldom, if ever, intended to bring direct advantage to local inhabitants, other than perhaps exposure to the Christian religion, a simple pretext used to give some legitimacy to the expedition.

Given that deprivations are bound to occur, and that justice or any sort of real advantage is unlikely to compensate local communities for the harms suffered, it is easy to see why imperialism and forceful conquest have been considered immoral and illegal for some time. On the basic racism that underlies the imperialist project of colonization, Henning Melber writes, "the colonial legacy has remained in most former colonizing nations, a chapter that has yet to be fundamentally questioned and critically explored in terms of the dominant ideology applied within these countries – that of civilizing the 'natives.'"[19]

In general, mass violence is an undeniable part of colonialism. But it is also present in neocolonialism and often expressed and presented in terms of development (see Chapter 4). But power and dominance – in the context of conceptual notions such as development, progress, and modernism – are still viewed as absolute paradigms rather than being questioned and revised.[20] Most "civilizing missions" must, therefore, be viewed as forms of predatory capitalism.[21] Because these phenomena, civilizing missions, are neither acknowledged nor rectified, the mindset that produces them is not eliminated. Aside from the formal definition of genocide – which lends a specific perspective to law as practised in the International Court of Justice, the International Criminal Court, and the various ad hoc tribunals they have spawned – there may be a "south perspective on genocide."[22]

Perhaps the clearest of the ongoing examples of the denial of individual, communitarian, and basic collective human rights is Israel's ongoing and unpunished attacks on Palestinians, described briefly in Chapter 5. Sonja Karkar addresses the question of "selectivity in remembering and labeling":

A quarter of a century ago, on September 16, 1982, Ariel Sharon, then Israel's defense minister, gave orders to root out "2,000 terrorists" he claimed were hiding in the Palestinian refugee camps of Sabra and Shatila in Lebanon. After a day of bombardment, what ensued, at the hands of the Lebanese right-wing Christian militia known as the Phalangists – armed and trained by the Israeli army – was a massacre so awful that people who know about it cannot forget it. The photos are gruesome reminders – charred, decapitated, indecently violated corpses ... For the victims and the handful of survivors, it was a 36-hours holocaust without mercy. It was deliberate, it was planned and it was overseen. But to this day, the killers have gone unpunished.[23]

Nor is this the only example of selectivity in the naming of atrocities. Take, for example, the cases of Darfur and the Democratic Republic of Congo (DRC), where a quarter million and five million people were killed, respectively. While one case of genocide can be openly discussed and condemned, the other remains in the shadows. Alejandro Bendaña explains: "The answer is simple: in Sudan, the U.S. has a geopolitical nemesis to confront: Arabs and their Chinese business partners. In the Congo, it is U.S. allies and European and U.S. corporate interests that benefit from the slaughter."[24] However, it would be a mistake to equate this case with that of Palestine. Although US economic interests are at stake in both cases, Israel's practices are perhaps the only modern example of a nationalist mission based on cultural (and religious) values and a common historical tradition that appears to stop at nothing and that proceeds in defiance not only of individual, communitarian, and collective human rights but also of both domestic and international law. In contrast, neocolonialism and the economic oppression it fosters are far less blatant, and those who carry them out are often careful to establish and observe legal trade regimes.

National States and International Law: A Brief Overview

> Flouting international law's bedrock principle of established states' territorial integrity, national movements from Slovenia to Eritrea have forced international institutions and governments to reckon with, ratify, and in some respects even defend their separatist claims.
>
> – Diane Orentlicher, "Separation Anxiety: International Responses to Ethno-Separatist Claims"

Before turning to the topic of self-determination, it is necessary to consider the legal position of nationalism and national states. From the legal point of view, states are defined in both objective and subjective terms. They are defined by both factual historical data and "a shared sense of communal solidarity," the sentiment that Will Kymlicka identifies as patriotism.[25] Neither entirely subjective nor completely objective aspects of nationalism are sufficient to establish a state. The history of the concept in law can be traced back to the principle of self-determination, which emphasizes popular sovereignty, and this understanding was initially established in international law at the time of the Treaty of Versailles, in 1919.[26] States alone were the original subjects of international law, and the basic characteristics of statehood are listed in Article 1 of the 1933 *Montevideo Convention on the Rights and Duties of States:* "The state as a person of international law should possess the following qualifications: (a) a permanent population; (b) a defined territory; (c) government; and (d) the capacity to enter into relations with other states."[27]

The problem, however, is that no specific UN body is empowered to research and assess whether these circumstances do obtain when a nation aspires to statehood. In addition, some have suggested that it should be possible to confirm statehood exceptionally in cases where these conditions are not present.[28] Because international law holds a "fortress-like conception of state sovereignty," the main principle is noninterference rather than the protection and defence of individual and collective human rights.[29] Self-determination, at least until after the Second World War, was not therefore intended to apply to all "would-be" nations in all continents: "Although classical international law had not discriminated on grounds of race or continent, nineteenth-century positivism introduced a distinction between 'civilized nations,' principally the same European powers that created and shaped international law, and others." Importantly, international law bound and protected only the former. This doctrinal move conveniently advanced Europe's acquisition of sovereignty over African territory."[30] Essentially, existing national states were entrenched within their specific borders, clear evidence of the "objective" principles of self-determination. It is only when the "subjective" aspect of the principle came to embody decolonization that the concept of self-determination of *peoples* emerged for dependent territories.

Self-Determination, Development, and Collective Human Rights

Whereas for some the "self" in self-determination can only be the singular, individual human being, for others the right to collective self-determination, that is, the claim of a group of people to choose the form of government under which they will live, must be treated as a myth, in the Levi-Straussian sense (that is, as a blueprint for living); not as an enforceable or enforced legal, political or moral right.

– Rodolfo Stavenhagen, "Self-Determination:
Right or Demon"

The subjective aspect of self-determination represents the most serious attack on the fortress of state sovereignty. The problem of secession or of how to decide "the will of the people" – for example, who votes, those who want to separate or all of the state's inhabitants? And are decisions final when reached? – has no ready answer. Diane Orentlicher cites a common concern, voiced by a US official: "No tribal entity was too small to have ambitions for self-determination."[31]

After the Second World War, the *self* in *self-determination* was transformed from its earlier meaning and viewed strictly in territorial terms. Orentlicher writes, "the postwar rendering of self-determination thus was transformed from a principle of state-making into a corrective to historical injustice of alien subjugation."[32] The UN General Assembly's Resolution 1514 (XV) not only confirms the right of peoples to emancipation from imperial rule, but it also offers several options for the newly formed nation such as "independent statehood, free association with an independent state, and integration with an independent state."[33] In addition, and especially because outright colonization has been banned officially, self-determination has a new meaning: it is now increasingly understood as democratic governance within nation-states.[34]

The recent transformation of the concept of self-determination does not necessarily represent a positive move toward collective human rights. The main problem is that democracy, as it exists today in some of the most influential Western states and in developing countries, is often limited to sporadic and, often, manipulated voting: it is not the form of democracy that J.R. Engel defines as thick democracy (see Chapter 6), that is, as an ideal worthy of respect. Democracy is often simply another marketing campaign in which those best able to afford the high-cost "advertising" of a campaign and other forms of public manipulation achieve a degree of power, for which they are seldom prepared.

Equally problematic is the practice of setting Western-style democracy as the most desirable form of governance – in fact, the only justifiable and defensible form – to facilitate the conceptual move from ensuring true democracy within one's borders to the often-voiced belief that democracy should obtain in all states globally. Finally, it is even less acceptable to conclude that Western-style democracy ought, therefore, to be imposed by Western states or Western coalitions upon peoples who are not so governed.

At any rate, according to the UN, there are many degrees of self-determination.[35] Frederich Kirgis lists separate aspects of self-determination, two of which are particularly relevant to my argument:

> (6) The right of limited autonomy, short of secession, for groups defined territorially or by common ethnic, religious or linguistic bonds – as in autonomous areas within confederations.
>
> (7) Rights of minority groups within a larger political entity, as recognized in Article 27 of the Covenant on Civil and Political Rights and in the General Assembly's 1992 Declaration on the Rights of Persons Belonging to National or Ethnic, Religious or Linguistic Minorities.[36]

In Chapter 2, I contrasted communitarian rights with collective rights. Indigenous and local communities are the only communities in which self-determination can be explicitly connected to basic collective rights; the clear right these communities posses to cultural integrity cannot be separated from rights deemed basic and collective. Acknowledging this is not an affirmation of the romanticized notion of the "noble savage."[37] I am simply recognizing the right of such peoples to territorial integrity, which acquires a special significance in their case and is expressed explicitly in several international law instruments. For instance, Article 1(2) of the *International Covenant on Civil and Political Rights* states that "all peoples may, for their own ends, freely dispose of their natural wealth and resources without prejudice to any obligation arising out of international economic cooperation based upon the principle of mutual benefit, and international law. *In no case may a people be deprived of its own means of subsistence*" (my emphasis). Even a cursory overview of some of the legal instruments pertinent to indigenous and local communities confirms that the law is prepared at least in principle to treat such peoples in a way that recognizes their *sui generis* relationship – human, cultural, and religious – to the land, and does so in a way that never applies to others anywhere. Thus, I am simply acknowledging that these communities alone, at this time, are considered bearers of basic collective human rights. The rest of humanity does not share this privilege.

The differential treatment of indigenous and local peoples is certainly appropriate, because they are especially vulnerable to alterations to their territories and their climate. This should not, however, stop us from acknowledging that we all share the same biological characteristics and vulnerabilities, even though the greater economic capabilities of industrialized nations provides some temporary and partial protection. Similar considerations should extend to rights that are truly universal. In fact, the most salient point regarding the sui generis rights of indigenous peoples is that their hard-won self-determination and territorial integrity are becoming increasingly meaningless because the quantitative territorial integrity to which they are entitled (to ensure their cultural integrity) must be joined to the right to qualitative (ecological) integrity to preserve their cultural integrity. As biological entities and as specific indigenous persons and communities, such people need a safe habitat that is biologically diverse in its historical development, if their rights as entrenched in law are to be respected. Self-determination, even self-government, will therefore remain an empty promise of special rights so long as the global economy and global governance conflict with what such rights require – that is, so long as trade law and development law do not impose robust restraints on the activities of corporate legal entities.

SELF-DETERMINATION, STATE MAKING, AND COLLECTIVE RIGHTS: ISRAEL AND PALESTINE

> Palestine was in 1914 an undivided part of the Ottoman Empire, without separate status. It was occupied by British troops in 1917 and came to be disposed of as part of a post-war settlement. The difficulty in achieving such a settlement was that by 1917 Britain had incurred conflicting obligations with respect to Palestine.
>
> – James Crawford, "Israel (1948-1949) and Palestine (1998-1999)"

Because I have touched repeatedly on the present situation of Palestine and the state of Israel, it is worth discussing the complexity of the move from the right to self-determination of peoples (the topic of this section) to the actual creation of states, a quite different proposition. The history of Israel and Palestine that James Crawford details is such an inextricable mixture of politics and law, arguments and counterarguments that it is indeed hard for a non-lawyer to follow the complex reasoning that has led to the present impasse.

Yet, despite the procedural and legal complexities, it is encouraging to note that the peremptory norm regarding the "right to self-determination of peoples" permits one to understand that "in these respects at least, statehood was a normative concept in the international system and not merely a descriptive one."[38]

In November 1917, Lord Balfour, speaking on behalf of the British War Cabinet, said: "His Majesty's Government view with favour the establishment in Palestine of a national home for the Jewish people, and will use their best endeavours to facilitate the achievement of this object, it being clearly understood that nothing shall be done which may prejudice the civil and religious rights of existing non-Jewish communities in Palestine, or the rights and political status enjoyed by Jews in any other country."[39] Lord Balfour's somewhat ambiguous statement eventually formed part of the *Mandate for Palestine*. The *Treaty of Sevres* of 1920 supported it as well.[40] The question of Palestine was referred to the United Nations in 1947, and the UN adopted Resolution 181(II), which included the division of Palestine into an Arab and a Jewish state, united by economic concerns, and the establishment of the international city of Jerusalem.[41]

I consider the latter particularly relevant because the status of Jerusalem is a grave source of contention today. I can personally attest to the success of such a move, the creation of a free city-state. The establishment of the Free City of Trieste, my birthplace, between 1947 and 1954 represented a period of peace and security after ongoing territorial disputes between Yugoslavia and Italy.[42] The solution, like the one that should have been reached for Jerusalem, was dictated by numbers of ethnic residents and the wishes of residents.

Decisions regarding Palestine's division were also reached according to population numbers and choice; however, "on May 1948, Jews constituted about 42 percent of the population of Palestine: they were allocated 56 percent of the area, including the barren area of Negev."[43] Crawford examines the most plausible arguments for and against the creation of the state of Israel, but that wealth of detail cannot be reproduced here. Several import points do emerge from his work, however. First, "Palestine in 1949 ... constituted a self-determination unit in international law"; second, "the Palestine Mandate has been challenged on several grounds ... especially as it 'constituted a trust over the same territory, the beneficiaries of which were two distinct and predictably antagonistic peoples.'"[44] Even without the space to assess the legality of various positions and arguments in the moves and countermoves reported by Crawford, self-determination appears to be foundational from the point of view of international equity, even if the principle of self-determination was not entrenched in law before 1948. Article 22 of the *International Covenant on Economic, Social and Cultural Rights* states that "the well-being and development of such peoples [i.e., the inhabitants of the territories concerned] form[ed] a sacred trust of civilization."[45] And it seems clear that only the "Arab inhabitants of Palestine" would fit that description, not the "constructive inhabitants," that is, immigrants, beyond the original 42 percent of the area. In addition, at the time of the ceasefire in 1948, Israel's Declaration of Independence," although "partly relying upon Resolution 181(II)," declared that "Israel was not created pursuant either to an authoritative disposition of the territory, or to a valid and subsisting authorization."[46] The territory claimed by Israel was "substantially greater" than the one decided by the "partition resolution," and it did not comply with the required "protection of minorities." As well, the situation of Jerusalem was not solved, and no Arab state was created at the time: "Thus Israel was created by the use of force, without the consent of any previous sovereign and without complying with any valid act of disposition."[47]

There were also a number of legal problems in the creation of the Palestinian state, despite the absence of any particular rule of law establishing that designation.[48] At any rate, the UN General Assembly's Resolution 43/177 was invoked in 1988 in support of Palestine's statehood, and over one hundred states recognized Palestine by 1993. Clearly, much more can and should be said regarding the legality of both Israel and Palestine, but many of the conditions that represent full statehood, especially for Palestine, are subject to continuous obstacles on the ground. However, as John Quigley notes: "Whether or not Palestine is a state is not a question for Israel to decide. The determination turns on objective criteria, with recognition by states providing significant evidence as to whether these criteria are met. Applying these criteria, Palestine has a plausible claim to statehood because it controls territory, and has the capacity to engage in international relations.'[49] The closest thing to a *terra firma* in the multitude of arguments and counterarguments remains the peremptory norm cited by Crawford at the outset, that is, the right to the self-determination of peoples.[50] The United Nations, at least in this regard, has a strong record of specific collective human rights protection.

The Role of NGOs, Transnational Organizations, and Civil Society

Community-based organizations are only the first link in the chain that is required to ensure that local human rights experiences of human rights impacts on the further normative development of human rights. The second link in the chain are local human rights NGOs – private organizations that are independent from the government and the market, and have chosen as their primary aim the promotion and protection of human rights ... International non-governmental human rights organizations are the third link in the chain ... organizations with an international membership that act across national borders in defense of the human rights of a wide variety of individuals and groups.

– Koen de Feyter, "Localising Human Rights"

What role can civil society play in regard to collective rights? Because my primary focus is on the legal aspects of rights, while the moral aspects of the problem come second, I have so far focused on a top-down approach to the subject. "Civil society organizations cannot ... make law directly," but perhaps they should.[51] The three links mentioned by Koen de Feyter suggest ways in which civil society could get involved in the defence of human rights. I argue, in contrast, that there are several difficulties in localizing human rights, as de Feyter proposes.

Harms to various local communities are indeed the most evident examples of human rights violations. They are cited often to support the contention that human rights are not well protected today. Cases such as that of the Awas Tingni or Ogoni "involve essentially collective claims by politically and economically marginalized communities living off their land and challenging governmental decisions allowing that land (and its natural resources) to be used in ways with which they disagree."[52] However, although the cases and the many events that manifest human rights breaches occur in various locations and are, at times, tried nationally, they are often present in international courts. In either case, these cases are tried either under international laws or under the specific provisions of a country's domestic laws. As Chapter 2 showed, even the full acknowledgment of the *sui generis* rights of indigenous peoples in a country such as Ecuador does not translate into local recognition and justice. At this time, we are simply waiting to see what the International Court of Justice will be able to do to protect indigenous peoples.[53]

Therefore, when the role of civil society in the defence of its own rights is considered, the first thing to note is that, under globalization and the supremacy of trade, even the forums that should be able to promote human rights are essentially powerless. De Feyter acknowledges that unless local community organizations are connected to other national or international organizations, they cannot be, at this time, "a force for change."[54] This is true of civil society in general, as it appears to have little influence either before or after the fact of human rights violations. Legislators, at best, "hear" some cases or allow them to sit at the table of various commissions or institutional organizations empowered to deliberate on development activities in specific regions.

The actual drafting of domestic legal regimes for the protection of human rights of all communities is also beyond the reach of local organizations. This problem is particularly grave, because law curricula do not include considerations of public health or the ecological effects of economic activities.[55] This, however, is the stage where local input based on the specific expertise of local communities would be most useful, as would the input of independent medical experts. Expertise that is general, as it applies to the effects of various chemicals and other substances and processes, would be most useful if it could be heard and entrenched in domestic and even international law long before the harms that arise from exposure to industrial activities are technically assessed by so-called experts hired or promoted by industry, as is most often the case.[56]

The lack of expertise represents a grave lacuna in the law, for it leads to inappropriately conceived and worded regulatory regimes. Harms that might have been prevented are allowed to happen. After the fact, local communities such as the Awas Tingni and Ogoni have to wait for years for hearings and compensation for what is often an incompensable harm. Nevertheless, both of these cases indicate that some progress regarding human rights is being made.

In other words, traditional local knowledge that would most accurately predict the results of industrial development in an area is not given a voice *before* decisions are made that will have an impact upon the local community. In addition, their voice is not easily heard even after the operations of the corporate body in question have resulted in harms to both people and environment. De Feyter is therefore correct to emphasize the need for links between local communities and domestic NGOs.[57] The importance of domestic and international law regarding human rights cannot be overstated. As Chaloka Beyani states, "Many writers are united in the opinion that the function of international law in the field of human rights is set to minimum standards against which municipal legal systems can be measured appropriately."[58]

If standards are not set internationally and adopted institutionally in the domestic setting, it is clear that the connection between local communities, domestic NGOs, and international NGOs is the necessary link that de Feyter indicates in the opening passage of this section. He argues that local community organizations represent the weakest link in that chain, despite the belief that "civil society is the engine behind a normative agenda seeking to establish and enforce contracts from below. Ordinary people can and should make and monitor laws."[59] There is yet another avenue that local communities can, and in fact do, follow to be heard – engaging in disruptive or even forceful confrontations with industrial developers. They do so at some peril to their own safety, but these strategies most often capture the interest of the media, which then become, in turn, part of the transnational advocacy network, which includes a number of like-minded actors.[60]

At the international level, there are many well-known and respected organizations such as Amnesty International, Médecins Sans Frontières, and Greenpeace, to name but a few, that mobilize public opinion and support the work of intellectuals and organizations by disseminating local information that is often viewed as too radical by local domestic media. The presence of UN special rapporteurs is also invaluable in this regard, as is the authoritative voice of the World Health Organization. Yet both are not heard enough and, in the case of the latter, always after the fact.[61] Although the UN's rapporteurs are often strong in their presentation of human rights abuses, the UN itself is far too weak in the necessary follow-up and corrective work. Most of the time, no changes are imposed on the guilty party or government.

Nevertheless, although NGOs (like multinational corporations) possess international legal personality, according to human rights conventions, they are also recognized "as functional, derivative and limited subjects of international law," for they possess certain fundamental rights, such as the right to association, freedom of speech, and procedural rights in the sense of *locus standi* before international human rights courts and monitoring bodies.[62] According to Article 71 of the *Charter of the United Nations*, NGOs are also accorded rights of participation in the work of the *International Covenant on Economic, Social and Cultural Rights* and its suborgans, such as "observer status" and "rights of petition and oral contribution," rights that multinational corporations, for the most part, do not possess.[63]

The issues these organizations espouse and support are precisely those that support collective human rights; therefore, they are vitally important. With the increasing withdrawal of the state, which is now most often prevented from providing services to its citizens because of globalization and such institutions as NAFTA and the World Trade Organization, these associations are the only voices left to fill the void – or at least to denounce it to the global community.

The Lack of Moral Debate in Democracies and Elsewhere

> Since the beginning of international law in the modern sense, the relationship between morals and law attracted the interest of lawyers and philosophers alike. Victoria, Grotius and Christian Wolff were cited as references for fundamental rules which are higher in authority than law stipulated in treaties or developed in custom.
>
> – Stefan Kadelbach, "*Jus Cogens*, Obligations *Erga Omnes* and Other Rules"

Jus Cogens norms and the *erga omnes* obligations they impose were discussed in the first part of this book. At best, some of their mandates may be incorporated in the national constitutions or charter of rights of various countries. From that position, these rules can be applied by the appropriate courts when cases that appear before them involve the grave issues to which jus cogens pertains. But aside from judgments in which the highest moral principles are invoked, moral debate, unlike voting, is not an essential part of democratic governance. Parties can support different platforms, but the moral content of the platforms is seldom teased out for discussion within each party. The opposing party may well attack the other party's platform but, again, the arguments proposed against it are most often factual, in the sense that the perceived advantages of one platform over another may be outlined and defended. Essentially, what is said to be at stake is, at best, the fairness of the allotted preference satisfaction of various stakeholders, whose rights are emphasized. The closest these platforms come to moral argument is the defence of racial, ethnic, or gender diversity or, perhaps, attacks on the personal sexual morality of a party's representative. The effects of any policy on basic collective human rights is seldom central to the arguments of the parties, especially in countries such as the United States and Canada, where one party alone is the winner and coalitions that may include, for instance, Green parties are unknown.

Recently, however, arguments about the impact of climate change have started to bring the rights of humankind into political discourse everywhere.

In all cases, however, the local and national effects of policies intended to mitigate global warming are the first consideration, despite the present state of scientific knowledge on the topic and the heroic efforts of Al Gore and other scientists and political figures to bring the situation to the attention of civil society and governments.

Civil society presents moral arguments through shouted slogans and placards waved in demonstrations when national elections take place and especially when G8 or G20 meetings take centre stage. These actions, however, although publicly acknowledged and permitted (at least until riot police are sent in to "control" crowds), are never treated as arguments to be heard, debated, and evaluated until the best moral argument prevails, in the sense that it may be incorporated into policies and legal regimes. Both "sides" of demonstrations are viewed primarily as the expression of legitimate interests or preferences. There is no effort to judge them. Hearing these arguments and being allowed to express them is the highest test of democracy. The final settlement of the dispute is left to the ballot. A case in point is the abortion issue, where a dated and morally debatable legal precedent is allowed to hold sway as the last word.[64] This precedent is viewed as sufficient to defend a politically correct preference, even in a country such as Canada, where the majority would like to revisit the country's current position, and perhaps even in the United States, where the position is viewed as unworthy of renewed discussion, although neither country has so far allowed a referendum on the topic.

In general, some arguments are allowed to prevail, even though political positions may be a more accurate description of the issues, as when demo-cratic governments refrain from judging the policies of the Israeli government for what they are – brutal forms of apartheid, war crimes, and crimes against humanity – for fear of being accused of anti-Semitism, despite the illogical status of the accusation. Similarly, the argument in support of the reproductive rights for women, a benign sounding position, is effectively, *mutatis mutandis*, the right to *patria potestas* (power of the father) of Roman times.

At election time, there may not be a party that offers any of the options requested by civil society at the time when demonstrations and placards were much in evidence. Basic collective rights, then, may not be included in any party platform when citizens vote. That is the case in Canada. Votes can be cast in favour of the Green Party, but they are wasted because the party has no member in Parliament. In a similar vein, a conscientious objector to nuclear power would find no party for which to vote, either in the United States or in Canada.

This is why I do not lament the prevalence of one or another moral theory in today's liberal democracies. In Part 1 of the discussion on moral community, I propose both Kantian and Gewirthian theories. In this chapter, I turn even further back in the history of moral theory, all the way to Aristotle. For the present purpose, the doctrine chosen is not as important as the fact that none is ever presented to voters or to governing bodies in justification of a political platform or for the enactment of a legal regime.

It may be useful to return to Aristotle once again to contrast his ideal polis with the highest example from modern governance today – that is, democracy as it is actually practised rather than the "thick" democracy ideal proposed by Ron Engel (see Chapter 5).

COMMUNITY OVER INDIVIDUALS AND JUSTICE

> One can even say that those who are most responsible for the
> well-being of the community bear the clearest resemblance, among
> political men, to the unmoved mover. For the divine is, in its own
> way, a cause of the goodness of the universe, and the more respon-
> sible one is for the goodness of one's community, the more
> closely one approximates this condition.
>
> – Richard Kraut, *Aristotle on the Human Good*

Political power and office should be shared equally among equals, but it is certain virtues, a certain excellence, that makes each one of these citizens equals who must share power for the greater benefit of the community and, therefore, who must govern in turn. Richard Kraut, in his discussion of Aristotle, states: "Justice, construed as a specific virtue, requires equal treatment ... and so when citizens are equally deserving of political power, they must take turns governing and being governed."[65]

The first difference between Aristotelian governance and today's (mostly) neoliberal democracies is clear. According to Aristotle, citizens should participate in the governance of the state for the common good, but only when they are deserving. Each person must be habituated to virtue (including intellectual virtue) and determined to seek it for the whole community of citizens. Today, in Western democracies, holders of public office are determined not only by wealth – their own and that of whomever else can be convinced to contribute – but also by the untiring work of "orators" – that is, spin doctors, speechwriters, and political advisers who work to ensure the victory of their candidate.[66] For the most part, the high-sounding words of the political campaign, the commitment to the "people" and the assurances of high moral standards all come from paid promoters, speechwriters, and others, not the candidates. Essentially, then, those who rule today do not need to develop their highest intellectual virtues by contemplating or practising the theoretical disciplines – mathematics, physics and, most of all, theology, Aristotle's "first philosophy."[67]

Although the most important of these disciplines is the study of the first cause, the study of nature (physics) is almost as important. Although all of these disciplines are superior to the practical sciences, the latter are also necessary to the pursuit of the political life.[68] The point is that not everyone is suited to pursuing the ideal of happiness, which involves the highest virtue and the highest subjects of study. What is required is doing one's best in "the realm of theory or the realm of practice."[69] The latter, intended as one's choice to pursue the political life, permits one to achieve happiness insofar as one can.

The pursuit of happiness through moral or intellectual activity is, however, basic. By making the interests of their communities *primary*, political rulers are not only seeking their own happiness but also, first and foremost, that of their communities. We need to keep in mind, however, that the community today must include the community of humankind, wherever they may reside, for rulers who ignore the global implications of their actions to promote their own state's advantage, at the expense of any and all others, cannot be moral or just.

ARISTOTLE RECONSIDERED IN THE DEFENCE OF COLLECTIVE RIGHTS

Throughout Aristotle's writings, and with particular frequency in the biological works, we find the rule that "Nature does nothing in vain" or "to no purpose." In a well-known passage of the De Caelo ... there is a variation on this: God and nature, Aristotle tells us, do nothing in vain ... That is, Nature, not only the natures of individual things but an immanent God (not dissimilar to that of On Philosophy), must work in a law-like fashion.

– John Rist, *The Mind of Aristotle*

Humanity is exposed to grave environmental harms because of four fundamental lacunae in globalized governance:

1   a lack of principled governance that recognizes the basic importance of human nature
2   a lack of understanding of interconnectedness and teleology in the laws or nature and their relation to human nature itself
3   a lack of emphasis on limits *(horos)* as a basic requirement of a human life worth living
4   a weak understanding of true democracy, as understood by Aristotle.

These four "missing" aspects of governance are also additional to the basic necessity of having international or transnational legal instruments or, in other words, cosmopolitanism that supports universal principles. There are laws for individual states, but the problems that need addressing are global in scope, and no state can solve them on its own. Municipal laws must internalize international legal rules within their constitutions in order for these principles to be operational within the state. But the formulation of these instruments must first be international, and only secondarily must they be incorporated into municipal law.

All four lacunae stem from the lack of appropriate limits to growth. This fundamental oversight results, for instance, in climate change. The ferocious resistance of some of the greatest polluters to the imposition of any limits whatsoever – on the grounds that they limit economic growth and corporate enrichment – tells its own story. The United States' decades-long history of resistance to even the idea of climate change tells another.[70]

Problems also stem from lack of acceptance of the interconnectedness of natural systems. Recognition of this interconnectedness conflicts with the pursuit of growth and enrichment that is the ultimate goal of most so-called democratic governance. Corporate crime, including crimes against humanity and even genocide, runs apace with development, especially in the case of the extractive and mining industries. The latter's operations often spell the demise of indigenous and local communities who depend on the services of the ecosystems that are exploited for gain, with little or no regard for the consequences.[71]

More importantly, no system of governance today fully accepts the existence of a definable human nature, let alone one with the Aristotelian connotations of moral and intellectual excellence. If it is considered at all, human nature today is the subject of self-serving individuals and nonuniversalizable, except insofar as choosing and consuming are its defining characteristics in an increasingly homogenized and globalized world. Unrestrained, unprincipled, and limitless choice, therefore, represents the ideal, and the democratically chosen leadership who follows this analysis clearly does not include any of these aspects of justice recommended by Aristotle.

Finally, the lack of both limits and principles combines with yet another form of greed: the quest for power. The quest for power is its own global disaster, one that should be considered in addition to globally engendered environmental disasters and the fact that inappropriate enrichment is making the life of impoverished populations impossibly harsh (especially, but not exclusively, in developing countries). From the illegal annexations of Palestinian territory, to the corporate-funded ethnic cleansing of Sudan and other areas in sub-Saharan Africa, to the forcible transfer of the Chagossians, to the tar sands of Alberta, Canada, the quest for power and unsustainable growth is widespread. A serious reconsideration of Aristotelian doctrine in all its aspects is necessary to avert global tragedy; sadly, it is unlikely to happen today.

Neither Aristotle nor many of the major moral theorists we know today spoke of or even envisaged the possibility of basic collective rights in our sense, but universal moral principles were essential to their thought, and these principles are lacking in global governance today. We have only considered democracy, which is viewed as the most desirable form of governance today. All other forms of governance must, therefore, be judged as even less close to a morally defensible ideal.

Cosmopolitanism and Sovereign Rights in Conflict

> Sovereignty is only a legitimate claim insofar as it seeks to guarantee the basic rights and satisfy the basic needs of humanity, in line with universally agreed principles and standards.
>
> – Margot Salomon, *Global Responsibility for Human Rights*

The history of cosmopolitanism and true universality is far longer than the existence of sovereign states. Yet today the very existence of international law and the international community imposes responsibilities on states well beyond their own borders.[72] Many problems arise regarding the responsibility of sovereign states. A state's conduct may not comply with international obligations, and it may impose damages on other states. In either or both cases, the objective element of "material or moral damage" is required. There is also the question of "aggravated state responsibility."[73] This sort of moral or legal obligation is of a different kind than the ordinary responsibility of states, for aggravated state responsibility "arises when a State violates a rule laying down a community obligation, that is, either a customary obligation *erga omnes* protecting such fundamental values as peace, human rights or self-determination of peoples, or an obligation *erga omnes contractantes* laid down in a multilateral treaty safeguarding those fundamental values."[74]

Both human rights and humanitarian law, following the provisions of *Charter of the United Nations* and the adoption of the international covenants on rights in 1966, cover aspects of the basic collective human rights under discussion. Values such as the prohibition of the use of force, the support for self-determination of peoples, and the acknowledgment of large-scale violations of human rights take on a collective dimension that clearly separates these forms of state responsibility from other ordinary wrongs. Hence, the use of terms such as the *cooperation of states* indicates the collective aspects of their responsibility. Beyond limits on state sovereignty, recognition of the interdependence of states is a foundational aspect of the development of international law. In fact, "in 1923, the Permanent Court of International Justice affirmed what Judge Weeramantry felt was necessary to reaffirm in 1996, and that is that 'the sovereignty of states would be proportionally diminished and restricted as international law developed.'"[75] Therefore, the defence of basic collective human rights is not a position that stands against present legal regimes but rather one that indicates and details the parameters of the eventual goal of the long-anticipated "development" of international law. This development is already in evidence when the global community speaks openly to criticize any state that does not practise democracy; however, it stops short of expressing a forceful condemnation of those states that still promote and practise immoral and illegal policies (such as the state of Israel). It is as if the moral vigilance of the international community ends, at best, at the ballot box. Whatever decisions, no matter how indefensible, a new democratically elected government makes are *ipso facto* rendered "right" (in the sense of justifiable and morally correct) because they emerged from an elected government. In conclusion:

> [Although,] under the Charter, UN Member States relinquish a degree
> of their sovereignty, and in its stead accept international cooperation
> in the respect for, and observance of, human rights as a common

purpose of their contemporary, collective activities. The international community does not seem at this time to extend its obligation to recognize the emerging *erga omnes* responsibility to force states to implement *jus cogens* norms as their gravest moral and legal obligations.[76]

World Law *(Weltinnenrecht)* and the Development of International Law

> World law may be defined as a body of law that transcends the notion of strictly inter-state law but does not exclude it; that is World Law encompasses in its scope and application state and non-state actors, transactions and situations of most different kinds beyond the state or national level.
>
> – Jost Delbrück, "Prospects for a 'World (Internal) Law'?"

Although no firm dates can be offered to trace the development of international law and divide it into hard and fast periods, there is some rough agreement among international legal scholars that there are "three major stages in the development of the international system: first, the so-called classical period that is ... often referred to as the 'Westphalian System'; second, the period of the international organization of the community of states; ... and third, the present period of globalization."[77]

The earliest period began with the Westphalian Peace Treaty of 1648 and was characterized by the principle of sovereignty. International law was based primarily on bilateral treaties, so that state obligations required state consent to occur. The main principle was that of the independence of states, which ensured the self-protection of each state from the others. This limited movement from complete independence to some form of interdependence was a portent of things to come.

During the second half of the nineteenth century, the recognition of the essential interdependence of states led to institutionalized interdependence, opening the second period. The League of Nations was founded in 1919, echoing Kant's Federation of the Free States.[78] But Kant's moral and political vision was obscured (and still is) by the reality of powerful states that used international legal instruments to promote "their own national interests."[79] However, the de facto limitation on the sovereign freedom of action of member states remains, at least in principle, in the present movement toward an international law of cooperation.[80]

The third period has been shaped by the forces of globalization and will be discussed below.

THE ROLE OF THE UNITED NATIONS AND COLLECTIVE HUMAN RIGHTS

> The traditional approach to enforcement in international law has been state-centric. As Damrosch has written, "States are violators and states are victims of violations of international law." The mechanisms of remedying such violations, as exemplified by UN Charter provisions for ensuring international peace and security, were similarly state-centric.
>
>   – Theodor Meron, *The Humanization of International Law*

The role of the UN in the promotion of human rights is made particularly difficult by the fact that the nations it comprises are not often in agreement regarding the subject.[81] The UN *Charter* – established for several purposes, one of which is the promotion of human rights – includes few explicit clauses, other than the prohibition of discrimination.[82] The earlier doctrine of non-intervention in the domestic affairs of states posed an obstacle to the promotion of human rights, although that emphasis has undergone a dramatic transformation.[83]

Part of the United Nations' mandate is "the promotion of democracy, election monitoring and nation-building."[84] In fact, many regional instruments are based on the view that democracy is necessary to qualify a state for participation in regional state meetings, and the provisions demand "periodic elections with universal and equal suffrage."[85] Even if we agree that representative democracy and periodic, free elections with universal suffrage are necessary, we need to understand that such civil rights are not sufficient, for they do not include clearly principled positions, debate on the issues or, most often, the basic collective rights supported by the *International Covenant on Economic, Social and Cultural Rights*. One could argue that democracy and civil rights are better than the opposite, but exclusive emphasis on these rights permits other violations to remain unobserved and free from condemnation, so long as the other procedural conditions are fulfilled. The roots of the present difficulties and the limitations in the UN's promotion and defence of human rights lie in the origin and early history of the organization.

THE INFLUENCE OF THE UN'S EARLY HISTORY

> In this organization a major role was to be given to the most
> powerful allies fighting against the Axis Powers, namely, the USA,
> the USSR, as well as Britain and France (which still had huge col-
> onial empires) and China, which was to be associated with them.
> They were allotted the role of world policemen, responsible for
> enforcing peace.
>
> – Antonio Cassese, *International Law*, 3rd ed.

On the basis of the understanding outlined by Antonio Cassese, the "grand design" of the UN included the elimination of the use of force to resolve international disputes, the regulation of unilateral action and military and political alliances, the promotion of economic and social cooperation to avoid grave inequalities, the elimination of colonial empires in favour of the self-determination of peoples, and the promotion of free trade and world markets, the main goals of American neoliberalism.[86]

Although this laundry list of desiderata appeared to be supportive of various aspects of collective human rights, some of the main points were the cause of many of the organization's future problems. First among them was the predominance of the United States within the structure, particularly its unparalleled industrial and military power. Then there were the other great powers, who, rightly or wrongly, continued to dominate the policies of the UN, starting with the veto power they exercised within the Security Council. The great powers' resistance to the restraints of the law – that is, their refusal to subject disputes about the interpretation of the *Charter* to the International Court of Justice – was particularly problematic.[87] However, the United States of Theodore Roosevelt and the 1945 Yalta meeting is not the United States of today. Nor is the role of international "policemen" appropriate at this time, if it ever was. The Security Council is highly selective in what it tolerates and what it condemns, and the domination of the "superpowers" is constantly in evidence.[88]

In addition to the gross human rights violations that have taken place in Darfur, Democratic Republic of Congo and Palestine have not generated a decisive Security Council resolution, and the question of what constitutes self-defence is also increasingly unclear. The use of force or aggression to settle interstate disputes was proscribed, but self-defence "was envisaged as an exception to this centralized collective security system."[89] The doctrine of pre-emptive military strikes was viewed by the UN and the European Union as inappropriate and dangerous, but the United States and the United Kingdom attacked Iraq for this reason in 2003, but without a formal appeal to self-defence.[90]

Peace was and continues to be viewed as the supreme value (note that Article 51 of the UN *Charter* only permits the use of force in response to an ongoing aggression).[91] However, it seems that the UN has not been able to do well in its support of peace, given the numerous internal and external conflicts that plague the world today. It is particularly galling that these conflicts are based, for the most part, in unilateral actions and military and political alliances that should have been replaced by peace and cooperation following the inception of the United Nations. Similarly, indirect aggression – that is, the support of insurgents (supported by the United States, Israel, and South Africa) – rather than direct military attack is proscribed by Article 51 as well.[92] Nevertheless, the use of force to stop another state should be legitimate "in respect to grave circumstance, namely: war crimes, genocide, and crimes against humanity," and it may also be permitted for communities and peoples whose self-determination is forcibly denied.[93]

The other major goal of the UN – the elimination of colonies – has been more successful. European countries have lost their dependent peoples, although the results of decolonization have not been uniformly positive. One could view this uneven success as yet another result of the power structure underlying the UN. The Security Council has included some colonizers, to be sure, but the most powerful, the United States, has not claimed dependent nations, with the exception of Native peoples in some sense. Hence, the First Nations of Canada and the Native peoples of the United States are the main communities whose self-determination is not yet fully satisfactory.

Although the UN has successfully achieved one of its main goals, and although it maintains a strong emphasis on the promotion and protection of human rights, the main aspects of basic collective human rights are not faring well in the world today. Industrialization and globalization, together with the promotion of economic development, have not proven to be a panacea but rather an insidious and, to some extent, unrecognized threat to the UN's program to affirm universal human rights (see Chapter 4).

The Overall Primacy of Economics and Basic Collective Rights

Increasingly, global capital claims a new order of international rights for itself in ways that have profound distinctive impacts on the human rights of human beings everywhere ... Protection of the rights of the foreign investor is to be of such a high order as to deconstruct all traditional newly emergent human rights as "trade destroying" policy obstacles that need to be overcome in the very title of making the future of human rights secure.

– Upendra Baxi, *The Future of Human Rights*

This brief paragraph emphasizes the main principle of the era of globalization, a phenomenon that has increasingly been in the public eye since the Second World War. At that time, "the then existing community of states decidedly committed itself to an all embracing liberalization of world trade."[94] Globalization cannot simply be understood as a market phenomenon, because it is the "unfettered global capitalism" that it fosters that evokes both concern and resistance on the part of people in all continents, particularly as it becomes clear that the formulation of the *Declaration on the Right to Development* – insisting as it does "that the individual is the subject of development, not its object" – has missed its mark.[95]

When entire nations become the objects of development, the collective rights of their peoples are no longer even a remote consideration. Chapter 4 explores the true impact of so-called development and Bhupinder Chimni's criticism of Amartya Sen's conception of freedom and development. The right of peoples to say no to hazardous economic and industrial development is nonexistent in practice. The right to consent is either watered down to a pro forma right to consultation or simply ignored altogether as a requirement for projects.[96] Thus, the public protection that was the main obligation and duty of states – at least within the domestic sphere – has been eliminated by free trade deals and agreements. Modern states, for the most part, are not allowed to protect even the health and safety of their own citizens if there is a perceived threat. Note, for instance, the states of the European Union in the question of hormone-laced meats,[97] or consider Canada, which, in its efforts to eliminate hazardous gasoline additives, is in conflict with the mandates of the *North American Free Trade Act*. Ethyl Corporation, a US company, sued the Canadian government for US$250 million. It obtained, in 1998, a settlement of US$11 million for the Canadian ban on the gasoline additive MMT, a nerve toxin.[98]

It can be said that the principal raison d'être of states is the physical security and protection of their citizens.[99] One could even argue that the legitimacy of the state itself is compromised by the "withdrawal of states from fulfilling public tasks."[100] Globalization therefore may also be understood as "a process of denationalization."[101] This withdrawal and the ongoing process of denationalization transfer the "production of public goods" to nonstate entities, who lack not only any democratic legitimacy but also the obligation to foster the public good.

It is not the protection of collective human rights that is nonstate entities' mandate or primary focus but rather the promotion of the economic interests of the most powerful Western states. What of development? For the most part, what is being developed is the capital and the influence of multinational corporations, not the human rights of developing countries. Upendra Baxi puts it well when he refers to globalization as the new paradigm: "The new paradigm may succeed only if it can render unproblematic the voices of suffering. This occurs in many modes. One such is the rationality reform, through the production of epistemologies that normalize risk (there is no escape from risk), ideologize it (some grave risks are justified for the sake of 'progress,' 'development,' 'security')."[102] This new paradigm also involves questioning causation, particularly in environmental and public health issues, and questioning even the smallest amount of compensation in cases where "judicial activism" is viewed as a further obstacle.[103]

Essentially, these aspects of globalization and the imposition of this new paradigm are accompanied by political resistance to recognizing group rights and the right to self-determination of indigenous peoples and other local communities.[104] It is, therefore, worth repeating that the mantra of development is followed by neither the freedom nor the "flourishing" of the people for whom it is intended. On the contrary, the freedom to choose their lifestyle is often taken away from these people, and those who flourish are distant shareholders and corporate managers. The help and assistance these people need for a life of dignity does not come from any corporate practice, and there is, at this time, no binding mandate for multinational corporations to plan and execute their projects while giving primacy to collective, basic human rights.[105]

PART 3

Toward a New Cosmopolitanism

7
World Law or International Legal Instruments? Toward the Protection of Basic Collective Human Rights

> The rights enshrined in Article 27 are not only framed in individualistic terms. The interests they aspire to protect can be comprehended in universal terms, as features of existence that are essential to what it means to be a human being: the capacity to participate in one's culture, to hold and exercise political beliefs, and to speak to others in a common language, plausibly possess universal value. That is, cultural, religious and linguistic affiliations help shape who we are. They constitute important features of what it means to be human.
>
> – Patrick Macklem, "Minority Rights in International Law"

Most scholars refer to communities and collectives interchangeably, whereas I suggest that communities are significant parts of the collectivity of humankind (see Chapters 1 and 2). In addition, although "cultural, religious and linguistic affiliations" do, as Patrick Macklem suggests, constitute important features of humanity, in the sense that everyone has some affiliation in regard to those special components of human existence, my argument is that there are other *basic* features of humanity that transcend communal and cultural groupings, because they are shared by all. The need for healthful food, air, and water and, in general, for a safe habitat – in other words, for the protection of one's life, health, and normal development – comes even before linguistic, cultural, and religious choices or traditions. In fact, they need to be understood as basic, because all people on Earth share precisely the *same* basic human needs, whatever their colour, gender, ethnicity, or religion.

Unless these basic needs are met, the other choices or traditions may not even be practised, nor will actions protected by the *International Covenant on Civil and Political Rights*.[1] Both sorts of rights are "universal in significance," and both sets of rights are "constituent features of human identity, shared by members of majorities and minorities alike," as Macklem says of specific minority rights.[2] Perhaps, according to the language of Article 27 of the *Universal Declaration of Human Rights* – which states that minority members of a community "shall not be denied the right" to practise their culture and religion and use their own language[3] (although Rapporteur Daniel Capotorti argues that states should practice "active and sustained intervention" to ensure that these rights can be protected) – positive measures are not mandated.

The present task, therefore, is to find any positives in a global situation that, for the most part, shows little support for basic collective human rights. I show that existing case law holds some hope for advancement, at least for the rights of indigenous and local peoples. I then reconsider existing international instruments and international governance to isolate documents that may support the basic defence of humanity. Finally, I attempt to discover any legal reason that may be used as a bastion for that defence.

The Ongoing Development of Human Rights Case Law

> The states have sued in both their *parens patriae* and proprietary capacities. As quasi-sovereigns and as property owners, they allege that Defendants' emissions, by contributing to global warming, "constitute a substantial and unreasonable interference with public rights in the plaintiffs' jurisdiction, including, inter alia, the right to public comfort and safety, the right to protection of vital natural resources and public property, and the right to use, enjoy, and preserve the aesthetic and ecological values of the natural world.
>
> – *State of Connecticut, et al. v. American Electric Power Company*

State of Connecticut, et al. v. American Electric Power Company (2009) is the latest and, arguably, the most successful case to date against pollution in general and climate change in particular that clearly defends collective rights, even though the connection between ecological degradation and harms to human life and health could be more clearly articulated ("the right to comfort and safety" comes close). Before discussing the case in detail, it is useful to show what constitutes the correct standard – that is, a successfully argued case for the protection of human beings, of no specific ethnicity or background. The cases I examine do not have the same universality, but some of the decisions were based on considerations of various aspects of the collective human rights defended in these pages. These cases involve indigenous peoples and minorities, because only they can offer a defence of some aspects of the basic collective human rights that are the focus of this book.

The protection of indigenous and local communities has a history of slow but ongoing progress, which began after the First World War, when "the League of Nations system was designed to accommodate nationals who belonged to 'racial, religious or linguistic minorities' living within the newly emerged or enlarged states."[4] The next period was characterized by the affirmation of the United Nations *Charter*, which was intended to establish universally valid human rights, with no specific provisions for minorities. After the adoption of the *Convention on Genocide* in 1948, several commissions worked on minority issues, and two working groups studied indigenous populations, establishing the two international decades for indigenous peoples, which ran from 1995 to 2004 and from 2005 to 2015.[5] The *Declaration on the Rights of Indigenous Peoples* was adopted by the UN General Assembly in 2007, despite the abstentions of eleven states and the objections of the United States, Canada, Australia, and New Zealand.

These instruments are not monitored by the UN, however, so their implementation is left to the will of individual states. As well, the rights entrenched in them do tend to be specific, but they are often individual rights. Thus, it is important to note that the rights protected even by weak and unenforced instruments are, at best, either individual or communitarian rather than collective. Although it is useful to review the judicial history of these provisions, these cases and instruments at best present a partial history of whatever progress might have been made regarding basic human rights.

We need to acknowledge that even the best, most useful, and respectful resolutions of actions brought by indigenous and local communities represent the failure of legal regimes and government bureaucracies to protect these peoples. Although "access to justice" is certainly a necessary component of the protection of human rights in general and of minority rights in particular, it is not sufficient.[6] I isolate existing legal instruments or institutions that may mandate, or at least support, the required protection *ab initio*, from the beginning. The case law is still evolving, but several of the existing cases present and defend the universal values I am seeking to promote.[7]

CASES WITH DIRECT REFERENCE TO BASIC COLLECTIVE HUMAN RIGHTS

The American Convention provides that every person has a right to have his life respected (Article 4(1)). The Inter-American Court interpreted the right to life to have an additional dimension in the Yakye Axa case. In that case the court stated that, essentially, the fundamental right to life is broader than freedom from arbitrary deprivation of life. The Court specified that the right to life includes the right to live a *vida digna,* or a dignified existence.

– Jo Pasqualucci, "The Evolution of International Indigenous Rights"[8]

The decision cited above on a case brought to the Inter-American Court of Human Rights by the Yakye Axa indigenous community in 2005 imposes certain obligations on states to ensure that at least the basic requirements of a dignified life are made available to indigenous peoples. The case therefore promotes an agenda that is congruent with the promotion of basic human rights in general. A similar protection seems to be advocated in *Moiwana Village v. Suriname,* heard by the same court in the same year.[9] The court supported the connection between a group's identity and the effects of "an attack on their physical integrity" caused by forced displacement.[10] In *Moiwana Village, physical integrity* was understood in the dual sense of the physical integrity of individuals within the community and the integrity of the community as a whole. Unlike the case involving the people of Chagos, these more recent cases indicate, minimally, a clear procedural progress, for indigenous people's access to justice is not denied.

In addition to hearing specific cases, the Inter-American Court of Human Rights can intervene to provide immediate protection "to prevent imminent danger."[11] The court did so in *Massacre de Plan de Sanchez v. Guatemala* (2004) and *Kankuamo Indigenous Peoples v. Colombia* (2004).[12] In the former case, the immediate threat arose when the life and physical integrity of certain witnesses was under attack. The court ordered the government of Guatemala to protect them. The government was also to secure the protection of six hundred community members living on the Kankuamo Indigenous Reserve in Colombia who had been threatened by paramilitaries and other irregular groups. These groups were killing community members and driving them from their lands on a regular basis.[13]

In addition to mandating immediate state protection for such communities, the indirect but no less imminent danger posed by attacks on these communities' natural resources is also in the sights of that court. This was the case when the government of Nicaragua "granted logging rights on untitled indigenous lands to a Korean company."[14] It was likewise the case when the "government of Belize granted logging rights and oil exploration rights on a Mayan reservation to a private company."[15] The Inter-American Court of Human Rights recognized that the basic subsistence of such communities is tied to their lands, as is their cultural and religious life: "Access to their ancestral lands and the natural resources on those lands is directly linked to their ability to obtain adequate food and clean drinking water."[16]

This statement is particularly germane to the defence of basic human rights proposed in this book. Paradoxically, it is only in indigenous case law that one may find examples of the following: (1) the connection between the right to life and natural resources; (2) the need to protect peoples, at least in principle, from the relentless intrusion of corporate raiders; and (3) the obligation of states to offer such protection to *all* their citizens. At least in theory, the rest of humankind is considered less at risk or perhaps better able to protect itself from the disguised physical aggression represented by industrial activities and the ecoviolence they bring, whenever and wherever they pursue their economic goals and practise their activities. I argue that neither of these claims is entirely true for most of humankind, although those who enjoy economic advantages are no doubt protected, at least partially and for some time. Both chemical exposure and climate change, however, affect all of humanity to varying degrees.

INVESTMENTS AND THE POLICE POWERS DOCTRINE

> Adopting a human rights framework allows to better define and articulate state obligations to respect, to protect and to fulfill environmental health. Not only do states have the obligation to refrain from acts which encroach upon people's health, such as activities causing environmental pollution *(obligation to respect)*, but they also have the obligation to take legislative action and other measures to protect people from health infringements by third parties *(obligation to protect)*. Finally, states also have the *obligation to fulfill* environmental health, by providing a safe environment.
>
> – Valentina Vladi, "Reconciling Environmental
>   Health and Investors' Rights in International
>   Investment Law"

The interface between environment and health emerges from a number of nonenvironmental settings, where the environment and health are often viewed as forms of indirect appropriation (e.g., when a corporation faces restraints on the sale and promotion of hazardous products), when regulatory regimes limit the investment advantages that may arise from the activities of technical and other extractive industries. Some of these cases have appeared in arbitration tribunals and address basic human rights.[17]

  One such case is that against Chemtura Corporation, which deals with the question of "whether the government of Canada should pay compensation to a US company for its ban of an agro-chemical called Lindane."[18] The case has not been resolved, but the response of Chemtura Corporation includes the expected disclaimers: the complaint was "not based on a rigorous risk assessment," and it "was motivated by a politically charged conflict."[19] Yet the WHO described the product as "moderately hazardous," and the Commission for Environmental Cooperation released an action plan, according to which "the parties commit to eliminate or ban the use of Lindane."[20]

In a similar case, *Methanex Corporation v. United States of America*, heard by the NAFTA Arbitral Tribunal in 2005, a Canadian corporation argued that the California regulations prohibiting the use of a gasoline additive were unfair to Canada.[21] Scientific evidence indicated that "MTBE (methyl/tertiary-butyl ether) contaminated ground water, and was difficult and expensive to clean up."[22] In this case, an appeal was made to police powers to restrain the use of the chemical, hence moving beyond the maxim of *sic utere tuo ut alterum non laedas* (use that which is yours so as not to injure others).

These cases rest on various due process issues such as the use of *indirect discrimination* to describe the way each country treats the products of another in trade. Ostensibly, all the cases originate from a desire to protect health and basic rights; however, the merits of scientific evidence are seldom the focus of the arbitrations. Trade remains the main focus, and at best some reasonable manner of resolving the problems is sought. These reasonable solutions do not, however, address the basic issue: why are trade-oriented institutions involved in the resolution of cases in which the *only* issue should be the scientific research connecting the product in question with public health and basic collective human rights?

It bears repeating: although basic collective human rights are entrenched in all human rights declarations and related covenants, the right appealed to by corporate plaintiffs is that of receiving fair treatment in their goal of profit maximization. Profit maximization is neither a legal principle nor a right, and it does not appear as such in any international legal instrument. In addition, these tribunals pose an even greater risk to collective human rights than the resolution of cases without any regard for the science involved. By making trade concerns superior to the obligations of states, outlined by Valentina Vladi above, NAFTA, the World Trade Organization, and other such tribunals discourage states from taking a stronger position against corporate offenders to protect the physical security of their citizens. There are two ancient doctrines that spell out clearly the king's obligation to his citizens – the public trust doctrine and the *parens patriae* (parent of the nation) doctrine – and both defend the ultimate collective rights of citizens.

From the Inuit Circumpolar Conference Petition and *Kivalina* to *State of Connecticut v. American Electric Power*

> The impacts of climate change, caused by acts and omissions by the United States, violate the Inuit's fundamental human rights protected by the American Declaration of the Rights and Duties of Man and other international instruments. These include their rights on behalf of culture, to property, to the preservation of health, life, physical integrity, security, and the means of subsistence, and to residence and the inviolability of the home.
>
> – Sheila Watt-Cloutier and others, "Petition to the
> Inter-American Commission on Human Rights"

In the last few years, the effects of climate change have been felt increasingly all over the world, but Arctic peoples and other indigenous groups from southern continents and regions, together with the inhabitants of islands and coastal cities, have been the sentinels, the proverbial canaries in the mine.[23] Their efforts to gain justice or at least redress for the harms they have suffered have been publicized and are well known, but little success can be reported.

Arctic peoples suffer the effects of climate change in a particularly brutal manner. As they see their rights to a traditional way of life disappear, they are also watching animals and their territories disappear because of pollution and glacial melts.

In a frozen land, where even small changes in the climate can be
significant, the rapid changes being wrought by global warming are
nothing short of catastrophic. Global warming is forcing the Inuit
to shoulder the burden of the rest of the world's development with
no corresponding benefit ... Inuit Qaujimajatuqangit [IQ] tells the
Inuit that the weather is not just warmer in the Arctic, but the entire
familiar landscape is metamorphosing into an unknown land.[24]

Contrast this passage, from a petition written by Artic peoples, with the terse
response of the Inter-American Commission on Human Rights (Organization
of American States), which declined to rule on the complaint "that global
warming caused by the United States violates their right to sustain traditional
ways" because "there was insufficient evidence of harm."[25]

The petition had been filed in December 2005 by Sheila Watt-Cloutier,
chair of the Inuit Circumpolar Conference, on behalf of the 155,000 Inuit
of Canada, Greenland, Russia, and the United States. The petition painstakingly takes the reader through familiar territory, problems addressed in this
book, such as recent harms to their traditional hunting and gathering culture,
to their economy, to their social and cultural practices, and to Inuit traditional
knowledge regarding climate conditions.[26] The petition also reviews well-
known facts and scientific evidence about global warming and the particular
vulnerability of the Arctic. To ignore the melting of polar ice sheets and
glaciers, rising sea levels (a hazard the Arctic shares with island and coastal
states), the alteration of species and habitats, and changed conditions that
amount to a physical and intellectual attack on life is to exhibit not only unacceptable ignorance but also wilful blindness.[27] To claim that there is insufficient evidence is a criminal approach to the reality of the Inuit's conditions.[28]

The petition also cites the conditions of Shishmaref, Alaska (see my
discussion of the Kivalina Case in Chapter 2), and the ongoing erosion of
that settlement. It also refers to the Lubicon case, and the importance of the
UN Human Rights Committee's decision in that case based on the right to
enjoy culture, as a violation of Article 27 of the *International Covenant on Civil
and Political Rights,* despite the fact that not much has changed for the Lubicon
since then.[29] I argue, albeit with far less support from legal precedent in either
international or domestic law, that the right to life, health, and normal function should be considered first, as the most basic human right.[30] The petition
states: "International health and environmental law also lend support to the
American Declaration's right to health. The preamble of the Constitution of

the World Health Organization (WHO) recognizes that, "[t]he enjoyment of the highest attainable standard of health is one of the fundamental rights of every human being."[31] Given the main focus of this book, the reference to health is particularly important. It indicates what the law should prescribe as a general obligation and what is perhaps the most important aspect of the Arctic peoples' plight: their survival, both individual and collective. It is clear that James Anaya and other scholars involved in drafting the document emphasize threats to cultural survival because the right to cultural integrity is included in several international instruments. By contrast, the right to health is seldom, if ever, coupled with environmental degradation or pollution of any kind.

Sheila Watt-Cloutier was, however, nominated, along with Al Gore, for a Nobel Prize, and on 20 June 2007, she won the 2007 Mahbub ul Haq Award for Outstanding Contribution to Human Development at the UN. Niamh Collier-Smith, a spokeswoman for the United Nations Development Programme, told CBC News that "Sheila Watt-Cloutier's dedication and her tireless work with the Inuit people, especially in the fact of devastating climate change, is a real inspiration to us all."[32]

The situation of the Native village of Kivalina (see Chapter 2), particularly the effect of relocation on their traditional culture, which is tied to a particular territory, bears obvious similarities to that of the Inuit.[33] In neither case, however, was the parens patriae doctrine invoked. Both the international legal case (the petition) and the claimants' case in the domestic case were based a combination of the classic position presented in *Rylands v. Fletcher* and the principles expounded in *Trail Smelter Arbitration*.[34] Neither case is cited specifically, but the addition of other components because of indigenous communities' *sui generis* position, that is, the protection of their rights to culture and religious practice, complete the petition. Still, *Trail Smelter Arbitration* is foundational for all environmental cases. Russel Miller argues, "The *Trail Smelter* principles persist in international instruments, casebooks and scholarly footnotes, as the *locus classicus* of international environmental law. So it is not at all surprising that one need only scratch the surface to find trace elements of these *Trail Smelter* principles in global climate change regimes."[35]

The question is whether Nunavut and other Arctic communities are indeed nations with their own boundaries and rights. Is Nunavut a nation in the sense that it could participate in international law meetings separate from Canada? It might be worth considering, from the standpoint of *lex ferenda* (future law) whether self-governance will entitle the Inuit to more legal protection than they enjoy as a separate minority within Canada. In fact, the thrust of Miller's argument is precisely the important role played by nonstate actors in both the *Trail Smelter Arbitration* case and climate change, a precedent that may help their case: "The rise of these non-state actors suggests a new world order in which the nation states' Westphalian prerogative is increasingly suspect. The literature is right to remind us that non-state actor involvement in international affairs is nothing new. But the nature and degree of the contemporary involvement of non-state actors is a genuine phenomenon."[36]

Nongovernmental organizations and major corporate individuals play a determining role in climate change negotiations. This pressure is new but is also based on *Trail Smelter* itself. During that case, the Citizens Protection Association, a Washington residents' group that would not allow the issue of Canadian pollution to rest, took a forceful stance and forced the case to be reopened in 1933. They refused the $350,000 judgment proposed by the International Joint Commission as compensation and insisted on additional investigations.[37] In contrast, corporate mining and smelting interests (on the US side) tried unsuccessfully to side with the Canadians. In other words, the *Trail Smelter Arbitration* "transcended its formal framework, as a dispute between the United States and Canada, to encompass the clash of interests between non-state actors in an environmental NGO, facing off against global industrial interests on the international plane. This clash of non-state actors is paradigmatic of contemporary international environmental law."[38] This reality is endemic to globalization: the main focus is on economic outcomes, without any regard for the serious human rights violations that result from corporate activities.

For Arctic peoples, the effects of the extended ecological footprint of a globalized economy are so severe and so diffuse that it would be extremely hard to bring home the responsibility for these results to either corporate individuals or complicit governments. This is especially true since the connection between environmental harms and medical harms has been ignored by courts and legislators, from *Trail Smelter* on. This ignorance might have been justified in 1933, even in 1941, but it is an anachronism today, when the connection between exposure to industrial products and processes and human health are backed by solid research from the World Health Organization, epidemiology, and other scientific research. Yet this connection is still overlooked, as is the accelerating damage caused by climate change, in a clear case of wilful blindness.[39]

The strong presence of NGOs in current environmental debates can, however, be used profitably by Nunavut. Nongovernmental organizations, now as then, "advised and even participated as members of government delegations."[40] Today, they are even more vocal and powerful. They are, for instance, much in evidence at climate change meetings: "The tiny nation of Vanuatu turned its delegation over to an NGO, with expertise in international law ... thereby making itself and the other sea-level island states major players in the fight to control global warming."[41] In fact, by the year 2000, when the sixth session of the UNFCCC Conference of the Parties (COP6) was convened in The Hague, "representatives of NGOs outnumbered representatives of states."[42] Hence, even if the self-governing nation of Nunavut does not have the full credentials of a state, the present operation of international law permits the participation of a much greater constituency, at least in the area of Climate Change: "Any Body or Agency, whether national or international, governmental or non-governmental, which is qualified in matters covered by the Convention, and which has informed the secretariat of its wish to be represented at a session of the Conference of the Parties as an observer, may be so admitted."[43]

The tone of the discourse, however, changes radically in *State of Connecticut, et al., v. America, Electric Power Company, Inc. et al.* (2009). Several trusts – the Open Air Institute, the Open Space Conservancy, and the Audubon Society of New Hampshire – joined with the states of Connecticut, New York, California, Iowa, New Jersey, Rhode Island, Vermont, and Wisconsin, as well as the City of New York, against several electrical power companies. These states and trusts jointly claimed that "the ongoing contributions to the public nuisance of global warming" are causing "and will continue to cause serious harms affecting human health and natural resources."[44] Although the defendants claimed the whole issue was a "non-justiciable political question" – for which the defendants lacked standing or that they attempted to displace federal common law – the Court of Appeals rejected their arguments. The states itemized, singly and collectively, the harms of climate change, which, they argued, will produce "substantial adverse effects on their environment's residents and property" and which will cost each state billions of dollars. As an example, "the reduction of California's mountain snowpack, the single largest freshwater source critical to sustaining water to the State's 34 million residents during the half of each year, when there is nominal precipitation" is certainly a "substantial adverse effect."[45] The states also listed several significant cases of "increased illnesses and deaths caused by prolonged heat wave" and harms caused by smog and poor air quality. They explicitly noted the impacts on "property, ecology and public health."[46] Finally, the trusts explained "how the ecological value of specific properties in which they have an interest will be diminished or destroyed by global warming."[47]

The connection between ecological values and public health is particularly relevant, as is the argument presented to the court. Well beyond the expected focus on economic impacts and property values (although these are also a significant part of the states and trusts' argument) is the rejection of the "political question" doctrine, especially the use of the parens patriae doctrine. This doctrine offers the first new approach to the problems discussed, although it is a principle rather than a legal instrument, either domestic or international.

THE PARENS PATRIAE DOCTRINE: AN OLD PRINCIPLE WITH A NOVEL APPLICATION

> *Parens patriae* is an ancient common law prerogative which "is inherent in the supreme power of every state ... [and is] often necessary to be exercised in the interests of humanity and for the prevention of injury to those who cannot protect themselves."
>
> – *State of Connecticut, et al., v. America, Electric Power Company, Inc. et al.* (2009)[48]

Protective jurisprudence has a history that dates back to the Middle Ages. In its most recent instantiations, the parens patriae doctrine has been used to support judicial decisions that deal with the protection of those who cannot speak for themselves, especially in the case of health issues.[49] The language of these judgments is extremely suggestive and worthy of attentive study.

The doctrine of parens patriae, despite its Roman name, is entirely a common law doctrine; for instance, although the Canadian Supreme Court makes use of it, it does not exist in Quebec law.[50] It is perhaps an anomaly that a doctrine with a Roman name and origin is presently only found in the common law, as Morin indicates in his description of the doctrine's historical background.[51] Until 1873, a fundamental dichotomy prevailed in Britain's legal system. From the Middle Ages, royal tribunals used the *commune ley,* but the great majority of cases were heard by lords and the local courts. Only rarely did the king, as fountain of justice, participate in court cases, and he did so through the person of his chancellor, who until the sixteenth century was also his confessor, hence the use of the Latin phrase *parens patriae.*[52]

The chancellor's goal was the promotion and the triumph of equity principles, learned in his study of Roman law. The rules guiding these judgments and their results eventually became codified, and precedent was born.[53] The doctrine of parens patriae was used in custody and guardianship matters involving a lord and a minor, perhaps one whose father might have been a tenant of the lord before his death. In these cases, guardianship was required until the child could be recognized as a tenant in his father's stead, at age fourteen.

The Court of Wards and Liveries was instituted by Parliament in 1540 and remained in operation for some time.[54] The concept of royal protection was substituted in the sixteenth century by the Court of Chancery, which kept the concept of wardship alive and introduced a novel move in 1792, when it forbade a violent father from interrupting his son's schooling and from continuing with his guardianship.[55] Although the Court of Wards was abolished, the concept of wardship remained as an aspect of parens patriae jurisdiction: "In time wardship became substantively and procedurally assimilated to the *parens patriae* jurisdiction, lost its connection with property, and became purely protective in nature."[56]

The origins of the doctrine of parens patriae explain both its Latin roots and its evolution from the protection of a minor's economic interests to the protection of children's interests, *simpliciter.* Does its development render the doctrine applicable to the protection of human beings in general? The classic statement of the modern principles that govern state intervention in the best interests of the child is Judge Rand's judgment in the Supreme Court of Canada case *Hepton et al. v. Maat et al.* (1957):

> The view of the child's welfare conceives it to lie, first, within the warmth and security of the home provided by his parents; when through a failure, with or without parental fault, to furnish that protection, that welfare is threatened, the community, represented by the Sovereign, is, on the broadest social and national grounds, justified in displacing the parents and assuming their duties. This in substance, is the rule of law established for centuries and in the

light of which the common law courts and the Court of Chancery, following their differing rules, dealt with custody.[57]

Judge La Forest likewise ties recent cases to their British background in *E. (Mrs.) v. Eve* (1986): "It will be obvious from these provisions that the Supreme Court of Prince Edward Island has the same *Parens Patriae* jurisdiction as was vested in the Lord Chancellor in England and exercised by the Court of Chancery there."[58] The increasingly wide reach of the doctrine has given the courts the ability to protect children from injury. In the English case *Re X (a minor)*, for instance, Judge Latey cited "a passage from Chambers on Infancy (1842), p. 20 that indicates that protection may be accorded against prospective as well/as present harms."[59]

This statement brings us a lot closer to the possibility of protecting health. If prospective harm is an explicit part of the parens patriae doctrine, then the doctrine is not simply a juridical tool to be used after some crime has been committed or to prevent some obvious injustice. The doctrine could be an especially powerful instrument when there is an unconsented medical treatment at issue, for it could be used "to prevent ... damage being done." In the United States, this approach was taken up in *Stump v. Sparkman* (1978).[60] In another US case, *Matter of Sallmaier*, heard in 1976, the court stated: "The jurisdiction of the Court in this proceeding arises *not by statute*, but from the common law jurisdiction of the Supreme Court to act as *parens patriae* with respect to incompetents."[61]

Essentially, there are two possible approaches included in the doctrine: the "best interest" approach and the "substituted judgment" approach.[62] What is relevant is that neither approach requires a person to protect. In fact, parens patriae only comes into effect when the individuals in need of protection cannot legally think or decide for themselves or protect their own interests. Because the doctrine has been applied in the case of incompetents, or those who are not able to protect themselves from harm, it is particularly appropriate for protecting from harm unborn generations and those who are first harmed by any exposure – in other words, children and infants, as the research of the World Health Organization and other epidemiologists and scientists indicates.[63] This research has shown that the particular physical configuration and growth pattern of children makes them particularly vulnerable to all forms of pollution, whether chemical or air- or water-based. Temperature variability is also particularly hazardous for infants and children, as are the droughts and floods endemic to climate change and the vector-borne diseases that follow global warming.[64] Although even a cursory consideration of the general collective of humankind indicates that all citizens are affected to varying degrees, pregnant women, infants and children, and the elderly are sure to be the first to suffer grave effects from climate change, as do the poor and other vulnerable populations.

In *Georgia v. Tenn. Copper Co.*, in 1907, the United States Supreme Court affirmed that "the state has an interest independent of and behind the titles of its citizens, in all the earth and air within its domain. It has the last word as to whether ... its inhabitants shall breathe pure air."[65] In the second seminal case for parens patriae standing in the United States, *Snapp & Son, Inc., v. Puerto Rico*, the court noted that there had been a "line of cases ... in which States successfully sought to represent the interests of their citizens in enjoining public nuisance."[66] In order to maintain a parens patriae action, a state must (1) "articulate an interest apart from the interests of particular private parties, i.e., the State must be more than a nominal party"; (2) "express a quasi-sovereign interest"; and (3) have "alleged injury to a sufficiently substantial segment of its population." The court in *Snapp & Son* also identified the two kinds of quasi-sovereign interests as follows: (1) "protecting the health and well-being ... of its residents" and (2) "securing observance of the terms under which [the state participates in the federal system."[67] Only health and well-being are relevant for protecting basic collective human rights anywhere.

The first possible difficulty of widening the use of the parens patriae doctrine is that "quasi-sovereign states" must acquire the parental standing necessary to legislate or use it for the protection of all, or even a significant segment of their people. If the doctrine is used elsewhere for protection from environmental harms, especially in a global setting and to deal with the international effects of climate change, it should be incorporated within international law and, when collective human rights breaches occur, in international courts. The question that arises is, which entity should, logically and legally, take the place of the parent, whose responsibility for dependent children indicates the applicability of the doctrine? In the case of the European Union, perhaps it could be said that all the citizens of the states within it are in a position similar to that of citizens of individual states. But it is much harder to envisage a similar "parental" role for the UN, even aside from the fact that, to my knowledge, this doctrine has not been appealed to by either the UN or the European Union in any environmental case thus far.

Nevertheless, my self-appointed task for this chapter was not only to seek out what may be already available to protect basic collective human rights but also to propose any doctrine, principle, or instrument that *may*, in the future, be involved to fulfill that role. The doctrine of parens patriae has now been used domestically to protect these rights. It has been used to acknowledge the state's responsibility to ensure that its citizens are not exposed to health hazards, which are the inescapable result of environmental exposures.

The Public Trust Doctrine: A Discussion

> In the case of the equation of the public trust doctrine and the police power, where the state purports to act pursuant to police powers but rests its powers on the property rights of the public, the fallacy is not well concealed, and the potential for state intrusion upon the private rights of individuals is limited only by the vision of those who would extend the reach of the public trust doctrine.
>
> – James Huffman, "Fish Out of Water: The Public Trust
> Doctrine in a Constitutional Democracy"

Perhaps it is the position (i.e., Huffman's) that must be clarified and ongoing debates regarding the public trust doctrine (the principle that certain resources are reserved for public use) that suggested, in the previous case, the use of a different (albeit related) tool, the parens patriae doctrine, to better protect the rights of the collective. James Huffman, arguing against Joseph Sax, sees the public trust doctrine as property law.[68] His main point is that because the public trust doctrine is traditionally and explicitly part of property law, legal scholars who seek to extend it to other fields such as "trust, constitutional, administrative and police power law" are mistaken.[69]

Huffman does, however, acknowledge the birth of the public trust doctrine in English common law.[70] Like parens patriae, the doctrine originated when the king and other noblemen held rights and power and when the common people needed to protect their own rights to the commons, such as land and waters, from the sole discretion of the king. Public trust implied that the king could not alienate the public rights to the use of those waters and lands.[71] Given this history, *pace* Huffman, it seems appropriate to understand the doctrine as a form of restraint on private rights, particularly the private rights of legal persons, and on democratic decisions that favour majoritarian preferences on the use of the commons over those of minorities, distant peoples, and future human beings.

In *Illinois Central R. v. Illinois* (1892), the US Supreme Court decided that the grant of submerged lands to the railroad violated "a trust for the people that they may enjoy the navigation of the waters, carry on commerce over them, and have liberty of fishing therein freed from the obstruction or inter-ference of private parties."[72] Of course, at that time, the full impact of the interference of private property on public rights to the commons was not fully appreciated, and future scientific research could not have been antici-pated. Today, however, it would be even more appropriate to invoke the doctrine to protect basic collective human rights. Nevertheless, given the debate about its true meaning and use and the procedural issues that surround the public trust doctrine, one can perhaps appreciate why the drafters of *State of Connecticut, et al., v. America, Electric Power Company* chose not to employ it and instead used a doctrine, parens patriae, whose connection to property has long since been abandoned.

The important point is that the historical basis of the public trust doctrine, like that of parens patriae, indicates that an all-powerful sovereign's policies and decisions were limited by the basic needs of his people, long before the modern emphasis on legal human rights. In other words, common law offers two possible options for the protection of collective human rights or general welfare (see Chapter 1).[73] At least in principle, either could be used to support and defend basic collective human rights.

Mary Christina Wood, discussing US law, presents a different position from Huffman on the issue. She "proposes a paradigm shift away from the current system of natural resource management, a system driven by political discretion, to one that is infused with public trust principles and policies across all branches of government and at all jurisdictional levels."[74] The first step is not to think of the public trust doctrine simply as another form of property right. In reference to environmental laws, particularly laws regarding the commons, she warns that "we have won many victories, but we are losing the planet."[75] To support her position, she cites a number of familiar statistics, including exposure to chemical and other pollutants from the womb on and the "loss of life and ecosystem on the planet," all of which she terms ecological bankruptcy.[76]

Given the global reach of ecological bankruptcy, it is not simply US law that suffers from administrative dysfunction. The severity and number of grave difficulties cited by Wood are such that they indicate a similar dysfunc-tion at the international level. The latter should be the most appropriate level from which to address the following global problems, listed by Wood, that affect basic collective rights:

- "The modern environmental administrative state is geared almost entirely to the legalization of natural resource damage."[77]

- "Agencies have created a regulatory complexity that is mind-boggling ... the complexity – legal baklava, so to speak – carries several perils for environmental policy. It distracts agencies from seeing the macro picture of resource health."[78]
- "Agencies regularly confront and succumb to political pressure to issue permits and sanction other harmful actions."[79]
- "The public has become disenfranchised within this system of environmental laws ... Standard environmental analyses contain acronyms, technical findings and conclusions that are unduly complex and incomprehensible to the average citizen."[80]
- "The judiciary has lost its potency as a third branch of government speaking in the environmental realm. This is primarily due to the tendency of courts to invoke the administrative deference doctrine."[81]

As in international law, political discretion and deference to the most powerful states and corporations trumps scientific research and moral obligation. It is not inappropriate to term this situation a form of institutional decay.[82] Therefore, despite acknowledged difficulties in isolating "a firm source of legal obligation," aiming for a fiduciary obligation, one that rests on the historical foundation of the public trust doctrine, is a good move, one that ought to prevail in some way in international law.[83] For the latter to happen, however, it would be necessary to secure an understanding of who would be "king," the entity upon whom the legal obligation would rest. The United Nations appears to be the only candidate for this role. However, it is well known that the UN is both an actor and a stage, and it is the latter role that would pose a problem.

Nevertheless, if the UN is to represent the global community, not only all states but also all people, then allegiance and compliance with its mandates, including its declaration and the findings of special commissions and rapporteurs, needs to rest on an assurance of protection and respect for global collective rights. Without the latter, it would be unrealistic to assume the legitimacy of an international legal order headed by the UN. Perhaps we could assume a fiduciary obligation on the part of the UN based on international legal regimes, an obligation similar to that owed by the Canadian government to First Nations. In Canada, the protection of First Nations, individually and collectively (as a community), provides the most solid "last word" in cases where their welfare is at stake. Thus, like the parens patriae doctrine, to understand the fiduciary basis of the public trust doctrine appears to provide desirable and possible doctrines as first steps toward the protection of the commons and of basic collective rights.

A Review of the Argument

> A new jurisprudence of rights, the explicit purpose of which is to mitigate the moral poverty of legal positivism, has quietly acknowledged the natural law part of its genealogy.
>
> – Costas Douzinas, *The End of Human Rights*

Costas Douzinas notes that although many view the international recognition of human rights as marking "the end of the ignorant past," "more human rights violations have been committed in this rights-obsessed century than at any other point in history."[84] Moreover, "when nature is no longer the standard of right, all individual desires can be turned into rights."[85]

It is appropriate to return to a discussion of natural law, given the argument I presented in Chapter 1 and natural law's ongoing presence in international law. Basic collective rights are indeed based on the nature of biological individuals and on the laws of nature, both of which are fundamentally unchanging. The connection between collective human rights and the abused commons, as I have noted repeatedly, is not present either in international or domestic law in a way that can protect these rights. Therefore, the quest for a magic bullet, a legal instrument or regime to resolve ongoing problems, did not prove to be a fruitful approach to finding more robust protections for basic collective rights. There are a number of good conventions – for instance, as I have noted in these pages, especially their preambles – but there are no existing regimes for monitoring and implementation.

A number of cases likewise presage real progress. The best among them, *State of Connecticut, et al. v. American Electric Power Company*, may even influence the final disposition of the *Kivalina* case and the Inuit petition currently before the European Commission of Human Rights. What the best case has to offer, however, is a return to traditional obligations and standards in the defence of principles that today may be termed *jus cogens* norms. Furthermore, appeals to strong fundamental norms give rise to what no king of old accepted: responsibilities that we now understand to be *erga omnes*, that is, obligations that extend to the entire international community. Is a return to traditional principles and standards enough to bring about progress?

Douzinas certainly thinks so, and perhaps this somewhat anachronistic answer is the best available and a new beginning.

Before offering my preliminary conclusions, a review of my argument is in order. In the opening chapters of Part 1, I attempted to ground collective basic rights and the public good in international law. I thus recognized right from the start the foundational aspect of jus cogens norms and the erga omnes obligations they support. Chapter 2 detailed the prevailing lawlessness fostered by globalization and by the proliferation of individual human rights, free from any standard provided by nature. It also exposed two of the major issues facing the world today: the effects of climate change and the increasing presence of hunger, which is itself one of the consequences of global warming in several continents. Responses to both issues reveal a lack of recognition of the public good that has resulted in the business-as-usual orientation of the lawless world described by Philippe Sands. A consideration of the issues, rather than simply the theory, in turn revealed that laws do exist, in both domestic and international regimes. On the ground, however, the general practice tends to be for states, legal entities, and others to attempt to circumvent these laws or to interpret them in ways that mitigate or eliminate whatever threat they may present to prevailing political and economic interests.

In addition, every effort to resolve the problems that confront us ends up, for the most part, mired in the usual procedures, subject to the same limiting deferences. Most of all, those who could resolve these problems are unable to think outside the box, even in regard to such obvious issues as the connection between human life, health, normal development, the habitat the humans in question inhabit. It is disheartening to note that even piling on more cases, learned jurisprudence, and explicitly protective legal instruments is insufficient to bring about progress.

Chapter 3 reprised the discussion of Chapter 1 to draw out the differences between communities and the collective and to show that indigenous peoples and other land-based minorities, at least in principle, enjoy the sort of legal framework that connects the integrity of their territories with that of their community and, at times, even with the physical integrity of individuals within their community. This acknowledgment is based on their particularity, on their status as *sui generis* communities. Therefore, indigenous peoples can serve as models in two senses: first, the traditional lifestyle of some of these communities supports basic collective human rights; second, these communities can function as guides, not to force a return to a lifestyle most of us have long since abandoned, but to help us understand what sort of natural limits must be accepted to stop destroying the planet and, ultimately, ourselves.

But as for other legal conventions, the protection of indigenous peoples' communitarian rights is often neglected, even in countries that are at the forefront of modern-day understandings of ecological necessities. These countries (e.g., Ecuador) may possess excellent constitutions, strong in the protection of nature itself, as well as the indigenous peoples who depend upon it. Yet there, too, these countries see indigenous peoples injured and decimated for political and trade-related reasons, decided beyond their own borders.

Part 2 examined more closely existing practices and instruments that may offer some hope for the protection of basic collective human rights. Chapter 4 considered the UN's Millennium Goals and the right to development. Both are clearly insufficient to ensure the protection we seek, although the existence of such documents can be considered a step forward, a tool in a limited arsenal of protective documents. Similarly, the principle of the common heritage of mankind and the emerging framework convention on public health appear as a beacon of hope, although neither has been used in any existing case to protect basic human rights.[86]

Perhaps one of the most hopeful ideals is the presence of democratic institutions in much of the world today. Democracy remains the most touted, promoted, and desired form of government everywhere. But Chapter 5 provides evidence of more disillusion than progress. The most powerful Western states today, the same states that proclaim themselves willing to wage war to ensure the prevalence of democracy in other countries and the protection of human rights everywhere, are involved in some of the most egregious violations of human rights in history. Examples include forced displacements, extraordinary renditions, and neocolonialism, not only through the spread of economic globalization but also through the return of imperialism and the support of nationalism in allied states, a practice that would not be tolerated in an unallied state.

In Chapter 6, I considered whether the existence of the United Nations, the presence of democracy in all of its most powerful states, and the participation of NGOs in both the design and the implementation of protective instruments will help to build a world and moral community based on cosmopolitanism. Will they be enough in a globalized world based on the preferences of the majority? Is world law possible? The chapter briefly reviewed the available jurisprudence, most of which related to indigenous communities. However, the best court judgment available today – *State of Connecticut, et al.*

v. American Electric Power Company, Inc. et al. (2009) – returns to standards and principles (and to the recognition of nonderogable state obligations) that could and should be repeated in the obligations of the international community. In international law, that would mean an appeal to erga omnes obligations. In general, the case suggests that the public good *must* be acknowledged as primary. Whether the appeal is to the parens patriae doctrine or the doctrine of the public trust, the move must be toward principles and standards and away from preferences and economic interests.

Perhaps, then, our effort to transform and reform should be aimed at what Mary Christina Wood terms the disfunctionality of the present legal infrastructures rather than at examining specific instruments and successful cases. The problems are systemic, embedded in the way law tends to operate in all settings. Hence, Wood is correct when she asks for a radical paradigm shift to save the planet and life on Earth.

Conclusion

In the spirit of attempting a paradigm shift as suggested at the end of the previous chapter, it is necessary to move beyond existing legal regimes. Against the background of what are usually (on the domestic plane) called constitutions, I will approach the subject of the common good from the opposite side and look at the phenomena discussed under the heading "the constitutionalization of international law." The basic premise of the constitutionalist school is that the international community is a legal community. A legal community is governed by rules and principles, not by power. The most fundamental norms may be global constitutional law.[1]

The *parens patriae* doctrine and the doctrine of the public trust can be invoked when the issue under consideration affects the citizens of a sovereign state. As noted, both doctrines require a central power, a government that can be held accountable for the illegitimate harms that citizens suffer and that generate the suit. As well, an international constitution based on non-derogable principles such as *jus cogens* norms may represent the central, unitary authority required to provide the focus for the responsibility and obligations that follow.

The idea of the "kingship" of the UN, however, suffers from several drawbacks. Primary among them is its political composition, the history of which was described briefly above. If some countries have the right to veto the protection of human rights, then political obligations rather than the legal and moral right are the UN's ultimate responsibility. To draw a parallel from history: the king's allegiance was primarily to the noblemen that supported him, not to the public good or to the protection of the weak or most vulnerable. Can the UN be reformed to eliminate this anomaly? Probably, but not as quickly as the ongoing disasters affecting the collectivity need to be addressed.

Yet a commitment to principles over politics appears to be one of the major transformative needs listed by Wood.[2] In that sense, the *Charter of the*

United Nations itself, as the central instrument upon which to base a possible UN constitution, is

> a different, merely treaty-related, type of higher law. According to Art. 103 of the UN-Charter, its provisions (and arguably secondary acts such as Security Council decisions) prevail in the event of a conflict between the Charter-obligations of Member States and obligations under any other agreement. However, UN-Acts privileged by Art.103 UN-Charter still rank below *jus cogens* and would have to give way in case of conflict. Consequently, a hierarchy of norms *within* international law exists.[3]

Another question related to the central institution that would be responsible for these doctrines is the status of the collective itself. The global problems that threaten the collective's survival cannot be solved entirely, or even primarily, at the domestic level. Even in the best of cases within democratic countries, citizens can only vote for what happens within each country and, in most cases, only within certain limits. For instance, the use and even the production of nuclear power is among the most hazardous activities in existence, as both the World Health Organization and the International Court of Justice have argued. Yet, to my knowledge, there is no effective voting choice in any major Western democracy that would allow voters to mark a clear *no* to the use of nuclear power.

Therefore, while citizens are not incompetent in the sense required for the application of parens patriae, they are nevertheless almost totally impotent when it comes to many aspects of policy making (e.g., on the most controversial issues, no referenda or other serious polling of public opinion is allowed). Hence, parens patriae is not only appropriate for defending the rights of future generations or infants and children today, but it is also equally desirable for the collective, the world citizenry, including the poor and vulnerable in developing countries and everyone else. There is little or no power of self-defence for the collective, given the dysfunctionality of many basic human rights regimes and the abdication of most modern states from their obligations (in favour of various free trade agreements). Finally, the lacunae or limitations of the scientific education of legislators and judges complete the list of the complex difficulties faced by those who need urgent protection of their basic rights.

I have traced the effects of all of the above, especially in the narratives of the case law regarding indigenous peoples. However, the international legal instruments that view the collective as primary – that is, the UNESCO instruments of the common heritage of mankind or, in general, legal instruments regarding public health, especially the recently proposed Framework Convention on the Right to Public Health – are seldom used in the jurisprudence. More specifically, even the *Declaration on the Rights of Indigenous Peoples* of 2007 is not supported by global consensus, although it has the sponsorship and support of the UN.

Laws in the public interest are, almost by definition, *not* laws that support the most powerful forces in globalization; however, Anne Peters and others argue that "the UN Charter is the constitutional document of international law."[4] Hence, despite the problems in ascribing a pivotal role to the UN, it seems to remain the best possibility for a central governing institution at the head of an inclusive transnational constitutionalism, given that existing laws do not function as they should to protect the collective. A world law would require a central figure to administer and enforce it and, at this time, the UN and its *Charter* appear to be the only recognized reference points in international law.[5] As well, there are many domestic instantiations of its mandates, which is especially significant because, at the same time, "state sovereignty is gradually being complemented, if not substituted, by other guiding principles, notably the 'global common interest' and/or rule of law,' and/or 'human security.'"[6]

Perhaps this preliminary discussion has laid down clearly enough the reasons for appealing to a world law as a starting point toward a solution for the multiple difficulties encountered in the quest for the protection of basic collective human rights. World law could herald the move toward a radical transformation of the current forms of governance (as Richard Falk advocates in his early and later work).[7]

WORLD LAW, COSMOPOLITANISM, AND AN INTERNATIONAL CONSTITUTION?

> Because the idea of a constitution is associated with the quest for a legitimate one, the constitutionalist reconstruction *provokes the pressing question of the legitimacy of global governance.* In consequence, the constitutionalist reconstruction of international law rather helps than blocks the revelation of existing legitimacy deficiencies in this body of law, which can obviously no longer rely on state sovereignty and consent alone.
>
> – Anne Peters, "Global Constitutionalism in a Nutshell"

There is no need to once again elaborate the many ways in which both state sovereignty and democratic consent, as they exist today, have failed to meet the main obligations of state democracies, that is, the protection of fundamental human rights. My argument concludes by proposing the UN as the most desirable central authority and, I now add, its *Charter* as the most appropriate constitution. Part of the "work" of the UN has been, and is, assisting in constitution building, particularly in the context of decolonization in recent and not so recent years.[8] International society, as a collective, needs a totally different approach to deal effectively with its problems, an approach that goes beyond positivism, coupled with sovereign states that may or may not want to collaborate and join and ratify the treaties that benefit the collectivity.

Despite its weaknesses, the UN's unitary position and authority may, at least in principle, deflect the fragmentation of rules and instruments that exist today in international law, as well as the all-encompassing power of trade-oriented institutions. The UN and its organs and commission can provide a united line of protection for the rights of the collective, and it can do so in ways that even the most progressive state constitution and related domestic legal infrastructures cannot. Onora O'Neill explains its necessity well:

> A global system of a plurality of more-or-less sovereign States whose inhabitants' lives are restricted for many purposes to their own state, can injure many lives. Even if each state were more or less internally just, and they rarely are, States may injure those whom they exclude, and a system of States may systematically or gratuitously injure outsiders by wars and international conflict and by economic structures that control and limit access to the means of life.[9]

O'Neill's passage touches on the difference between globalization and cosmopolitanism. While the former is primarily procedural in its structures and influenced primarily by powerful, market-oriented powers, the latter is based primarily on substantive moral principles of justice that include but also transcend the economic realm and rely on Kantian principles. States may or may not be fully just within their own borders, but they may well injure those outside their borders by exclusionary practices, which are *direct* injuries.[10] The practices outlined in the previous chapters are *indirect* injuries. These injuries are a form of indirect injustice because "destroying parts of natural and manmade environments injure those whose lives depend on them." In addition, "the principles of destroying natural and manmade environments, in the sense of destroying their reproductive and regenerative powers, is not universalizable."[11]

Ecological and biological integrity is precisely what O'Neill terms "regenerative and reproductive powers" or true sustainability: "Environmental justice is therefore a matter of transforming natural and manmade systems only in ways that do not systematically or gratuitously destroy the reproductive and regenerative powers of the natural world, so do not inflict indirect injury."[12] In O'Neill's terms, moral principles constitute the blueprint and the specifications, which define the product to be produced. In a similar sense, strategies based on principles are not tools to use to achieve just aims, but they do define what forms those tools may take. O'Neill writes: "The move from abstract and inconclusive principles of justice towards just institutions, policies and practices is analogous to moves from design specification towards finished product."[13]

The finished product of this book – a strategy for just and ecologically sensitive institutions – may not yet be achievable, but at least a prototype of what the finished product may look like and what it may achieve can emerge. At this point, we are still at the blueprint and specification stage. In contrast to the procedural thrust of liberal governance (with its avoidance of moral absolutes or clear commitment to a specified common good, beyond the economic advantage of the most powerful groups, states, and institutions), cosmopolitanism recognizes the porousness of borders, despite their logic of inclusion and exclusion. Because it recognizes the existence of nonderogable obligations beyond borders, its scope includes "distant strangers and future generations."[14] Cosmopolitanism based on Kantianism can supply the principles and guidelines absent in the thinking of even the best among the advocates of liberal democracy, who seldom seek out the roots of injustice: "The idea that our economic policies and the global economic institutions we impose make us causally and morally responsible for the perpetuation and even aggravation of world hunger, by contrast, is an idea rarely taken seriously by established intellectuals and politicians in the developed world."[15]

John Rawls's work on justice distorts this basic reality: "like the existing global economic order, that of Rawls's Society of Peoples is then shaped by free bargaining."[16] The strategies required to overcome free bargaining will be discussed further. For now, the main point is that every practice that bears the prefix or qualifier *free* is, *ipso facto*, not so, in the universal sense. Being free to pursue harmful practices does not render those who are harmed free. Freedom can be considered an obstacle to global justice, not a constructive component of it. Rawls's liberalism and his studies of justice and the law of peoples emphasize and support this very lack of substantive, principled approaches, a situation that must be transcended because it supports globalization and all its inherent injustices.[17]

The alternative to globalization that I propose is a form of Kantian cosmopolitanism, an approach that embodies respect for near and distant persons and future generations as well. In contrast, the principles that Rawls embraces and that support fairness are said "to be internal to liberal societies."[18] At best, these principles attempt to mitigate some of the evils fostered by liberalism. They make no attempt to reach all the way to the destructive foundation on which these theories and practices rest: "a pattern of derivation shows that inclusive principles of indifference to and neglect of others also cannot be universalized."[19] To proceed from blueprints to specifics, it is important to ensure that the starting point is compatible with and supportive of the final goal. A Kantian form of cosmopolitanism provides this initial blueprint.

In addition, the need for a world law is implicit in Richard Falk's contention that the world is a whole. Thomas Pogge's example of global famine (see Chapter 6) supports Falk's contention that the world as a whole has arrived at a Grotian moment.[20] But thus far we have been unable or unwilling to even attempt to reach across the normative abyss that is before us. As Falk writes, "A neo-liberal world order based on the functional imperatives of the market is not likely to be a Grotian moment in the normative sense."[21] Falk's main point coincides with my argument: while Grotius was able to "articulate a normative bridge between past and future" at a critical historical moment, the present world order is both unable and unwilling to do so. Falk notes that the present world order "reflects mainly economistic priorities and that the state system has lost much of its credibility in problem solving, in the face of "the rise of market forces."[22] Falk adds: "We currently confront in this era of economic and cultural globalization a more profound normative vacuum: the dominating logic of the market in a world of greatly uneven social, economic, and political conditions and without any built-in reliable means to ensure that a continuing global economic growth does not at some point and in certain respects cause decisive ecological damage."[23]

Given his clear understanding of many of the forces I have identified as causative of global dysfunction, it is important to consider what Falk proposes as an antidote, if not cure. While he does not appeal directly to Kantian cosmopolitanism, his proposals include "an International Criminal Court with broad powers of investigation and effective procedures to ensure implementation ... without being subject to political controls" and a "strong and effective U.N. (with) an environment program capable of protecting the global commons" and ensuring "respect for fundamental obligations to uphold human rights." However, because "the state appears to have lost its creativity and autonomy," as well as its ability to initiate "a new normative order," "the European Union is one exploration of another sort of agency."[24] Falk's argument makes it clear that although he thinks people should be heard and involved in the transformation necessary to produce a normative framework, he concedes that we have been "lulled to ideological sleep by a mixture of consumerist allurements and a deadening market-driven ideological consensus."[25] Pulling ourselves up by our own bootstraps to the demanding normativity required to prevent global disaster appears to be an impossibility.

The UN *Charter* and Its Constitutional Potential

> Because the *Charter* is the constitution of the international community, member states are obliged to maintain a certain minimum ability to safeguard international peace ... The guiding idea is that a council reform should advance as much as possible the aims and purposes of the international community as set out in the *Charter*. It should promote in particular the maintenance of international peace and the protection of the "dignity and worth of the human person."
>
> – Bardo Fassbender, "The United Nations Charter as Constitution of the International Community"

It has been argued that "the Charter has had a constitutional quality *ab initio*."[26] But what is a constitution? Scholars of different backgrounds and eras have proposed different definitions. For instance, Konrad Hesse defines a constitution as "the legal fundamental order of a public community": a constitution "determines the guiding principles according to which political unity shall be constituted and governmental tasks shall be performed. It establishes procedures to resolve conflicts in the community and organizes and structures the formation of political unity and governmental activity. It creates the foundations and sets forth the essential features of the legal order as a whole."[27]

It is important to note that some common law countries do not share the European preoccupation with the theory of constitutions. The United Kingdom has no constitution, although the United States does.[28] James

Madison, for instance, distinguished between "a constitution established by the people and unalterable by the government and a law established by the government and alterable by the government."[29] Bardo Fassbender adds that "constitutions almost always present a complex of fundamental norms governing the organization and performance of governmental functions in a given state ... and relationships between state authorities and citizens."[30] This passage raises two questions with which I have been dealing in one form or another throughout this book: (1) What is the extent of the sovereign power of states? and (2) Who should be the citizens of the collective, whose human rights require urgent protection?

Historically, Jean Bodin framed the power of sovereign state as a necessary step in the formation of modern territorial states. He did not, however, view their power as "limitless."[31] Bodin clearly saw the sovereign state as bound by the tenets of natural law.[32] A further confirmation of this limitation can be found in Emmerique de Vattel's work, as natural law also mandated the principle of *neminem laedere* (not to do damage to someone else) and *pacta sunt servanda* (agreements must be kept).[33]

In recent times, the UN *Charter* itself recognizes the "sovereign equality of member states."[34] However, it also asserts the UN's right to interfere with that sovereignty, should state policies "endanger international peace and security."[35] In addition, the *Charter* provides an obligation to all member states "to promote respect for human rights without discrimination on the basis of race, sex or nationality."[36] Hence, the second question is answered, for it is recognized that the protection of human rights is a seamless concept, that is, one that is not limited by either the physical location or the ethnic or religious background of the citizens who constitute the world's collective.

However, this theoretical agreement between sovereignty and the protection of human rights, while correct in principle, does not appear to correspond to our present reality.[37] Kant himself believed that "the freedom of the individual can only be safeguarded within a lawful society, which Kant understood to be the 'res publica' or the 'good state.'"[38] In contrast to theory, however, the reality is that legal systems, domestic and international, are dysfunctional; they cannot offer solid protection of basic rights.[39] Jost Delbrück adds that although "the binding nature of international human rights norms is accepted ... there are no adequately functioning courts of law, an economic and social achievement that would allow for the implementation of economic and social rights; or sufficiently well-trained legal persons who could respond to the demands of the international human rights norms."[40]

Richard Falk, faced with this reality, proposes a complete change in the world order, an idea that I share.[41] Nevertheless, as we move from here to there, the urgency of collective protection suggests a direction and interim measures of the kind to which Fassbender and Delbrück appear to support. Their proposed use of the UN *Charter* and of world law and a constitution seem to be the best next step available, even as we wait for a complete overhaul of the present world order.

AN INTERNATIONAL CONSTITUTION OR A UN WORLD ENVIRONMENTAL ORGANIZATION?

> A constitution consists of the fundamental rules governing a political community and is generally but not always in written form. In contrast, *constitutionalism* refers to the broader set of qualities or values associated with the liberal conception of a constitution, such as limited government and the dignity of the individual.
>
> – Daniel Bodansky, "Is There an International Environmental Constitution?"

Appealing to the UN and its *Charter* means, essentially, seeking an international constitution, one that would be applicable to all member states. It would mean acknowledging that "a constitution is a higher body of law, typically of an enduring nature, setting the fundamental rules of a political community."[42] Constitutionalism is indeed understood as the possibility of designing and enacting a higher law. Applying this novel approach to international environmental law is something that is, increasingly, viewed as desirable.[43]

There are a number of reasons for seeking a totally new way of understanding, designing, and applying international environmental law. The first and most obvious is the lack of consideration granted to most environmental issues and cases today. Human rights problems, for instance, are at best treated as torts rather than as grave crimes. One can understand the difficulties facing the International Court of Justice and the International Criminal Court when there are so many clear and obvious cases of crimes against humanity or genocide competing for their attention. People who have been attacked with machetes clearly need more immediate attention than those whose attacks consist of toxic exposures that result in slowly developing diseases, although they may be equally fatal in the end. The second reason is that a constitutional form of governance "could help to compensate for the declining role of state consent."[44] Constitutional governance may be at least a partial answer to Falk's concern about a Grotian moment, for international law would acquire a "stronger normative footing."[45] Finally, the third reason is that much of the discourse on various aspects of a world law emphasizes the role of constitutions as providing substantive rules for basic human rights protection, beyond procedural rules.[46] That, of course, is precisely why we are seeking a better institutional and organization regime, perhaps even another court, with the capacity to handle issues and cases that do not take precedence today.

Another positive aspect of pursuing this approach is that is bears similarities to the supranational form of governance that prevails in the European Union, without, however, eliminating the sovereignty of the individual states. Bodansky adds: "Constitutions are sometimes depicted as limitations on public power. Yet they, in fact, serve dual functions, both constituting and constraining power."[47] In sum, the specific aspect of constitutionalism that makes it "hierarchically superior to ordinary law" renders it capable of protecting the basic human rights of the collective, and the environment itself, in ways that cannot yet be found in today's law regimes.[48]

Before exploring how this new order would function at the practical level, it is useful to trace the background of an idea – the establishment of a World Environmental Organization – that has been building for some time in the work of several scholars. The most recent and explicit proposal has been promoted and organized by Judge Amedeo Postiglione and the International Court of the Environment Foundation.

THE IDEA OF A WORLD ENVIRONMENTAL ORGANIZATION

Environmental problems, however, were no concern in 1945, with the term "environment" not even appearing in the UN Charter. It was only in 1972 that UNEP [United Nations Environment Programme] was set up as a mere programme, without legal personality, without budge, and – according to its founding instruments – with only a small secretariat," which is no comparison to the other specialized organizations that can avail themselves of more resources, hence, influence.

– Frank Biermann, "The Rationale for a World Environmental Organization"

The need for an environmental organization with, at least, parity with other important UN organizations and organs is obvious, as is the lack of awareness of the impact of global environmental problems on human rights. The idea of a World Environmental Organization (WEO) emerged right after the Rio Conference of 1992.[49] Steve Charnovitz compares the lack of support for an environmental regime with support for trade organizations such as the World Trade Organization and their ongoing growth and power. Since the 1990s, "many analysis have called for correcting 'this organizational dysfunction in environmental regimes.'"[50]

Several variations on the theme of the WEO or other possible organizations were proposed by a number of scholars from the 1990s onward.[51] Despite their different histories and backgrounds, all of these proposals were overlooked at the 2002 World Summit on Sustainable Development and at the 2002 Johannesburg Summit.[52] In contrast, most governments were discussing, organizing, the promoting trade through the World Trade Organization: "it seems noteworthy that the Governments were willing to delve into the management of the trading system while not paying much attention to needed improvements in environmental governance."[53]

This book proposes some of the reasons for this dissonance. It is clear that, to effectively correct this situation, an organization would have to be intrusive; it would have to restrain the sovereign power of states to pursue their interests and their perceived advantage. I use the term *perceived advantage* because all trade policies are enacted, as they usually are, for the short-term advancement of the party in power, and the enterprises that support the party are, for the most part, harmful to those who are the real responsibility of each state: its collective citizenry. The basic rights of the latter would be protected by an organization committed to their health and to that of their habitat. In addition, the global aspect of such an organization would be a far better match for the worldwide reach of present attacks on humankind than a legal instrument limited by the borders of any one country. International environmental law, even at best, is "inter-national," or between nations, especially since the vital connection between ecological safety and basic human rights has not been established.

Is this proposed solution fated to remain theoretical, or is there a movement toward official sanctioning of such an organization? The International Court of the Environment Foundation (ICEF) has been working for many years to render such an organization practicable.

GLOBAL ENVIRONMENTAL GOVERNANCE: THE PROPOSAL OF
JUDGE AMEDEO POSTIGLIONE AND THE ICEF

> The need for strengthening environmental governance is urged by
> the inadequacy for the actions presently carried out in the context
> of the U.N. system, including its organs, agencies and programme,
> to deal in a coordinated and most effective fashion with the most
> relevant outstanding issues of environmental protection and the
> achievement of sustainable development in a global perspective.
>
> – Francesco Francioni et al., "Options and Modalities
>   for the Improvement of International Environmental
>   Governance"

Judge Postiglione met with a number of other legal scholars, European Union
government officials, and judges in various courts in Europe and elsewhere
on 20-21 May 2010 in Rome, Italy, at the Offices of the Ministry of Foreign
Affairs, for yet another ICEF convention.[54] His 2010 publication, *Global Environmental Governance*, lists several reasons why he feels an international
court of the environment is necessary: to connect human rights and the environment and to affirm both individual and collective rights, based on the
"responsibility to protect," as both a procedural and a substantive right.[55]
These rights are based on the "absolute priority of the sustainability of life
on earth," because viewing the environment as a necessity leads, in turn, to
the "necessity for *erga omnes* mandatory norms."[56] These few words, combined
with the three options outlined below, give a taste of the publication and its
detailed analysis of the need for environmental governance.

In Part 4, Postiglione reviews the possible options that could be advanced
to operationalize the new organization. The first is "the establishment of a
new U.N. Specialized Agency for the Environment (UNEO). This is the preferred Option of the group." It would inherit "competences ... presently
owned and exercised by the UNEP," but it would also act as an umbrella
organization, coordinating environmental initiatives within the UN system.
The proposed Convention of the UNEO should be presented as "an initiative
of the European Union"; thus, the European Union's member states would
represent an initial "negotiating block."[57]

The United Nations Environmental Organization (UNEO) would have
the same membership as the UN and would have its own juridical personality
as a "specialized agency of the United Nations."[58] The new organization would

strive to coordinate all "common environmental policies" and harmonize the "global environmental action" pursued.[59] Because the coordination of most relevant existing multilateral environmental agreements (MEAs) is a difficult task, Postiglione views these moves only as "process."[60] The UNEO would emerge as the "main permanent multilateral forum for environmental negotiation"; "provide capacity building to a national judiciary"; "provide assistance in the development of regional and bilateral agreements"; and "assist and advice "on the resolution of environmental disputes."[61]

This option has a few disadvantages. The first is the need for voluntary and non-voluntary funding. Second, it would be necessary to adopt an international treaty to institute the organization and a dispute settlement system coordinated with other pre-existing judicial systems.[62]

The second option is a "reinforcement of the existing system (EUNEP), or an Enhanced UNEP," which would be put in place by means of a new resolution of the UN General Assembly.[63] This would entail "expanding the existing functions and improving [the UNEP] administrative structure and funding,"[64] The second option would eliminate the need "to create a new bureaucratic machinery"; the transition from UNEP to EUNEP could be fairly simple; and the role of the new UN agency would gain strength through its proposed connection with the Global Environmental Fund.[65] However, the low visibility of the current UNEP at the international level would persist. It would also be hard for the UNEP to gain the "environmental authority" it presently lacks. And, finally, such "enhancement would not help to coordinate the proliferating 'Conferences of the Parties' and MEAs [multilateral environmental agreements] as the UNEP already acts as the Secretariat of the latter."[66]

Finally, the third option is the "establishment of a new international organization for the protection of the environment (WEO)." It would be instituted through an international ministerial, which could be convened by the European Union. Its membership should be open to all states, and it would promote "co-ordination with the UN institutions, agencies and programmes" and perhaps act as a secretariat to several MEAs. As well, its administrative structure should include a dispute settlement authority, including a court of first instance and a Court of Appeal, with three or five judges chosen not only on the basis of their competence and independence but also from a wide geographical area.[67]

The main advantage of a WEO would be the creation of a global environmental system, which may provide coherence and coordination for environmental protection. However, the strength and rigidity of this approach would not appeal to many states. Although the World Trade Organization has a similar strength, it is appealing to states because it enhances their political and economic interests.[68] The suggestion that the WEO "should also try to establish a preferential relationship with the WTO" is unrealistic and naive.[69] It is obvious that any strong environmental organization, to be effective, would necessarily be in direct conflict with the World Trade Organization and other trade-oriented institutions.

The possibility of collaborating with the World Trade Organization or of involving industry in the construction of such a radically new organization would undermine any positive role this institution may play in the protection of the environment and basic human rights. Nevertheless, the ICEF can boast of a strong and growing movement, one that appears to have the potential for a real impact, even in the preliminary stage. This is more evident in Europe, where there is already an implicit acceptance of various forms of supranational governance, which is not yet accepted in Asia, Africa, or America. Despite its limitations and problems, the very existence of this initiative, with its growing momentum and its widespread support, merits its mention as a possible first step in the defence of the commons.

The Next Steps

> It is sufficient to mention a few key words to make the reader recall the great debates which have profoundly influenced, if not changed, global life: self-determinations of peoples, decolonization, human rights, fight against racial discrimination, definition of aggression, nuclear arms, utilization of outer space and the sea-bed ("common heritage of mankind"), global environmental problems, especially the use of non-renewable resources and the protection of particularly vulnerable areas (Antarctica, tropical forests). In all these discussions, the UN regarded itself as the "natural forum"; and indeed, no other body could have claimed a similar legitimacy.
>
> – Bardo Fassbender, "The United Nations Charter as Constitution of the International Community"

As Bardo Fassbender states, the *Charter of the United Nations* was intended, designed, and used to provide basic principles and support universal law. In reviewing Fassbender's analysis, I also agree with his assessment of the role the *Charter* has played in the great debates named and more besides, such as the *Convention on the Rights of the Child* and the *Declaration on the Rights of Indigenous Peoples*.

However, despite the UN's pronouncements, the Arctic and Antarctica continue to be severely affected by climate change, tropical forests are being systematically eliminated, and the connection between environmental problems and the basic rights of humanity, of which the UN proclaims itself to be the champion, is still unrecognized for the most part. The UN *Charter* opens with a strong appeal that is universal: "We the Peoples of the United Nations, determined to save succeeding generations from the scourge of war, which twice in our lifetime has brought untold sorrow to mankind."[70] The aim is the protection of future generations, and the object to be eliminated is the greatest scourge of the era during which the UN came into existence – that is, war. Aggression, however, is still not well defined today, and the most common and widespread forms of violence today include economic oppression and the deprivation of basic rights of the collective, through climate change, deprivation of natural resources, and increasingly hazardous industrial activities. The novel peril to which humankind is progressively exposed was not known over sixty years ago. If the *Charter* is to become the living constitution of a newly recognized world law and global community, its definitions and principles must be re-examined. Chapter XVIII and Articles 108 and 109 of the *Charter* indicate that amendments were consonant with its design and expected by its drafters. After all, even a *jus cogens* norm can be modified by another rule of the same character.[71]

The most basic problem beyond definitions and basic principles, however, appears to be the composition of the UN Security Council, which tends to work against the basic requirements and goals of the *Charter*, that is, global governance "based on peace and the protection of the dignity and worth of the human person."[72] Hence, a change in the Security Council's rights and composition would be an amendment with lasting and wide-reaching effects. The possibility of amendments and the limitations on the sovereignty of states embedded in the *Charter* render it a possible future global constitution. *The Charter* would, if amended, be capable of restructuring international law and effecting a transformation oriented to the protection of collective human rights. In contrast, the present composition of the Security Council clearly militates against the achievement of the main goal of the *Charter* – the maintenance of peace – as is evidenced by a number of ongoing conflicts and gross violations of the "dignity of the human person."

Therefore, we can only hope that the next steps, at least the most desirable ones, will be possible, regardless of whether the focus is on the role of the UN and the *Charter* as world law and an emergent world constitution. These amendments ought to be the first and most important target for future transformations. The UN could make use of its own organs (such as the World Health Organization), and it should support its own rapporteurs and the results of its own commissions' findings, without the strangling effect of its own Security Council and its outmoded and unjust veto system.

Perhaps the UN should also liberate itself from the vestiges of old allegiances and old wars and embrace its own self-determination in order to fulfill its original mandate and its possible destiny in the future of international law. Only then will the basic rights and human dignity of the collective find their promised champion. In fact, the UN should be the focal point for a world law, with the *Charter* as a world constitution. The UN has a lot in its favour, including (1) the intentions of the original drafters of the *Charter*; (2) its quasi-democratic composition; (3) its openness to amendments, consonant with its need to cover emerging issues and situations; and (4) the principled background of most of its documents, declarations, and reports. In addition, the UN *Charter* carries a high degree of authority, both moral and legal. Joseph Raz discusses the relationship between morality and the law and the "necessary obligation to obey the law."[73] Raz also notes that Thomists and some non-Thomists such as Gerald Dworkin start with the obligation to obey all laws, except for "marginal cases of law to which duty does not apply."[74] However, he neglects to point out that, for Thomas Aquinas himself, obedience to the law, which is normally mandatory, ceases to be if the law in question is not just – that is, if it is not aimed at the common good. When a state is radically unjust, then the obligation is to disobey, not to be in any way complicit in its wrongful aims, because the state's legitimacy is lost when the common good is not served by its rulers. Speaking of man's obligation to obey a prince, Aquinas says clearly, "if he commands what is unjust, his subjects are not bound to obey him."[75]

Justice, in turn, is determined by the adherence of laws to the common good. This understanding of natural law, based on the biological or scientific observations of Aristotle, to a large extent, defends the theory from the objections of constructivism, which is based on Western ideals. Aristotle was a Greek. (For those who persist in viewing natural law as primarily a Christian theory, one should bear in mind that Jesus was a birth citizen of the Middle East, not the West.) A just law is a man-made code that squares with the moral law or the law of God. An unjust law is a code that is out of harmony with the moral law. To put it in the terms of St. Thomas Aquinas: an unjust law is a human law that is not rooted in eternal law and natural law. Any law that uplifts human personality is just; any law that degrades human personality is unjust.[76] Essentially, then, the moral authority of the *Charter* and of all UN instruments is ultimately based on whether they are intended to support the common good.

What about their legal authority? Raz states that "the law has come to be seen as subject to change in response to changing circumstances, and to changing moral beliefs. It has become the way 'we,' 'society' discharge our obligations to each other in an environment of relatively rapid social change."[77] Thus, law in general, is not only the expression of a moral ideal, which in turn provides its legitimacy, it is also "the authoritative voice of a political community," against a background of multiple communities and a "decline in the role of custom."[78] Because Raz writes of the political community rather than a state, it may be appropriate to see the political community, rather than a state, as the global collective of subjects of international law. Finally, the legal aspects of world law and of its constitution must be emphasized and strengthened. Their legal authority is undermined by their political dependence and geopolitical commitments. This weakness must be remedied in order not to harm or diminish the global moral authority of the UN and to ensure its ability to protect the collective.

Will some form of a WEO or other global environmental organization, based on the present UN or working as one of its organs, indeed be the solid step forward envisaged by members of the ICEF and other scholars? The question is integral to this book, because my goal is to unite environmental considerations with the basic rights of the collective. Hence the question I propose needs to be framed as follows: is an organization that aims to set apart the protection of the environment as a major component of the UN system necessary for both the commons and basic human rights? A higher profile for environmental concerns, and perhaps even a separate court to adjudicate cases with both speed and competence, would be a very good thing indeed. What must be understood, however, is that even the inception and full success of such an organization would not be sufficient to accomplish what I have proposed in these pages.

The inescapable connection between the environment and the basic survival rights of humankind are perhaps alluded to, but not clearly established, by any form of WEO. In fact, in some sense, the establishment of a separate organization may even create the impression that such a step is all that is needed. In fact, the interface between human rights and ecological conditions should be explicitly introduced right in the Charter and at the forefront of other basic international instruments, such as the *International Covenant on Civil and Political Rights* and the *International Covenant on Economic, Social and Cultural Rights,* as is recommended by some of those who advocate an enhanced World Health Organization and even a Framework Convention on Public Health.[79]

Thus, although it is vital to give at least parity (if not primacy) to ecological issues, in comparison with trade and economic ones, it is insufficient to do so if such issues are not linked explicitly to collective and individual human rights. I refer to the global moral authority of the UN: a wider and clearer understanding of the reach of human rights based on recent science should be the first and most important step toward achieving it. The second, or concomitant, step proposed by the supporters of a WEO would then be completing and rendering operational the understanding of human rights promoted by the *Charter.*

Cosmopolitanism, Global Citizenship, and World Governance

> Legally, the term *citizenship* now denotes a constitutionally defined relationship between an individual and a nation state, in which the individual receives a guarantee of certain civic rights in exchange for certain civic duties and responsibilities.
>
> > – Michael Karlberg, "Discourse Identity and Global Citizenship"

The main point is that many are questioning liberal democracy's ability to deal effectively with globalization and its problems, especially environmental degradation.[80] This issue is particularly grave when even democracy itself, in its present instantiation – that is, in conjunction with neoliberalism in the West – cannot deal effectively with collective human rights issues under the supraconstitutional governance of major trade and financial organizations. As Stephen Clarkson argues, even the best and most sensitive domestic constitutions no longer provide the last word on human rights issues, if and when a possible trade conflict is found within its mandates.[81] Hence, in that sense, there are already-existing organizations that embody centralized forms of global governance, over and above presently existing states.

Thus, to propose that cosmopolitan principles are foundational to global governance for the protection of collective rights is not to attempt a totally new form of governance. Rather, it is an effort to show why existing global institutions do not support the primacy of collective human rights and, therefore, why they are both inappropriate and insufficient to perform their task. For instance, the authors of the "Roadmap for Integrating Human Rights into the World Bank Group" acknowledge the relevance of human rights to the objectives and operations of the World Bank, but admit that integration, desirable though it is, has yet to come.[82] In contrast, no such report exists at this time for either the World Trade Organization or for NAFTA.

Some hold that democracy can indeed "spread across territorial borders" as a form of "double democratization," and this seems to be the main goal of the transformation of governance.[83] My analysis, however, points in the opposite direction, as does the work of others, for instance, Richard Falk.[84] At any rate, as Angel Saiz writes, "the urgency and complexity of the environmental challenge demands a supranational mechanism that has the benefit of political and financial independence."[85] However, Saiz does not acknowledge that states can no longer claim full independence, precisely because of the presence of a supraconstitution enforced by trade-oriented organizations. States' constitutional mandates can be (and are regularly) superseded by the legal decisions of nontransparent, nonelected institutions.

Peter Furia, nevertheless, discusses cosmopolitanism as many see it – that is, as elitist and unpopular, as neither understood nor accepted by most people given their (well-founded) suspicions about existing supranational institutions. He cites Alexander Wendt:

> In Europe, mass opinion is considerably more nationalistic and anti-integration than elite opinion. The same is true of the United States, where there is a deeply rooted populist culture of isolationism that is hostile to the UN, NAFTA, WTO, and international involvement generally ... In sum, then, to the extent that a perception of transnational community is being born, it is much more a community of capital and states than of peoples ... they [peoples] are hostile to the whole idea of transnational community in the first place.[86]

Distrust of "the UN, NAFTA, WTO" suggests the two main conclusions that are tentatively proposed in this work. First, the UN is viewed as one of the politically controlled major institutions from which most of the threats to peoples' collective rights originate. It should, however, be considered a defender of such rights, in opposition to NAFTA and the World Trade Organization. Second, even peoples' own states appear preferable to an unprincipled and opaque supranationalism that could include some of the most uncontrollable transnational corporate actors as the ultimate sources of power.

Furia defines cosmopolitanism as "the belief that humanity as a whole constitutes the relevant identity group and that concrete moral and political obligations arise from this identification." This definition is consonant with my defence of the human collectivity as well. Furia adds some further distinctions: "At one extreme, we would have the hypothetical 'universalist,' who believes that anything that tends to divide humanity into sub-groups is, by definition, bad. At the other extreme, we would have the hypothetical 'multi-nationalist,' whose moral commitment is to groupness, alterity, diversity as such."[87] In Chapter 1 of this book, I argued that these are not necessarily positions in conflict, provided that cosmopolitan universalism is viewed as the main principle in defence of what all humanity shares as a collectivity of biological beings, with the same basic needs. In contrast, communities and other diverse groups, while *all* worthy of the same respect for their humanity, may differentiate themselves by holding specific positions and beliefs, not all of which may be worthy of our collective support, when judged from the standpoint of the defence of basic rights. Hence, that defence must be taken to be the final criterion for morally just governance. Finally, it is still an open question whether the UN, as the only presently existing institution with the capacity to promote responsibility for collective rights, could be transformed into an organization that could deliver on what it promotes and affirms, thus differentiating itself drastically from NAFTA, the World Trade Organization, and the International Monetary Fund on questions related to human rights,[88] or whether some version of a World Environmental Organization may provide a useful, positive first step.

Notes

INTRODUCTION
1 Westra (2004a).
2 R. Westra (2010, 105).
3 Westra (2004a).

CHAPTER 1: INDIVIDUAL RIGHTS AND COLLECTIVE RIGHTS IN CONFLICT
1 Wood (1998).
2 Hardin (1968).
3 Wood (1998, 81).
4 Shue (1996).
5 Westra (2004a).
6 Boyle (2007, 471).
7 Westra (2009b, especially Chaps. 1 and 6); see also Michelot (2006, 428).
8 Westra (2007)
9 Atapattu (2002-3).
10 Leopold (1949, 203).
11 *Gabčíkovo-Nagymaros Project*, [1997].
12 Vasak (1979).
13 Vasak (1977, 29).
14 Galenkamp (1998, 20).
15 Stavenhagen (1990, 258).
16 Galenkamp (1998, 38).
17 See *Guerra and Others v. Italy*, [1998]; *López Ostra v. Spain*, [1994]; and *Fadeyeva v. Russia*, [2005] for some related cases.
18 Newman (2004); Kymlicka (1995); Gewirth (1978); Anaya (2004); Shavarsh (2007); Isaac (2002).
19 Anaya (2004, 52-53).
20 Newman (2004, 158).
21 Brownsword (2004, 216).
22 Shue (1996, 27n4).

23 Ibid., 18n4 and 19n4.

24 Ibid., 23n4.

25 UN, *Universal Declaration of Human Rights* (1948); *International Covenant on Economic, Social and Cultural Rights* (1966); and *International Covenant on Civil and Political Rights* (1966).

26 (Pogge 2001, 7). Pogge's statistics are drawn from the United Nations Development Programme's *Human Development Reports* for 1998, 1999, and 2000.

27 See Fidler (2001); Westra (2000); McMichael (2000); Epstein (1978).

28 O'Neill (1996).

29 Ibid., 175.

30 Ibid., 176.

31 Ibid., 179.

32 Soskolne and Bertollini (1999).

33 Brown-Weiss (1992).

34 Westra et al. (2000).

35 O'Neill (1996, 193n16).

36 Shue (1996, 19n4).

37 Gewirth (1982).

38 Ibid., 5.

39 Ibid., 7.

40 Ibid., 5.

41 Beyleveld and Brownsword (2001, 71).

42 Shue (1996, 19n4).

43 Gewirth (1982, 54n23); see also Beyleveld and Brownsword (2001, 70n29).

44 Mathieu (1996, 28, emphasis added); see also Beyleveld and Brownsword (2001, 158n29).

45 Marquis (1989).

46 Beyleveld and Brownsword (2001, 158n29).

47 Ibid., 112n29.

48 Gewirth (1982, 112n25); see also Singer (1976); DeGrazia (1995).

49 Regan (1983).

50 DeGrazia (1995).

51 Westra (1994, 96-97).

52 On preferences, see Westra (2000).

53 Ibid., 39.

54 See Bedau (1979) on survival and Matthews and Pratt (1985) on subsistence.

55 Donnelly (1989, 38).

56 On constraint, see Brownsword (2004, 214).

57 See *Alien Torts Claim Act* jurisprudence, for instance, in Westra (2009b, Chap. 6)

58 See, for instance, Scott (2008); Atapattu (2002-3, 65).

59 See Goldin Rosenberg (2007).

60   Finnis (1980, 152).
61   Ibid., 136-38.
62   Ibid., 164.
63   Brownsword (2008a, 1).
64   Ibid., 6-7.
65   Anaya (2004, 131-40); see also Westra (2007, Chap. 2).
66   Brownsword (2008a, 8).
67   Westra (2004b).
68   Brown (2008).
69   See Jones (1970, 326) for general information.
70   Pogge (1992, n70).
71   Brownsword (2008a).
72   Ibid., 55.
73   See Pogge (2001).
74   Pogge (1992, 56).
75   Ibid., 63.
76   Ibid.
77   Shue (1996, 18).
78   See Atapattu (2002-3).
79   Feinberg (1973).
80   Newman (2004, 128).
81   Ibid.
82   Aquinas (1953, 95).
83   See also Westra (2004a, Chap. 1).
84   Held (1970, 165-68).
85   Newman (2004, 128) writes, "The argument here is for moral rights held by collectivities."
86   Westra (2006).
87   Raz (1997, 84).
88   Newman (2004, 132).
89   Ibid., 159.
90   Brand and Sekler (2009, 5, 6).
91   Howard and Donnelly (1993, 66, 67).
92   Dworkin (1977, 272-73).
93   Donnelly (1989, 70).
94   Ibid., 64.
95   Ibid. To be fair, Donnelly recognizes that Western market practices can be blamed for creating the necessity for human rights.
96   Falk (1984, 131).
97   Westra (2004a); see also Kössler (2008).
98   Kössler (2008, 35).

99 Depelchin (2008, 22).

100 Schabas (2000).

101 Schaller (2008, 80-81).

102 Westra (2006).

103 Beyleveld and Brownsword (2001, 105-10).

104 Brownsword (2008b, 200).

105 Westra (2006, 2009a).

106 Grandjean and Landrigan (2006).

107 Beyleveld and Brownsword (2001, 123).

108 Grandjean and Landrigan (2006).

109 Gewirth (1978, 141) writes: "Children are potential agents in that, with normal maturation, they will attain the characteristics of control, choice, knowledge, and reflective intention that enter into the generic features of action."

110 Beyleveld and Brownsword (2001, 127).

111 Brownsword (2008a, Chap. 2).

112 Boyd (2003, especially Chap. 11).

113 See, for instance, Swedish Ministry of the Environment (2001, 130; 2002).

114 Boyd (2003, 291).

115 Ibid.

116 Ibid., 293.

117 Westra (2004a, especially Chap. 2).

118 See, for instance, *Pappajohn v. the Queen*, [1980]; *R. v. DeSousa*, [1992]; and *Sansregret v. The Queen*, [1985].

119 Sunstein (1990, 407, 408-10).

120 Ibid., 419.

121 For examples, see ICJ, *Application of the Convention of 1902*, [1958], separate opinion of Judge Moreno Quintana; ICJ, *Right of Passage over Indian Territory*, [1960], dissenting opinion of Judge Fernandes; ICJ, *South West Africa (Ethiopia v. South Africa)*, [1966], dissenting opinion of Judge Tanaka; ICJ, *North Sea Continental Shelf (Federal Republic of Germany/Denmark) (Federal Republic of Germany/Netherlands)*, [1969], dissenting opinion of Judge Tanaka; ICJ, *Legal Consequences for States*, [1971], separate opinion of Vice-President Ammoun; ICJ, *Military and Paramilitary Activities*, [1986], separate opinion of President Negendra Singh and separate opinion of Judge Sette-Cama; ICJ, *Gabčíkovo-Nagymaros Project*, [1997], separate opinion of Vice-President Weeramantry.

122 Kadelbach (2006, 34).

123 Shrader-Frechette (1982).

124 Shrader-Frechette (1982, 15, 25-44; 1993); Draper (1991).

125 Draper (1991); Wilson (1992); Colborn, Dumanoski, and Myers (1996).

126 Wasserstrom (1985); McMahan (2009, 141); Bok (1985).

127 Handl (1985, 49).

128   Ragazzi (1998, 173).
129   *Nuclear Tests (Australia v. France)*, [1974], and *Nuclear Tests (New Zealand v. France)*, [1974].
130   *Nuclear Tests (New Zealand v. France)*, [1974], 494; Ragazzi (1998, 175).
131   Ragazzi (1998, 175).
132   *Treaty Banning Nuclear Weapons Tests* (1963).
133   Ragazzi (1998, 177).
134   Cited in ibid., 179.
135   ICJ, *Barcelona Traction*, [1970].
136   *Legality of the Threat of Nuclear Weapons*, Advisory Opinion, [1996].
137   Cited in Kindred et al. (2000, 363).
138   *Legality of the Threat of Nuclear Weapons*, Advisory Opinion, [1996].
139   Falk (1998, 172).
140   Ibid.
141   Ibid., 173.
142   Ibid., 174.
143   Ibid., 175.
144   Kindred et al. (2000, 631).
145   Goerner (1994); Caldwell (1993).
146   Deets (1998, 1).
147   ICJ, *Gabčíkovo-Nagymaros Project (Hungary v. Slovakia)*, [1997].
148   Peel (2001, 82).
149   Ibid.
150   Deets (1998, 17).
151   *Gabčíkovo-Nagymaros Project*, [1997], separate opinion of Weeramantry.
152   UN, *Declaration on the Right to Development* (1986); UN, *Declaration of the United Nations Conference* (1972) *(Stockholm Declaration)*.
153   *Gabčíkovo-Nagymaros Project*, [1997], separate opinion of Weeramantry.
154   Velasquez (1998).
155   Ibid., 330.
156   Ibid.
157   Brown-Weiss (1990).
158   *Canterbury v. Spence* (1972) (my emphasis).
159   *Gabčíkovo-Nagymaros Project*, [1997].
160   Ibid., 17.
161   Tesón (1998).
162   Ibid., 128.
163   *Gabčíkovo-Nagymaros Project*, [1997], separate opinion of Weeramantry, 17.
164   *Legality of the Threat of Nuclear Weapons*, [1996]; see also a discussion of the ecological implications and environmental justice in Westra (2009b, Chap. 6).
165   See Kadelbach (2006, 36-37).

166 Ibid., 36; see also UN, International Law Commission, *Third Report on State Responsibility* (2000, paras. 374, 379).

167 Talmon (2006).

168 GFCC, Order of 24 June 2003, 2 BvR 685/03, BVerf GE 108, p. 129, para. 67; Brownlie (2003a, 489); GFCC, Order of 26 October 2004, BvR 955/00, pp. 175-83 at 128.

169 Talmon (2006).

170 Brownsword (2008a, Chap 4).

171 Westra (2004b).

172 Brownsword (2008, 10).

CHAPTER 2: THE COMMON GOOD AND THE PUBLIC INTEREST

1 See also Barboza (2001, 358) and Spinedi (2000, 106-7).

2 UN, International Law Commission, *First Report on State Responsibility* (1998, para. 97); Wyler (2002, 1148).

3 Pellet (1997, 287; 2006, 421).

4 Tomuschat (2006, 425).

5 On Israel's status, see UN, Commission on Human Rights, *Report of the Special Rapporteur* (2004); UN, Commission on Human Rights, *Report of the Special Rapporteur* (2005); UN, Human Rights Council, *Report of the Special Rapporteur* (2008); see also Westra (2009b, Chap. 6).

6 See, for example, ICJ, *Application of the Convention on the Prevention and Punishment of the Crime of Genocide*, [1996], 595, and ICJ, *Armed Activities on the Territory of the Congo*, [2005]. On the illegal employment of child soldiers, see ICJ, *Armed Activities of the Territory of the Congo (New Application 2002)*, [2006]. On the illegal treatment of prisoners, see *Rasul v. Bush* (2004), and see *Zadvydas v. Davis* (2001) on the prohibition of torture. Finally, on the seldom-used nonrecognition of states in breach of United Nations declarations and treaties, see Dugard (1987).

7 See also Weil (1983) and the dissenting opinion of Judge Tanaka in ICJ, *South West Africa*, [1966], 298.

8 On jus cogens and positive law, see Tunkin (1971, 107); Alexidze (1969, 145); Akehurst (1974-75, 281-85).

9 Dugard (1987, 149).

10 Baxi (1999).

11 Onuf and Birney (1974, 187).

12 Dugard (1987, 152).

13 See Dugard (1987, 133-34).

14 Ibid., 135.

15 Ibid.

16 ICJ, *Legal Consequences for States*, [1971]; see discussion in Dugard (1987, 136); see also Higgins (1972) and Ragazzi (1998, 164-69).

17 Dugard (1987, 139); Ragazzi (1998, 182-86).

18 Dugard (1987, 139).

19 ICJ, *Barcelona Traction*, [1970], Second Phase.

20 Salomon (2007, 19); see also UN, Commission on Human Rights, *Interim Report of the UN Special Representative* (2006).

21 Salomon (2007, 19); see also Steger (2003, 48).

22 Leader (2004, 53-68); Grandjean and Landrigan (2006); Westra (2006, Chap. 2).

23 *Oxford English Dictionary*, 2nd ed., *s.v.* "nature" also cites Artistotle in this regard.

24 Ragazzi (1997, 183). *Intrinsic evils* refers to "life, physical and mental integrity and human dignity," which, Ragazzi adds, are "essentially [the goods] ... protected by the four examples of obligations *erga omnes* given in the Barcelona case."

25 Ibid., 187.

26 Salomon (2007, 1).

27 Ragazzi (2007).

28 See discussion in Ragazzi (1997, 200-3).

29 Ragazzi (1997, 203).

30 "*Pacta sunt servanda* and custom" (Kadelbach, 2006, 29).

31 Ibid.

32 On Article 53, see Salomon (2007, 15-25).

33 Tomuschat (1993-94, 211).

34 Cassese (2005, 396).

35 Salomon (2007, 14).

36 Tomuschat (1999, 59); see also the discussion in Salomon (2007, 23).

37 Sands (2005).

38 Westra (2006, 2009b); Gostin (2008b, 3); Heinzerling (2008); Myers (1993); Salomon (2007, 24).

39 Salomon (2007, 24).

40 Ibid.

41 Westra (2004a).

42 As cited in Sands (2005, 70).

43 Ibid.

44 Bederman (2001, 176).

45 Ibid.

46 Kindred et al. (2000, 11).

47 Bederman (2001, 173).

48 Ibid., 179.

49 Reinisch (2001).

50 Postiglione (2001, 95-10).

51 Private communication with author, 1 June 2008, Ottawa, Ontario.

52 Westra (1998, Chap. 5).

53   Ibid. and Westra (2007, Appendix 2).

54   Ibid.

55   *Wiwa v. Royal Dutch Petroleum Co.* (2002).

56   EC, *Council Directive 83/129/EEC,* [1983]; Charnovitz (1994).

57   Ward v. Canada (Attorney General), [2002].

58   Shue (1996).

59   Postiglione (2001, 68-71).

60   Ibid., 71, my translation.

61   Ibid., 68-71.

62   Ibid., 78.

63   ECJ, *Handelskwekerij G.J. Bier BV v. Mines de Potasse d'Alsace,* [1976].

64   Westra (2006); Soskolne and Bertollini (1999).

65   Terry (2001, 111).

66   Sands (2005, 97).

67   Ibid., 87-97.

68   Ibid.

69   Ibid., 100n71.

70   Colborn, Dumanoski, and Myers (1996).

71   Falk (1964).

72   Sands (2005, 86-94).

73   Ibid.

74   *Native Village of Kivalina v. ExxonMobil Corp., et al.* (2008) *[Kivalina]*.

75   Ibid., para. 1.

76   Ibid., para. 4.

77   Ibid.

78   *Convention for the Protection of Human Rights and Fundamental Freedoms* (1950), art. 8.1.

79   *Kivalina,* para. 3.

80   Ibid., para. 2.

81   *People of State of California v. General Motors Corp.* (2007).

82   *Kivalina,* para. 5.

83   28 U.S.C. s. 1331.

84   28 U.S.C. s. 1367(a).

85   *Kivalina,* paras. 7-9.

86   See, for instance, BP (n.d.) and Chevron (n.d.).

87   *Kivalina,* para. 39.

88   Ibid., para. 41.

89   Ibid., para. 247.

90   Ibid.

91   Ibid., para. 189.

92   Ibid., para. 190.

93 Ibid., paras. 192 and 194.

94 IPCC (2007); see also Hassol (2004); Westra (2007, Chap. 8).

95 *Kivalina*, para. 125; see IPCC (2007).

96 WHO, *WHO Framework Convention on Tobacco Control* (2003).

97 *Kivalina*, para. 250.

98 Ibid., para. 252.

99 *Pappajohn v. The Queen*, [1980].

100 *Kivalina*, paras. 264-67.

101 Ibid., paras. 236-38.

102 Ibid.

103 Westra (2009a); Luban (2004); Aminazadej (2007, 231); Sachs (2004).

104 Smithfield is the world's largest pork producer, with 12 billion in sales annually. See Diebel (2009).

105 Ibid.

106 Ibid.

107 Ibid.

108 On collateral damage, see Leader (2004).

109 Bullard (1994).

110 Bullard (2001).

111 Boyd (2003).

112 Bourette (2000).

113 Ibbitson (2000); Machine (2000).

114 For these case studies, see Baxi (1998) and Westra (1998).

115 On risks, see Hiskes (1998).

116 Gbadegesin (2001); Westra (1998); Baxi (1998); Gaylord and Bell (1995); Bullard (1994).

117 Westra (1998, Chap. 3); Pogge (2001).

118 Burkitt (1991).

119 Nikiforuk (2000).

120 Westra (1998); Westra et al. (2000); Daily (1997); Noss (1992).

121 Rapport (1995); Callicott (1999).

122 Westra (2000).

123 Nikiforuk (2000).

124 Eisnitz (1997); Davis (1996); Cohen (1998).

125 Regan (1983); Singer (1975).

126 Pogge (2001).

127 Pimentel and Goodland (2000); Pimentel (1991); Daly (1996); Brown (1995); Kendall and Pimentel (1994).

128 Epstein (1989).

129 Mitchell, Gray, and Sequin (2000).

130 Rifkin (1992); Singer (1976).

131 Mitchell, Gray, and Sequin (2000).
132 Callicott (1980).
133 Ibid., 60.
134 Rifkin (1992); Singer (1976); Rachels (1997).
135 Eisnitz (1997); Cohen (1998); Davis (1996).
136 Rifkin (1992).
137 McCalman, Penny, and Cook (1998).
138 *R. v. United Keno Hill Mines Ltd.* (1980), cited in *R. v. Village of 100 Mile House,* [1993].
139 Canadian Environmental Law Association (2000).
140 Ibid., para. 1.
141 Mellon and Fondriest (2001, 1).
142 Ibid., 2.
143 Canadian Environmental Law Association (2000).
144 Ibid., para. 4.
145 Ibid.
146 See Shiva (1989).
147 See also Baxi and Paul (1986) for a discussion of this case.
148 Scovazzi (1991).
149 Baxi and Paul (1986).
150 Ibid., 29.
151 Ibid., 31.
152 Scovazzi (1991, 406).
153 *Charan Lal Sahu v. Union of India* (1990).
154 *South West Africa Cases (Ethiopia v. South Africa; Liberia v. South Africa),* [1966], separate opinion of Judge Tanaka; see discussion in Salomon (2007, 161-65).
155 *International Covenant on Economic, Social and Cultural Rights* (1976), Preamble, para. 2.
156 ICJ, *Legality of the Threat or Use of Nuclear Weapons,* [1996], 226, para. 79; ICJ, *Legal Consequences of the Construction,* [2004]; ICJ, *Armed Activities on the Territory of the Congo (New Application: 2002),* [2006], para. 64.
157 Salomon (2007, 168).
158 ICJ, *South West Africa,* [1966], dissenting opinion of Judge Tanaka, 297.
159 Higgins (1998, 167); see also discussion in Salomon (2007, 174-75).

CHAPTER 3: COMMUNITIES AND COLLECTIVES

The section "Plan Colombia and the Indigenous Peoples of the Colombia-Ecuador Border Region" is based on the research of Rebekah Myers, University of Windsor.
1 See also Kymlicka (1989).
2 Bosselman (2008); see also the Earth Charter, a "soft law" instrument on this issue, http://www.earthcharterinaction.org/.

3   Galenkamp (1998, 31).

4   Ibid., 32.

5   Ibid., 33.

6   Ibid. 34.

7   Ibid., 43-45.

8   Dworkin (1977).

9   Shue (1996).

10 Galenkamp (1998, 47).

11 Ragazzi (1998); Salomon (2007); Tomuschat (2006).

12 On community of rights, see Brownsword (2008a).

13 Ibid.

14 Newman (2004, 135).

15 Salomon (2007).

16 UN, Commission on Human Rights, Sub-Commission on Prevention of Discrimination and Protection of Minorities, "Draft United Nations Declaration on the Rights of Indigenous Peoples" (1994).

17 See, for instance, the arrow impossibility theorem, based on four reasonable conditions to provide "a transitive ranking of social states": Newman (2004, 136-37).

18 Ibid., 140.

19 Grammon, with Groulx (2009, 2n1).

20 *R. v. Powley*, [1999].

21 *R. v. Powley*, [2003].

22 Grammond, with Groulx (2009, 2).

23 Ibid.

24 Grammond (2008, 487).

25 Grammond, with Groulx (2009, 3).

26 Metcalf (2004).

27 ILO, *Convention No. 169* (1989), entered into force 5 September 1991.

28 Metcalf (2004, 103); see also UN, Commission on Human Rights, Sub-Commission on Prevention of Discrimination and Protection of Minorities, *Study of the Problem of Discrimination against Indigenous Populations by Special Rapporteur, Mr. José Martinez Cobo* (1986), para. 379, which has the following definition: "Indigenous communities, peoples and nations are those which, having a historical continuity with pre-invasion and pre-colonial societies that developed on their territories, consider themselves distinct from other sectors of the societies now prevailing in those territories, or parts of them. They form at present non-dominant sectors of society and are determined to preserve, develop and transmit to future generations their ancestral territories, and their ethnic identity as the basis of their continued existence as peoples, in accordance with their own cultural patterns, social institutions and legal systems."

29 *Convention on Biological Diversity* (1992).

30 Anaya (2004).

31 Ibid.

32 See, for instance, Baxi (1998).

33 Anaya (2004, 16-17); see also Grotius (1984).

34 *Pace* Anaya (2004).

35 Ibid. See also Thomas Aquinas (1953), who termed any law that did not promote and protect the interests of all citizens a form of violence by a sovereign or law-maker; it was, therefore, the citizen's obligation not only *not* to obey the law but also to actively oppose it. See Westra (2004a, 38); see also King Jr. (1990).

36 De Vattel (1916 [1758]); Anaya (2004, 20).

37 Westra (2006, Chap. 7).

38 See, for instance, ibid., Chap. 10, and the Introduction to the Earth Charter at http://www.globalecointegrity.net.

39 Anaya (2004, 223). See also UN, Commission on Human Rights, *Report of the Special Rapporteur on the Situation of Human Rights and Fundamental Freedoms* (2002), paras. 102, 109, 103.

40 Anaya (2004, 223-24).

41 UN, CERD, *Report* (1992).

42 Ibid., 45.

43 OAS, Inter-American Commission on Human Rights, *Report on the Situation of Human Rights in Ecuador* (1997), Chap. VII.

44 See Metcalf (2004); Anaya (2004).

45 ILO, *Convention No. 169*; Shue (1996).

46 Tamburlini, von Ehrenstein, and Bertollini (2002); see also Westra (2006, Chap. 2); and Gewirth (1982).

47 Noss (1992).

48 Westra (1994, 1998).

49 European Environment Agency (EEA) (2005, 6).

50 Ibid.

51 Mittelstaedt (2005); Scott (2008).

52 EEA (2005, 23).

53 Rogan and Regan (2003).

54 EEA (2005, 24).

55 Colborn, Dumanoski, and Myers (1996).

56 EEA (2005, 11).

57 Westra (1998); see also *Wiwa v. Royal Royal Dutch Petroleum Co., et al.* (2000).

58 OAS, Inter-American Commission on Human Rights, "Proposed American Declaration on the Rights of Indigenous Peoples" (1997).

59 Metcalf (2004, 106).

60 Ibid., 107.

61   *Convention on Biological Diversity* (1992); *Convention to Combat Desertification* (1994).

62   Metcalf (2004, 104); *Declaration on the Establishment of the Arctic Council* (1996).

63   Halewood (1999).

64   Shelton (1994).

65   *Convention on the Rights of the Child* (1989).

66   Anaya (2004).

67   Ibid., 100-3.

68   Wallace (1994, 25-30).

69   Anaya (2004, 104).

70   Ibid., 2.

71   Cassese (1995, 114); Lenin (1969).

72   Cassese (1995, 16-17).

73   Lenin (1969, 160).

74   Cassese (1995, 19).

75   Ibid., 33.

76   Ibid., 25.

77   Ibid., 37; see also Grenville (1974, 198).

78   Cassese (1995, 43-47).

79   *International Covenant on Economic, Social and Cultural Rights* (1976); *International Covenant on Civil and Political Rights* (1996).

80   Cassese (1995, 56).

81   Ibid., 65.

82   UN, Security Council, Res. 435 (1978). Namibia's independence was declared on 21 March 1990. See also Schmidt-Jortzig (1991).

83   UN, *Declaration on the Granting of Independence to Colonial Countries and Peoples* (1961).

84   Cassese (1995, 92).

85   Ibid., 93n74.

86   Date-Bah (1998).

87   Gilbert (1994, 123).

88   Ibid.

89   Brownlie (2003b, 1, 5).

90   Metcalf (2004, 125).

91   UN, Commission on Human Rights, Sub-Commission on Prevention of Discrimination and Protection of Minorities, Resolution 1994/45, Annex "Draft United Nations Declaration" (1994).

92   Brownsword (2008a).

93   See, for instance, *Aguinda v. Texaco* (1996); *Sarei et al. v. Rio Tinto PLC* (2002); *Cherokee Nations v. Georgia* (1831); *Wiwa v. Royal Dutch Petroleum* Co., et al. (2000).

94   Newman (2004, 58).

95   Ibid., 159.
96   Réaume (1988, 2).
97   Tabachnick (2009, 165).
98   Ibid., 168.
99   Ibid., 166-67.
100 Ibid., 170.
101 Westra (2007).
102 Soskolne and Bertollini (1999).
103 Kay and Regier (2000); Kay and Schneider (1994); Karr (1993, 2000); Karr and Chu (1999); Rees and Wackernagel (1996); Goodland and Daly (1995); Miller and Westra (2002); Westra (1994, 1998). In 2000, the final group definition of integrity was published by Island Press (Pimentel, Westra, and Noss 2000), and in 2008 the fifteenth anniversary of the group's meetings was celebrated with a volume that included both law and public policy concerns (Westra, Bosselmann, and Westra 2008).
104 Raz (1984, 195).
105 Réaume (1988, 5).
106 Grandjean and Landrigan (2006); Gostin (2008b, 487-95).
107 Gostin (2008b, 487).
108 See R. v. Cuerrier, [1988].
109 Westra (2004).
110 Gostin (2008b, 491); Heinzerling (2008).
111 Rees and Wackernagel (1996)
112 See also Constitution of the Federal Republic of Brazil, art. 8, XVII, art. 4(4), and art. 198, cited in Pallemaerts (1986, 374).
113 Wiessner (1999, 81).
114 Ibid.
115 Mayers (2009).
116 Cited in Mayers (2009, 15).
117 Congressional Research Service, Library of Congress (2001, 9).
118 Ibid.; see also discussion in Mayers (2009, 16).
119 Oldham and Massey (2002, 3).
120 WRITENET (2008, 5).
121 UN, Declaration on the Rights of Indigenous Peoples (2007).
122 Ibid., art. 8.
123 Acosta (2007). See also Tenebaum (2002); Wolcott (2002); the Cultural Survival website; Anya (2004, 134); OAS, Inter-American Commission on Human Rights, Report on the Situation (1997).
124 Oldham and Massey (2002, 1-2).
125 Ibid., 2.
126 Ibid., 3.

127   *Venancio Aguasanta Arias et al. v. DynCorp et al.* (2001).

128   Ibid., 3.

129   Ibid.

130   Williams, Kroes, and Munro (2000); see also Roundup Ultra Sample Label, 1999.

131   For the Quebec case, see *114957 Canada Ltéé (Spraytech, Societé d'arrosage) v. Hudson (Town)*, [2001].

132   Pentassuglia (2009, 4).

133   Ibid.

134   See the high commissioner for human rights' response to UN, Secretary General, *Larger Freedom* (2005).

135   See, for instance, *Guerra and Others v. Italy*, [1998]; *López Ostra v. Spain*, [1994]; *Fadeyeva v. Russia*, [2005]; *Oneryildiz v. Turkey*, (2004).

136   UN, Human Rights Committee, *Omniyak and the Lubicon Lake Band v. Canada* (1990).

137   UN, Human Rights Committee, *General Comment Adopted by the Human Rights Committee under Article 40* (1994), para. 7.

138   UN, Human Rights Committee, *Lovelace v. Canada* (1981).

139   Anaya (2004, 136).

140   Ibid, 5.

141   Ibid., 7.

142   *Mayagna (Sumo) Awas Tingni v. Nicaragua* (2001).

143   Ibid., 21.

144   Anaya and Grossmann (2002, 9).

145   Ibid., 17.

146   Ibid., 19.

147   Ibid.

148   1995, Constitution of Nicaragua.

149   Ibid.

150   Ibid., 66.

151   Ibid., 48. Law 445, 13 December 2002.

152   Ibid., 71.

153   Ibid.

154   Anaya (2000, 190).

155   Ibid., 190-91.

156   UN, Human Rights Committee, *Ivan Kitok v. Sweden* (1988) *[Kitok]*.

157   Ibid., submitted under the optional protocol of the *International Covenant on Civil and Political Rights*, art. 5, para. 4.2.

158   Ibid., para. 2.2.

159   Ibid., para. 4.3.

160   Morse (2002).

161   *Kitok*, para. 9.8.

162 Citing the *ratio decidendi* of *Lovelace v. Canada* (1977).

163 Sandler (2006, 6).

164 Ibid.

165 ICJ, "Aerial Herbicide Spraying" (2008). The court fixed 29 April 2009 as a time limit for the filing of the memorial by Ecuador and 29 March 2010 as the time limit for the filing of a countermemorial by Colombia.

166 ICJ, "Equador Institutes Proceedings" (2008).

167 Ibid.

168 Pavlakos (2008, 164).

169 Ibid., 165.

170 Kant (2002, para. 4:429).

171 Raz (2005-6, 1018).

CHAPTER 4: COLLECTIVE BASIC RIGHTS TODAY

1 Salomon (2007); Steiner and Alston (2000); UN, Commission on Human Rights, *Report of the Working Group* (2006); UN, Commission on Human Rights, *Report of the High-Level Task Force* (2005).

2 Cassese (2005, 49).

3 Ibid., 52, citing de Vattel (1916 [1758]), "A dwarf is as much a man as a giant; a small republic is no less a sovereign state as the most powerful kingdom."

4 Cassese (2005, 55).

5 Ibid., 57.

6 See ICJ, *Legal Consequences of the Construction of a Wall*, [2004], as forceful conquest "does not transfer a legal title of sovereignty" (Cassese 2005, 57).

7 Cassese (2005, 357-63).

8 Ibid., 358.

9 Ibid., 360.

10 Ibid., 361, and see also 364n8n9.

11 *Bancoult v. McNamara* (2004); Westra (2007, App. 2); *Revenga* (2005).

12 See Cassese (2005, 368-69) for a discussion of the acceptance of the universally known principle of *volenti non fit injuria*.

13 Pogge (2008).

14 Etzioni (2009, para. 3).

15 UN, *United Nations Millennium Declaration* (2000).

16 Alston (2005).

17 Dellapenna (2008).

18 Licari, Nemer, and Tamburlini (2005); Tamburlini, von Ehrenstein, and Bertollini (2002).

19 World Health Organization, Commission on Social Determinants of Health (2008); Gostin (2008b).

20 Kunitz (2000).

21 UN, Commission on Human Rights, *Right to Development* (2000).

22 Ibid., para. 4.

23 Ibid.

24 Sen (1999, esp. 231).

25 UN, Commission on Human Rights, *Right to Development* (2000), para. 6.

26 UN, Human Rights Committee, *Omniyak and the Lubicon Lake Band v. Canada,* (1996); *Chagos Islanders v. Attorney General,* [2003]; *Aguinda v. Texaco* (1996); *Aguinda v. Texaco, Inc.* (2001); *Alvarez-Machain v. United States,* (2003); *Bancoult v. McNamara* (2003); *Doe/Roe v. Unocal Corp* (2000); *Filartiga v. Pena Irala* (1980); *Jota v. Texaco Inc.* (1998); *Maria Aguinda and others* (2002).

27 UN, Commission on Human Rights, *Right to Development* (2000), para. 4.

28 Ibid., para. 8.

29 See, for instance, *Presbyterian Church of Sudan, Rev. John Gaduel and others v. Talisman Energy Inc.* (2003).

30 Westra (2007, App. 2).

31 UN, World Conference on Human Rights, *Vienna Declaration;* see also *Charter of the United Nations,* art. 56.

32 Pilkington (2009).

33 UN, Commission on Human Rights, *Right to Development* (2000), para. 15.

34 Ibid.

35 On basic human rights, see Shue (1996).

36 Rees and Wackernagel (1996); Rees and Westra (2003).

37 Chimni (2008, 2).

38 Ibid., 3-4.

39 Sen (1999, 18, 116).

40 Chimni (2008, 8).

41 Sen (1999, 123).

42 See Dellapenna (2008).

43 Chimni (2008, 11); see also Stewart and Deneulin (2002, 64).

44 Secretariat of the United Nations Convention to Combat Desertification (2009, 11), foreword by Executive Secretary Luc Gnacadja.

45 Ibid., 111, Preface by Elena Espinoza, Spain.

46 Ibid., 15.

47 Ibid., 4.

48 Ibid.

49 Ibid.

50 Sen (1999).

51 Secretariat of the United Nations Convention to Combat Desertification (2009).

52 See also the resolution on the environment and security adopted by the Ministerial Council of the Organization for Security and Co-operation in Europe (OSCE) as the *Madrid Declaration on Environment and Security* (2007).

53　Secretariat of the United Nations Convention to Combat Desertification (2009, 5).
54　Ibid., 6.
55　Ibid. See also the discussion of this duality in relation to indigenous people's rights in Westra (2007, Chap. 2).
56　Secretariat of the United Nations Convention to Combat Desertification (2009, 7).
57　Ibid.
58　Ibid., 8.
59　Ibid., 31.
60　SIDYM (2006).
61　Cassese (2005, 19).
62　Ibid.
63　Cassese (1987, 123).
64　Ibid.
65　Ibid., 176.
66　Ibid.
67　Ibid., 177.
68　Ibid., 178.
69　Ibid., 189.
70　Birnie and Boyle (1992, 118); see also Birnie and Boyle (2002, 97-100).
71　Daily (1997); Westra et al. (2000, Chap. 1).
72　Larschan and Brennan (1983, 306).
73　Ibid., 310.
74　Noss (1992); Westra (1994); Ulanowicz (1997); Daily (1997).
75　*Black's Law Dictionary*, 5th ed., 1173.
76　ICJ, *Fisheries Jurisdiction*, [1973], 97.
77　Westra (1998).
78　Cheng (1980, 337).
79　Larschan and Brennan (1983, 323).
80　Ibid., 322.
81　Cheng (1980, 337).
82　Birnie and Boyle (2002, 97-100).
83　Ibid.
84　Wood (1996, 307).
85　Westra (2004b).
86　Wood (1996, 311).
87　Ibid., 312-13.
88　Westra (1998); see also Rockefeller (2002).
89　Soskolne and Bertollini (1999); Tamburlini, von Ehrenstein, and Bertollini (2002).
90　Francioni (2006), translated by the author.
91　Ibid., 699.

92 Ibid., 701.
93 Scovazzi (2009b, 12).
94 Ibid.
95 Ibid., 13.
96 *International Covenant on Economic, Social and Cultural Rights* (1976) *[ICESCR]*.
97 Meier (2006).
98 Steiner and Alston (2000, 246).
99 See, for instance, Westra (2006, App. 2) for the reports of five developing countries to the WHO on their respective compliance with the mandates of the convention; UN, Commission on Human Rights, *Convention on the Rights of the Child* (1989).
100 *ICESCR*, art. 2(1).
101 UN, Office of the High Commissioner for Human Rights, *Manual on Human Rights Reporting* (1997).
102 Meier (2006, 752).
103 Ibid., n238.
104 Ibid., 739.
105 Ibid., 239; see also Institute of Medicine (1988); Raeburn and MacFarlane (2003). Note that the 1986 *Ottawa Charter for Health Promotion* added "health promotion" to "health protection."
106 Meier (2006, 741, 742).
107 McMichael (1995); Patz (2005); Susser and Susser (1996).
108 Wald (2007); Ratner (2007).
109 Westra (2004a).
110 Westra (2009b).
111 Vitousek et al. (1986); Angermeier and Karr (1994).
112 Westra (2006). I define ecojustice by including intergenerational and intragenerational issues and, specifically, by recognizing that the most vulnerable groups must be included in that definition.
113 Gostin (2008b, 6).
114 Ibid., 23.
115 Ibid.; Garrett and Rosenstein (2005).
116 Gostin (2008b, 234).
117 Ibid., 235; see also Westra (2009a).
118 Rifkin (1992); Cassuto (2010).
119 Gostin (2008b, 238).
120 Backman et al. (2008, 2047).
121 Gostin (2008b, 246); see also Fidler (2005); Forrest (2000); Taylor (1997).
122 WHO (2005, 9).
123 Grandjean and Landrigan (2006).
124 Boyd (2003).

CHAPTER 5: GLOBALIZATION, DEMOCRACY, AND COLLECTIVE RIGHTS

1   Jonas (1984).
2   UN, Human Rights Council, *Report of the Special Rapporteur* (2008); see also Amnesty International (2009); Westra (2009b, Chap. 6).
3   Westra (2009b).
4   Engel (2010).
5   Westra (2010b).
6   Engel (2010, 2).
7   Ibid., 5.
8   Ibid.
9   Sand (2009b).
10 Scovazzi (2009a).
11 UN, Human Rights Committee, *Consideration of Reports* (2006), 16.
12 Scovazzi (2009a, 893-96). This discussion is based Scovazzi's report of the case, and direct quotes are translated from the Italian by the author.
13 Ibid., 894.
14 Ibid.
15 See Council of Europe, Parliamentary Assembly, *Alleged Secret Detentions* (2006), 36.
16 Scovazzi (2009a, 894-95).
17 Council of Europe, Parliamentary Assembly, *Alleged Secret Detentions* (2006), 132.
18 *Convention against Torture and Other Inhuman, Cruel or Degrading Treatment or Punishment* (1984), as does art. 4 of the *International Covenant on Civil and Political Rights* (1966) and the *American Convention on Human Rights* (1969).
19 *American Convention on Human Rights*, art. 27.
20 Winkler (2008, 40).
21 Ibid.
22 Ibid., 41.
23 Ibid., 42.
24 Rice (2005).
25 Ibid.; see also Waterman (2005).
26 Rice (2005).
27 Winkler (2008, 46-47).
28 Ibid., 48; see also *Prosecutor v. Furundzjia* (1999).
29 Winkler (2008, 340).
30 Ibid., 35; see also Grey (2005).
31 Ibid., 337.
32 Ibid., 338.
33 Ibid., 339, citing Pither (2008, 394).
34 *Arar v. Ashcroft* (2006); see also Sage (2006).

35 UN, Human Rights Council, *Report of the Special Rapporteur on the Promotion and Protection of Human Rights* (2007).

36 *Bancoult v. McNamara* (2003), 22. The history and details of this and subsequent decisions regarding the Diego Garcia case may be found in Sand (2009b).

37 Ibid., 22(c)-23.

38 Ibid., 31-33.

39 *Federal Employees Liability Reform and Tort Compensation Act of 1988*, Pub. L. No. 100-694, 102 Stat. 4563 (1988) (codified at 28 U.S.C. ss. 2671-2680).

40 *Bancoult v. McNamara* (2004), para. 42.

41 Ibid., para. 47.

42 Steiner and Alston (2000, 1072).

43 *Filártiga v. Peña-Irala* (1980).

44 Ibid. See also *United States v. Smith* (1920).

45 Terry (2001, 110).

46 Ibid., 133.

47 See Steyn (2004).

48 Sand (2009a, 115).

49 Ibid., 117.

50 Ibid., 118.

51 Ibid., 119, 120, 124, 127.

52 *R (Bancoult) v. Secretary of State for Foreign and Commonwealth Affairs,* [2008].

53 Ibid., para. 5.

54 British Indian Ocean Territories Order 1965 SI No. 1920.

55 Ibid., para. 6.

56 *Chagos Islanders v. Attorney General,* [2003].

57 Ibid., para. 10.

58 Ibid., para. 17.

59 Ibid., para. 28.

60 Ibid., para. 44; see Blackstone (1809, 137).

61 Salomon refers to Donnelly (2003, 201).

62 Salomon (2007, 130).

63 Ibid., 132.

64 Ibid., 150.

65 Salomon (2007, 151); *Marrakesh Agreement Establishing the World Trade Organization* (1994).

66 Howse and Mutua (2000, 13, 21).

67 Salomon (2007, 155).

68 Ibid., 157.

69 Kymlicka (1995, 45, 44-47).

70 Galenkamp (1998, 156).

71 Ibid., 157.

72 Ibid., 158.

73 Kymlicka (1995, 44).

74 Galenkamp (1998, 167).

75 Kymlicka (1998, 47).

76 Ibid., 49.

77 Scott (2001, 50).

78 Ibid., 51.

79 Ibid., 52.

80 Alston (2002, 824).

81 Peers (2001). See also the discussion in Alston (2002, 825).

82 Art. 15.1(c) states: "To benefit from the protection of the moral and material interests resulting from any scientific, literary or artistic production of which he is the author."

83 Alston (2002, 826).

84 Falk (1984, 48).

85 On the Third World Forum, see ibid., 50.

86 Owens (1959).

87 Kymlicka (1989, 107).

88 Ibid., 124

89 Ibid., 128; see also Dworkin (1989); Rawls (1993).

90 Kymlicka (1989, 129).

91 Falk (1984, 178).

92 UN, Commission on Human Rights, *Report of the Special Rapporteur* (2005, 6).

93 ICJ, *Legal Consequences of the Construction of a Wall*, [2004], "Relevant International Humanitarian Law and Human Rights Instruments," paras. 123-37.

94 Ibid.

95 Martin, Fagin, and Warner (2005, 1472).

96 UN, Commission on Human Rights, *Report of the Special Rapporteur* (2005).

97 In UN, Commission on Human Rights, *Report of the Special Rapporteur* (2004, III(6)). John Dugard terms it "annexation under the guise of security."

98 Crawford (1999).

99 Ibid., 100; UN, *Appointment and Terms of Reference* (1948).

100 Crawford (1999, 100).

101 Ibid., 110.

102 *Palestinian Declaration of Independence* (1988), para. 10; see also Crawford (1999, 111-12).

103 Boyle (1990, 303).

104 Crawford (1999, 112).

105 UN, Commission on Human Rights, *Report of the Special Rapporteur* (2005, VI(19)).

106 Ibid., VI(18).

107 Ibid.
108 UN, Commission on Human Rights, *Report of the Special Rapporteur* (2005, VI(17)).
109 UN, Human Rights Council, *Report of the Special Rapporteur on the Situation of Human Rights in the Palestinian Territories* (2008), para. 58.
110 Neumann (2005); see also Pappe (2006).
111 Amnesty International (2009).
112 Ibid., 3.
113 Ibid.

CHAPTER 6: COSMOPOLITANISM, THE MORAL COMMUNITY, AND COLLECTIVE HUMAN RIGHTS

1 Ford et al. (2006); see also Westra (2007).
2 Gilbert (1998, 5); see also Guiberneau (1996, 43).
3 Gilbert (1998, 6).
4 Ibid., 8.
5 Ibid., 9.
6 Ibid., 11.
7 Ibid., 12.
8 Devlin (1959, 137).
9 Hart (1998, [1959]).
10 Ibid., 52.
11 Ibid.
12 Ibid., 133-53.
13 Ibid., 152-53.
14 Ibid., 154.
15 Ibid., 166.
16 Ibid., 169.
17 Melber (2005); Abugre (2008).
18 Pimentel and Goodland (2000).
19 Melber (2008, 266).
20 Ibid., 267.
21 Ibid.
22 Schabas (2000); Bendafia (2008).
23 Karkar (2007).
24 Bendaña (2008, 280).
25 Orentlicher (2001, 1249); Kymlicka (1989); see also Stalin (1913): "A nation is a historically evolved stable community of language, territory, economic life and a psychological make-up manifested in a community of culture."
26 Orentlicher (2001).
27 *Montevideo Convention on the Rights and Duties of States* (1933), art. 1.
28 Higgins (1963, 11-57).

29 Orentlicher (2001, 1252).

30 Ibid., 1253.

31 As cited in Orentlicher (2001, 1256); see also Kindred et al. (2000, 13): "A permanent population is necessary, although there is no minimum requirement. Canada recognized Nauru, which in 1982 had a population of 8,421, and the Seychelles, which in 1983 had a population of 69,000."

32 Orentlicher (2001, 1256).

33 *Declaration on the Granting of Independence* (1961); see also Steiner and Alston (2000, 1265) and Orentlicher (2001).

34 Orentilicher (2001, 1256).

35 Kirgis (2001, 1270).

36 Ibid., 1271.

37 Ruru (2009).

38 Crawford (1999, 95).

39 U.K., H.C., "Palestine Royal Commission Report," Cmd 5479, in *Sessional Papers*, vol. 14 (1936-37) 19 at 22, and see, generally, Stein (1961).

40 Crawford (1999, 98); see also *Treaty of Sèvres* (1920), art. 97. Turkey agreed, and in 1923 Turkey ratified the *Treaty of Lausanne*.

41 UN, *Question of Palestine* (1947). The relinquishment of the mandate was authorized by the *Palestine Act, 1948* (U.K.), 11 & 12 Geo. VI, c. 27, s.1.

42 Crawford (1999, 123).

43 Ibid., 103n39.

44 Ibid., 104.

45 Ibid., 105; *International Covenant on Economic, Social and Cultural Rights* (1996).

46 Crawford (1999, 103).

47 Ibid.

48 Ibid., 114.

49 Quigley (1997, 724).

50 Crawford (1999, 124).

51 De Feyter (2007, 81).

52 Ibid., 74. See also *Mayagna (Sumo) Awas Tingni Community v. Nicaragua* (2001) and *Social and Economic Rights Action Center and the Centre for Economic and Social Rights v. Nigeria* (2001).

53 See ICJ, "Letter from the Ambassador" (2008).

54 Ibid., 78.

55 J. Christopher Weeramantry, talk to the faculty, University of Ottawa, October 2009; see also Westra (2009a).

56 See Grandjean and Landrigan (2006) and Gostin (2008a).

57 Gostin (2008a); see also Appigyei-Atua (2002).

58 Beyani (1999, 22-23); see also Higgins (1994, Chaps. 6 and 7) and Brownlie (1988).

59 De Feyter (2007, 81); see also Gready (2004, 8).

60 De Feyter (2007, 81); see also Kenk and Sikkink (1998), who list many groups and organizations that are part of those networks, including the media and intellectuals.

61 Gostin (2008a).

62 Delbrück (2001-2).

63 Ibid., 413.

64 See *Roe v. Wade* (1973).

65 Kraut (1989, 98).

66 I believe the European Union is somewhat better than North America and other countries in this regard, because of the predominance of the transnational principled aspect found in its governance. See Westra (2004a).

67 Aristotle (1961, VI, 1, 1026a, 18-19).

68 Kraut (1989, 74-75).

69 Ibid., 75.

70 Westra (2007, Chap. 8).

71 Ibid., Chap. 4.

72 Cassese (2007, 245-77).

73 Ibid., 252, 253, 262.

74 Ibid, 262.

75 Salomon (2007, 26); see also ICJ, *Legality of the Threat,* [1996], dissenting opinion of Judge Weeramanty, 495.

76 Salomon (2007, 21).

77 Delbrück (2001-2, 403).

78 Ibid., 405.

79 Ibid., 406.

80 Ibid., 407.

81 Meron (2006, 473).

82 Ibid., 483.

83 Ibid.

84 Ibid., 486.

85 Ibid. See, for instance, *Charter of the Organization of the American States* (1948), art. 2(b); and OAS, *Inter-American Democratic Charter of Lima* (2001), art. 1.

86 Cassese (2007, 317-18).

87 Ibid., 320.

88 Ibid., 323.

89 Ibid., 324.

90 Ibid., 361.

91 Ibid., 362. Cassese suggests several ways to modify the prohibition while retaining the best part of its restraining powers.

92 Ibid., 365.

93 Ibid., 374.

94 Delbrück (2001-2, 408); see also Held et al. (1999, 16).

95 Delbrück (2001-2, 409); Baxi (2002, 153).

96 See, for instance, Goodall and Counsell (2008).

97 WTO, *EC Measures Concerning Meat* (1998).

98 See Hughes, Lucas, and Tilleman (2003, 650-51).

99 Gostin (2008a).

100 Delbrück (2001-2, 409).

101 Ibid.

102 Baxi (2002, 152).

103 Ibid.

104 Delbrück (2002, 411).

105 In contrast, see Baxi's (2002) "Magna Carta for Global Capital."

CHAPTER 7: WORLD LAW OR INTERNATIONAL LEGAL INSTRUMENTS?

1 Westra (2004a).

2 Macklem (2008, 9).

3 UN, Commission on Human Rights, Sub-Commission on Prevention of Discrimination and Protection of Minorities, *Study of the Rights of Persons* (1977); see also Choleminski (1998).

4 Pentassuglia (2009, 2).

5 Ibid., 4.

6 On access to justice, see ibid., 149-80.

7 See ibid for the evolution of case law.

8 Pasqualucci is referring to *Yakye Axa Indigenous Community v. Paraguay* (2005).

9 *Moiwana Village v. Suriname* (2005).

10 Pentassuglia (2009, 152); see also *Chagos Islanders v. Attorney General*, [2003], ch. 5, ss. 3, 3a, and 3b.

11 Pasqualucci (2006, 315).

12 *Massacre de Plan de Sanchez v. Guatemala* (2004); *Kankuamo Indigenous Peoples v. Colombia* (2004).

13 Pasqualucci (2006, 316).

14 Ibid., 97; see also *Mayagna (Sumo) Awas Tigni Community v. Nicaragua* (2001), also discussed in Chapter 5.

15 Pasqualucci (2006, 97); see OAS, *Maya Indigenous Community of the Toledo District v. Belize* (2004).

16 Pasqualucci (2006, 97); see also *Yakye Axa Indigenous Community*, (2005), para. 167.

17 Vladi (2010, 5).

18 Ibid. See also *Crompton Corporation v. Government of Canada* (2001).

19 Vladi (2010, 6).

20 Commission for Environmental Cooperation (2006).

21 *Methanex Corporation v. United States of America* (2005).

22 Vladi (2010, 8).

23 Westra (2007).

24 Watt-Cloutier and others (2005).

25 Revkin (2006, 9).

26 Westra (2004, 7-21).

27 In a recent speech to the American Geographical Union, Al Gore acknowledged "the end of the age of print," and with it much of the desire for real information and the ability to think and weigh issues. Print has been supplanted by television's emphasis on entertainment. Gore added, "There is now wilful blindness among both the public and the politicians." See Hoffman (2007).

28 Westra (2004).

29 Watt-Cloutier and others (2005, 76).

30 Westra (2006, Chap. 1).

31 Watt-Cloutier and others (2005, 86).

32 SIKU News (2007).

33 *Native Village of Kivalina v. ExxonMobil* (2008).

34 *Rylands v. Fletcher* (1865-68); *Trail Smelter Arbitration (U.S. v. Canada)* (1941).

35 Miller (2006, 167).

36 Ibid., 168; see also Paust (2004).

37 Miller (2006, 169).

38 Ibid., 171; see also Brown-Weiss (1997).

39 Westra (2004, Chap. 5).

40 Miller (2006, 171).

41 Mathews (1997, 51).

42 Betsill (2002, 49).

43 *Kyoto Protocol*, art. 7, para. 6, art. 13, para. 8. The Inuit of Nunavut as well as other Inuit also have a voice in the Intergovernmental Panel on Climate Change.

44 *State of Connecticut, et al., v. America, Electric Power Company, Inc. et al* (2009), 3.

45 Ibid., 8.

46 Ibid., 9.

47 Ibid., 10.

48 Citing *Late Corporation of the Church of Jesus Christ of Latter-Day Saints v. United States*, 136 U.S. 1, 57 (1).

49 See *E. (Mrs.) v. Eve*, [1986]; *Winnipeg Child and Family Services (Northwest Area) v. G. (D.F.)*, [1997].

50 Morin (1990); *Droit de la Famine*, [1988].

51 Morin (1990).

52 Ibid., 830; see also Baker (1979, 273).

53 Morin (1990).

54 Morin (1990, 32); see also *Court of Wards Act 1540*, 32 Henry VIII, c. 46, and *Wards and Liveries Act 1541*, 33 Henry VIII, c. 22.

55 *Skinner v. Warner* (1792).

56 La Forest, J., in *E. (Mrs.) v. Eve*, [1986].

57 *Hepton et al. v. Maat et al.*, [1957], Rand, J., 607-8.

58 La Forest, J., in in *E. (Mrs.) v. Eve*, [1986], 39.

59 *Re X (a minor)*, [1975]; cited in La Forest, J., *E. (Mrs.) v. Eve*, [1986], para. 44.

60 *Stump v. Sparkman* (1978).

61 *Matter of Sallmaier* (1976), para. 991; quoting *Moore v. Flagg*, 137 App.Div. 338, 122 N.Y.S. 174; Matter of Weberlist, 79 Misc.2d 753, 360 N.Y.S.2d 783 (my emphasis).

62 La Forest, J., in in *E. (Mrs.) v. Eve*, [1986], para. 64

63 Licari, Nemer, and Tamburlin (2005); Grandjean and Landrigan (2006); Westra (2006).

64 Patz et al. (2005).

65 *Georgia v. Tenn. Copper Co.*, (1907, 237).

66 *Snapp & Son, Inc. v. Puerto Rico* (1982, 4n10).

67 Ibid., 41n11.

68 Huffman (2003, 2).

69 Ibid., 3.

70 Ibid., 4 and 22n146.

71 Ibid., 22.

72 *Illinois Central R. v. Illinois* (1892), 23.

73 Newman (2004, 127).

74 Wood (2009, 43).

75 Ibid., 56; see also Speth (2008).

76 Wood (2009, 47).

77 Ibid., 55.

78 Ibid., 57.

79 Ibid.

80 Ibid., 61.

81 Ibid.

82 Ibid., 62.

83 Ibid., 63.

84 Douzinas (2000, 9).

85 Ibid., 11.

86 On this framework convention, see Gostin (2008a).

CONCLUSION

1 Peters (2005, 541); see also ICJ, *Barcelona Traction, Light and Power Company* (1970), Second Phase Judgment.

2　Wood (2009).

3　Peters (2005, 539). See also Delbrück (1997); ICJ, *Application of the Convention on the Prevention and Punishment of the Crimes of Genocide*, [1993], separate opinion of Judge ad hoc Lauterpacht.

4　Peters (2005, 538); Fassbender (1998).

5　Delbrück (1997).

6　Peters (2005, 541).

7　See Falk (1964, 1970, 1984, 1998).

8　Sripati (2009).

9　O'Neill (1996, 172).

10　Ibid., 175.

11　Ibid., 176.

12　Ibid., 177. This is what is argued from a scientific and a moral point of view in the work of the Global Ecological Integrity Project. See Pimentel, Westra, and Noss (2000); Karr (2000); Noss and Cooperrider (1994); Westra (1998).

13　O'Neill (1996, 181).

14　Ibid., 113.

15　Pogge (2001, 15).

16　Ibid., 16.

17　Pogge (2001, 22); see Rawls (1971, 1993).

18　O'Neill (1999, 47).

19　Ibid., 193.

20　Falk (1998, 4).

21　Ibid., 14.

22　Ibid., 28.

23　Ibid., 26.

24　Ibid., 27-29.

25　Ibid., 30.

26　See, for example, Harry S. Truman, Speech, 26 June 1945, in United Nations Information Organization (1945, 680).

27　Cited in Fassbender (1998, 532-33).

28　Damaska (1990).

29　Cited in Hamilton and Rossiter (1961, 331-32).

30　Fassbender (1998, 536).

31　Delbrück (1981-82, 567, 570).

32　Ibid.; see Bodin (1962, 104).

33　De Vattel (1980).

34　*Charter of the United Nations*, art. 2, para. 1.

35　Delbrück (1981-82, 571); see also *Charter of the United Nations*, c. 7.

36　Delbrück (1981-82, 571); see also *Charter of the United Nations*, art. 1, para. 3; art. 13, para. 1; art. 55, para. 1.

37 Delbrück (1981-82, 527).
38 Ibid., 573.
39 Wood (2009).
40 Delbrück (1981-82, 576).
41 Falk (1970, 1998); but see also Westra (2010a, 168). I view the choice currently facing us as one between "barbarism and socialism."
42 Bodansky (2009, 566); see also Peters (2006).
43 Bodansky (2009); see also Charnovitz (2005) and Postiglione (2010).
44 Bodansky (2009, 567).
45 Ibid., 568.
46 Westra (2011); Bodansky (2009, 570).
47 Bodansky (2009, 572).
48 Ibid., 573.
49 Charnovitz (2005, 87).
50 Ibid., 88.
51 Palmer (1992); Esty (1999); Biermann (2000); Whally and Zissimos (2001).
52 Charnovitz (2005, 89).
53 Ibid., 90.
54 Postiglione (2010).
55 Ibid., 85, 87, 89.
56 Ibid., 5, 11.
57 Ibid.
58 Ibid., 9.
59 Ibid., 10.
60 Ibid.
61 Ibid., 13.
62 Ibid., 27, 29.
63 Ibid., 30.
64 Ibid.
65 Ibid., 33.
66 Ibid., 34.
67 Ibid., 36.
68 Ibid., 38.
69 Ibid., 39.
70 *Charter of the United Nations*, as signed in 1945 and amended in 1965, 1968, and 1973.
71 *Vienna Convention on the Law of Treaties* (1980), art. 53; see also discussion in Fassbender (1998, 600).
72 Fassbender (1998, 606).
73 Raz (2009, 169).
74 Ibid., 171.

75   Aquinas (n.d, Bk. II, Pt. I, Q. 104, A. 6, reply Obj. 3).
76   See King Jr. (1990, 71).
77   Raz (2009, 99).
78   Ibid.
79   Gostin (2008a).
80   Saiz (2005, 165).
81   Clarkson (2003).
82   Herbertson, Thompson, and Goodland (2010).
83   Held and McGraw (2002).
84   Falk (2002).
85   Saiz (2005, 167).
86   Wendt (1999, 129); see also discussion in Furia (2005).
87   Furia (2005, 339).
88   This is a position for which I have also argued in Westra (2011).

Works Cited

CASES CITED

AFRICA

Social and Economic Rights Action Center and the Center for Economic and Social Rights v. Nigeria, African Commission on Human and People's Rights, Communication No. 155/96 (2001).

AMERICAS

Kankuamo Indigenous Peoples v. Colombia (Provisional Measures Order), Order of 5 July 2004, Inter-Am. Ct. H.R. (Ser. E).

Massacre de Plan de Sanchez v. Guatemala (Reparations), (2004), Inter-Am. Ct. H.R. (Ser. C), No. 116.

Mayagna (Sumo) Awas Tingni Community v. Nicaragua, (2001), Inter-Am. Ct. H.R. (Ser. C), No. 79.

Moiwana Village v. Suriname, (2005), Inter-Am. Ct. H.R. (Ser. C), No. 124.

Yakye Axa Indigenous Community v. Paraguay, (2005), Inter-Am. Ct. H.R. (Ser. C), No. 125.

CANADA

114957 Canada Ltée (Spraytech, Societé d'arrosage) v. Hudson (Town), 2001, SCC 40, [2001] 2 S.C.R. 241.

Droit de la Famille, 323, [1988] R.J.Q. 1542 (C.A.).

E. (Mrs.) v. Eve, [1986] 2 S.C.R. 388.

Hepton et al. v. Maat et al., [1957] S.C.R. 606.

Pappajohn v. The Queen, [1980] 2 S.C.R. 120.

R. v. Cuerrier, [1988] 2 S.C.R. 371.

R. v. DeSousa, [1992] 2 S.C.R. 944.

R. v. Powley, [1999] 1. C.N.L.R. 153 (Ont. Ct. (Prov. Div.)).

R. v. Powley, 2003 SCC 43, [2003] 2 S.C.R. 207.

R. v. Village of 100 Mile House, [1993] B.C.J. No. 2848 (Prov. Ct.) (QL).

Sansregret v. The Queen, [1985] 1 S.C.R. 570.

Ward v. Canada (Attorney General), [2002] 1 S.C.R. 569.

Winnipeg Child and Family Services (Northwest Area) v. G. (D.F.), [1997] 3 S.C.R. 925.

Europe

Fadeyeva v. Russia, no. 55723/00, [2005] 55723/00 E.C.H.R. 376.

Guerra and Others v. Italy, no. 14967/89, [1998], 26 E.H.R.R. 357.

López Ostra v. Spain, no. 16798/90 [1994], 20 E.C.H.R. 277.

Oneryildiz v. Turkey, (2004) 41 E.C.H.R. 325.

India

Charan Lal Sahu v. Union of India, (1990) 1 SCC 613.

International

Crompton Corporation v. Government of Canada, NAFTA dispute, "Notion of Intent to Submit a Claim to Arbitration Under Section B of Chapter 11 of NAFTA," 6 November 2001, http://www.naftalaw.org/.

Methanex Corporation v. United States of America, NAFTA Arbitral Tribunal, Final Award, 3 August 2005.

Trail Smelter Arbitration (U.S. v. Canada), Arbitral Tribunal, 16 April 1938, 11 March 1941, 3 U.N.R.I.A. 1905 (1941).

European Court of Justice (ECJ)

Handelskwekerij G.J. Bier BV v. Mines de Potasse d'Alsace, C-21/76, [1976] E.C.R. 1735.

International Criminal Tribunal for the Former Yugoslavia

Prosecutor v. Furundzjia, Case No. IT-95-17/1, 38 I.L.M. 349 (1999).

International Court of Justice (ICJ)

"Aerial Herbicide Spraying (Ecuador v. Colombia)," Unofficial Press Release No. 2008/13, 2 June 2008.

Application of the Convention of 1902 Governing the Guardianship of Infants (Netherlands v. Sweden), [1958] I.C.J. Rep. 55, separate opinion of Judge Moreno Quintana.

Application of the Convention on the Prevention and Punishment of the Crime of Genocide (Bosnia-Herzegovina v. Yugoslavia, [1996] I.C.J. Rep. 595; [1993], Order, of the Court of Provisional Measures, I.C.J. Rep. 3, 29, 32, Further Requests for the Indication of Provisional Measures, separate opinion of Judge ad hoc Lauterpacht.*Armed Activities on the Territory of the Congo (Democratic Republic of the Congo v. Uganda)*, [2005] I.C.J. Reports 116.

Armed Activities on the Territory of the Congo (New Application: 2002) (Democratic Republic of the Congo v. Rwanda), [2006] I.C.J., general list No. 126.

Barcelona Traction, Light and Power Company, Limited (Belgium v. Spain) (New Application: 1962), [1970] I.C.J. Rep. 50.

"Ecuador Institutes Proceedings against Colombia with Regard to a Dispute Concerning the Alleged Aerial Spraying by Colombia of Toxic Herbicides over Ecuadorian Territory," Unofficial Press Release No. 2008/5, 1 April 2008.

Fisheries Jurisdiction (United Kingdom of Great Britain and Northern Ireland v. Iceland), [1973] I.C.J. Rep. 3.

Gabčíkovo-Nagymaros Project (Hungary v. Slovakia), [1997] I.C.J. Rep. 7, separate opinion of Vice-President Weeramantry.*Legal Consequences for States of the Continued Presence of South Africa in Namibia (South West Africa) notwithstanding Security Council Resolution 276 (1970)*, Advisory Opinion, [1971] I.C.J. Rep. 16, separate opinion of Vice-President Ammoun.

Legal Consequences of the Construction of a Wall in the Occupied Palestinian Territory, Advisory Opinion, [2004] I.C.J. Rep 4, 43 I.L.M 1009.

Legality of the Threat of Nuclear Weapons, Advisory Opinion, [1996] I.C.J. Rep. 226, declaration of President Bedjaoui and dissenting opinion of Judge Weeramanty.

"Letter from the Ambassador of Ecuador (Appointed) to the Kingdom of the Netherlands to the Registrar of the International Court of Justice," 31 March 2008, No. 4-4-3/08.

Military and Paramilitary Activities in and against Nicaragua (Nicaragua v. United States of America), [1986] I.C.J. Rep. 14, separate opinion of President Negendra Singh and separate opinion of Judge Sette-Cama.

North Sea Continental Shelf (Federal Republic of Germany v. Denmark) (Federal Republic of Germany/Netherlands), [1969] I.C.J. Rep. 3, dissenting opinion of Judge Tanaka.

Nuclear Tests (Australia v. France), [1974] I.C.J. Rep. 253.

Nuclear Tests (New Zealand v. France), [1974] I.C.J. Rep. 457.

Right of Passage over Indian Territory (Portugal v. India), [1960] I.C.J. Rep. 6, dissenting opinion of Judge Fernandes.

South West Africa (Ethiopia v. South Africa; Liberia v. South Africa), [1966] I.C.J. Rep. 6, dissenting opinion of Judge Tanaka.

UNITED KINGDOM

Chagos Islanders v. Attorney General, [2003] EWCH 2222 (QB), (2003) All E.R. (D) 166.

R (Bancoult) v. Secretary of State for Foreign and Commonwealth Affairs, [2007] Q.B. 1067 (Bancoult 1).

R (On the Application of Bancoult) v. Secretary of State for Foreign and Commonwealth Affairs, [2008] UKHL 61, on appeal from [2007] EWCA Civ. 498.

Re X (a minor), [1975] 1 All E.R. 697, [1975] Fam. 47.

Rylands v. Fletcher, 3 H & C. 744 (1865); L.R. 1 (Ex. 265) (1866); L.R. 3 H.L. 330 (1868).

Skinner v. Warner (1792), Dickens 799, 21 E.R. 473.

UNITED NATIONS, HUMAN RIGHTS COMMITTEE

–. *Ivan Kitok v. Sweden,* Communication No. 197/1985, UN GAOR, UN Doc. CCPR/
C/33/D/197/1985 (1988).

–. *Lovelace v. Canada,* Communication No. 24/1977, UN GAOR, 36th Sess., Supp. No.
40, UN Doc. A/36/40 (1981).

–. *Omniyak and the Lubicon Lake Band v. Canada,* Communication No. 167/1984, UN
GAOR, 1990, Supp. No 40, UN Doc. A/45/40 (1990).

UNITED STATES

Alvarez-Machain v. United States, 331 F.3d 604, 620 (9th Cir. 2003).

Aguinda v. Texaco, 945 F. Supp. 625 (S.D.N.Y. 1996); 1 and 2 F. Supp.2d 53 (S.D.N.Y.).

Aguinda v. Texaco, Inc., 142 F. Supp.2d 534 (S.D.N.Y. 2001).

Arar v. Ashcroft, 414 F. Supp.2d 250 (E.D.N.Y. 2006).

Bancoult v. McNamara, 217 F.R.D. 280 (D.D.C. 2003).

Bancoult v. McNamara, 370 F. Supp.2d 1 (D.C. Cir. 2004).

Canterbury v. Spence, 464 F.2d 772 (D.C. Cir. 1972).

Cherokee Nations v. Georgia, 30 US 1 (5 Pet. 1) (1831).

Doe/Roe v. Unocal Corp, 110 F. Supp.2d 1294, 1306 (C.D. Cal. 2000).

Filártiga v. Peña Irala, 630 F.2d 876 (2d Cir. 1980).

Georgia v. Tenn. Copper Co., 206 U.S. 230 (1907).

Illinois Central R. v. Illinois, 146 U.S. 387 (1892).

Jota v. Texaco Inc., 157 F.3d 153 (2d Cir. 1998).

*Maria Aguinda and others including the Federation of the Yagua People of the Lower Amazon
and Lower Napo v. Texaco, Inc.,* 303 F.3d 470 (2002).

Matter of Sallmaier, 378 N.Y.S.2d 989 (N.Y. Sup. Ct. 1976), para. 991.

Native Village of Kivalina v. ExxonMobil, et al., CV 08-1138 (N.D. Cal. 2008).

People of State of California v. General Motors Corporation, 2007 WL 2726871 (N.D. Cal.
2007).

Presbyterian Church of Sudan, Rev. John Gaduel and others v. Talisman Energy Inc., 244 F.
Supp.2d 289 (S.D.N.Y 2003).

Rasul v. Bush, 542 U.S. 466 (2004).

Roe v. Wade, 410 U.S. 35 (1973).

Sarei et al. v. Rio Tinto PLC, 221 F. Supp.2d 1116 (C.D. Cal 2002).

Snapp & Son, Inc. v. Puerto Rico ex rel. Baus, 458 U.S. 592 (1982).

State of Connecticut, et al. v. American Electric Power Company, Inc. et al., 582 F.3d 309
(2d Cir. 2009).

Stump v. Sparkman, 435 U.S. 349 (1978).

United States v. Smith, 18 U.S. 153, 5 L.Ed. 57 (1920).

Venancio Aguasanta Arias, et al. v. DynCorp et al., Civil Action No. 01-1908, Dist. Ct. D.C.
(2001).

Wiwa v. Royal Dutch Petroleum Co., No. 96 Civ. 8386, 2002 US Dist LEXIS 3293 (S.D.N.Y. 2002).

Wiwa v. Royal Dutch Petroleum Co., et al., 226 F.3d 88 (2d Cir. 2000).

Zadvydas v. Davis, 533 U.S. 678, 121 S. Ct. 249 (2001).

INTERNATIONAL DOCUMENTS AND DECISIONS

AGREEMENTS AND TREATIES

American Convention on Human Rights, 18 July 1978, O.A.S. T.S. No. 36, 1144 U.N.T.S. 123.

Charter of the Organization of American States, 30 April 1948, 119 U.N.T.S. 3 (entered into force 13 December 1951).

Charter of the United Nations, 24 October 1945, 1 U.N.T.S. XVI.

Convention against Torture and Other Cruel, Inhuman, or Degrading Treatment or Punishment, 10 December 1984, 1465 U.N.T.S. 85, 23 I.L.M. 1027 (1984) (entered into force 26 June 1987).

Convention for the Protection of Human Rights and Fundamental Freedoms, 4 November 1950, 213 U.N.T.S. 221 at 223, Eur. T.S. 5.

Convention on Biological Diversity, 5 June 1992, 1760 U.N.T.S. 9 (No. 30619), Can. T.S. 1993 No. 24, 31 I.L.M. 818.

Convention to Combat Desertification in those Countries Experiencing Serious Drought and/or Desertification, Particularly in Africa, 14 October 1994, 1954 U.N.T.S. 3, Can. T.S. 1996 No. 51, 33 I.L.M. 1332.

Declaration on the Establishment of the Arctic Council, Canada, Denmark, Finland, Iceland, Norway, Russian Federation, Sweden, and the United States, 19 September 1996, 35 I.L.M. 1387.

International Covenant on Civil and Political Rights, 19 December 1966, 999 U.N.T.S. 171, arts. 9-14, Can. T.S. 1976 No.47, 6 I.L.M. 368.

International Covenant on Economic, Social and Cultural Rights, 16 December 1966, 993 U.N.T.S. 3, 1976 Can. T.S. No.46 (1966) (entered into force 3 January 1976).

Kyoto Protocol to the United Nations Framework Convention on Climate Change, 11 December 1997, 37 I.L.M. 22 (1998).

Marrakesh Agreement Establishing the World Trade Organization, 15 April 1994, 1867 U.N.T.S. 31874 (entered into force 1 January 1995).

Montevideo Convention on the Rights and Duties of States, 26 December 1933, 49 Stat. 3097 (1934), 165 L.N.T.S. 10; 1934, 28 A.J.I.L. Supp. 75.

Palestinian Declaration of Independence, 15 November 1988, UN GAOR, 43d Sess., Annex 3 (Agenda Item 37), 13, UN Doc. A/43/827, S/20278 (1988), 27 I.L.M. 1668 (1988).

Treaty Banning Nuclear Weapons Tests in the Atmosphere, in Outer Space and under Water, 10 October 1963, 480 U.N.T.S 43.

Treaty of Sèvres, 10 August 1920, 118 BFSP 652.

Vienna Convention on the Law of Treaties, 27 January 1980, 115 U.N.T.S. 331, 8 I.L.M. 679 (signed in 1969).

COUNCIL OF EUROPE (CE)

Parliamentary Assembly. *Alleged Secret Detentions and Unlawful Inter-State Transfers Involving Council of Europe Member States*, Draft report – Part II, Rapporteur Dick Marty, Doc. AS/Jur (2006).

EUROPEAN COMMUNITIES (EC)

Council Directive 83/129/EEC of 28 March 1983 Concerning the Importation into Member States of Skins of Certain Seal Pups and Products Derived Therefrom, [1983] O.J. L 91/30.

EUROPEAN ENVIRONMENT AGENCY (EEA)

Environment and Health, EEA Report No. 10/2005 (2005).

GERMAN FEDERAL CONSTITUTIONAL COURT (GFCC)

Order of 24 June 2003, 2 BvR 685/03, BVerf GE 108.
Order of 26 October 2004, 2 BvR 955/00.

INTERNATIONAL LABOUR ORGANIZATION (ILO)

Convention No. 169, Indigenous and Tribal Peoples Convention, 1989.

ORGANIZATION FOR SECURITY AND CO-OPERATION IN EUROPE (OSCE)

Ministerial Council. *Madrid Declaration on Environment and Security*, MC.DOC/4/07 (30 November 2007).

ORGANIZATION OF AMERICAN STATES (OAS)

Inter-American Commission on Human Rights. *Inter-American Democratic Charter of Lima*, 11 September 2001.
–. *Maya Indigenous Community of the Toledo District v. Belize*, Case 12.053, Report No. 40/04 (2004), OR OEA/Ser.L/V/II.122, Doc. 5, rev. 1 at 727 (2006).
–. "Proposed American Declaration on the Rights of Indigenous Peoples," in *Annual Report of the Inter-American Court on Human Rights*, OR OEA/Ser.L/V/II.95, Doc. 6, rev. (1997).
–. *Report on the Situation of Human Rights in Ecuador*, OR OEA/Ser.L/V/II.96, Doc. 10, rev. 1 (1997).

UNITED NATIONS (UN)

Appointment and Terms of Reference of a United Nations Mediator in Palestine, GA Res. 186 (S-2), UN GAOR, UN Doc. A/553 (1948).

CERD (Committee on the Elimination of Racial Discrimination). *Report of the Committee on the Elimination of Racial Discrimination,* UN GAOR, 1992, 47th Sess., Supp. No. 18, UN Doc. A/47/18.

Commission on Human Rights. *Convention on the Rights of the Child,* GA Res. 44/25, UN GAOR, Supp. No. 49, UN Doc. A/44/49 (1989).

–. *Interim Report of the Special Representative of the Secretary-General on the Issue of Human Rights and Transnational Corporations and Other Business Enterprises,* UN ESCOR, 2006, UN Doc. E/CN.4/2006/97.

–. *Report of Special Rapporteur on the Situation of Human Rights and Fundamental Freedoms of Indigenous People, Mr. Rodolfo Stavenhagen, submitted pursuant to Commission on Resolution 2001/57,* UN ESCOR, 2002, UN Doc. E/CN.4/2002/97.

–. *Report of the Special Rapporteur of the Commission on Human Rights, John Dugard, on the Situation of Human Rights in the Palestinian Territories Occupied by Israel since 1967, Submitted in Accordance with Commission Resolution 1993/2 A,* UN ESCOR, 2004, UN Doc. E/CN.4/2004/6.

–. *Report of the Special Rapporteur on the Situation of Human Rights in the Palestinian Territories Occupied by Israel since 1967, John Dugard,* UN ESCOR, 2005, UN Doc. E/CN.4/2005/29/Add.1.

–. *Report of the Working Group on the Right to Development on Its Seventh Session (Geneva, 9-13 January 2006),* UN ESCOR, 2006, UN Doc. E/CN.4/2006/26.

–. *Report of the High-Level Task Force on the Implementation of the Right to Development on Its Second Meeting,* UN ESCOR, 2005, UN Doc. E/CN.4/2005/WG.18/TF/3.

–. *The Right to Development: Report of the Independent Expert on the Right to Development, Dr. Arjun Sengupta, Pursuant to General Assembly Resolution 54/175 and Commission on Human Rights Resolution E/CN.4/RES/2000/5,* UN ESCOR, 2000, UN Doc. E/CN.4/2000/WG.18/CRP.1.

–. *Study on the Right to the Truth: Report of the Office of the United Nations High Commissioner for Human Rights,* UN ESCOR, 2006, UN Doc. E/CN.4/2006/91.

Commission on Human Rights. Sub-Commission on Prevention of Discrimination and Protection of Minorities. *Resolution 1994/45,* Annex "Draft United Nations Declaration on the Rights of Indigenous Peoples," UN ESCOR, 1994, UN Doc. E/CN.4/1995/2, E/CN.4/Sub.2/1994/56 at 105 (1994).

–. *Study of the Problem of Discrimination against Indigenous Populations by Special Rapporteur, Mr. José Martinez Cobo,* UN ESCOR, 1986, UN Doc. E/CN/Sub.2/1986/7/Add.4.

–. *Study of the Rights of Persons Belonging to Ethnic, Religious and Linguistic Minorities: Mr. Francesco Capotorti,* UN ESCOR, 1977, UN Doc. E/CN.4/Sub.2/384.

Declaration of the United Nations Conference on the Human Environment, GA Res. 2994 (XXVII), UN Doc. A/Conf/48/14/Rev.1, reprinted in 11 ILM 1416 (1972) (Stockholm Declaration).

Declaration on the Granting of Independence to Colonial Countries and Peoples, GA Res. 1514 (XV), UN GAOR, 15th Sess., Supp. No. 16, UN Doc. A/4684 (1961) 166.

Declaration on the Right to Development, GA Res. 41/128, UN GAOR, UN Doc. A/RES/41/128 (1986).

Declaration on the Rights of Indigenous Peoples, GA Res. 61/295, UN GAOR, UN Doc. A/RES/61/295 (2007).

Human Rights Committee. *Consideration of Reports Submitted by States Parties under Article 40 of the Covenant: Concluding Observations of the Human Rights Committee, United States of America*, 2006, UN Doc. CCPR/C/USA/CO/3/Rev.1.

–. *General Comment Adopted by the Human Rights Committee under Article 40, Paragraph 4 of the International Covenant on Civil and Political Rights, Addendum*, General Comment, no. 23(50) (art. 7), UN Doc. CCPR/C/21/Rev.1/Add.5 (1994).

Human Rights Council. *Report of the Special Rapporteur on the Promotion and Protection of Human Rights and Fundamental Freedoms While Countering Terrorism, Martin Scheinin, Addendum, Mission to the United States of America*, UN GAOR, 6th Sess., UN Doc. A/HRC/6/17/Add.3 (2007).

–. *Report of the Special Rapporteur on the Situation of Human Rights in the Palestinian Territories Occupied since 1967, John Dugard*, UN GAOR, 7th Sess., UN Doc. A/HRC/7/17 (2008).

International Law Commission. "Draft Articles on State Responsibility." 1996. http://www.javier-leon-diaz.com/.

–. *First Report on State Responsibility by Mr. James Crawford, Special Rapporteur*, UN GAOR, 50th Sess., UN Doc. A/CN.4/490/Add.6 (1998).

–. *Third Report on State Responsibility by Mr. James Crawford, Special Rapporteur*, UN GAOR, 52d Sess., UN Doc. A/CN.4/507/Add. 4 (2000).

Office of the High Commissioner for Human Rights. *Manual on Human Rights Reporting under Six Major International Human Rights Instruments*, 1997, UN Doc. ST/HR/PUB/91/1 (Rev. 1).

Question of Palestine, UN GAOR, 1st Sess., UN Doc A/296 (1947).

Security Council. Res. 435 (1978) of 29 September 1978.

Secretary General. *Larger Freedom: Towards Development, Security and Human Rights for All*, UN Doc. A/59/2005 (31 March 2005).

United Nations Millennium Declaration, GA Res. 55/2, UN GAOR, 55th Sess., Supp. No. 49, UN Doc. A/RES/55/2 (2000).

Universal Declaration of Human Rights, GA Res. 217(III), UN GAOR, 3d Sess., Supp. No. 13, UN Doc. A/810 (1948) at 781.

World Conference on Human Rights. *Vienna Declaration and Program of Action*, UN GAOR, 48th Sess, UN Doc. A/Conf.157/24 (1993), reprinted in 32 I.L.M. 1661.

WORLD HEALTH ORGANIZATION (WHO)

WHO Framework Convention on Tobacco Control, 2003.

World Trade Organization (WTO)

EC Measures Concerning Meat and Meat Products (Hormones) (1998), WTO Doc. WT/
  DS26/AB/R, WT/DS48/AB/R (Appellate Body Report).

BOOKS AND ARTICLES

Abugre, Charles. 2008. "Behind Most Mass Violence Lurk Economic Interests." *Develop-ment Dialogue* 50 (December): 27-77.

Acosta, Andres Mejia. 2007. "Ecuador." Freedom House.com. http://www.freedomhouse.
  org/.

Akehurst, Michael. 1974-75. "The Hierarchy of the Sources of International Law." *British Yearbook of International Law* 47: 273-85.

Alexidze, Levan A. 1969. "Problem of *Jus Cogens* in Contemporary International Law." *Soviet Yearbook of International Law* 127: 149.

Alston, Philip. 2002. "Resisting the Merger and Acquisition of Human Rights by Trade Law: A Reply to Petersmann." *European Journal of International Law* 13, 4: 815-44.

–. 2005. "Ships Passing in the Night: The Current State of the Human Rights and Development Debate Seen Through the Lens of the Millennium Development Goals." *Human Rights Quarterly* 27, 3: 755-829.

Aminazadej, Sara C. 2007. "A Moral Imperative: The Human Rights Implications of Climate Change." *Hastings International and Comparative Law Review* 30, 2: 231-65.

Amnesty International. 2009. *Israel/Gaza, Operation "Cast Lead": 22 Days of Death and Destruction.* London: Amnesty International Publications.

Anaya, S. James. 2004. *Indigenous Peoples in International Law.* 2nd ed. New York: Oxford University Press.

Anaya, S. James, and Claudio Grossman. 2002. "The Case of Awas Tingni v. Nicaragua: A New Step in the International Law of Indigenous Peoples." *Arizona Journal of International and Comparative Law* 19, 1: 1-15.

Angermeier, Paul, and James R. Karr. 1994. "Biological Integrity versus Biological Diversity as Policy Directives." *BioScience* 44: 690-97.

Anghie, Antony. 2006. *Imperialism, Sovereignty and the Making of Human Rights.* Cambridge: Cambridge University Press.

Appiagyei-Atua, Kwadwo. 2002. "Human Rights, NGOs, and Their Role in the Promotion and Protection of Rights in Africa." *International Journal on Minority and Group Rights* 9, 3: 265-89.

Aquinas, Thomas. 1953. *The Political Ideas of St. Thomas Aquinas.* Edited by Dino Bigongiari. New York: Hafner.

–. 1988. *On Law, Morality and Politics.* Edited by W. Baumgarth and R.J Regan. Indianapolis, IN: Hackett Publishers.

–. N.d. *Summa Theologica.* http://www.sacred-texts.com/.

Aristotle. 1939. *De Caelo.* Translated by W.K.C Guthrie. Cambridge, MA. Loeb Classical Library/Harvard University Press.

–. 1961. *The Metaphysics: Books I-IX*. Translated by Hugh Tredennick. Cambridge, MA: Harvard/Loeb Classical Library.

–. 1992. *Nicomachean Ethics*. Translated by H. Rackhman. Cambridge, MA: Harvard/Loeb Classical Library.

Atapattu, Sumudu. 2002-3. "The Right to a Healthy Life or the Right to Die Polluted? The Emergence of a Human Right to a Healthy Environment under International Law." *Tulane Environmental Law Journal* 16, 1: 65-126.

Backman, Gunilla, Khosla P. Hunt, R. Jaramillo-Strouss, C. Fikre, B.M. Rumble, C. Revalin, D. Paez, and D.A. Pineda. 2008. "Health Systems and the Right to Health: An Assessment of 194 Countries." *The Lancet* 372, 9655: 2047-85.

Baker, John Hamilton. 1979. *An Introduction to English Legal History*. 2nd ed. London: Butterworths.

Barboza. 2001. "State Crimes: A Decaffeinated Coffee?" In *Liber Amicorum Georges Abi-Saab*, edited by Laurence Boisson de Chazournes and Vera Gowlland-Debbas, 357-76. Boston: Martimus Nijhoff Publishers.

Baxi, Upendra. 1998. "Voices of Suffering and the Future of Human Rights." *Transnational Law and Contemporary Problems* 8, 2: 125-69.

–. 2002. *The Future of Human Rights*. Oxford: Oxford University Press.

Baxi, Upendra, and Thomas Paul. 1986. *Mass Disasters and Multinational Liability: The Bhopal Case*. Delhi: Indian Law Institute.

Bedau, Hugo Adam. 1979. "Human Rights and Foreign Assistance Programs." In *Human Rights and US Foreign Policy*, edited by Peter G. Brown and Douglas MacLean, 29-44. Lexington, MA: Lexington Books.

Bederman, David J. 2001. *International Law Frameworks*. New York: Foundation Press.

Bendaña, Alejandro. 2008. "Is There a South Perspective on Genocide?" *Development Dialogue* 50: 279-91.

Betsill, Michele. 2002. "Environmental NGOs Meet the Sovereign State: The Kyoto Protocol Negotiations on Global Climate Change." *Colorado Journal of International Environmental Law and Policy* 13, 1: 49-64.

Beyani, Chaloka. 1999. "The Legal Premises for the International Protection of Human Rights." In *The Reality of International Law: Essays in Honour of Ian Brownlie*, edited by Guy S. Goodwin-Gill and Stefan Talmon, 21-36. Oxford: Clarendon Press.

Beyleveld, Deryck, and Roger Brownsword. 2001. *Human Dignity in Bioethics and Biolaw*. Oxford: Oxford University Press.

Biermann, Frank. 2000. "The Case for a World Environmental Organization." *Environment* 42, 9: 23-31.

–. 2005. "The Rationale for a World Environmental Organization." In *A World Environmental Organization*, edited by Frank Biermann and Steffen Bauer, 117-44. Aldershot, UK: Ashgate.

Birnie, Patricia W., and Alan E. Boyle. 1992. *International Law and the Environment*. New York: Clarendon Press.

–. 2002. *International Law and the Environment*. 2nd ed. Oxford: Oxford University Press.

Blackstone, William. 1809. *Commentaries on the Laws of England*. Vol. 1. 15th ed. Oxford: Clarendon Press.

Bodansky, Daniel. 2009. "Is There an International Environmental Constitution?" *Indiana Journal of Global Legal Studies* 16, 2: 565-84.

Bodin, Jean. 1962. *The First Booke of a Commonweale*. In *The Six Books of a Commanweale*, edited by Kenneth Douglas McRae and R. Knolles. Cambridge, MA: Harvard University Press.

Bok, Sissela. 1985. "Distrust, Secrecy, and the Arms *Race.*" *Ethics* 95, 3: 712-27.

Boniwa, Gersen. 2008. "'To Dominate the System and Not Be Dominated by It': Centre Indigena de Estudes e Perquisas (CINEP), and Ministry of Education, Brasilia, Brazil." *Poverty in Focus: Indigenising Development* 17 (May): 6-8

Bosselmann, Klaus. 2008. *The Principle of Sustainability: Transforming Law and Governance*. Aldershot, UK: Ashgate Publishing.

Bourette, Susan. 2000. "Ontario Ignored Water Alert." *Globe and Mail,* 8 June.

Boyd, David. 2003. *Unnatural Law*. Vancouver: UBC Press.

Boyle, Alan. 2007. "Human Rights of Environmental Rights? A Reassessment." *Fordham Environmental Law Review* 18, 3: 471-511.

Boyle, F.A. 1990. "The Creation of the State of Palestine." *European Journal of International Law* 1: 301-6.

BP. n.d. "Carbon Disclosure Project," "Greenhouse Gas Emissions Questionnaire – BP UK." http://www.cdproject.net/.

Brand, Ulrich, and Nicola Sekler. 2009. "Postneoliberalism: Catch-All Word or Valuable Analytical and Political Concept? Aims of a Beginning Debate." *Development Dialogue* 51, 1: 5-14.

Brown, Donald A. 1995. "The Role of Law in Sustainable Development and Environmental Protection Decision Making." In *Sustainable Development: Science, Ethics and Public Policy*, edited by John Lemons and Donald Brown, 64-76. Dordrecht, Netherlands: Kluwer Academic Press.

Brown, Garrette Wallace. 2008. "Moving from Cosmopolitan Legal Theory to Legal Practice: Models of Cosmopolitanism." *Legal Studies* 28, 3: 430-51.

Brownlie, Ian. 2003a. *Principles of Public International Law*. 6th ed. Oxford: Oxford University Press.

–. 2003b. "The Rights of Peoples in Modern International Law." In *The Rights of Peoples*, 6th ed., edited by J. Crawford, 1-16. Oxford: Oxford University Press.

Brownsword, Roger. 2004. "Technoregulation, Human Rights, and Human Dignity." In *Global Governance and the Quest for Justice: Human Rights*, Vol. 4, edited by Roger Brownsword, 203-34. Oxford: Hart Publishing.

–. 2008a. *Rights, Regulation and the Technological Revolution*. Oxford: Oxford University Press.

–. 2008b. "Rights, Responsibility and Stewardship: Beyond Consent." Paper presented at the inaugural conference for the European Association of Health Law, Royal Society of Edinburgh, 10-11 April.

Brown-Weiss, Edith. 1990. "Our Rights and Obligations to Future Generations for the Environment." *American Journal of International Law* 84: 198-207.

–. 1992. "Intergenerational Equity." In *Environmental Change and International Law*, edited by Edith Brown-Weiss, 385-412. New York: United Nations Press.

–. 1997. "The Changing Structure of International Law." *Georgetown Law Review: Res Ipsa Loquitury* 52 (Spring): 45-54.

Bullard, Robert. 1994. *Dumping in Dixie*. Boulder, CO: Westview Press.

–. 2001. "Decisionmaking." In *Faces of Environmental Racism*, edited by Laura Westra and Bill Lawson, 3-28. 2nd ed. Lanham, MD: Rowman Littlefield.

Burkitt, Denis. 1991. "Are Our Commonest Diseases Preventable?" *The Pharos of Alpha Omega Alpha Winter* 54, 1: 19-21.

Caldwell, Lynton. 1993. "The Ecosystem as a Criterion." In *Policy for Land and Ethics*, edited by Lynton Caldwell and Kristin Shrader-Frechett, 183-208. Lanham, MD: Rowman Littlefield.

Callicott, J. Baird. 1980. "*Animal Liberation: A Triangular Affair*." *Environmental Ethics* 2 (Winter): 311-38.

–. 1999. *The Land Ethic Revisited*. Albany, NY: SUNY Press.

Canadian Environmental Law Association. 2000. "Rural Ontario Industrial Hog Barns, Industrial Waste." *Intervenor* 25, 1. http://www.cela.ca/.

Cassese, Antonio. 1987. *International Law in a Divided World*. Oxford: Oxford University Press.

–. 1995. *Self-Determination of Peoples*. Cambridge: Cambridge University Press.

–. 2005. *International Law*. 2nd ed. Oxford: Oxford University Press.

–. 2007. *International Law*. 3rd ed. Oxford: Oxford University Press.

Cassuto, David. 2010. "Owning What You Eat: The Discourse of Food." In *Democracy, Ecological Integrity and International Law*, edited by J. Ronald Engel, Laura Westra, and K. Bosselmann, 306-32. Newcastle, UK: Cambridge Scholars Press.

Charnovitz, Steve. 1994. "Free Trade, Fair Trade, Green Trade: Defogging the Debate." *Cornell International Law Journal* 27: 459-525.

–. 2005. "Toward a World Environmental Organization: Reflections upon a Vital Debate." In *A World Environmental Organization*, edited by Frantz Biermann and Steffan Bauer, 87-116. Aldershot, UK: Ashgate.

Cheng, Bin. 1980. "The Legal Regime of Airspace and Outer Space in the Boundary Problem, Functionalism versus Spatialism: The Major Promises." *Annals of Air Space Law* 5: 323-37.

Chevron. n.d. "Caron Disclosure Project," "(CDP5) Greenhouse Gas Emissions Questionnaire 0: Chevron USA." http://cdproject.net/.

Chimni, Bhupinder. 2008. "The Sen Conception of Development and Contemporary International Law Discourse: Some Parallels." *Law and Development Review* 1, 1: 1-22. http://www.bepress.com/.

Choleminski, Ryszard. 1998. "State Duty towards Ethnic Minorities: Positive or Negative?" *Human Rights Quarterly* 10, 3: 344-71.

Cicero. 1928. *De Republica.* Translated by C.W. Keyes. Harvard, MA: Loeb Classical Library/Harvard University Press.

Clarkson, Stephen. 2003. "Global Governance and the Semi-Peripheral State: The WTO and NAFTA as Canada's External Constitution." In *Governing under Stress: Middle Powers and the Challenge of Globalization,* edited by Marjorie Griffin Cohen and Stephen Clarkson, 153-74. London: Zed Books.

Cohen, Robert. 1998. *Milk: The Deadly Poison.* Oradell, NJ: Argus Publishing.

Colborn, Theo, Dianne Dumanoski, and John Peterson Myers. 1996. *Our Stolen Future.* New York: Penguin Books.

Commission for Environmental Cooperation. 2006. "The North American Regional Action Plan (NARAP) on Lindane and Other Hexachlorocyclohexane (HCH) Isomers." 30 November. http://www.cec.org/.Congressional Research Service, Library of Congress. 2001. "Andean Regional Initiative (ARI): FY2002 Assistance for Colombia and Neighbours." fpc.state.gov/documents/organization/7948.pdf.

Crawford, James. 1999. "Israel (1948-1949) and Palestine (1998-1999): Two Studies in the Creation of States." In *The Reality of International Law,* edited by Guy Goodwin-Gill and Stefen Talmon, 95-124. Oxford: Clarendon Press.

Daily, Gretchen. 1997. "Natures Services." In *Societal Dependence on Natural Ecosystems,* edited by Paul Ehrlich and Gretchen Daily, 3-4. Washington, DC: Island Press.

Daly, Herman. 1996. *Beyond Growth.* Boston: Beacon Press.

Damaska, Mirjan R. 1990. "Reflections of American Constitutionalism." *American Journal of Comparative Law* 38: 421-44.

Damrosch, Lori. 1997. "Enforcing International Law through Non-Forcible Measures." *Collected Courses* 1, 269: 9-250.

Date-Bah, S.K. 1998. "Rights of Indigenous Peoples: Relation to National Resources Development: An African Perspective." *Journal of Energy and National Resources Law* 16, 4: 389-412.

Davis, Karen. 1996. *Prisoned Chickens, Poisoned Eggs: An Inside Look at the Poultry Industry.* Summertown, TN: Book Publishing.

Deets, Stephen. 1998. "Solving the Gabcikovo-Nagymaros Dam Conflict." East European Studies Meeting Reports, Woodrow Wilson Centre, Washington, DC.

de Feyter, Koen. 2007. "Localising Human Rights." In *Economic Globalisation and Human Rights,* edited by Wolfgang Benedek, Koem de Feyter, and Fabrizio Marella, 67-82. Cambridge: Cambridge University Press.

DeGrazia, David. 1995. *Taking Animals Seriously.* New York: Cambridge University Press.

Delbrück, Jost. 1981-82. "International Protection of Human Rights and State Sovereignty." *Indiana Law Journal* 57, 4: 567-78.

–, ed. 1997. *New Trends in International Lawmaking: International "Legislation" in the Public Interest*. Berlin: Duncker and Humblot.

–. 2001-2. "Prospects for a 'World (Internal) Law'? Legal Developments in a Changing International System." *Indiana Journal of Global Legal Studies* 9, 2: 401-12.

Dellapenna, Joseph. 2008. "A Human Right to Water: An Ethical Position or a Realizable Goal?" In *Reconciling Human Existence with Ecological Integrity*, edited by Laura Westra, Klaus Bosselmann, and Richard Westra, 183-94. London: Earthscan.

Depelchin, Jacques. 2008. "The History of Mass Violence since Colonial Times." *Development Dialogue* 50 (December): 13-32.

Dershowitz, Alan. 2003. *The Case for Israel*. Hoboken, NJ: John Wiley.

de Vattel, Emmerich. 1916 [1758]. *The Law of Nations*. Classics of International Law Series. Translated by J. Chitty. Philadelphia: J.W. Johnson and Co.

–. 1980. *The Law of Nations or, Principles of the Law of Nature, Applied to Conduct and Affairs of Nations and Sovereigns*. London: Book III.

Devlin, Patrick. 1959. "Morals and the Criminal Law." Maccabacan Lecture in Jurisprudence, read at the British Academy on 18 March. *Proceedings of the British Academy* 45: 129-51.

DeWet, Erika. 2004. "The Prohibition of Torture as an International Norm of *Jus Cogens* and Its Implications for National and Customary Law." *European Journal of International Law* 15, 1: 1, 97-122.

Diebel, Linda. 2009. "Mexican Outbreak Is Really 'NAFTA Flu,' Critics Say." *Toronto Star*, 1 May.

Donnelly, Jack. 1989. *Universal Human Rights in Theory and Practice*. Ithaca, NY: Cornell University Press.

–. 2003. *Universal Human Rights in Theory and Practice*. 2nd ed. Ithaca, NY: Cornell University Press.

Douzinas, Costas. 2000. *The End of Human Rights*. Oxford: Hart Publishing.

Draper, Elaine. 1991. *Risky Business*. Cambridge: Cambridge University Press.

Dugard, John. 1987. *Recognition and the United Nations*. Cambridge: Grotius Publications.

Dworkin, Ronald. 1977. *Taking Rights Seriously*. Cambridge, MA: Harvard University Press.

–. 1989. "Liberal Community." *California Law Review* 77, 3: 479-504.

Eisnitz, Gail. 1997. *Slaughterhouse: The Shocking Story of Greed, Neglect, and Inhumane Treatment Inside the US Meat Industry*. New York: Prometheus Books.

Engel, J. Ronald. 2010. "Contesting Democracy: Thick vs. Thin Interpretations of the Democratic Ideal." In *Democracy, Ecological Integrity and International Law*, edited by J. Ronald Engel, Laura Westra, and Klaus Bosselmann, 26-40. Newcastle upon Tyne: Cambridge Scholars Publishing.

Epstein, Richard A. 1989. "Justice across the Generations." *Texas Law Review* 67: 1465-83.

Epstein, Samuel. 1978. *The Politics of Cancer*. San Francisco: Sierra Club Books.

Esty, Daniel. 1999. "Toward Optimal Environmental Governance." *New York University Law Review* 74, 6: 1495-1574.

Etzioni, Amitai. 2009. "Spent: America after Consumerism." *New Republic,* 17 June. http://www.tnr.com/.

Falk, Richard A. 1964. *The Role of Domestic Courts in the International Legal Order.* Syracuse, NY: Syracuse University Press.

–. 1970. *The Status of the Law in International Society.* Princeton, NJ: Princeton University Press.

–. 1984. *Human Rights and State Sovereignty.* New York: Holmes and Meier Publishers.

–. 1998. *Law in an Emerging Global Village.* Ardsley, NY: Transnational Publishers.

–. 2002. "Interpreting the Interaction of Global Markets and Human Rights." In *Globalization and Human Rights,* edited by A. Brysk, 61–76. Berkeley: University of California Press.

Farr, William. *Vital Statistics: A Memorial Volume of Selections from Reports and Writings.* Edited by Noel A. Humphreys. London: Sanitary Institute, 1885.

Fassbender, Bardo. 1998. "The United Nations Charter as Constitution of the International Community." *Columbia Journal of Transnational Law* 36, 3: 529-620.

Feinberg, Joel. 1973. *Social Philosophy.* Englewood Cliffs, NJ: Prentice Hall.

Fidler, David P. 2001. *International Law and Public Health.* Ardsley, NY: Transnational Publishers.

–. 2005. "From International Sanitary Conventions to Global Health." *Chinese Journal of International Law* 4, 2: 325-92.

Finnis, John. 1980. *Natural Law and Natural Rights.* Oxford: Clarendon.

Ford, J., B. Smit, and J. Wandel. 2006. "Vulnerability to Climate Change in the Arctic: A Case Study from Arctic Bay, Canada." *Global Environmental Change* 16: 145-60.

Forrest, Michelle. 2000. "Using the Power of the World Health Organization: The International Health Regulations and the Future of the International Health Law." *Columbia Journal of Law and Social Problems* 33, 2: 153-80.

Francioni, Francesco. 2006. "Beni culturali: Diritto internazionale." In *Dizionario del diritto pubblico,* Vol. 1, edited by Antonio Cassese, 690-704. Milan: Giuffrè.

Francioni, Francesco, F. Lanzerini, M. Montini, and E. Morgera. 2010. "Options and Modalities for the Improvement of International Environmental Governance through the Establishment of a UN Environmental Organization." Paper presented at ICEF Conference, Rome, 20-21 May.

Furia, Peter A. 2005. "Global Citizenship Anyone? Cosmopolitanism, Privilege and Public Opinion." *Global Society* 19, 4: 331-59.

Galenkamp, Marlies. 1998. *Individualism versus Collectivism.* Rotterdam: Erasmus University.

Garrett, Laurie, and Scott Rosenstein. "Missed Opportunities: Governance of Global Infectious Diseases." *Harvard International Review* 27: 64-69.

Gaylord, Clarice, and Elizabeth Bell. 1995. "Environmental Justice: A National Priority." In *Faces of Environmental Racism,* edited by Laura Westra and Peter Wenz, 29-40. Lanham, MD: Rowman Littlefield.

Gbadegesin, Segun. 2001. "Multinational Corporations, Developed Nations and Environmental Racism: Toxic Waste, Oil Explorations and Ecocatastrophes." In *Faces of Environmental Racism*, 2nd ed., edited by Laura Westra and Bill Lawson, 187-202. Lanham, MD: Rowman Littlefield

Gewirth, Alan. 1978. *Reason and Morality*. Chicago: University of Chicago Press.

–. 1982. *Human Rights: Essays on Justification and Applications*. Chicago: University of Chicago Press.

Gilbert, Paul. 1994. *Terrorism, Security and Nationality*. London: Routledge.

–. 1998. *The Philosophy of Nationalism*. Boulder, CO: Westview Press.

Goedhuis, D. 1981. "Some Recent Trends in the Interpretation and the Implementation of the Rules of International Space Law." *Columbia Journal of Transnational Law* 19: 213-33.

Goerner, Sally. 1994. *Chaos and Evolving Ecological Universe*. Amsterdam: Gordon and Breach Science Publishers.

Goldin Rosenberg, Dorothy, executive producer. 2007. *Toxic Trespass*. Film produced for OISE. Ottawa: National Film Board of Canada.

Goodland, Robert, and Simon Counsell. 2008. "How the World Bank Could Be the World in Alleviation of Climate Change." In *Reconciling Human Existence with Ecological Integrity*, edited by Laura Westra, Klaus Bosselman, and Richard Westra, 219-43. London: Earthscan.

Goodland, Robert, and Herman Daly. 1995. "Universal Environmental Sustainability and the Principles of Integrity." In *Perspectives on Ecological Integrity*, edited by Laura Westra and John Lemons, 102-24. Dordrecht, Netherlands: Kluwer Academic.

Goodwin, Robert E. 1980. "No Moral Nukes." *Ethics* 90, 3: 417-49.

Gostin, Lawrence. 2008a. "Meeting Basic Survival Needs of the World's Least Healthy People: Toward a Framework Convention of Global Health." *Georgetown Law Journal* 96, 2: 331-92.

–. 2008b. *Public Health Law: Power, Duty and Restraint*. 2nd ed. Berkeley: University of California Press.

Grammond, Sebastien. 2008. "Disentangling 'Race' and Indigenous Status: The Role of Ethnicity." *Queen's Law Journal* 33, 2: 487-518.

–, with Lynne Groulx. 2009. "Finding Métis Communities." Paper presented at "Conference on Indigenous Peoples," University of Ottawa, 21 May.

Grandjean, Philippe, and Philip Landrigan. 2006. "Developmental Neurotoxicity of Industrial Chemicals." *The Lancet* 368, 9553: 2167-78.

Gready, P. 2004. *Fighting for Human Rights*. London: Routledge.

Grenville, J.A.S. 1974. *The Major International Treaties, 1914-1973: A History and Guide with Texts*. London: Methuen.

Grey, Stephen. 2005. "United States: Trade in Torture." *Le monde diplomatique*, April. http://mondediplo.com/.

Grotius. 1984. *The Law of War and Peace*. Classics of International Law. Translated by Francis W. Kelsey. Birmingham, AL: Legal Classics Library.

Guiberneau, Montserrat. 1996. *Nationalisms: The Nation State and Nationalism in the Twentieth Century.* Cambridge: Polity.

Halewood, Michael. 1999. "Indigenous and Local Knowledge in International Law: A Preface to *Sui Generis* Intellectual Property Protection." *McGill Law Review* 44, 4: 953-98.

Hamilton, Alexander, and Clinton Rossiter. *The Federalist Papers.* New York: New American Library, 1961.

Handl, Gunther. 1985. "Liability as an Obligation Established by a Primary Rule of International Law: Some Basic Reflections on the International Law Commission's Work." *Netherlands Year Book of International Law* 16: 49-79.

Hardin, Garrett, 1968. "The Tragedy of the Commons." *Science* 162, 3859: 1243-48.

Hart, H.L.A. 1998 [1959]. "Immorality and Treason." In *Morality and the Law,* edited by R.M. Baird and S.E. Rosenbaum, 47-53. Buffalo, NY: Prometheus Books.

Hassol, Susan Joy. 2004. *Impacts of a Warming Arctic: Arctic Climate Impact Assessment.* Cambridge: Cambridge University Press.

Heinzerling, Liza. 2008. "Climate Change, Human Health and the Post-Cautionary Principle." *Georgetown Law Journal* 96, 2: 445-60.

Held, David, and Antony McGraw. 2002. *Globalisation/Antiglobalisation.* Cambridge: Polity Press.

Held, David, Anthony McGrew, David Goldblatt, and Jonathan Perration. 1999. *Global Transformations: Politics, Economics and Culture.* Palo Alto, CA: Stanford University Press.

Held, Virginia. 1970. *The Public Interest and Individual Interests.* New York: Basic Books.

Herbertson, Kirk, Kim Thompson, and Robert Goodland. 2010. *A Roadmap for Integrating Human Rights into the World Bank Group.* Washington, DC: World Resources Institute. http://pdf.wri.org/.

Hertsgaard, Mark. 1999. *Earth Odyssey: Around the World in Search of Our Environmental Future.* New York: Broadway Books.

Higgins, Rosalyn. 1963. *The Development of International Law through the Political Organs of the United Nations.* London: Clarendon Press.

–. 1972. "The Advisory Opinion on Namibia: Which UN Resolutions Are Binding under Article 25 of the Charter?" *International and Comparative Law Quarterly* 2, 2: 270-86.

–. 1994. *Problems and Process: International Law and How We Use It.* Oxford: Clarendon Press.

Hiskes, Richard P. 1998. *Democracy, Risk and Community.* New York: Oxford University Press.

Hitler, Adolf. 1980. "18 September 1941." In *Adolf Hitler: Monologe im Führerhauptquartier,* edited by Werner Jochmann, 60-64. Hamburg: Albrecht Knaus Verlag.

Hoffman, Sarah. 2007. "Gore Speaks to 6,000 Earth Scientists in San Francisco." *Op.Ed. News.com,* 26 January.

Howard, Rhoda E., and Jack Donnelly. 1993. *Universal Human Rights in Theory and Practice*. Ithaca, NY: Cornell University Press.

Howse, Robert, and Makau Mutua. 2000. "Protecting Human Rights in a Global Economy: Challenges for the World Trade Organization." International Centre for Human Rights and Democratic Development, http://www.ichrdd.ca/.

Huffman, James L. 2003. "Fish Out of Water: The Public Trust Doctrine in a Constitutional Democracy." In *Symposium: Joseph Sax and the Public Trust*, Article 6. Berkeley, CA: Berkeley Electronic Press. http://www.bepress.com/.

Hughes, Elaine, Alastair R. Lucas, and William A. Tilleman. 2003. *Environmental Law and Policy*. 3rd ed. Toronto: Edmond Montgomery Publications.

Human Rights Watch. 2004. "The United States' 'Disappeared': The CIA's Long-Term 'Ghost Detainees.'" Briefing Paper. http://www.hrw.org/.

Ibbitson, John. 2000. "Harris's Denials Are Floundering." *Globe and Mail*, 8 June.

Institute of Medicine. 1988. *The Future of Public Health*. Washington, DC: Committee for the Study of the Future of Public Health, National Academy Press.

IPCC. 2007. "Summary for Policymakers." In *Climate Change 2007: The Physical Science Basis – Contribution of Working Group I to the Fourth Assessment Report of the Intergovernmental Panel on Climate Change*, edited by S. Solomon, D. Qin, M. Manning, Z. Chen, M. Marquis, K.B. Averyt, M. Tignor, and H.L. Miller, 1-18. Cambridge, UK: Cambridge University Press.

Isaac, Thomas. 2002. "Canadian Charter of Rights and Freedoms: The Challenge of the Individual and Collective Rights of Aboriginal People." *Windsor Yearbook of Access to Justice* 21: 431-54.

Jonas, Hans. 1984. *The Imperative of Responsibility*. Chicago: University of Chicago Press.

Jones, Walter T. 1970. *The Classical Mind*. San Diego, CA: Harcourt, Brace, Jovanovich.

Kadelbach, Stefan. 2006. "*Jus Cogens*, Obligations *Erga Omnes* and Other Rules – The Identification of Fundamental Norms." In *The Fundamental Rules of the International Legal Order*, edited by Christian Tomuschat and Jean-Marc Thouvenin, 21-40. Leiden, Netherlands: Martinus Nijhoff.

Kant, Immanuel. 1996 [1797]. *The Metaphysics of Morals*. Translated and edited by Mary Gregor. Cambridge: Cambridge University Press.

–. 2002. *Groundwork for the Metaphysics of Morals*. Edited by Thomas E. Hill Jr. and A. Zweig. Oxford: Oxford University Press.

Karkar, Sonja. 2007. "Sabra and Shatila: On Massacre, Atrocities and Holocausts." *Just Commentary* 7, 10: Article 107.

Karlberg, Michael. 2008. "Discourse Identity and Global Citizenship." *Peace Review* 20, 3: 310-20.

Karr, James. 1993. "Protecting Ecological Integrity: An Urgent Social Goal." *Yale Journal of International Law* 18, 1: 297-306.

–. 2000. "Ecological Integrity and Ecological Health Are Not the Same." In *Engineering within Ecological Constraints*, edited by Peter C. Schulze, National Academy of Engineering, 97-110. Washington, DC: National Academy Press.

Karr, James, and Ed Chu. 1999. *Restoring Life to Running Waters*. Washington, DC: Island Press.

Kay, James, and H. Regier. 2000. "Uncertainty, Complexity and Ecological Integrity: Insights from a Ecosystem Approach." In *Implementing Ecological Integrity*, edited by Philippe Crabbe, Alan Holland, Lech Ryszkowski, and Laura Westra, 121-56. NATO Science Series, Vol. 1. Dordrecht, Netherlands: Kluwer Academic Publishers.

Kay, James, and E. Schneider. 1994. "The Challenge of the Ecosystem Approach." *Alternatives* 20, 3: 1-6.

Kempton, Kate. 2005. "Bridge over Troubled Waters: Canadian Law on Aboriginal Treaty 'Water Rights.'" Paper on file with author.

Kendall, Harry W., and David Pimentel. 1994. "Constraints on the Expansion of the Global Food Supply." *AMBIO* 23, 3: 198-205.

Kenk, M., and K. Sikkink. 1998. *Activists beyond Borders*. Ithaca, NY: Cornell University Press.

Kindred Hugh M., Karin Michelson, René Provost, Ted L. McDorman, Armand L. DeMistral, and Sharon Ann Williams. 2000. *International Law*. 6th ed. Toronto: Emond Montgomery Publications.

King, Martin Luther, Jr. 1990, "Letter from a Birmingham Jail." In *Nonviolence in Theory and Practice*, edited by R. Holmes, 60-71. Belmont, CA: Wadsworth.

Kirgis, Frederick, Jr. 2001. "The Degrees of Self-Determination in the United Nations Era." In *International Human Rights in Context*, edited by Henry J. Steiner and Philip Alston, 1270-72. Oxford: Oxford University Press.

Kössler, Reinhart. 2008. "Violence, Legitimacy and Dynamics of Genocide: Notions of Mass Violence Examined." *Development Dialogue* 50 (December): 33-52.

Kraut, Richard. 1989. *Aristotle on the Human Good*. Princeton, NJ: Princeton University Press.

Kunitz, Stephen J. 2000. "Globalization, States and the Health of Indigenous Peoples." *American Journal of Public Health* 90, 10: 1531-39.

Kymlicka, Will. 1989. *Liberalism, Community, Culture*. Oxford: Oxford University Press.

–. 1995. *Multicultural Citizenship*. Oxford: Oxford University Press.

The Lancet. 2008. "The Right to Health: From Rhetoric to Reality." 372, (9655): 2001.

Larschan, Bradley, and Bonnie Brennan. 1983. "The Common Heritage of Mankind Principle in International Law." *Columbia Journal of Transnational Law* 21, 2: 305-38.

Lauterpacht, Hersch. 1947. *Recognition in International Law*. Cambridge: Cambridge University Press.

Leader, Sheldon. 2004. "Collateralism." In *Global Governance and the Quest for Justice*. Vol. 4, *Human Rights*, edited by Roger Brownsword, 53-68. Oxford: Hart Publishing.

Lenin, Vladimir I. 1969. "Thesis on the Socialist Revolution and the Right of Nations to Self-Determination." In *Selected Works*. London: Lawrence and Wishart.

Leopold, Aldo. 1949. *A Sand County Almanac*. New York: Oxford University Press.

Licari, Licia., Linda Nemer, and Georgia Tamburlini. 2005. *Children's Health and the Environment.* Copenhagen, Denmark: World Health Organization for Europe Office.

Lisska, Anthony. 1996. *Aquinas' Theory of Natural Law.* Oxford: Clarendon Press.

Luban, David. 2004. "A Theory of Crimes against Humanity." *Yale Journal of International Law* 29: 85-168.

Machine, R. 2000. "Water Sewage Not a Priority for SuperBuild." *Globe and Mail,* 8 June.

Macklem, Patrick. 2008. "Minority Rights in International Law." Legal Studies Research Paper No.08-19, University of Toronto.

Marquis, Donald. 1989. "Why Abortion Is Immoral." *Journal of Philosophy* 86, 4: 183-202.

Martin, Susan, Patricia Fagin, and John Warner. 2005. "Palestinian Refugees in Gaza." *Fordham International Law Journal* 28: 1457-78.

Mathews, Jessica T. 1997. "Power Shift." *Foreign Affairs* 76, 1: 50-55.

Mathieu, Deborah. 1996. *Preventing Prenatal Harm: Should the State Intervene?* 2nd ed. Washington, DC: Georgetown University Press.

Matthews, Robert, and Cranford Pratt. 1985. "Human Rights and Foreign Policy: Principles and Canadian Practice." *Human Rights Quarterly* 7, 2: 159-88.

Mayers, Rebekah. 2009. "Plan Colombia and the Dangers of Aerial Herbicides." Paper presented at the Law Faculty, University of Windsor, Ontario, 20 March.

McCalman, Ian, B. Penny, and M. Cook. 1998. *Mad Cows and Modernity.* Canberra, Australia: Humanities Research Centre, Australian National University.

McMahan John. 2009. *Killing in War.* Uehiro Series in Practical Ethics. Oxford: Oxford University Press.

McMichael, Anthony J. 1995. "The Health of Persons, Populations and Planets: Epidemiology Comes Full Circle." *Epidemiology* 6, 6: 633-36.

–. 2000. "Global Environmental Change in the Coming Century: How Sustainable Are Recent Health Gains?" In *Ecological Integrity: Integrating Environment, Conservation and Health,* edited by David Pimentel, Laura Westra, and Reed Noss, 245-60. Washington, DC: Island Press, 2000.

Meier, Benjamin Mason. 2006. "Employing Health Rights for Global Justice: The Promise of Public Health in Response to Insalubrious Ramifications of Globalization." *Cornell International Law Journal* 39, 3: 711-52.

Melber, Henning. 2005. "How to Come to Terms with the Past: Re-visiting the German Colonial Genocide in Namibia." *Afrika Spectrum* 1, 40: 139-48.

–. 2008. "Colonialism and Mass Violence: Integral Parts of Modernity." *Development Dialogue* 50, (December): 263-70.

Mellon, M., and D. Fondriest. 2001. "Pearls before Pigs." *Nucleus* 23, 1: 1-3.

Meron, Theodor. 2006. *The Humanization of International Law.* Leiden: Martinus Nijhoff Publishers.

Metcalf, Cherie. 2004. "Indigenous Rights and the Environment: Evolving International Law." *Ottawa Law Review* 35, 1: 101-40.

Michelot, Agnès. 2006. "Enjeux de la reconnaissance du statut de réfugié écologique pour la construction d'une nouvelle responsabilité internationale, Actes du colloque de Limoges sur 'Les réfugiés écologiques.'" *Revue Européenne de Droit de l'Environment,* 4 December: 428-45.

Miller, Peter, and Laura Westra, eds. 2002. *Just Integrity.* Lanham, MD: Rowman Littlefield.

Miller, Russell A. 2006. "Surprising Parallels between *Trail Smelter* and the Global Climate Change Regime." In *Transboundary Harm in International Law,* edited by Rebecca M. Bratspies and Russell A. Miller, 167-80. Cambridge: Cambridge University Press.

Mitchell, Alana, John Gray, and Real Seguin. 2000. "Fear of Farming." *Globe and Mail,* June 3.

Mittelstaedt, Martin. 2005. "Pollution Debate Born of Chemical Valley's Girl-Baby Boom." *Globe and Mail,* 15 November.

Morin, Michel. 1990. "La compténce parens patriae et le droit privé: Un emprunt inutile, un affront à l'histoire." *Revue de Barreau* 50, 5: 827-924.

Morse, Bradford. 2002. "Comparative Assessments of the Position of Indigenous Peoples in Quebec, Canada, and Abroad." http://papers.ssrn.com/.

Myers, Norman. 1993. "Environmental Refugees in a Globally Warmed World." *Bioscience* 43, 11: 752-61.

Neumann, Michael. 2005. *The Case against Israel.* Edinburgh: A.K. Press.

Newman, Dwight G. 2004. "Collective Interests and Collective Rights." *American Journal of Jurisprudence* 49: 127-63.

Nikiforuk, Andrew. 2000. "National Water Crisis Forecast: Study Blames Declining Supply on Lax Attitudes, Climate Change." *Globe and Mail,* 7 June. http://www.aquacareltd.com/.

Noss, R.F. 1992. "The Wildlands Project Land Conservation Strategy." In "The Wildlands Project: Plotting a North American Wilderness Recovery Strategy," special issue *Wild Earth,* 10: 10-25.

Noss, R.F., and A.Y. Cooperrider. 1994. *Saving Nature's Legacy.* Washington, DC: Island Press.

O'Neill, Onora. 1996. *Towards Justice and Virtue.* Cambridge: Cambridge University Press.

Oldham, John, and Rachel Massey. 2002. "Health and Environmental Effects of Herbicide Spray Campaigns in Colombia." Institute for Science and Interdisciplinary Studies Occasional Paper, Amherst, MA.

Onuf, N.G., and Richard K Birney. 1974. "Peremptory Norms of International Law." *Denver Journal of International Law and Policy* 4, 2: 187-98.

Orentlicher, Diane. 2001. "Separation Anxiety: International Responses to Ethno-Separatist Claims." In *International Human Rights in Context,* edited by Henry J. Steiner and P. Alston, 1249-57. Oxford: Oxford University Press.

Owens, Joseph. 1959. *A History of Ancient Western Philosophy.* New York: Applecroft Century Crofts.

Pallemaerts, Marc. 1986. "Development, Conservation and Indigenous Rights in Brazil." *Human Rights Quarterly* 8, 3: 374-400.

Palmer, Geoffrey. 1992. "New Ways to Make International Environmental Law." *American Journal of International Law* 86, 2: 259-83.

Pappe, Ilan. 2006. *The Ethnic Cleansing of Palestine*. Oxford: One World.

Pasqualucci, Jo M. 2006. "The Evolution of International Indigenous Rights: The Interamerican Human Rights System." *Human Rights Law Review* 6, 2: 281-322.

Patz, Jonathan, D. Campbell-Lendrum, T. Holloway et al. 2005. "Impact of Regional Climate Change on Human Health." *Nature* 438, 7066: 310-17.

Paust, Jordan. 2004. "The Reality of Private Rights, Duties, and Participation in the International Legal Process." *Michigan Journal of International Law* 25, 4: 1229-50.

Pavlakos, George. 2008. "Non-Individualism and Rights." In *The Tension between Group Rights and Human Rights*, edited by K. De Feyter and G. Pavlakos, 147-71. Oxford: Hart Publishing.

Peel, Jacqueline. 2001. "New State Responsibility Rules and Compliance with Multilateral Environmental Obligations: Some Case Studies of How the New Rules Might Apply in the International Environmental Context." *Review of European Community and International Environmental Law* 10, 1: 82-97.

Peers, Steve. 2001. "Fundamental Rights or Political Whim? WTO Law and the European Court of Justice." In *The EU and the WTO*, edited by Grainne de Burca and Joanne Scott eds., 111-30. Portland, OR: Oxford University Press.

Pellet, Alain. 1997. "Vive le crime! Remarques sur les degrés de l'illicite en droit international." In *International Law on the Eve of the Twenty-First Century: Views from the International Law Commission*, United Nations, 281-315. New York: United Nations.

–. 2006. "Conclusions." In *Fundamental Rules of the International Legal Order: Jus Cogens and Obligations Erga Omnes*, edited by Christian Tomuschat and Jean Marc Thouvenin, 417-24. Leiden: Martinus Nijhoff.

Pentassuglia, Gaetano. 2009. "Evolving Protection of Minority Groups: Global Challenges and the Role of International Jurisprudence." *International Community Law Review* 11, 2: 185-218.

Peters, Anne. 2005. "Global Constitutionalism in a Nutshell." In *Weltinnenrecht: Liber amicorum Jost Delbrück*, edited by Klaus Dicke and Jost Delbrück, 535-50. Berlin: Duncker and Humblot.

–. 2006. "Compensatory Constitutionalism: The Function and Potential of Fundamental International Norms and Structures." *Leiden Journal of International Law* 19, 3: 579-610.

Pilkington, Ed. 2009. "Shell Pays Out 15.5 m over Saro-Wiwa." *Globe and Mail,* 9 June.

Pimentel, David. 1991. "Conserving Biological Diversity in Agricultural/Forestry Systems." *Bioscience* 42, 5: 354-62.

Pimentel, David. 2006. "Soil Erosion: A Food and Environmental Threat." *Environment, Development and Sustainability* 8, 1: 119-37.

Pimentel, David, and Robert Goodland. 2000. "Environmental Sustainability and Integrity in the Agricultural Sector." In *Ecological Integrity: Integrating Environment, Conservation and Health,* edited by David Pimentel, Laura Westra, and Reed Noss, 121-37. Washington, DC: Island Press.

Pimentel, David, U. Stachow, and D.A. Takacs et al. 1992. "Conserving Biological Diversity in Agricultural/Forestry Systems." *Bioscience* 42, 5: 354-62.

Pimentel, David, Laura Westra, and Reed Noss. 2000. *Ecological Integrity: Integrating Environment, Conservation and Health.* Washington, DC: Island Press.

Pither, Kerry. 2008. *Dark Days: The Story of Four Canadians Tortured in the Name of Fighting Terror.* Toronto: Penguin.

Pogge, Thomas W. 1992. "Cosmopolitanism and Sovereignty." *Ethics* 103, 1: 48-75.

–. 2001. *Global Justice.* Oxford: Blackwell Publishers.

–. 2004. "The First United Nations Millennium Development Goal: A Cause for Celebration?" *Man and Development* 5, 3: 377-89.

–. 2008. "Aligned: Global Justice and Ecology." In *Reconciling Human Existence with Ecological Integrity,* edited by Laura Westra, Klaus Bosselmann, and Richard Westra, 147–58. London: Earthscan.

Postiglione, Amedeo. 2001. *Giustizia e ambiente globale:* Necessità di una corte internazionale. Milan: Giuffrè Editore.

–. 2010. *Global Environmental Governance.* Brussels: Bruylant.

Quigley, John. 1997. "The Israel-PLO Interim Agreements: Are They Treaties?" *Cornell International Law Journal* 30, 3: 717-40.

Rachels, James. 1997. "Vegetarianism and 'The Other Weight Problem.'" In *Environmental Ethics,* edited by Louis Pojman, 367-73. Belmont, CA: Wadsworth Publishing Company.

Raeburn, John, and Sarah MacFarlane. 2003. "Putting the Public into Public Health: Towards a More People-Centred Approach." In *Global Public Health: A New Era,* edited by Robert Beaglehole and Ruth Bonita, 267-82. Oxford: Oxford University Press.

Ragazzi, Maurizio. 1998. *The Concept of International Obligations Erga Omnes.* Oxford: Clarendon Press.

–. 2007. "Alexidze on *Jus Cogens* (Selected Consideration)." In *Theory and Practice of Contemporary International Law: Essays in Honour of Prof. Levan Alexidze on the 80th Birthday Anniversary,* 25-38. Tbilisi: Movatia.

Rapport, David J. 1995. "Ecosystem Health: More Than a Metaphor?" *Environmental Values* 4, 4: 287-309.

Ratner, Steven R. 2007. "Can We Compare Evils? The Enduring Debate on Genocide and Crimes against Humanity." *Washington University Global Studies Law Review* 6, 3: 583-89.

Rawls, John. 1971. *A Theory of Justice.* Cambridge, MA: Harvard University Press.

–. 1993. *Political Liberalism.* New York: Columbia University Press.

Raz, Joseph. 1984. "On the Nature of Rights." *Mind* 93, 370: 194-214.

–. 1997. "Rights and Politics." In *Law Values and Social Practices*, edited by John Tasioulas, 75-98. Aldershot, UK: Ashgate.

–. 2005-6. "The Problem of Authority: Revisiting the Service Conception." *Minnesota Law Review* 90, 4: 1003-44.

–. 2009. "About Morality and the Nature of Law." In *Between Authority and Interpretation*, edited by J. Raz, 166-81. Oxford: Oxford University Press.

Rees, William, and M. Wackernagel. 1996. *Our Ecological Footprint*. Gabriola Island, BC: New Society Publishers.

Rees, William, and Laura Westra. 2003. "When Consumption Does Violence: Can There Be Sustainability and Environmental Justice in a Resource-Limited World?" In *Just Sustainabilities: Development in an Unequal World*, edited by Julien Agyeman, Robert Evans, and Robert D. Bullard, 99-124. London: Earthscan.

Regan, Tom. 1983. *The Case for Animal Rights*. Berkeley: University of California Press.

Reinisch, August. 2001. "Governance without Accountability." *German Yearbook of International Law* 44: 270-306.

Revenga, Álvaro, director. 2005. *Sipakapa No Se Vende*. Guatemala: Caracol Productions.

Revkin, Andrew C. 2006. "World Briefing Americas: Inuit Climate Change Petition Rejected." *New York Times*, 16 December.

Rice, Condoleezza. "Renditions Save Lives." *Times Online*, 5 December. http://www.timesonline.co.uk/.

Rifkin, Jeremy. 1992. *Beyond Beef: The Rise and Fall of the Cattle Culture*. New York: Plume Books.

Rist, John. 1989. *The Mind of Aristotle*. Toronto: University of Toronto Press.

Rockefeller, Steven C. 2002. Foreword to *Just Ecological Integrity: The Ethics of Maintaining Planetary Life*, edited by Peter Miller and Laura Westra, x-xiv. Lanham, MD: Rowman Littlefield.

Rogan, Walter J., and Beth N. Ragan. 2003. "Evidence of Effects of Environmental Chemicals on the Endocrine System in Children." *Pediatrics* 112, 1: 247-52.

Ruru, Jacinta. 2009. "Review of L. Westra, 2007, *Environmental Justice and the Rights of Indigenous People*." *Environmental Law Journal* 21, 2: 385-87.

Sachs, Wolfgang. 2004. "Climate Change and Human Rights." In *Scripta Varia*. Vol. 106, *Interactions between Global Change and Human Health*, Pontifical Academy of Sciences, 349-68. Rome: Vatican City.

Sage, Michael V. 2006. "The Exploitation of Legal Loopholes in the Name of National Security: A Case Study on Extraordinary Rendition." *California Western International Law Journal* 37, 1: 142.

Saiz, Angel Valencia. 2005. "Globalisation, Cosmopolitanism and Ecological Citizenship." *Environmental Politics* 14, 2: 163-78.

Salomon, Margot. 2007. *Global Responsibility for Human Rights*. Oxford: Oxford University Press.

Sand, Peter H. 2009a. "Diego Garcia: British American Legal Black Hole in the Indian Ocean?" *Journal of Environmental Law* 21, 1: 113-37.

—. 2009b. *United States and Britain in Diego Gracia.* New York: Palgrave MacMillan.

Sandler, Ron. 2006. "Comments on Bill Lawson's 'Racist Property Holdings and Environmental Coalitions,' and Laura Westra's 'The Rights of Indigenous Peoples: Ecofootprint Crime and the Biological/Ecological Integrity Model.'" Paper presented at the American Philosophical Association, Newark, Delaware, 30 December.

Sands, Philippe. 2005. *Lawless World.* London: Allen Lane/Penguin Books.

Sax, Joseph. 1980. "Liberating the Public Trust Doctrine from Its Historical Shackles." *U.C. Davis Law Review* 14, 2: 185-94.

Schabas, William. 2000. *On Genocide.* Dordrecht, Netherlands: Kluwer Law Publishers.

Schaller, Dominik J. 2008. "Colonialism and Genocide: Raphael Lemkin's Concept of Genocide and Its Application to European Rule in Africa." *Development Dialogue* 50 (December): 75-94.

Schmidt-Jortzig, E. 1991. "The Constitution of Namibia: An Example of a State Emerging under Close Supervision and World Scrutiny." *German Yearbook of International Law* 34: 413-28.

Scott, Craig. 2001. "Translating Torture into International Tort: Conceptual Divides in the Debate on Corporate Accountability for Human Rights Harms." In *Torture as Tort,* edited by Craig Scott, 55-63. Oxford: Hart Publishing.

Scott, Dayna. 2008. "Confronting Chronic Pollution: A Socio-Legal Analysis of Risk and Precaution." *Osgoode Hall Law Journal* 46, 2: 293-343.

Scovazzi, Tullio. 1991. "Industrial Accidents and the Veil of Transnational Corporations." In *International Responsibility for Environmental Harm,* edited by Francesco Francioni and Tullio Scovazzi, 395-427. London: Graham and Trotman, Kluwer Academic Publishers.

—. 2009a. "Considerazioni in tema di segreto di stato e gravi violazioni dei diritti umani." In *Diritti Individuali e Giustizia Internazionale,* edited by Gabriella Venturini, and Stefania Bariatti. Milan, Italy: Giuffrè.

—. 2009b. "La Convention pour la sauvegarde du patrimoine culturel immatériél." Unpublished paper on file with the author.

Secretariat of the United Nations Convention to Combat Desertification. *Securitizing the Ground, Grounding Security.* Bonn, Germany: UNCCD. http://www.unccd.int/knowledge/docs/dldd_eng.pdf.

Sen, Amartya. 1999. *Development as Freedom.* Oxford: Oxford University Press.

Shavarsh, Kachatryan. 2007. "Problematic Issues Concerning the Freedom of Association and Group/Collective Rights in the Republic of Armenia." *Brigham Young University Law Review* 3: 639-64.

Shelton, Dinah. 1994. "Fair Play, Fair Pay: Preserving Traditional Knowledge and Biological Resources." *Yearbook of International Environmental Law* 5: 77.

Shiva, Vandana. 1989. *Staying Alive.* London: Zed Books.

Shrader-Frechette, Kristin. 1982. *Nuclear Power and Public Policy*. Dordrecht, Netherlands: Kluwer Academic.

–. 1993. *Burying Uncertainty*. Berkeley: University of California Press.

Shue, Henry. 1996. *Basic Rights: Subsistence, Affluence and American Foreign Policy*. Princeton, NJ: Princeton University Press.

SIDYM. 2006. "Conclusions." II International Symposium on Desertification and Migrations (El II Simposio Internacional sobre Desertificación y Migraciones), Almería, 25-27 October. http://www.sidym2006.com/.

SIKU News. 2007. "Another Award for Sheila Watt-Cloutier." *SIKU News*, 27 April. http://www.sikunews.com/.

Silva, Mario. 2009. "Extraordinary Rendition: A Challenge to Canada and the United States Legal Obligations under the Convention against Torture." *California Western International Law Journal* 39: 313-55.

Singer, Peter. 1975. *Animal Liberation*. New York: HarperCollins.

–. 1976. *Animal Rights and Human Obligations*. Englewood Cliffs, NJ: Prentice Hall.

Soskolne, Colin, and Roberto Bertollini. 1999. *Ecological Integrity and Sustainable Development: Cornerstones of Public Health*. Rome: World Health Organization.

Speth, James Gustave. 2008. *The Bridge at the End of the World: Capitalism, the Environment and Crossing from Crisis to Sustainability*. New Haven, CT: Yale University Press.

Spinedi, Marina. 2000. "La responsibilité de l'etat pour 'crime': Une responsibilité pénale?" In *Droit international pénal*, edited by Alain Pellet and Emmanuel Decaux, 106-7. Paris: Redone.

Sripati, Vijayashri. 2009. "UN Constitutional Assistance: An Emergent Policy Institution." Unpublished paper presented at Osgoode Hall Law School, York University, Toronto, Ontario, October.

Stalin, Joseph V. 1913. "Marxism and the National Question." *Prosveshcheniye* 3-5 (March-May). English translation at http://www.marxists.org/.

Stavenhagen, Rodolfo. 1990. "The Right to Cultural Identity." In *Human Rights in a Pluralistic World: Individuals and Collectivities*, edited by C. Berting, 255-58. London: Westport.

–. 1993. "Self-Determination: Right or Demon?" *IV Law and Society Trust* 67: 1-12.

Steger, M.B. 2003. *Globalization: A Very Short Introduction*. Oxford: Oxford University Press.

Stein, L. 1961. *The Balfour Declaration*. London: Valentine-Mitchell.

Steiner, Henry J., and Philip Alston. 2000. *International Human Rights in Context: Law, Politics and Morals*. 2nd ed. Oxford: Oxford University Press.

Stewart, F., and S. Deneulin. 2002. "Amartya Sen's Contribution to Development Thinking." *Studies in Comparative International Development* 37, 2: 61-70.

Steyn, Johan. 2004. "Guantanamo Bay: The Legal 'Black Hole.'" *International and Comparative Law Quarterly* 53, 1: 1-15.

Sunstein, Cass R. 1990. "Paradoxes of the Regulatory State." *University of Chicago Law Review* 57, 2: 407-44.

Susser, Mervyn, and Ezra Susser. 1996. "Choosing a Future for Epidemiology. II. From Black Box to Chinese Boxes and Eco-Epidemiology." *American Journal of Public Health* 86, 5: 674-77.

Swedish Ministry of the Environment. 2001. *The Swedish Environmental Objectives: Interim Targets and Action Strategies – Government Bill 2000/01.* Stockholm: Swedish Ministry of the Environment.

–. 2002. *Stockholm Thirty Years On: Progress Achieved and Challenges in International Environmental Cooperation.* Stockholm: Swedish Ministry of the Environment.

Tabachnick, David. 2009. "Writing on Water." In *Environmental Justice in the New Millennium,* edited by Filomina Chioma Steady, 165-88. New York: Palgrave-MacMillan.

Talmon, Stefan. 2006. "The Duty Not to Recognize as Lawful a Situation Created by the Illegal Use of Force or Other Serious Breaches of *Jus Cogens* Obligations: An Obligation without Real Substance?" In *The Fundamental Rule of the International Order,* edited by Christian Tomuschat and Jean-Marc Thouvenis, 99-126. Leiden, The Netherlands: Martinus Nijhoff.

Tamburlini, Gergio, Olga von Ehrenstein, and Roberto Bertollini. 2002. *Children's Health and the Environment: A Review of the Evidence.* EEA Report No. 29. Geneva: World Health Organization.

Taylor, Allyn L. 1997. "Controlling the Global Spread of Infectious Diseases: Toward a Reinforced Role for the International Health Regulations." *Houston Law Review* 33, 5: 1327-62.

Tenebaum, David. 2002. "Pesticides Coca-Killing Controversy." *Environmental Health Perspectives* 110, 5: A236.

Terry, John. 2001. "Taking Filartiga on the Road: Why Courts Outside the United States Should Accept Jurisdictions over Actions Involving Torture Committed Abroad." In *Torture as Tort: Comparative Perspectives on the Development of Transnational Human Rights Litigation,* edited by Craig Scott, 109-29. Oxford: Hart Publishing.

Tesón, Fernando R. 1998. "Two Mistakes About Democracy." *American Society of International Law Proceedings* 92: 126-31.

Tomei, Manuela, and Lee Swepston. 1996. *Indigenous and Tribal Peoples: A Guide to ILO Convention No. 169.* Geneva: International Labour Organization.

Tomuschat, Christian. 1993-94. "Obligations Arising for States Without or Against Their Will." *Rec. des Cours Academie de Droit International de la Haye* 241: 195-374

–. 1999. "International Law: Ensuring the Survival of Mankind on the Eve of a New Century." *Rec. des Cours Academie de Droit International de la Haye* 281: 9-438.

–. 2006. "Reconceptualizing the Debate on *Jus Cogens* and Obligations *Erga Omnes:* Concluding Observations." In *Fundamental Rules of the International Legal Order,* edited by Christian Tomuschat and Jean-Marc Thouvenen, 425-36. Leiden, the Netherlands: Martinus Nijhoff.

Tunkin, Gregory I. 1971. "*Jus Cogens* in Contemporary International Law." *University of Toledo Law Review* 3, 1: 107-18.

Ulanowicz, Robert. 1997. *Ecology: The Ascendant Perspective*. New York: Columbia University Press.

United Nations Information Organization, eds. 1945. *Documents of the United Nations Conference on International Organization*. New York: United Nations Information Organization.

Vasak, Karel. 1977. "A 30-Year Struggle: The Sustained Effort to Give the Force of Law to the Universal Declaration of Human Rights." *UNESCO Courier* (November): 29.

–. 1979. "For the Third Generation of Human Rights: The Rights of Solidarity." Inaugural lecture to the tenth study session of the International Institute of Human Rights, Strasbourg, France.

Velasquez, Manuel. 1998. *Business Ethics, Concepts and Cases*. Belmont: Prentice-Hall.

Vitousek, Paul M., Paul Ehrlich, Anne Ehrlich, and Patricia Matson. 1986. "Human Appropriation of the Products of Photosynthesis." *Bioscience* 36 (June): 368-73.

Vladi, Valentina. 2010. "Reconciling Environmental Health and Investors' Rights in International Investment Law." In *Democracy, Ecological Integrity and International Law*, edited by Ronald Engel, Laura Westra, and Klaus Bosselmann, 226-46. Cambridge: Cambridge Scholars Publishing.

Walcott, Judith. 2002. "Spraying Crops, Eradicating People." *Cultural Survival Quarterly, Indigenous Responses to Plan Colombia* 26, 4: 28-35.

Wald, Patricia M. 2007. "Genocide and Crimes against Humanity." *Washington University Global Studies Law Review* 6, 3: 621-33.

Wallace, Paul. 1994. *The Iroquois Book of Life: White Roots of Peace*. Santa Fe, NM: Clear Light Publishers.

Wasserstrom, Richard. 1985. "War, Nuclear War and Nuclear Deterrence: Some Conceptual and Moral Issues." In *Nuclear Deterrence, Ethics and Strategy*, edited by Richard Hardin, J. Mersheimer, Gerald Dworkin, and Robert Goodin, 15-36. Chicago: University of Chicago Press.

Waterman, Shaun. 2005. "Ex-CIA Lawyer Calls for Law on Renditions." *SPACE WAR*, 9 March. http://www.spacewar.com/.

Watt-Cloutier, Sheila, and others. 2005. "Petition to the Inter-American Commission on Human Rights Seeking Relief from Violations Resulting from Global Warming Caused by Acts and Omissions of the United States," 7 December.

Weil, Prosper. 1983. "Toward Relative Normativity in International Law?" *American Journal of International Law* 77, 3: 413-42.

Wendt, Alexander. 1999. "A Comment on Held's Cosmopolitanism." In *Democracy's Edges*, edited by Ian Shapiro and Casiano Harker-Cordon, 127-33. New York: Cambridge Press.

Westra, Laura. 1994. *An Environmental Proposal for Ethics: The Principle of Integrity*. Lanham, MD: Rowman Littlefield.

–. 1998. *Living in Integrity*. Lanham, MD: Roman Littlefield.

–. 2000. "The Disvalue of Contingent Valuation and the Accounting Expectation Gap." *Environmental Values* 9, 2: 153-71. Lancaster, UK: White Horse Press.

–. 2004a. *Ecoviolence and the Law: Supranational Normative Foundations of Ecocrime*. Ardsley, NY: Transnational Publishers.

–. 2004b. "Environmental Rights and Human Rights: The Final Enclosure Movement." In *Global Governance and the Quest for Justice*. Vol. 4, *Human Rights*, edited by Roger Brownsword, 107-20. Oxford: Hart Publisher.

–. 2006. *Environmental Justice and the Rights of Unborn and Future Generations*. London: Earthscan.

–. 2007. *Environmental Justice and the Rights of Indigenous Peoples*. London: Earthscan.

–. 2009a. "Biological Integrity, Ecological Integrity: The Right to Life and the Right to Health in Law." *Transnational Law and Contemporary Problems* 18, 1: 3-44.

–. 2009b. *Environmental Justice and the Rights of Ecological Refugees*. London: Earthscan Publishers.

–. 2010a. "Collective Human Rights: Public Health v. Structural and Ecological Violence (The Example of Ecuador v. Colombia)," *ILSA Journal of International and Comparative Law* 16, 2: 557-72.

–. 2010b. "Ecology and the Law: Democracy, Globalization and the Roots of Ecological Problems." In *Democracy, Ecological Integrity and International Law*, edited by J. Ronald Engel, Laura Westra, and Klaus Bosselmann, 8-25. Newcastle upon Tyne: Cambridge Scholars Publishing.

–. 2011. *Globalization, Violence and World Law*. Leiden, Netherlands: Brill.

Westra, Laura, Klaus Bosselmann, and Richard Westra, eds. 2008. *Reconciling Human Existence with Ecological Integrity*. London: Earthscan.

Westra, Laura, Peter Miller, James R. Karr, William E. Rees, and Robert E. Ulanowicz. 2000. "Ecological Integrity and the Aims of the Global Ecological Integrity Project." In *Ecological Integrity: Integrating Environment, Conservation and Health*, edited by David Pimentel, Laura Westra, and Reed F. Noss, 19-41. Washington, DC: Island Press.

Westra, Richard. 2010. *Political Economy and Globalization*. London: Routledge, Taylor Francis Group.

Whally, J., and B. Zissimos. 2001. "What Could a World Environment Organization Do?" *Global Environmental Politics* 1, 1: 29-34.

WHO. 2005. *International Health Regulations*. 2nd ed. Geneva: World Health Organization. http://www.who.int/.

Wiessner, Siegfrid. 1999. "Rights and Status of Indigenous Peoples: A Global Comparative and International Legal Analysis." *Harvard Human Rights Journal* 12: 57-128.

Williams, Gary M., R. Kroes, and K. Munro. 2000. "Safety Evaluation and Risk Assessment of the Herbicide Roundup and Its Active Ingredient, Glyphosate, for Humans." *Regulatory Toxicology and Pharmacology* 31, 2: 117-65.

Wilson, Edward O. 1992. *The Diversity of Life*. Cambridge, MA: Harvard University Press.

Winkler, Matteo. 2008. "When Extraordinary Means Illegal: International Law and European Reaction to the United States Rendition Program." *Loyola Los Angeles International and Comparative Law Review* 3, 1: 33-76.

Wood, James C. 1996. "Intergenerational Equity and Climate Change." *Georgetown International Environmental Law Review* 8, 2: 293-332.

Wood, E.M. 1998. "The Agrarian Origins of Capitalism." *Monthly Review* 50, 3: 14-31.

Wood, Mary Christina. 2009. "Advancing the Sovereign Trust of Government to Safeguard the Environment for Present and Future Generations (Part I): Ecological Realism and the Need for a Paradigm Shift." *Environment* 39, 1: 43-89.

World Health Organization. Commission on Social Determinants of Health. 2008. *Closing the Gap in a Generation: Health Equity through Action on the Social Determinants of Health.* Geneva: World Health Organization.

WRITENET. 2008. *The Ecuador-Colombia Border: Historical Links, Current Events, and Future Possibilities*, May. http://www.unhcr.org/.

Wyler, Eric. 2002. "From 'State Crime' to Responsibility for 'Serious Breaches of Obligations under Peremptory Norms of International Law.'" *European Journal of International Law* 13, 5: 1147-60.

Index

Printed and bound in Canada by Friesens

Set in Giovanni and Scala Sans by Artegraphica Design Co. Ltd.

Copy editor and proofreader: Lesley Erickson

Indexer: Natalie Boon